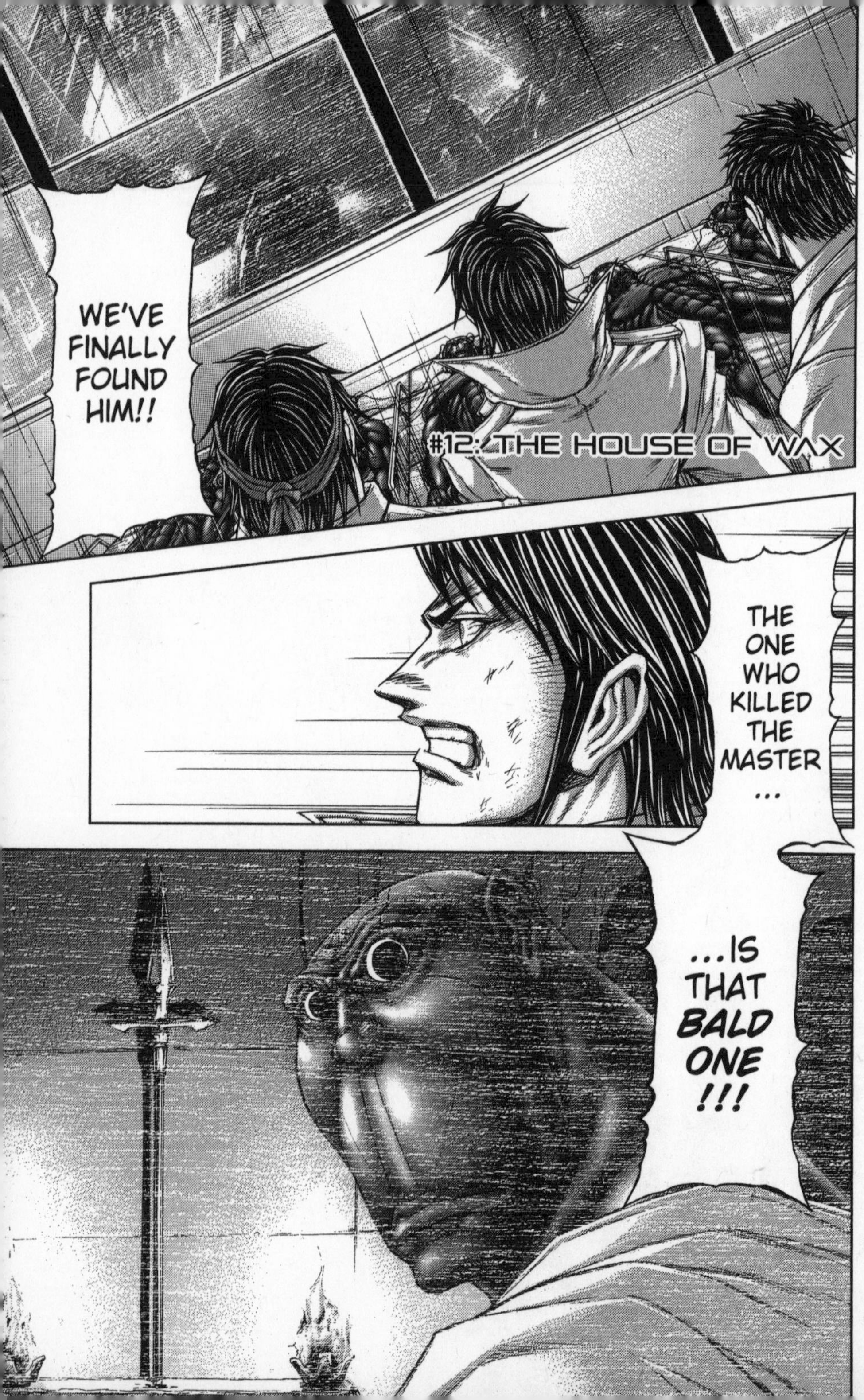
WE'VE FINALLY FOUND HIM!!
#12: THE HOUSE OF WAX
THE ONE WHO KILLED THE MASTER ...
...IS THAT BALD ONE !!!

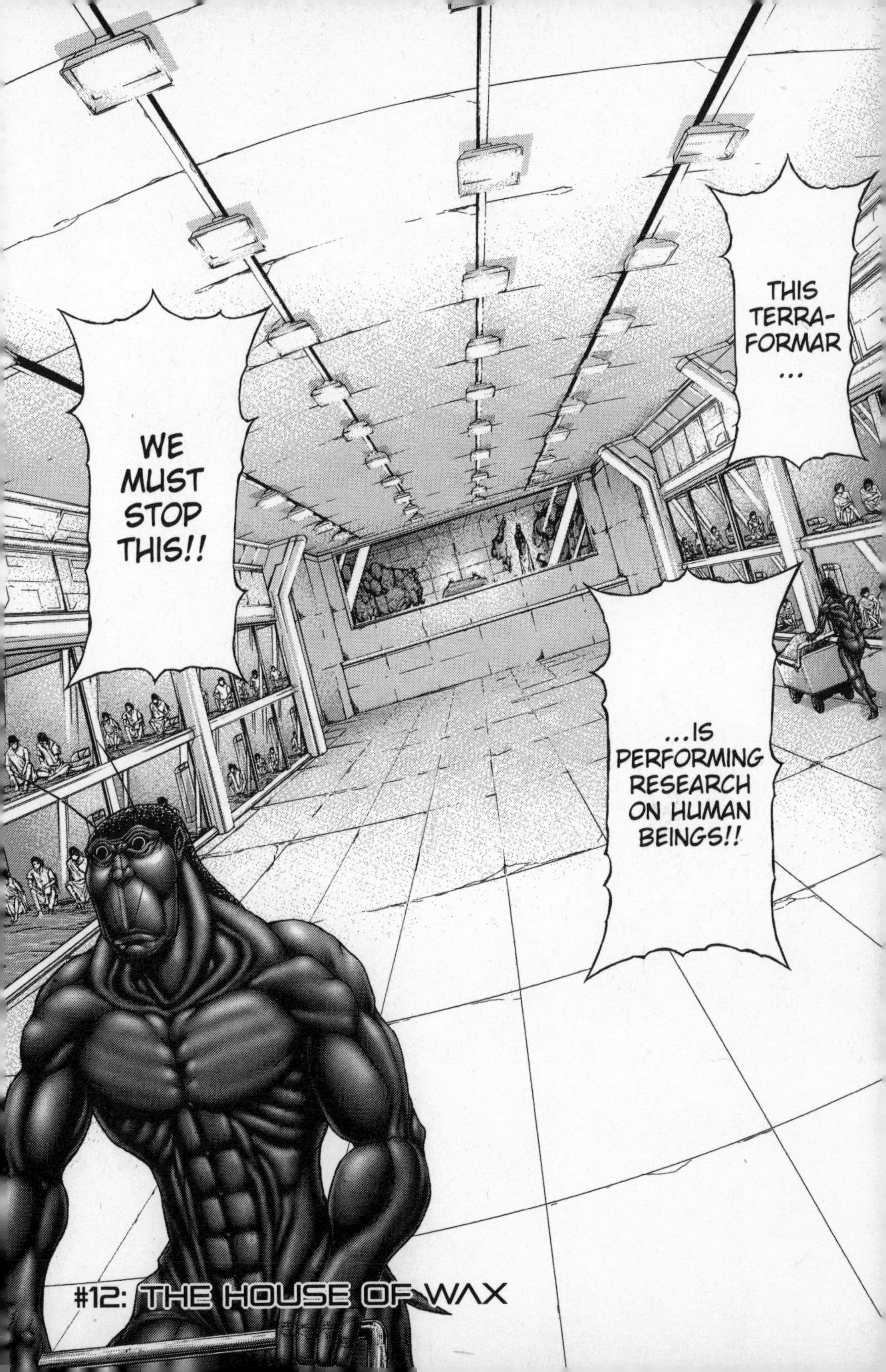
THIS TERRA-FORMAR...
...IS PERFORMING RESEARCH ON HUMAN BEINGS!!
WE MUST STOP THIS!!
#12: THE HOUSE OF WAX

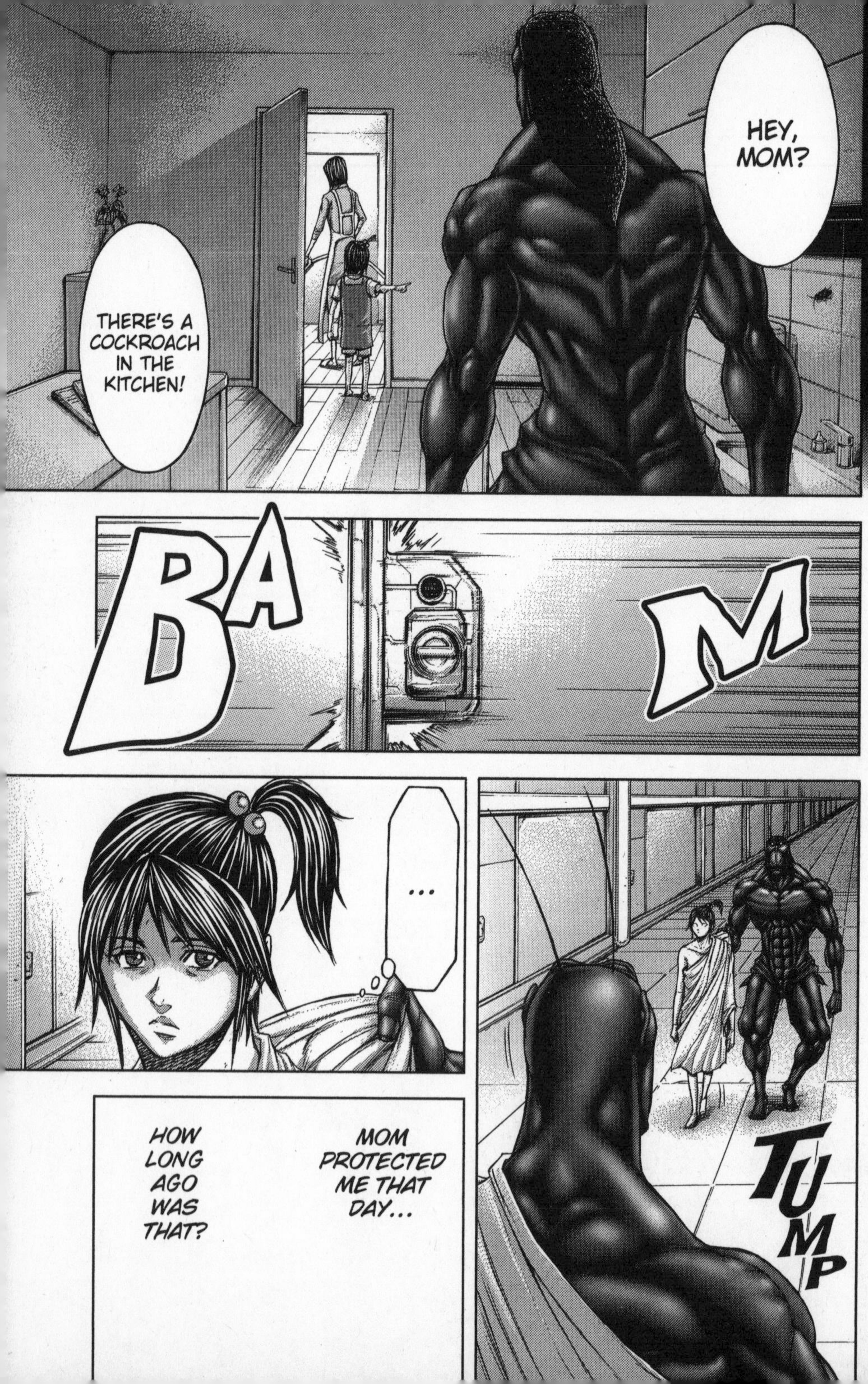
HEY, MOM?
THERE'S A COCKROACH IN THE KITCHEN!
BAM
TUMP
...
HOW LONG AGO WAS THAT?
MOM PROTECTED ME THAT DAY...

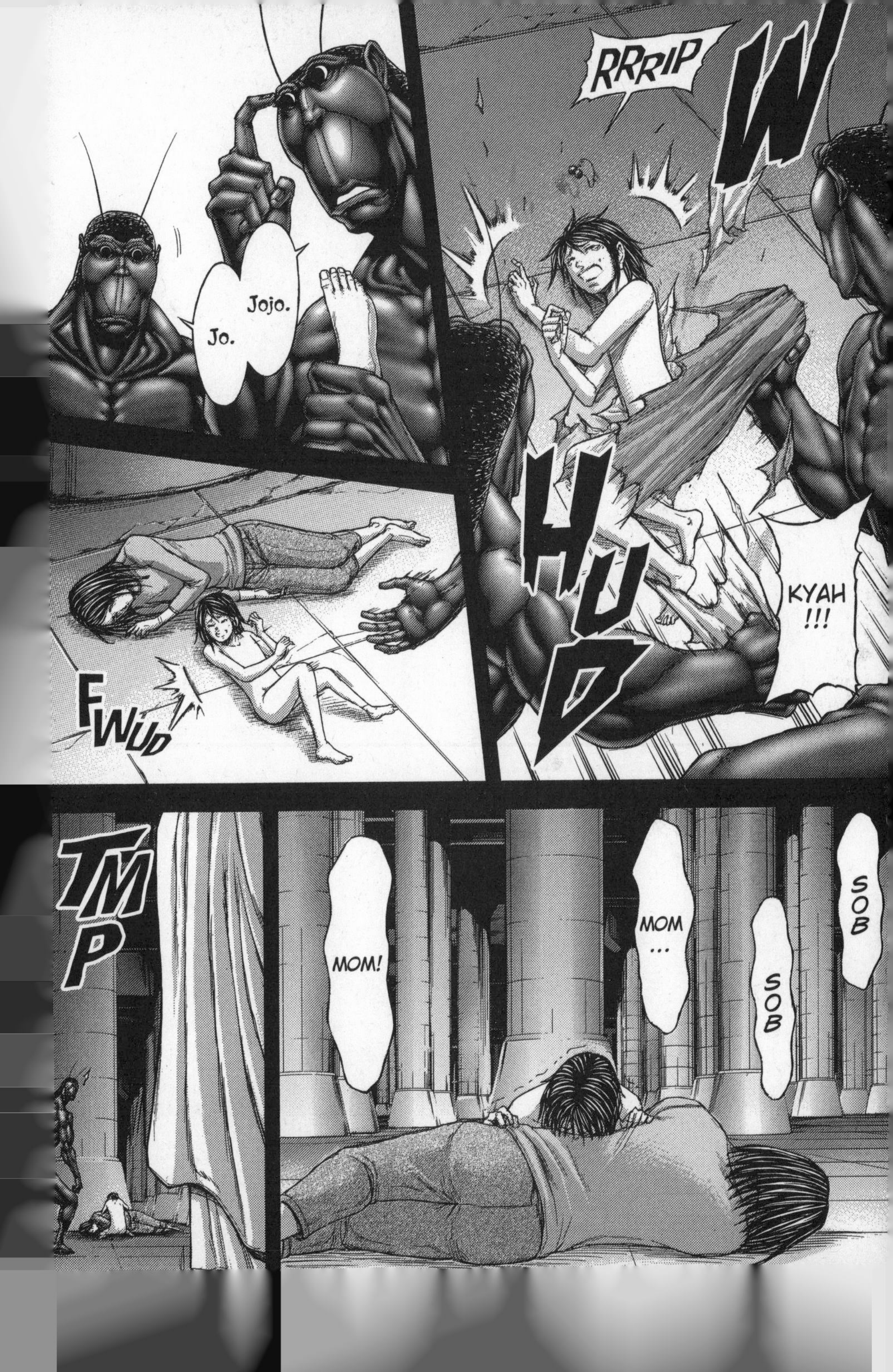
RRRIP
WHUD
KYAH!!!
Jojo. Jo.
FWUD
SOB
SOB
MOM...
MOM!
TMP

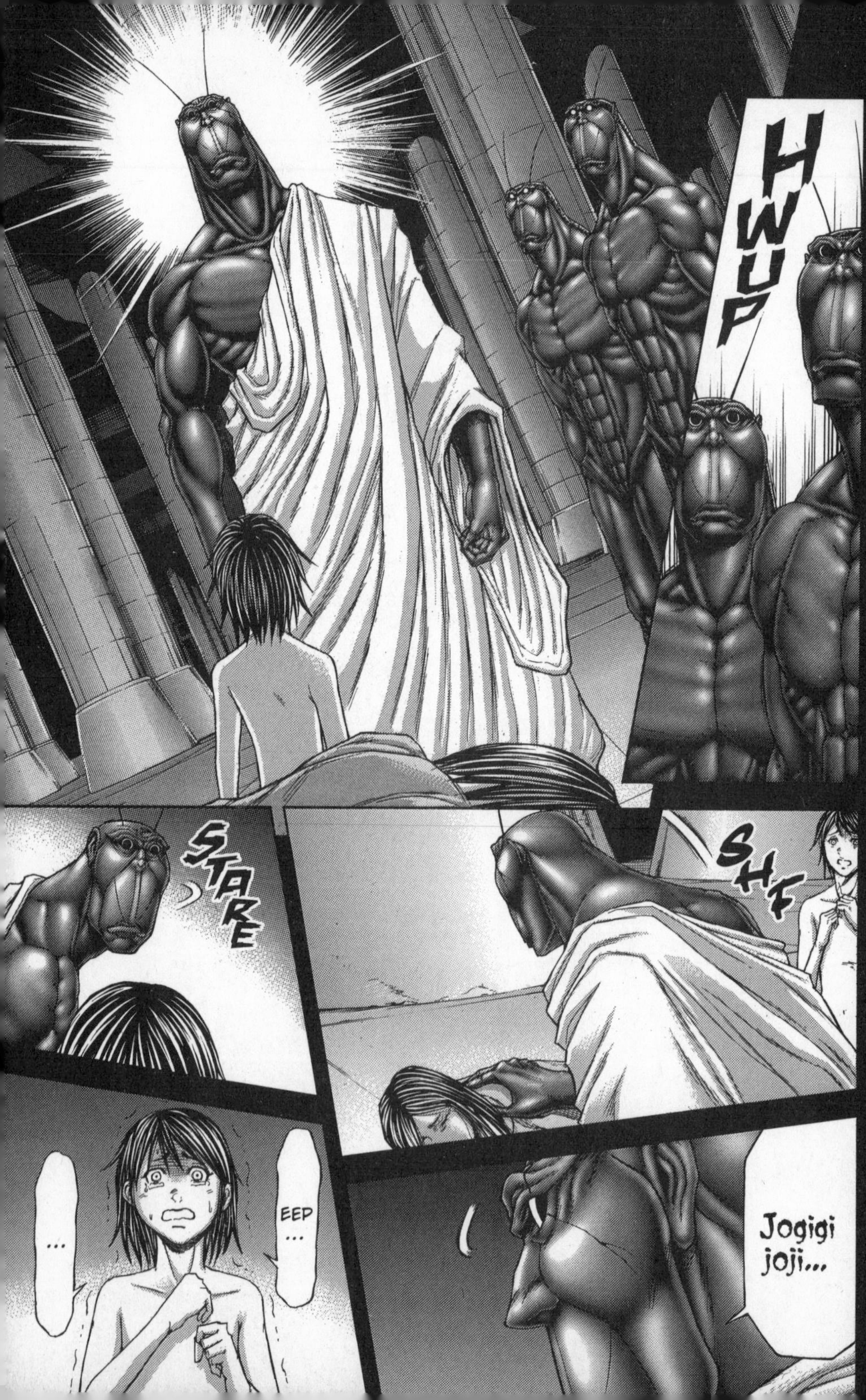
HWUP
SHF
STARE
Jogigi joji...
EEP ...
...

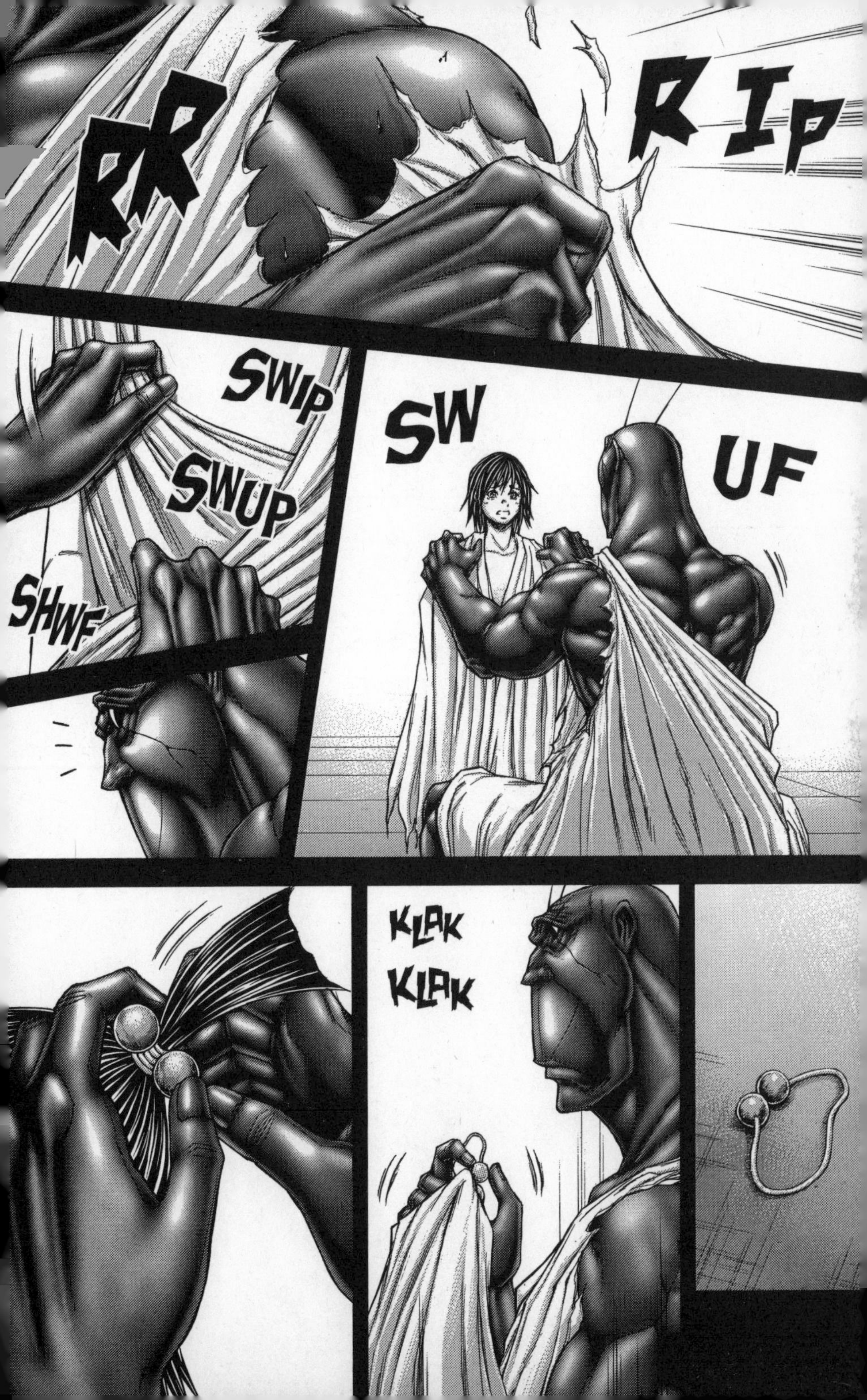
RIP
RR
SW
UF
SWIP
SWUP
SHWF
KLAK
KLAK

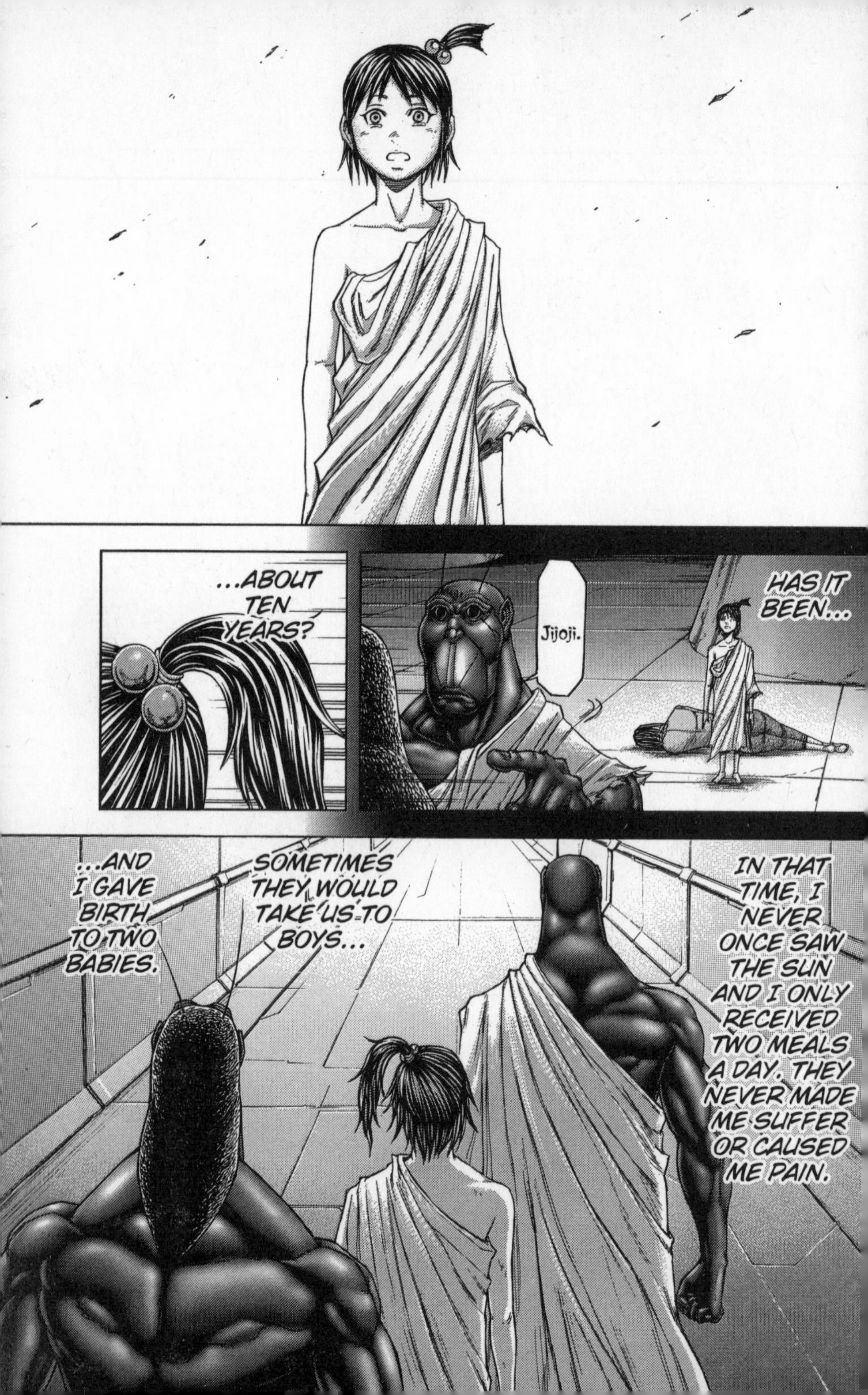
HAS IT BEEN...
Jijoji.
...ABOUT TEN YEARS?
IN THAT TIME, I NEVER ONCE SAW THE SUN AND I ONLY RECEIVED TWO MEALS A DAY. THEY NEVER MADE ME SUFFER OR CAUSED ME PAIN.
SOMETIMES THEY WOULD TAKE US TO BOYS...
...AND I GAVE BIRTH TO TWO BABIES.

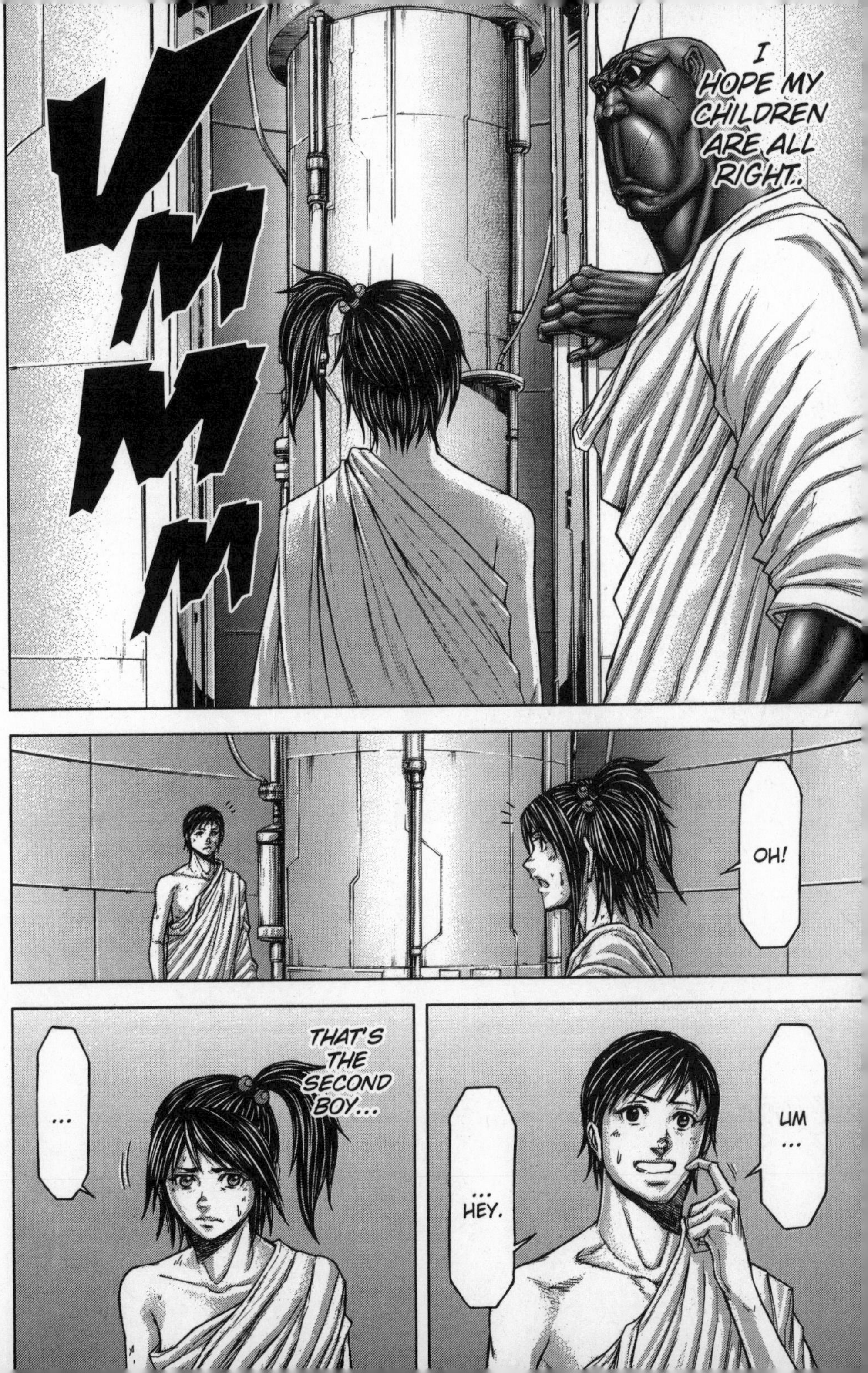
I HOPE MY CHILDREN ARE ALL RIGHT..
VMMM
OH!
UM ...
... HEY.
THAT'S THE SECOND BOY...
...

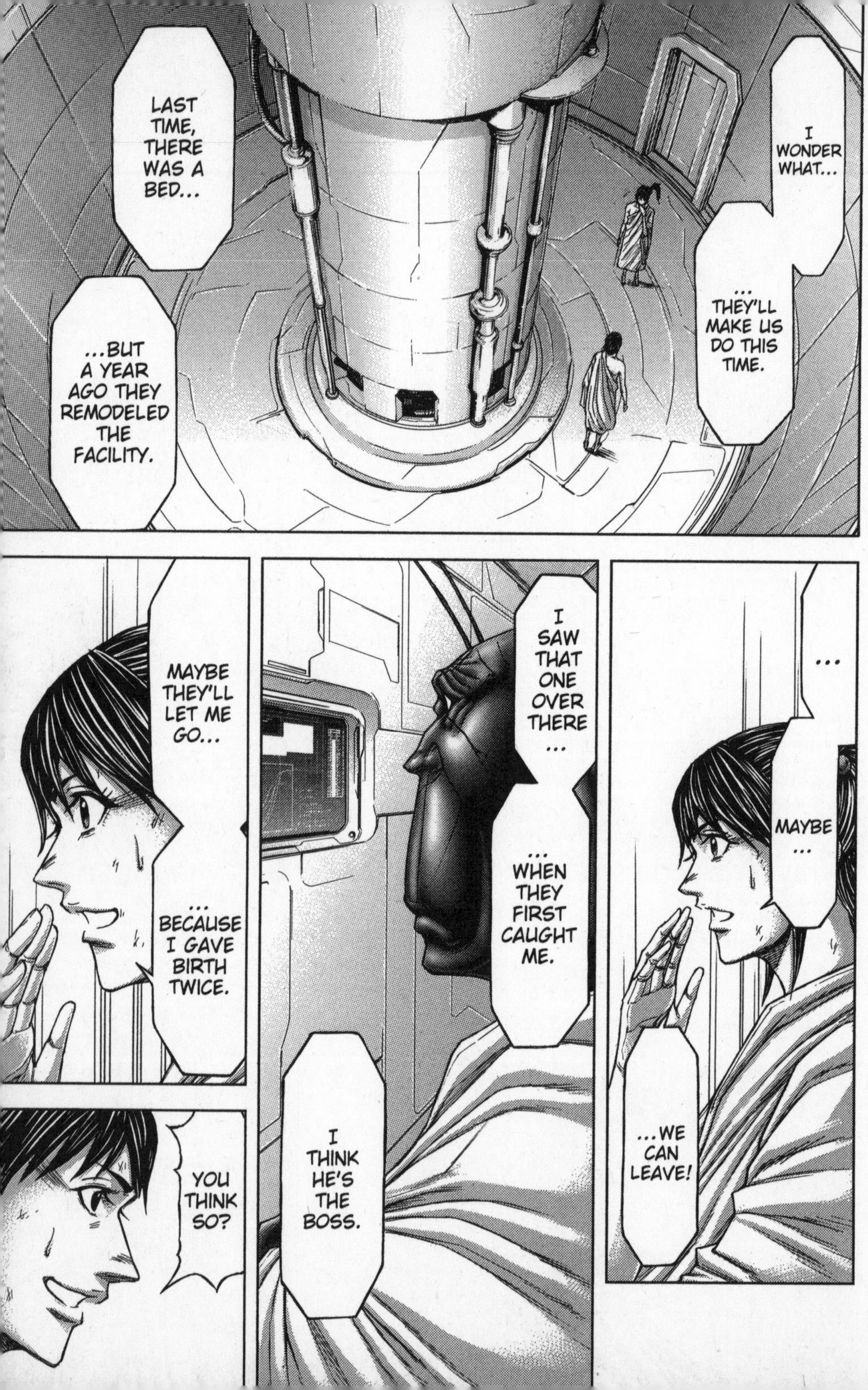
I WONDER WHAT...
...THEY'LL MAKE US DO THIS TIME.
LAST TIME, THERE WAS A BED...
...BUT A YEAR AGO THEY REMODELED THE FACILITY.
...
MAYBE...
...WE CAN LEAVE!
I SAW THAT ONE OVER THERE...
...WHEN THEY FIRST CAUGHT ME.
I THINK HE'S THE BOSS.
MAYBE THEY'LL LET ME GO...
...BECAUSE I GAVE BIRTH TWICE.
YOU THINK SO?

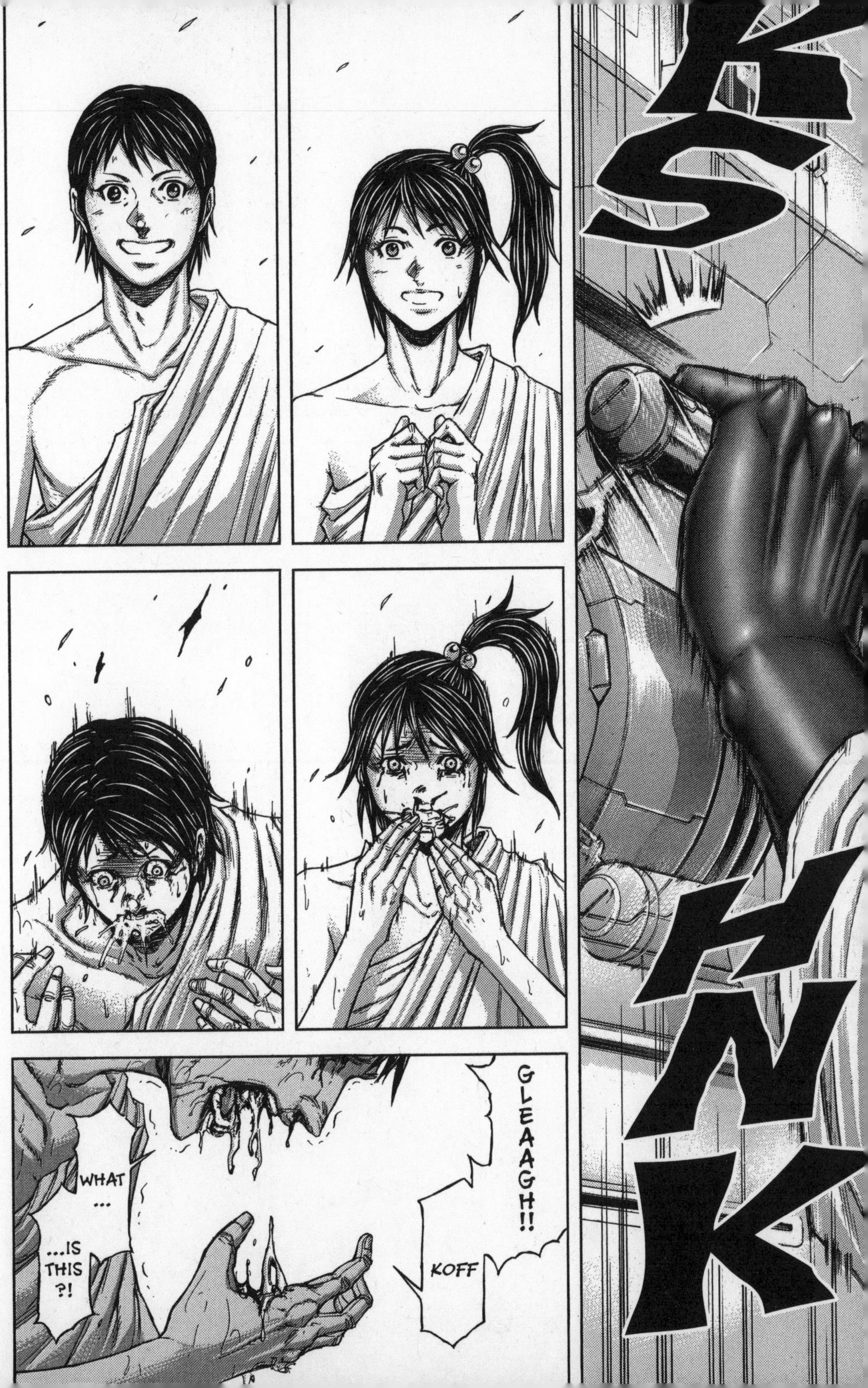
KSHNK
GLEAAGH!!
KOFF
WHAT ...
...IS THIS ?!

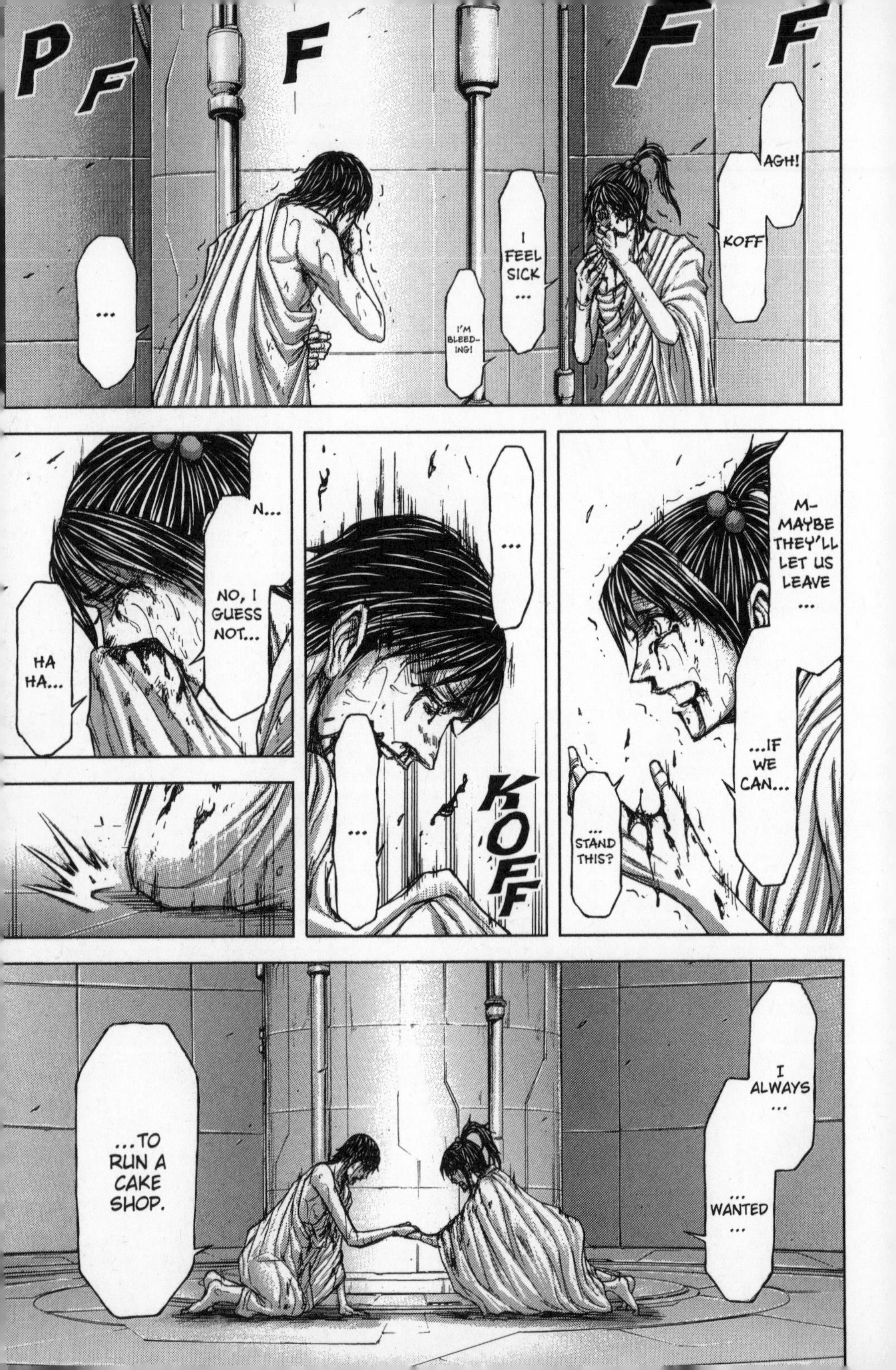
F
F
AGH!
KOFF
I FEEL SICK ...
I'M BLEEDING!
F
PF
...
M-MAYBE THEY'LL LET US LEAVE ...
...IF WE CAN...
... STAND THIS?
...
KOFF
...
N...
NO, I GUESS NOT...
HA HA...
I ALWAYS ...
... WANTED ...
...TO RUN A CAKE SHOP.

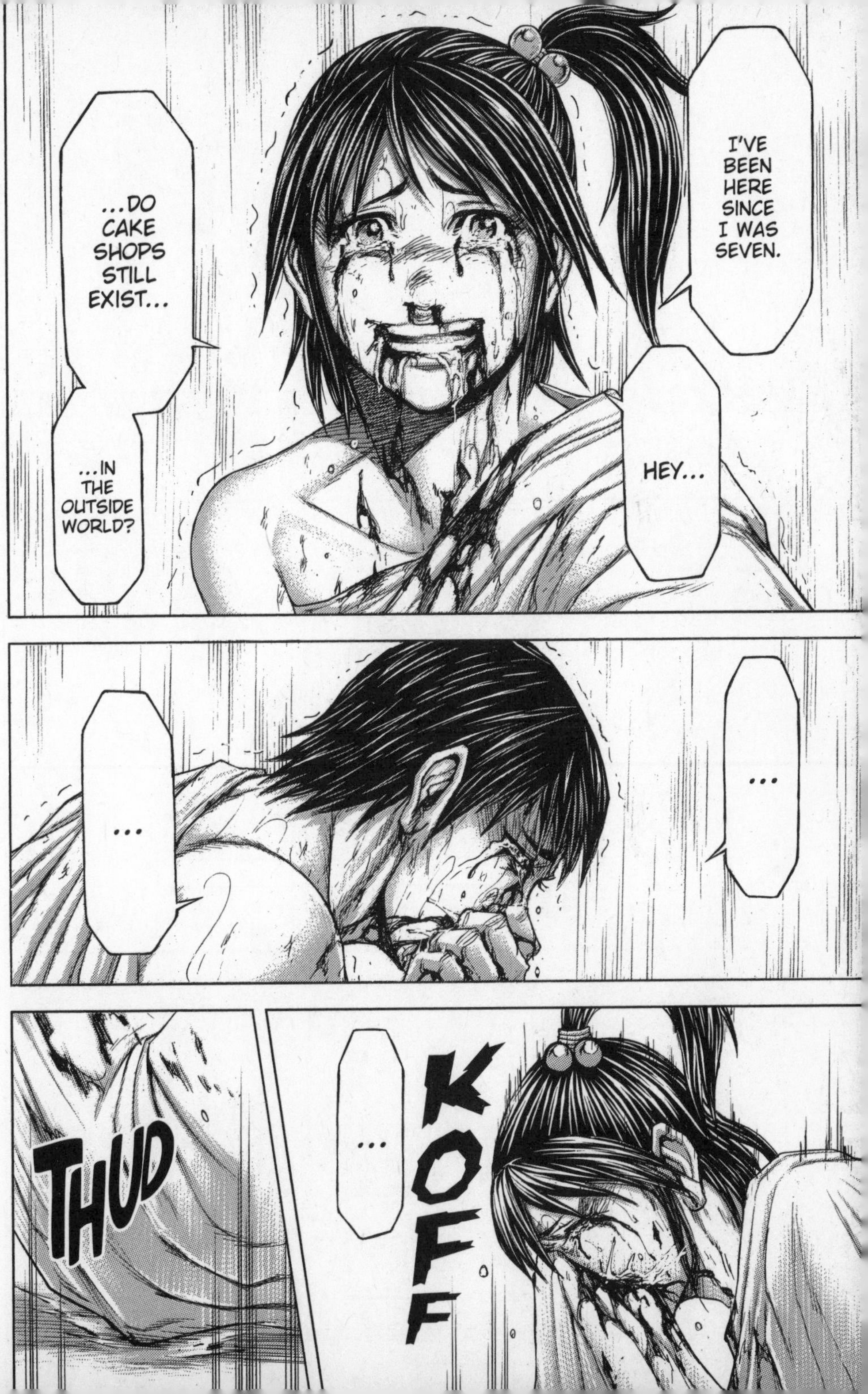
I'VE BEEN HERE SINCE I WAS SEVEN.
HEY...
...DO CAKE SHOPS STILL EXIST...
...IN THE OUTSIDE WORLD?
...
...
...
KOFF
THUD

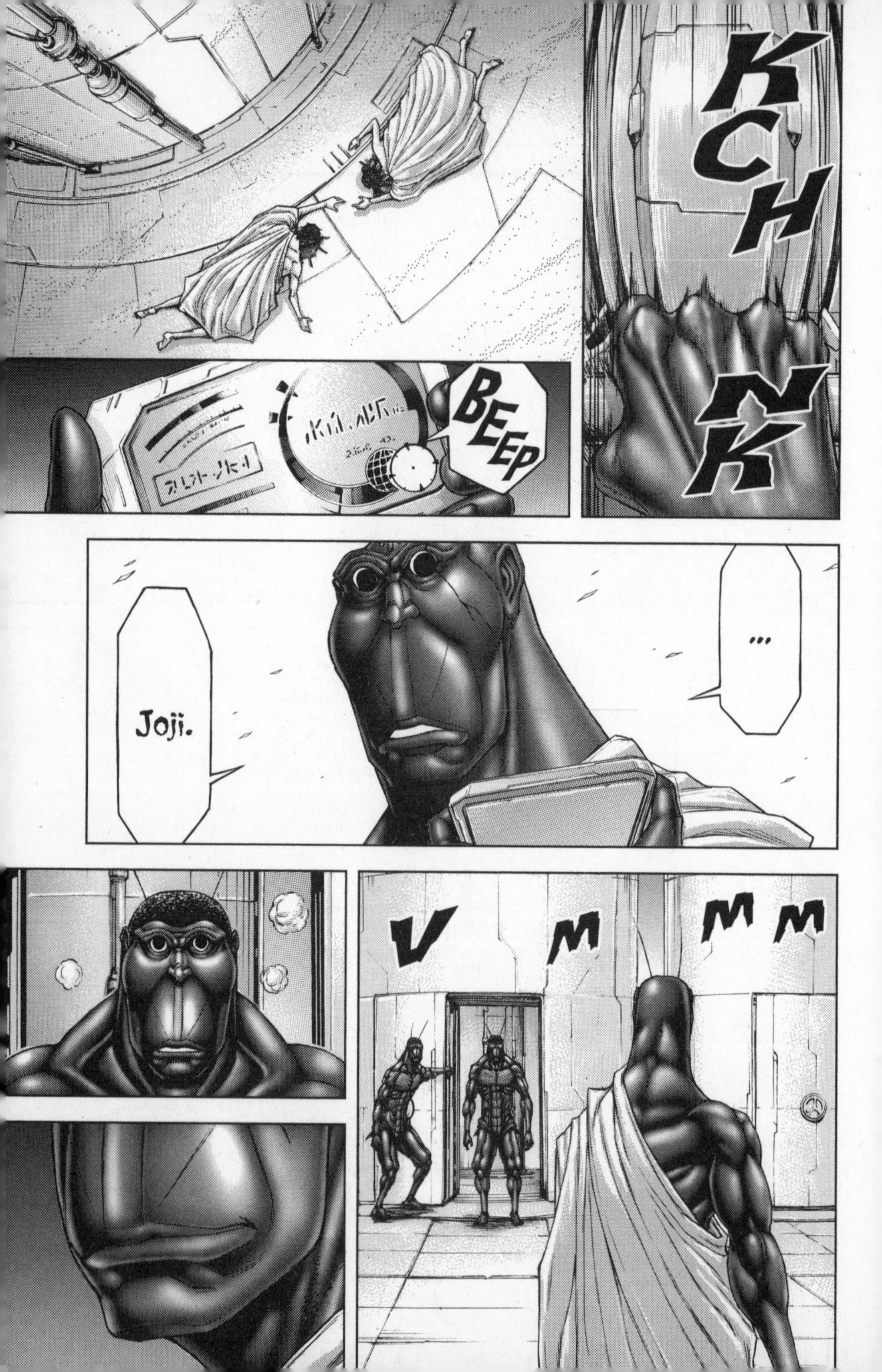
KCHNK
BEEP
...
Joji.
VMMM

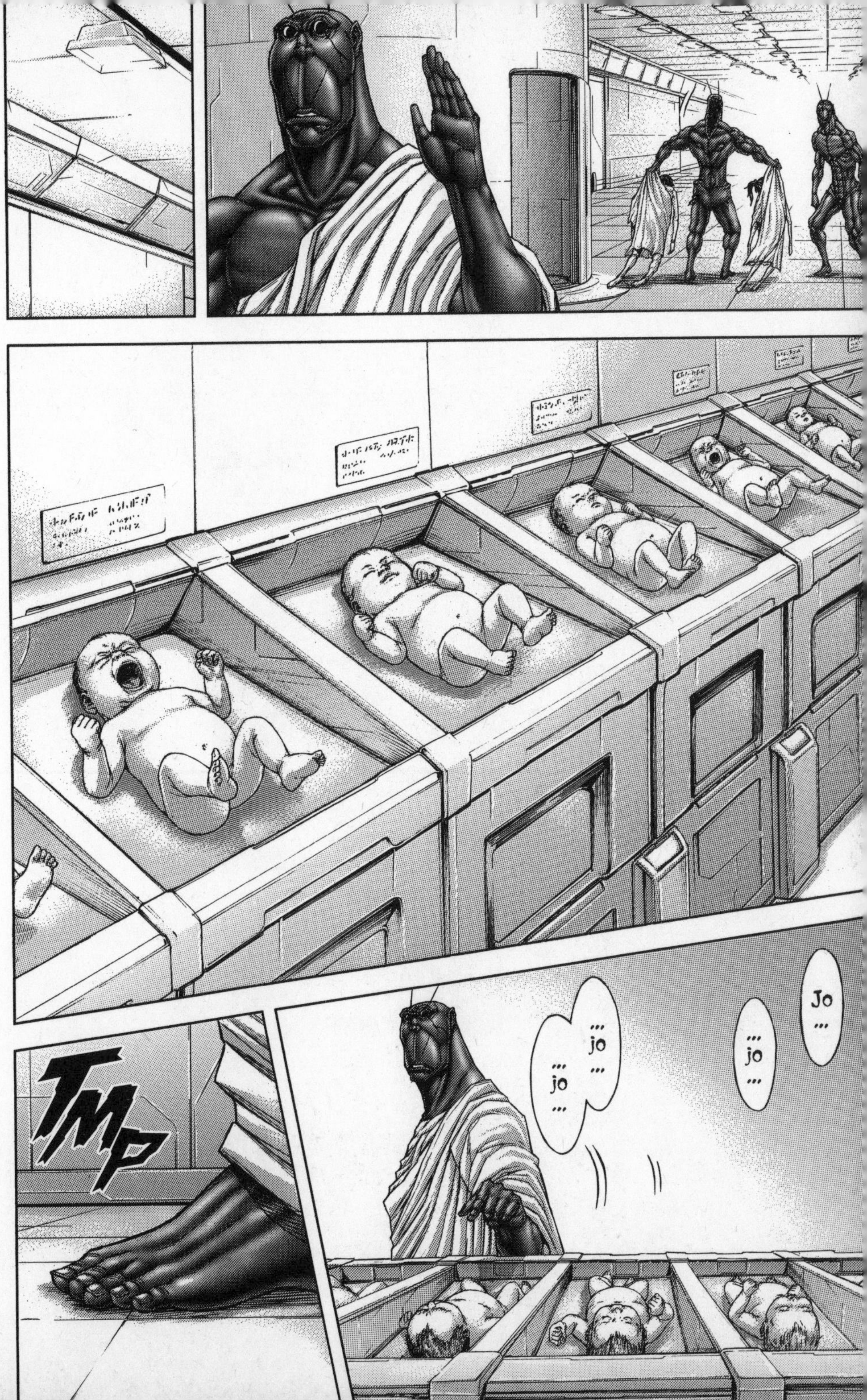
Jo ...
... jo ...
... jo ...
... jo ...
TMP

THIS LIFE-FORM PRAYS LIKE HUMANS DO...

...

Joji!!

...AND TALKS LIKE HUMANS...

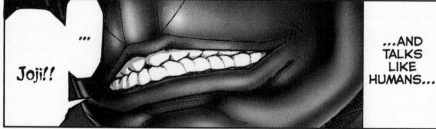

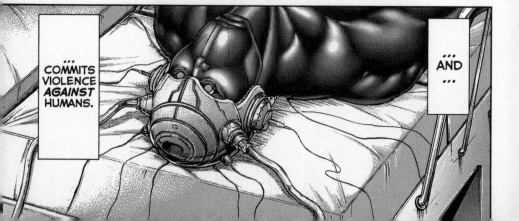

...COMMITS VIOLENCE *AGAINST* HUMANS.

... AND ...

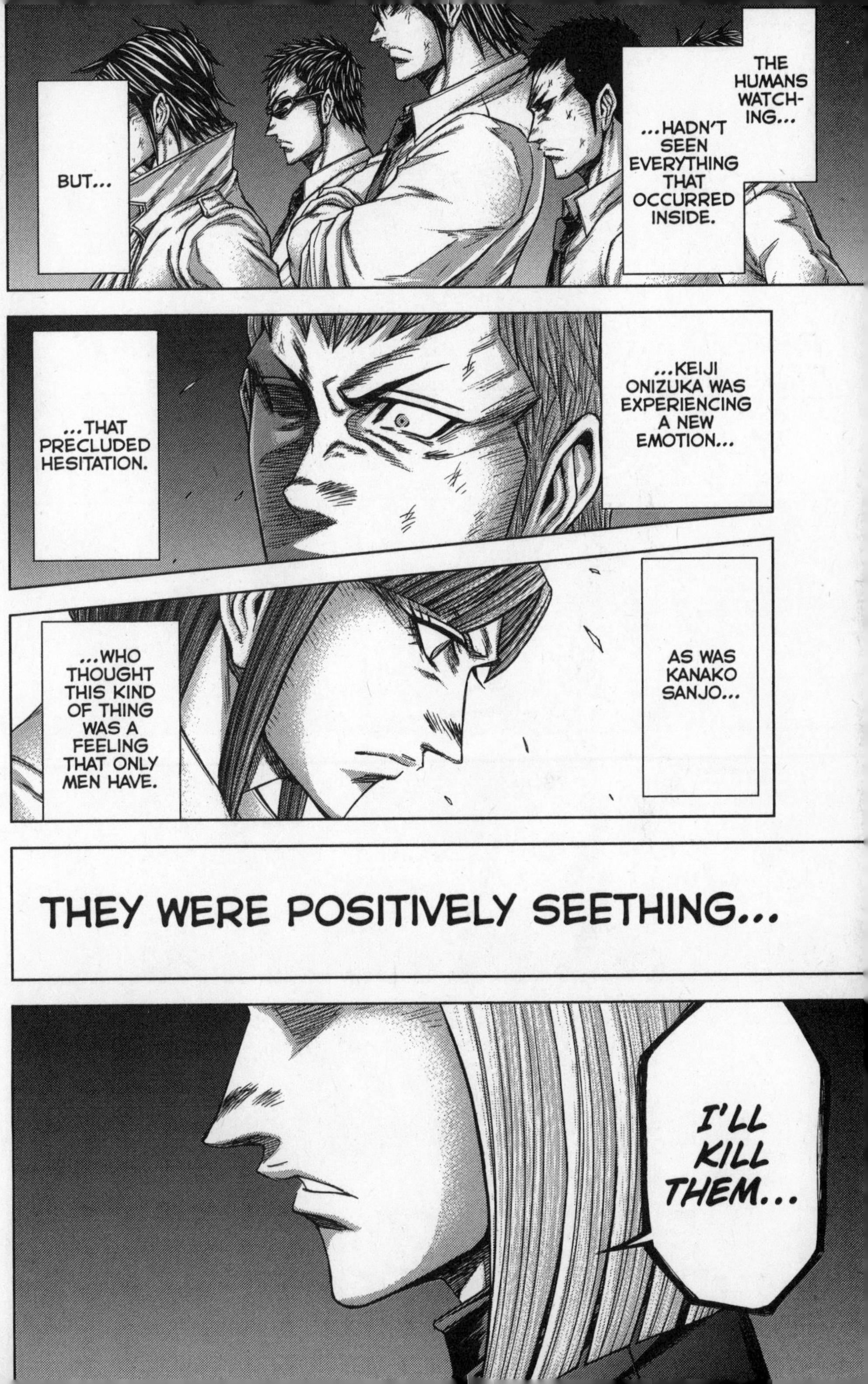
THE HUMANS WATCHING...
...HADN'T SEEN EVERYTHING THAT OCCURRED INSIDE.
BUT...
...KEIJI ONIZUKA WAS EXPERIENCING A NEW EMOTION...
...THAT PRECLUDED HESITATION.
AS WAS KANAKO SANJO...
...WHO THOUGHT THIS KIND OF THING WAS A FEELING THAT ONLY MEN HAVE.
THEY WERE POSITIVELY SEETHING...
I'LL KILL THEM...

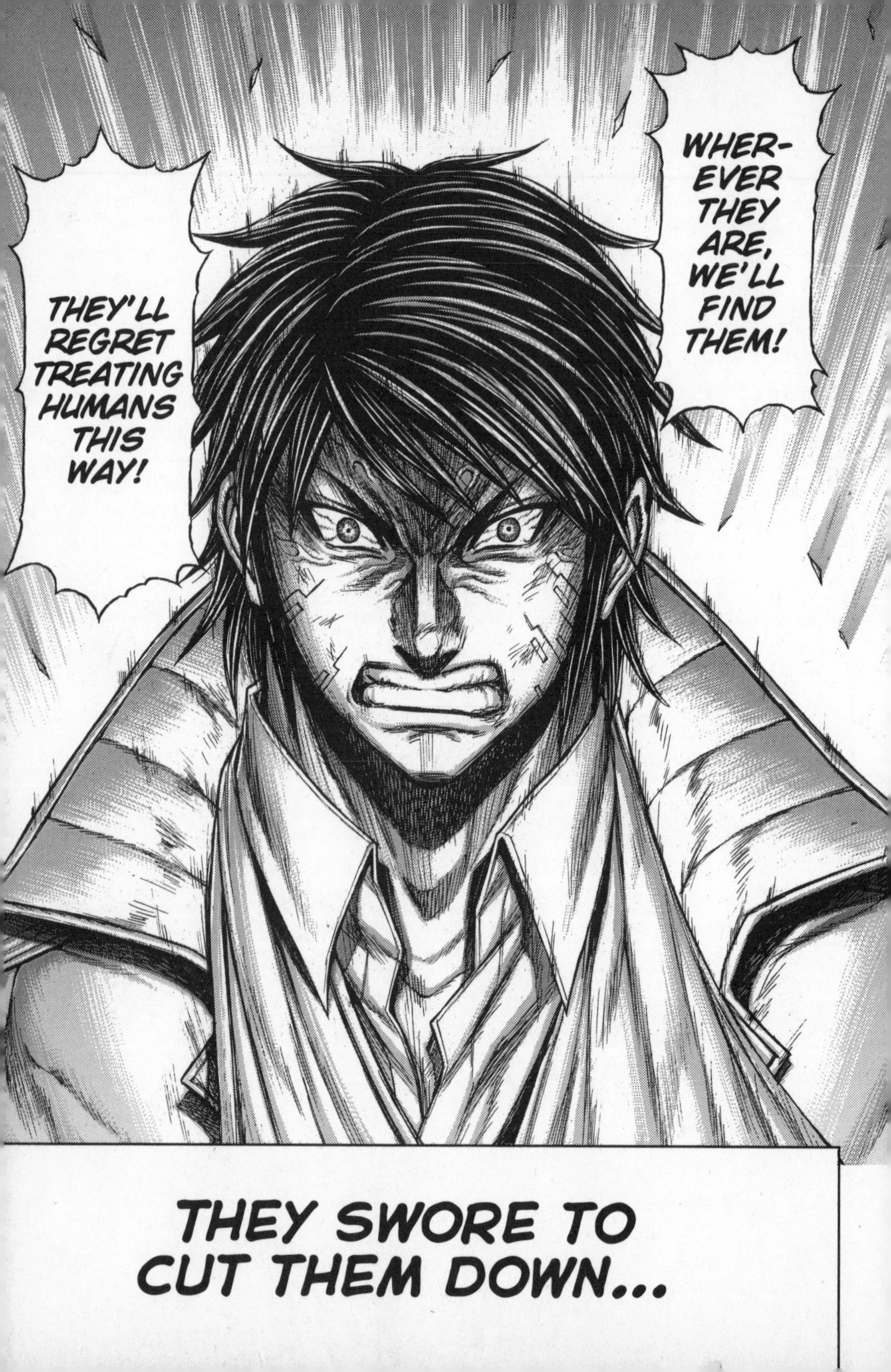
WHER-EVER THEY ARE, WE'LL FIND THEM!
THEY'LL REGRET TREATING HUMANS THIS WAY!
THEY SWORE TO CUT THEM DOWN...

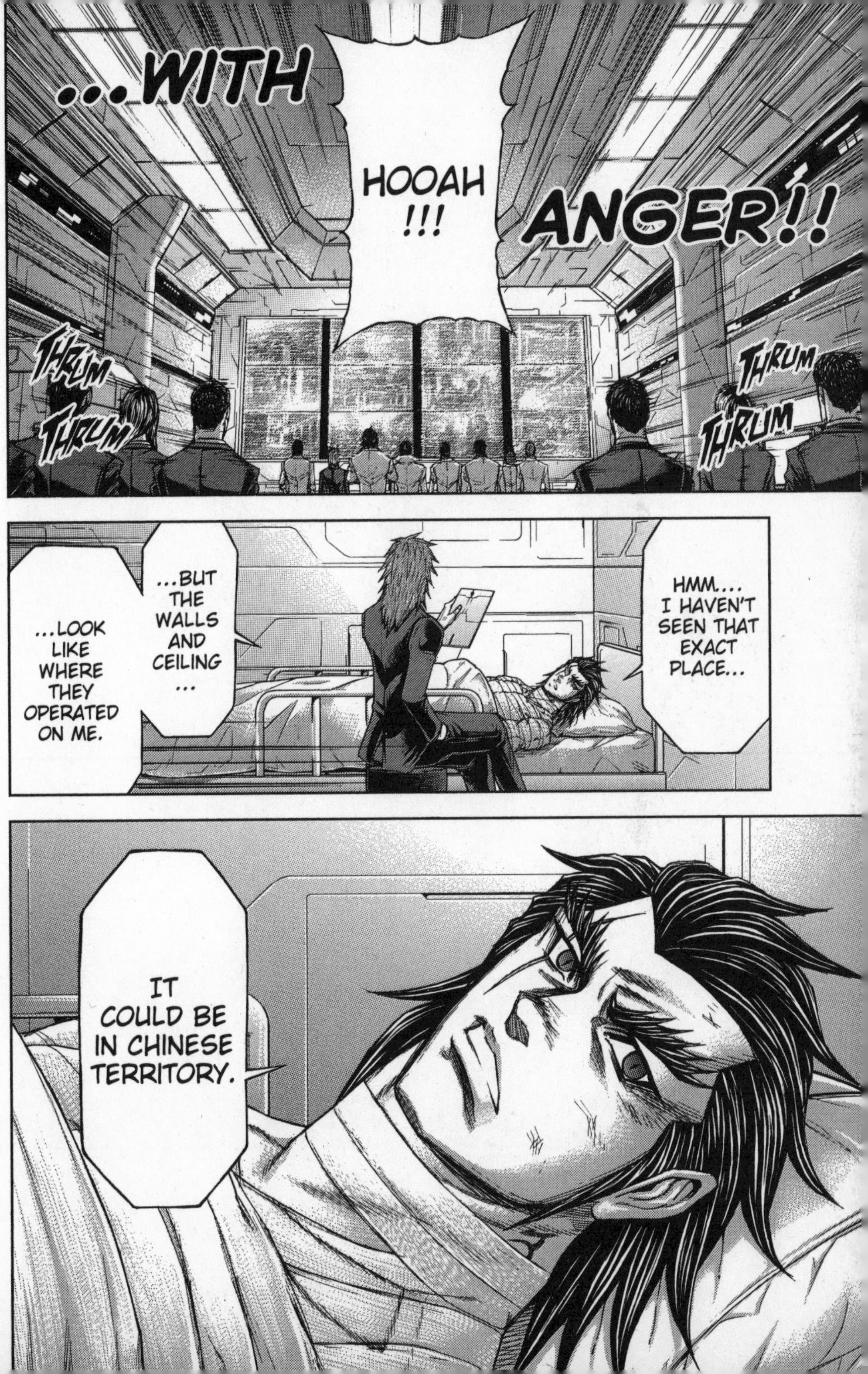
...WITH
HOOAH !!!
ANGER!!
THRUM THRUM
THRUM THRUM
HMM.... I HAVEN'T SEEN THAT EXACT PLACE...
...BUT THE WALLS AND CEILING ...
...LOOK LIKE WHERE THEY OPERATED ON ME.
IT COULD BE IN CHINESE TERRITORY.

#13: THE GHOST AREA

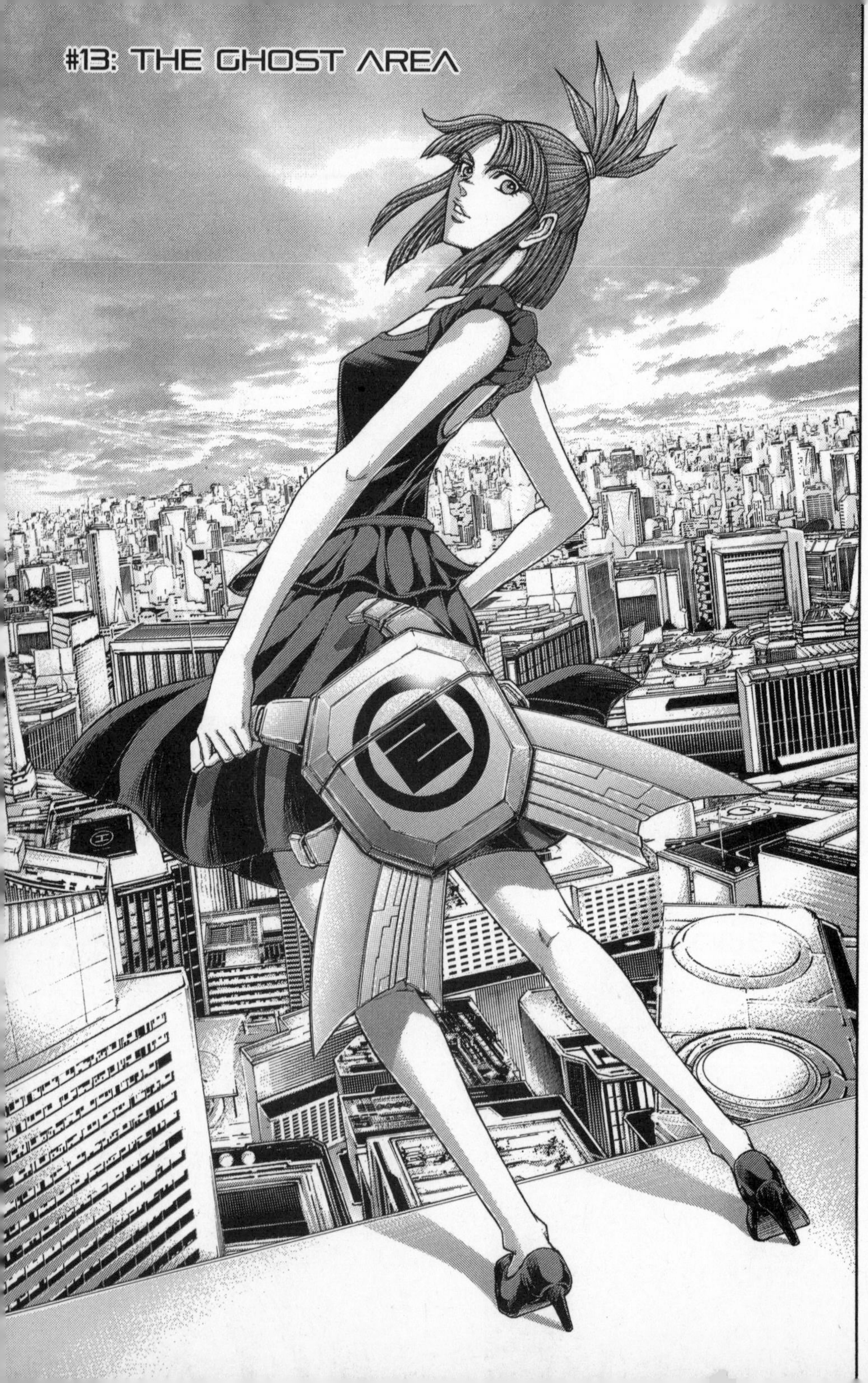

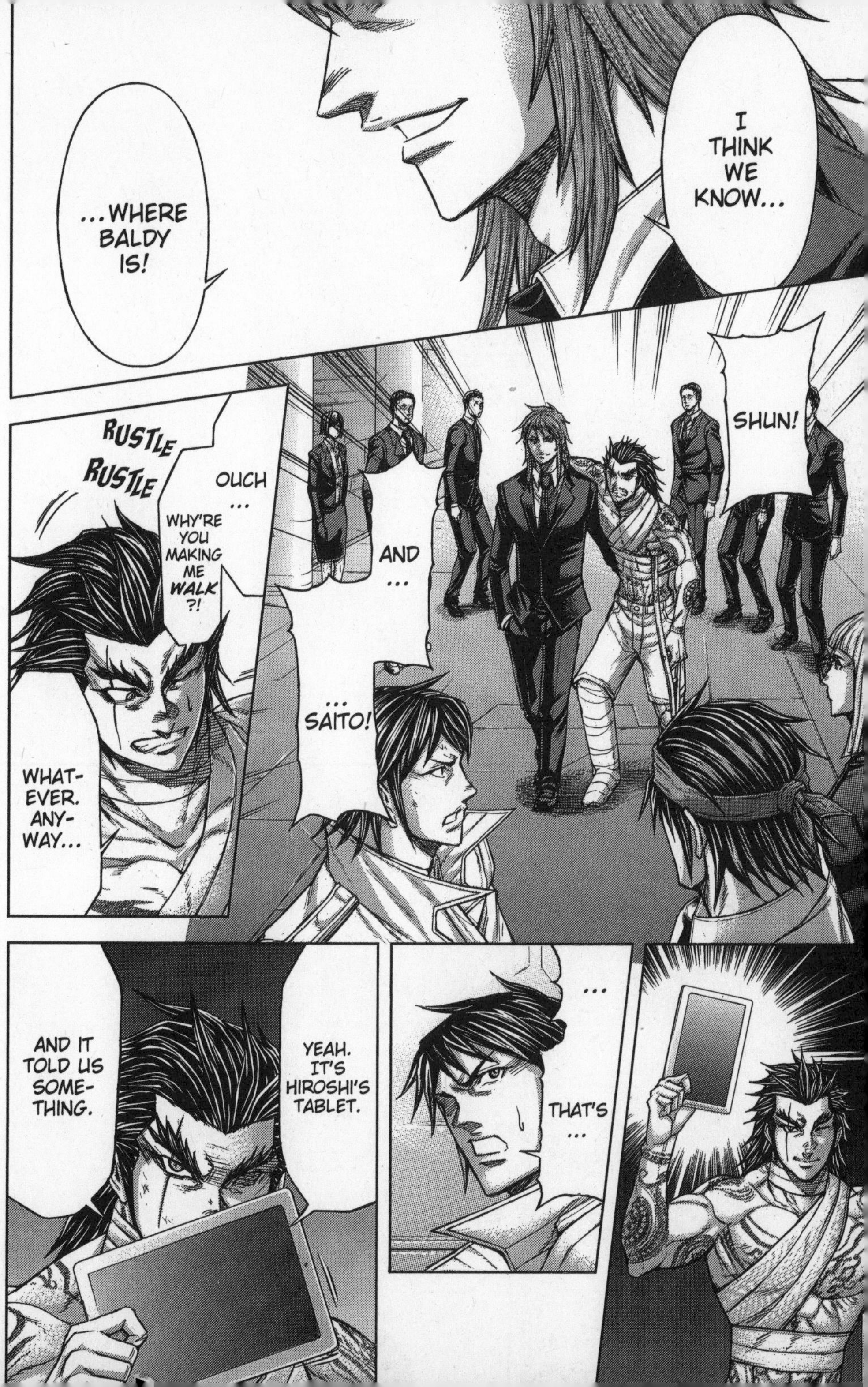
I THINK WE KNOW...
...WHERE BALDY IS!
SHUN!
AND...
...SAITO!
RUSTLE RUSTLE
OUCH...
WHY'RE YOU MAKING ME WALK?!
WHAT-EVER. ANY-WAY...
...
THAT'S...
YEAH. IT'S HIROSHI'S TABLET.
AND IT TOLD US SOME-THING.

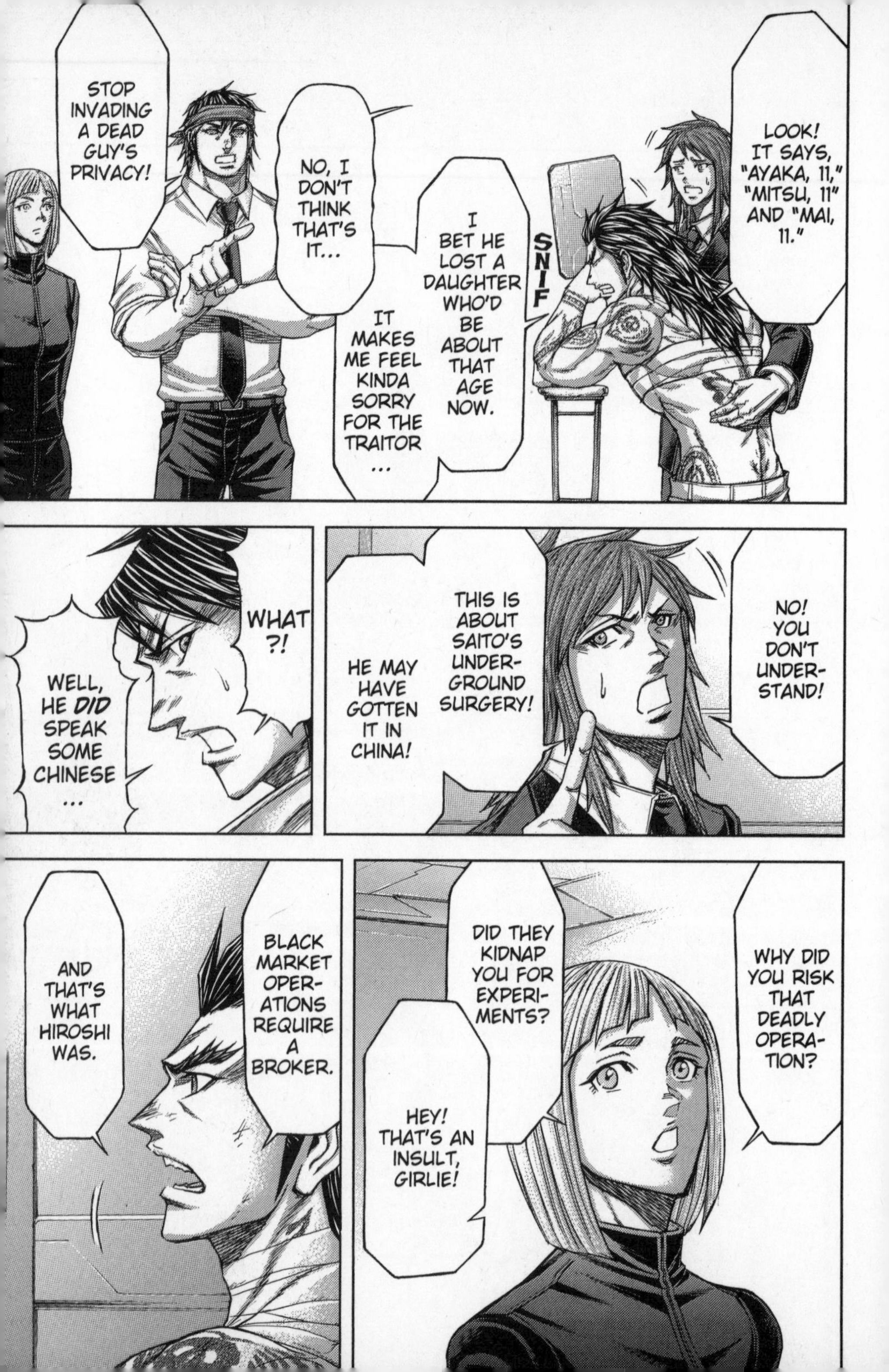
LOOK! IT SAYS, "AYAKA, 11," "MITSU, 11" AND "MAI, 11."
SNIF
I BET HE LOST A DAUGHTER WHO'D BE ABOUT THAT AGE NOW.
IT MAKES ME FEEL KINDA SORRY FOR THE TRAITOR...
NO, I DON'T THINK THAT'S IT...
STOP INVADING A DEAD GUY'S PRIVACY!
NO! YOU DON'T UNDER-STAND!
THIS IS ABOUT SAITO'S UNDER-GROUND SURGERY!
HE MAY HAVE GOTTEN IT IN CHINA!
WHAT?!
WELL, HE *DID* SPEAK SOME CHINESE...
WHY DID YOU RISK THAT DEADLY OPERA-TION?
DID THEY KIDNAP YOU FOR EXPERI-MENTS?
HEY! THAT'S AN INSULT, GIRLIE!
BLACK MARKET OPER-ATIONS REQUIRE A BROKER.
AND THAT'S WHAT HIROSHI WAS.

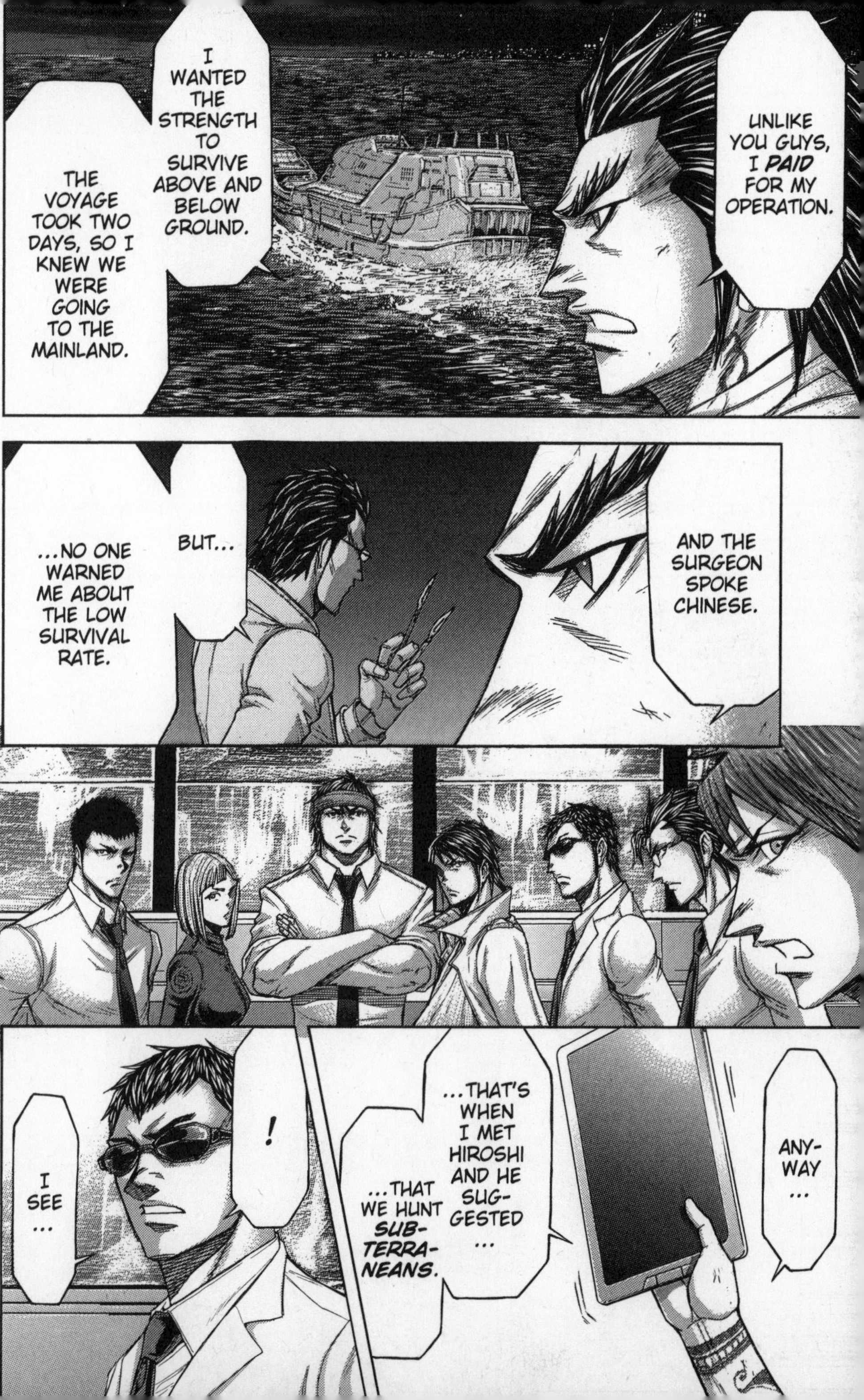
UNLIKE YOU GUYS, I PAID FOR MY OPERATION.
I WANTED THE STRENGTH TO SURVIVE ABOVE AND BELOW GROUND.
THE VOYAGE TOOK TWO DAYS, SO I KNEW WE WERE GOING TO THE MAINLAND.
AND THE SURGEON SPOKE CHINESE.
BUT...
...NO ONE WARNED ME ABOUT THE LOW SURVIVAL RATE.
ANYWAY...
...THAT'S WHEN I MET HIROSHI AND HE SUGGESTED...
...THAT WE HUNT SUBTERRANEANS.
!
I SEE...

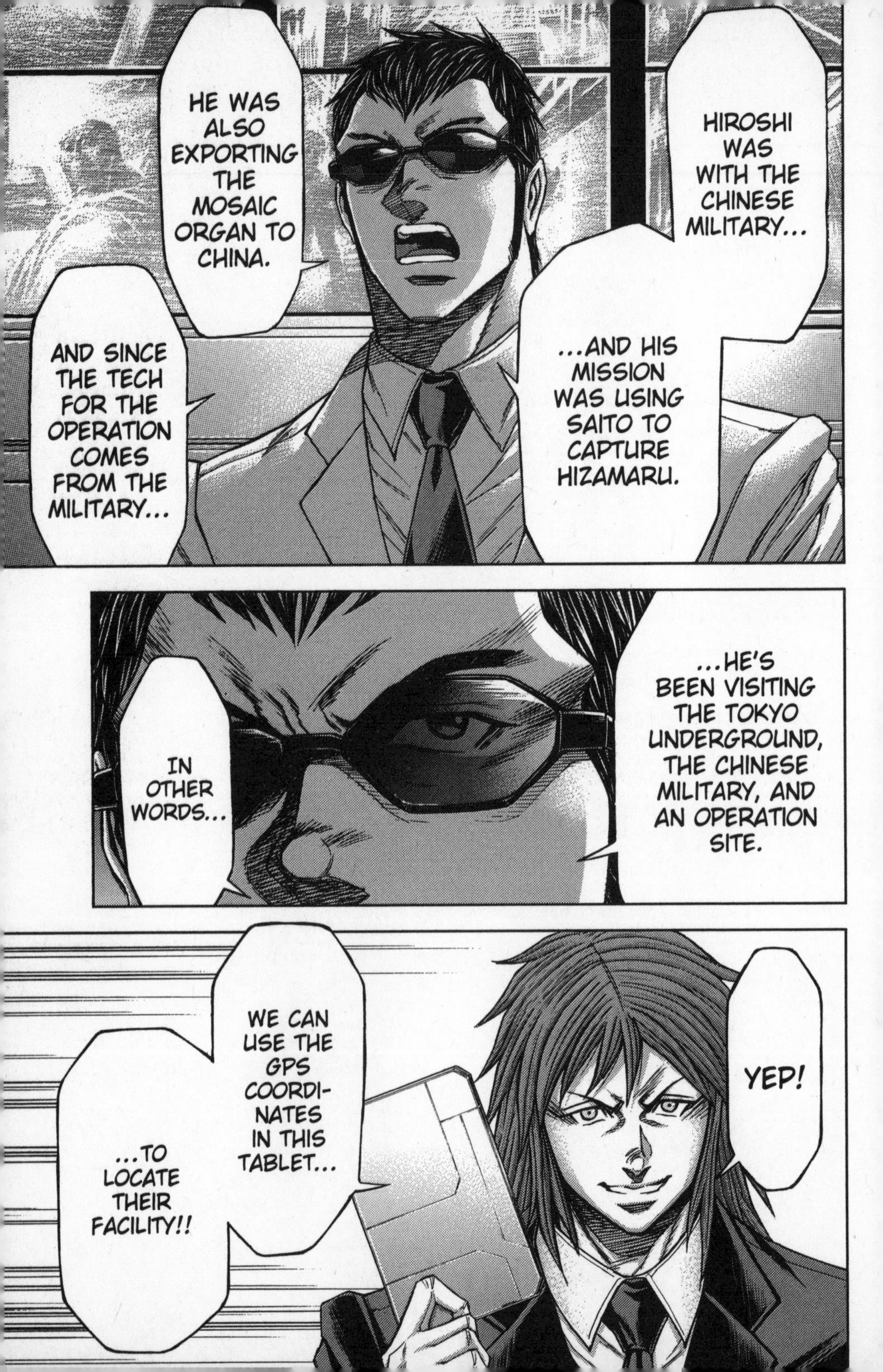
HIROSHI WAS WITH THE CHINESE MILITARY...
...AND HIS MISSION WAS USING SAITO TO CAPTURE HIZAMARU.
HE WAS ALSO EXPORTING THE MOSAIC ORGAN TO CHINA.
AND SINCE THE TECH FOR THE OPERATION COMES FROM THE MILITARY...
IN OTHER WORDS...
...HE'S BEEN VISITING THE TOKYO UNDERGROUND, THE CHINESE MILITARY, AND AN OPERATION SITE.
YEP!
WE CAN USE THE GPS COORDI-NATES IN THIS TABLET...
...TO LOCATE THEIR FACILITY!!

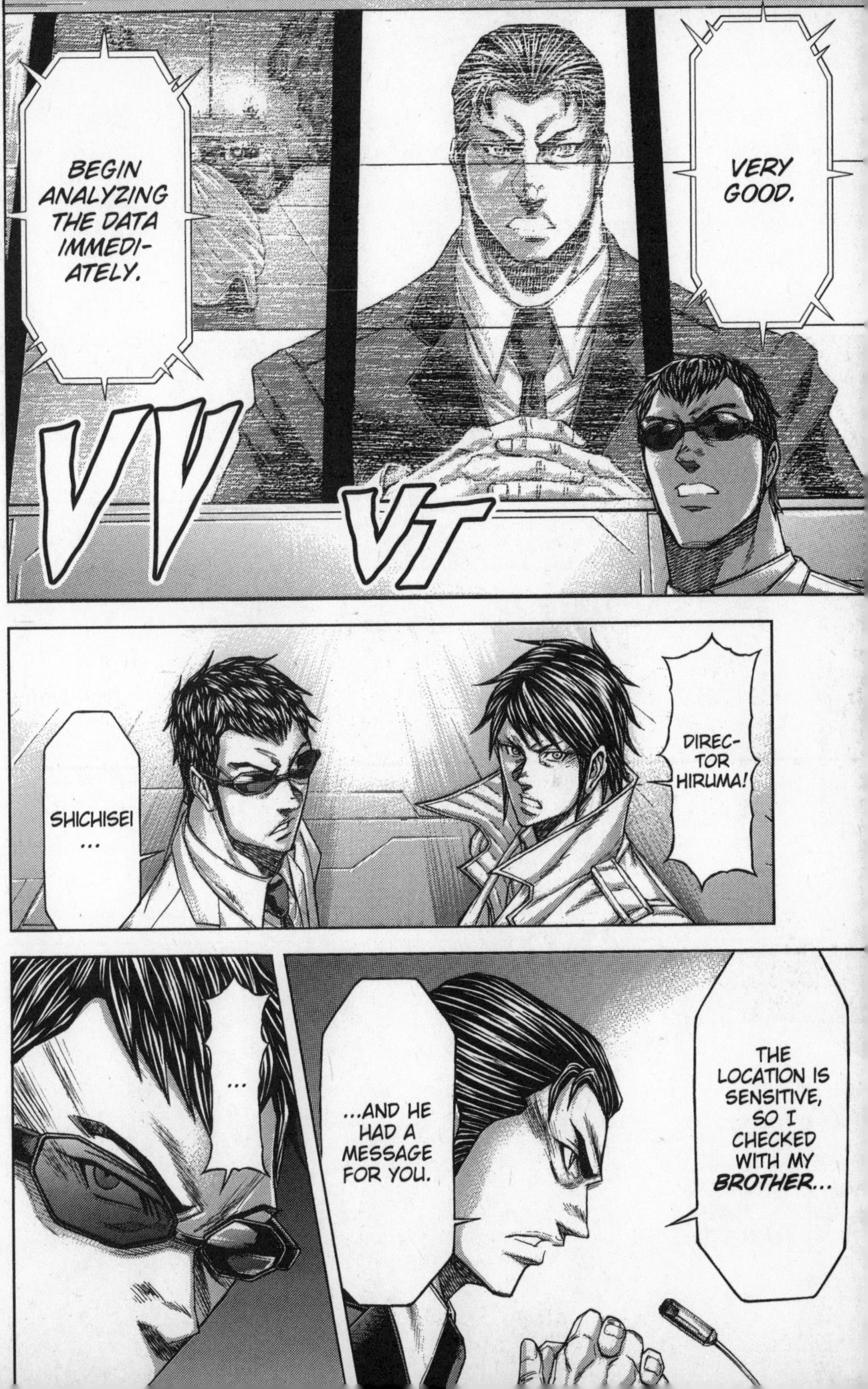
VERY GOOD.
BEGIN ANALYZING THE DATA IMMEDIATELY.
VV VT
DIRECTOR HIRUMA!
SHICHISEI ...
THE LOCATION IS SENSITIVE, SO I CHECKED WITH MY *BROTHER*...
...AND HE HAD A MESSAGE FOR YOU.
...

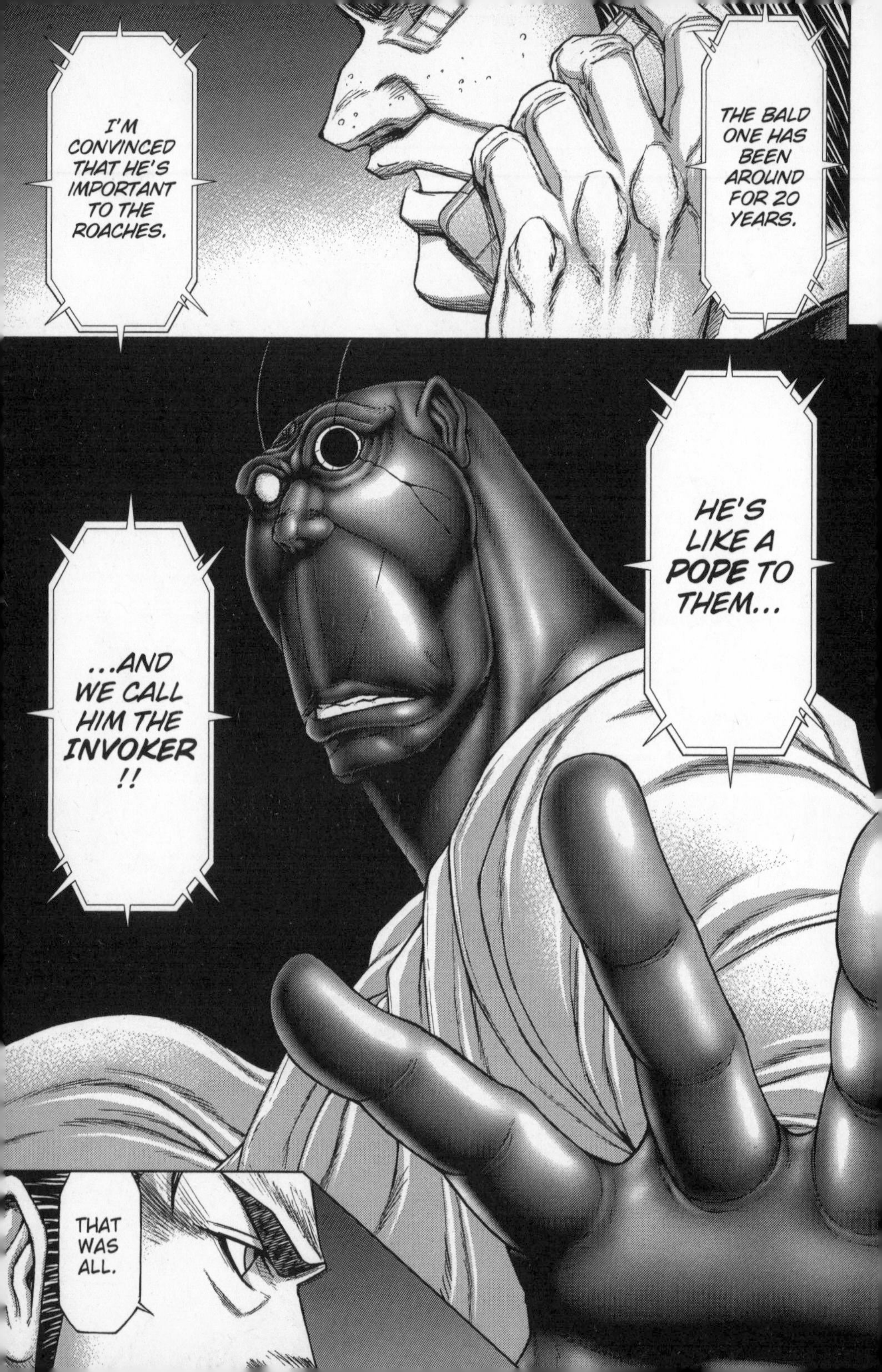
THE BALD ONE HAS BEEN AROUND FOR 20 YEARS.
I'M CONVINCED THAT HE'S IMPORTANT TO THE ROACHES.
HE'S LIKE A **POPE** TO THEM...
...AND WE CALL HIM THE **INVOKER** !!
THAT WAS ALL.

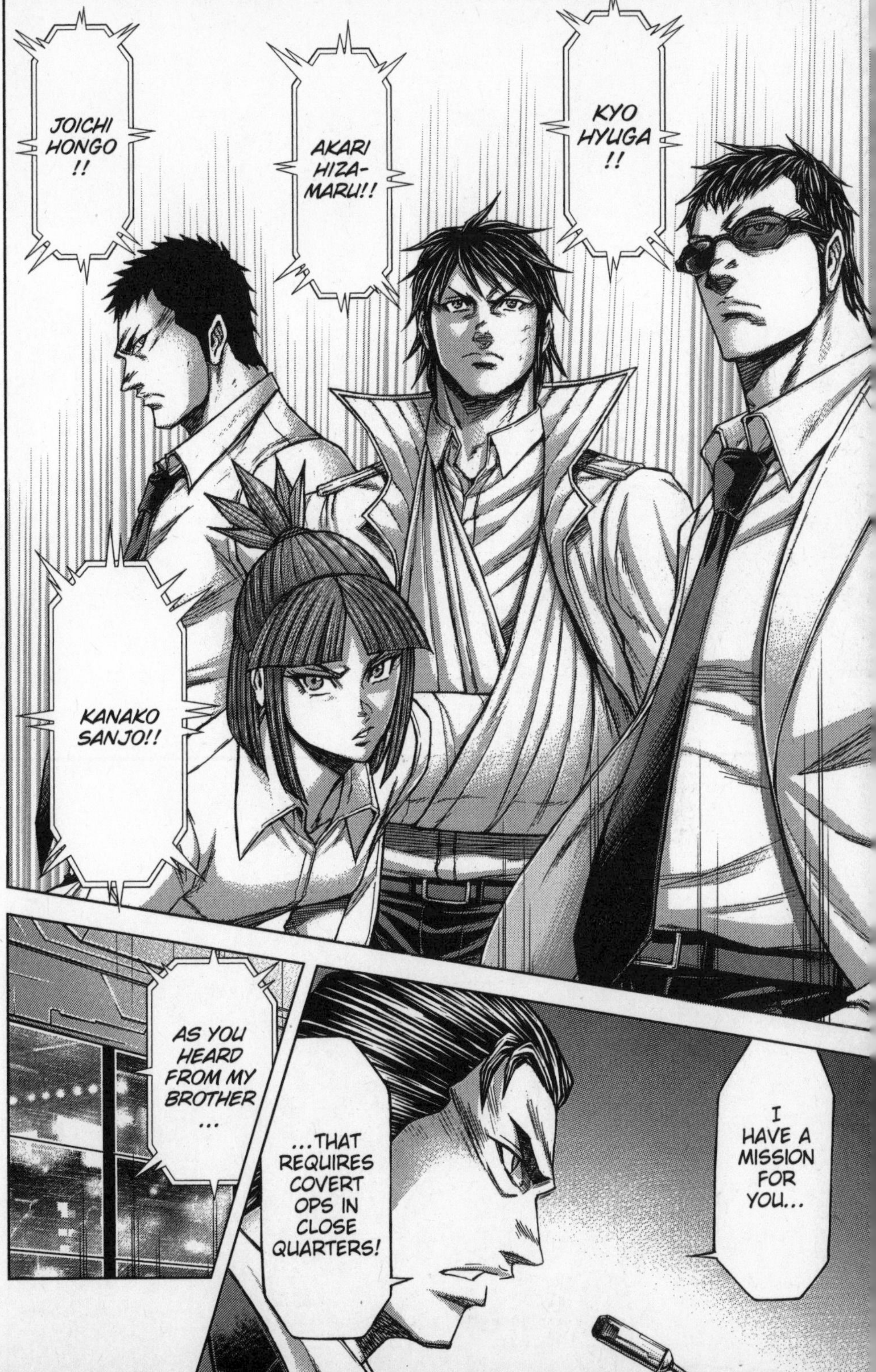
KYO HYUGA!!
AKARI HIZA-MARU!!
JOICHI HONGO!!
KANAKO SANJO!!
I HAVE A MISSION FOR YOU...
...THAT REQUIRES COVERT OPS IN CLOSE QUARTERS!
AS YOU HEARD FROM MY BROTHER...

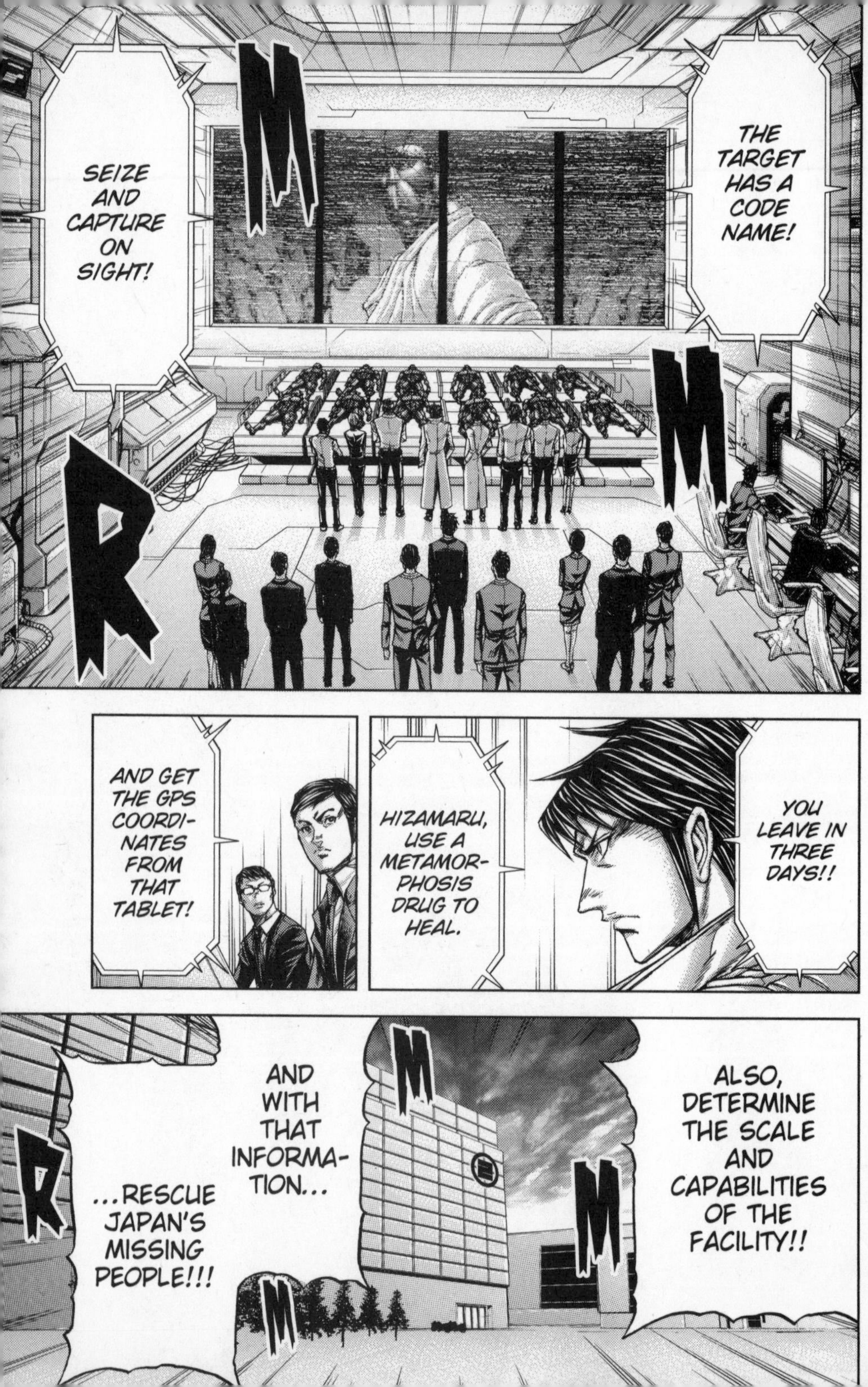
THE TARGET HAS A CODE NAME!
SEIZE AND CAPTURE ON SIGHT!
M
M
R
YOU LEAVE IN THREE DAYS!!
HIZAMARU, USE A METAMORPHOSIS DRUG TO HEAL.
AND GET THE GPS COORDINATES FROM THAT TABLET!
ALSO, DETERMINE THE SCALE AND CAPABILITIES OF THE FACILITY!!
M
M
AND WITH THAT INFORMATION...
M
...RESCUE JAPAN'S MISSING PEOPLE!!!
R

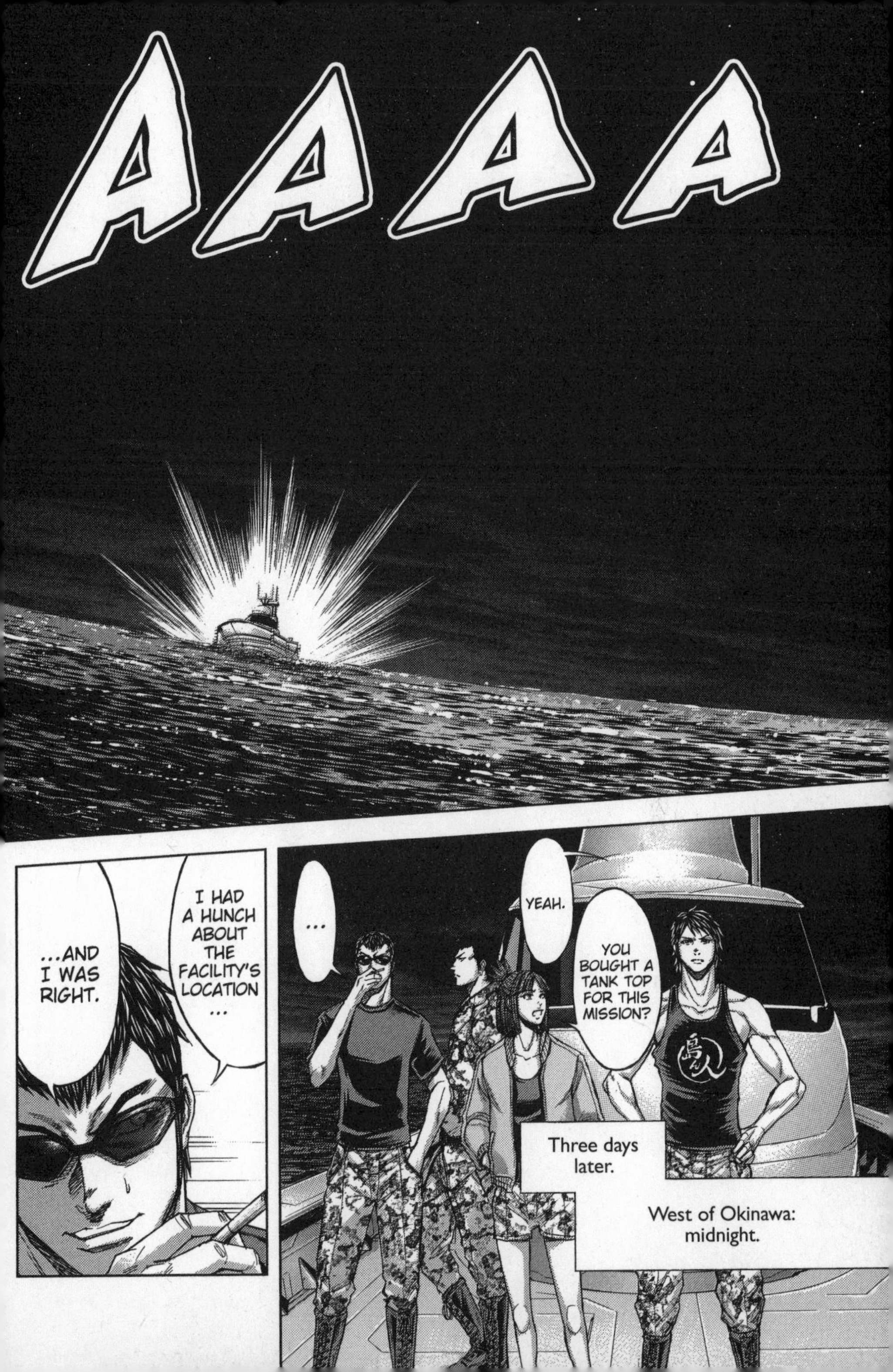
AAAA
YOU BOUGHT A TANK TOP FOR THIS MISSION?
YEAH.
...
Three days later.
West of Okinawa: midnight.
I HAD A HUNCH ABOUT THE FACILITY'S LOCATION...
...AND I WAS RIGHT.

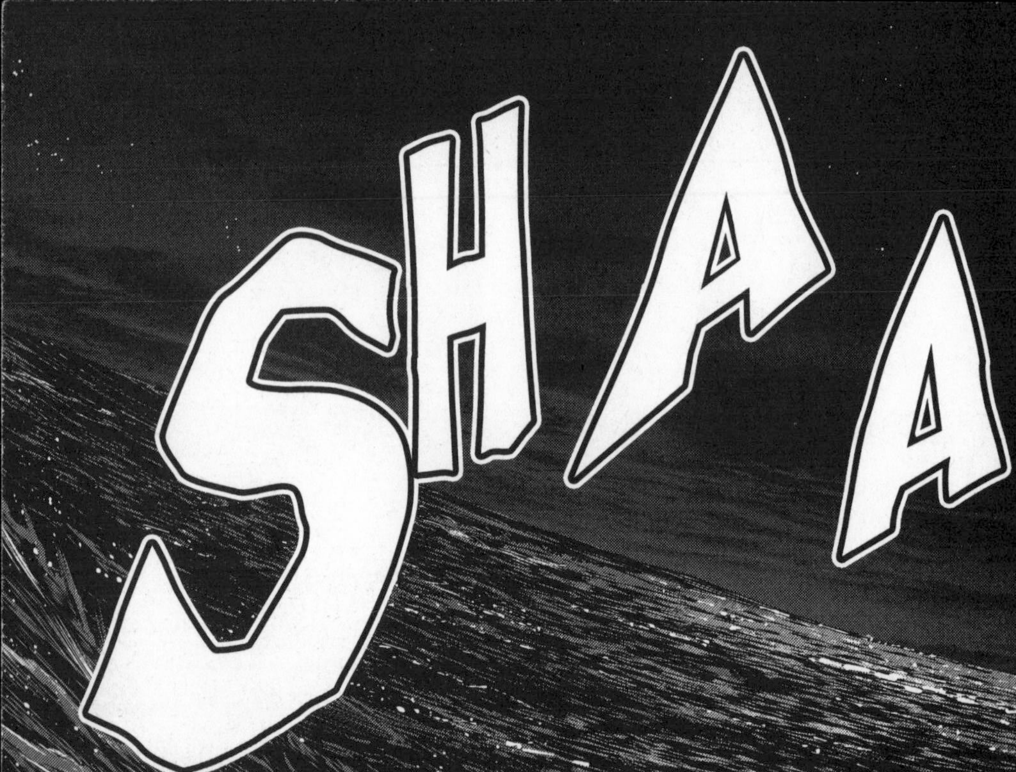
SHAA
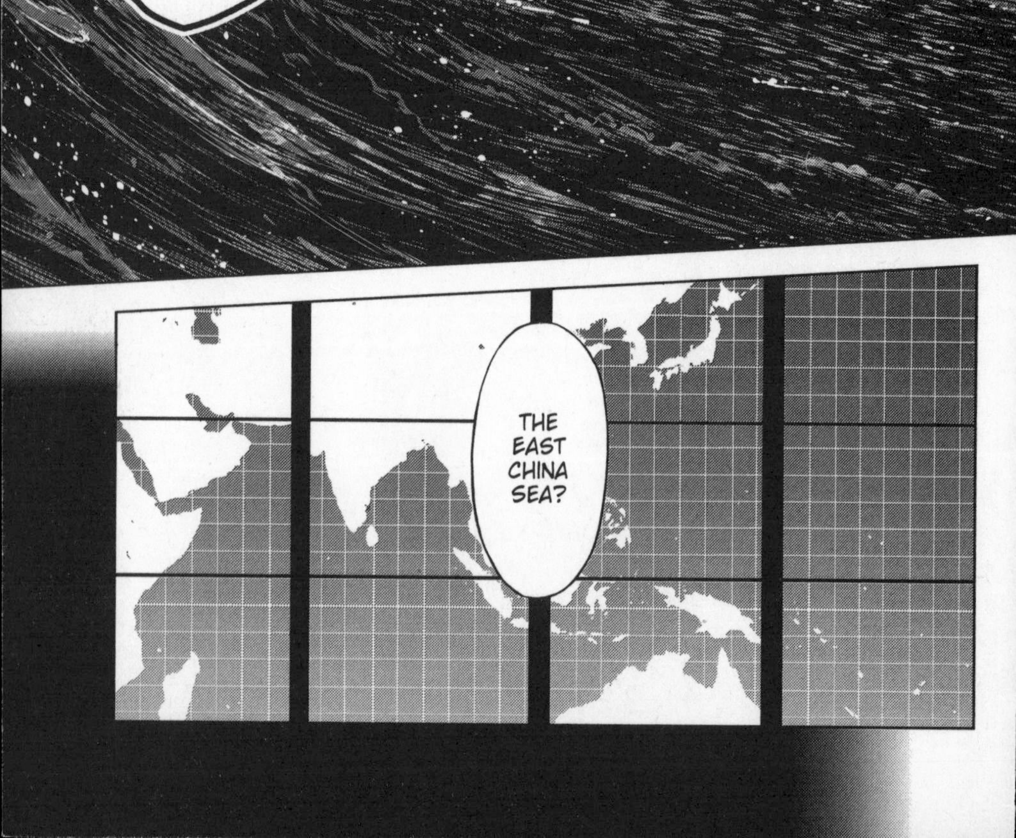
THE EAST CHINA SEA?

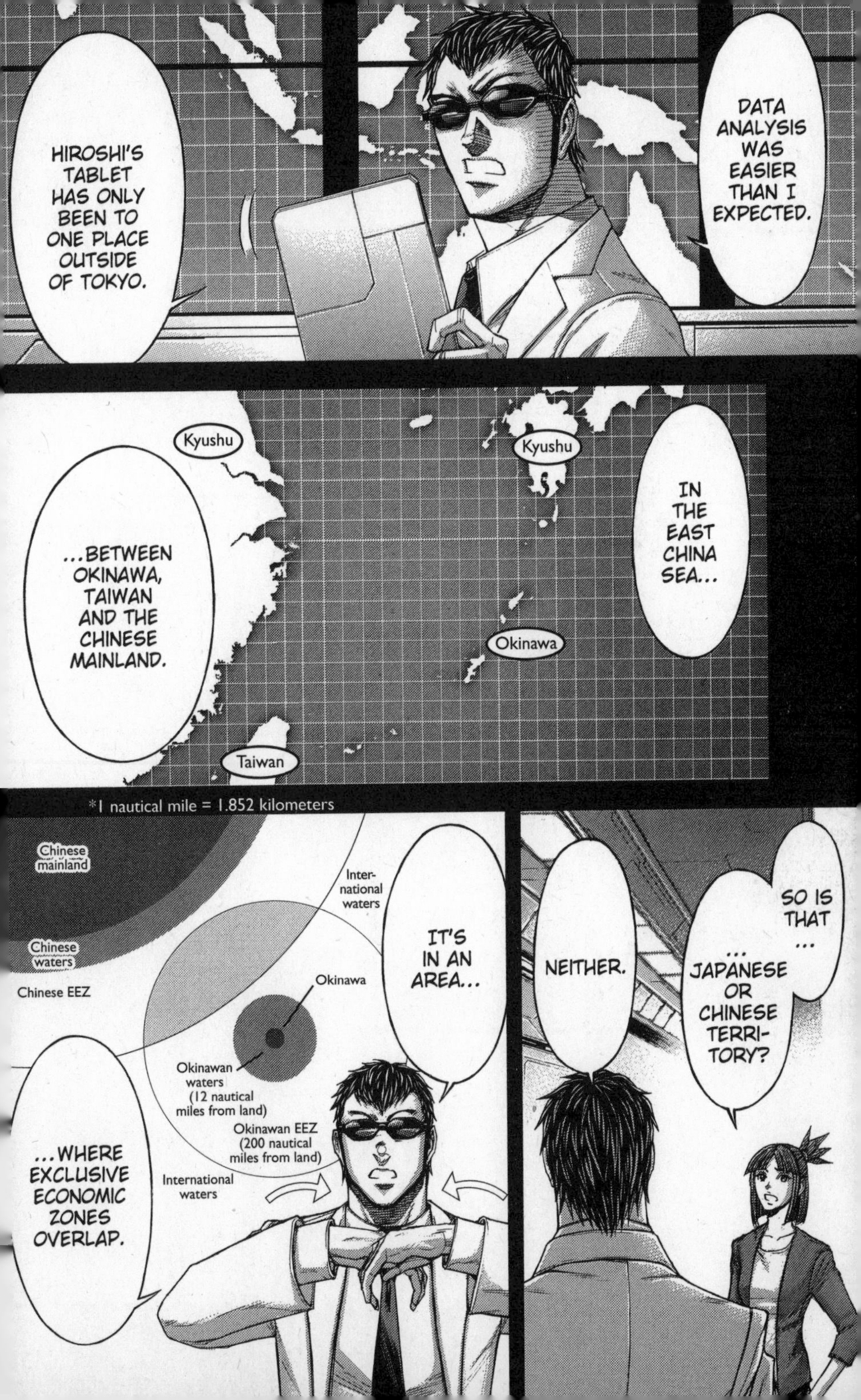
DATA ANALYSIS WAS EASIER THAN I EXPECTED.
HIROSHI'S TABLET HAS ONLY BEEN TO ONE PLACE OUTSIDE OF TOKYO.
IN THE EAST CHINA SEA...
Kyushu
Kyushu
Okinawa
Taiwan
...BETWEEN OKINAWA, TAIWAN AND THE CHINESE MAINLAND.
*1 nautical mile = 1.852 kilometers
SO IS THAT ... JAPANESE OR CHINESE TERRITORY?
NEITHER.
IT'S IN AN AREA...
Chinese mainland
International waters
Chinese waters
Okinawa
Chinese EEZ
Okinawan waters (12 nautical miles from land)
Okinawan EEZ (200 nautical miles from land)
International waters
...WHERE EXCLUSIVE ECONOMIC ZONES OVERLAP.

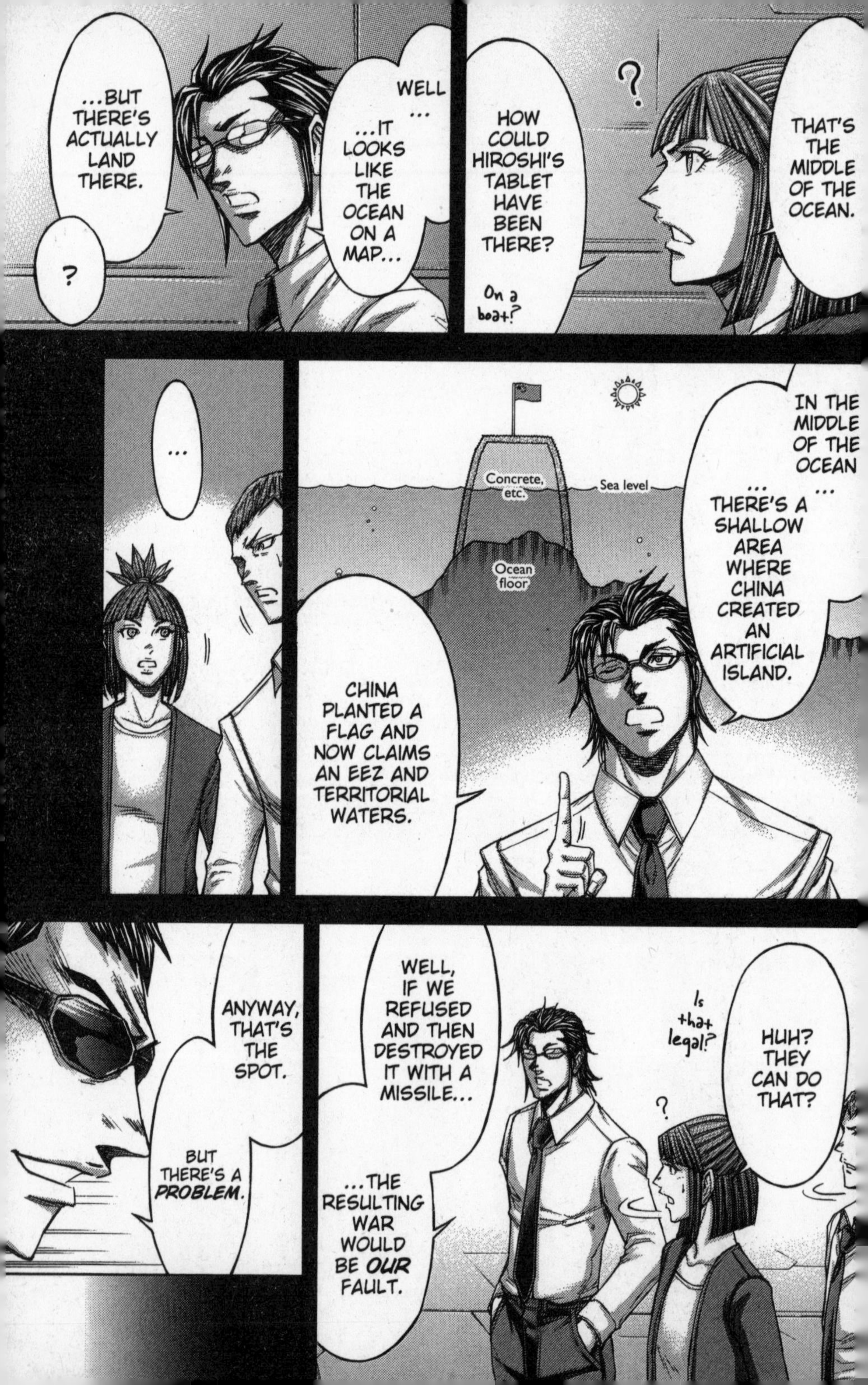
THAT'S THE MIDDLE OF THE OCEAN.
?
HOW COULD HIROSHI'S TABLET HAVE BEEN THERE?
On a boat?
WELL ...
...IT LOOKS LIKE THE OCEAN ON A MAP...
...BUT THERE'S ACTUALLY LAND THERE.
?
IN THE MIDDLE OF THE OCEAN ... THERE'S A SHALLOW AREA WHERE CHINA CREATED AN ARTIFICIAL ISLAND.
Concrete, etc.
Sea level
Ocean floor
CHINA PLANTED A FLAG AND NOW CLAIMS AN EEZ AND TERRITORIAL WATERS.
...
HUH? THEY CAN DO THAT?
Is that legal?
?
WELL, IF WE REFUSED AND THEN DESTROYED IT WITH A MISSILE...
...THE RESULTING WAR WOULD BE *OUR* FAULT.
ANYWAY, THAT'S THE SPOT.
BUT THERE'S A *PROBLEM*.

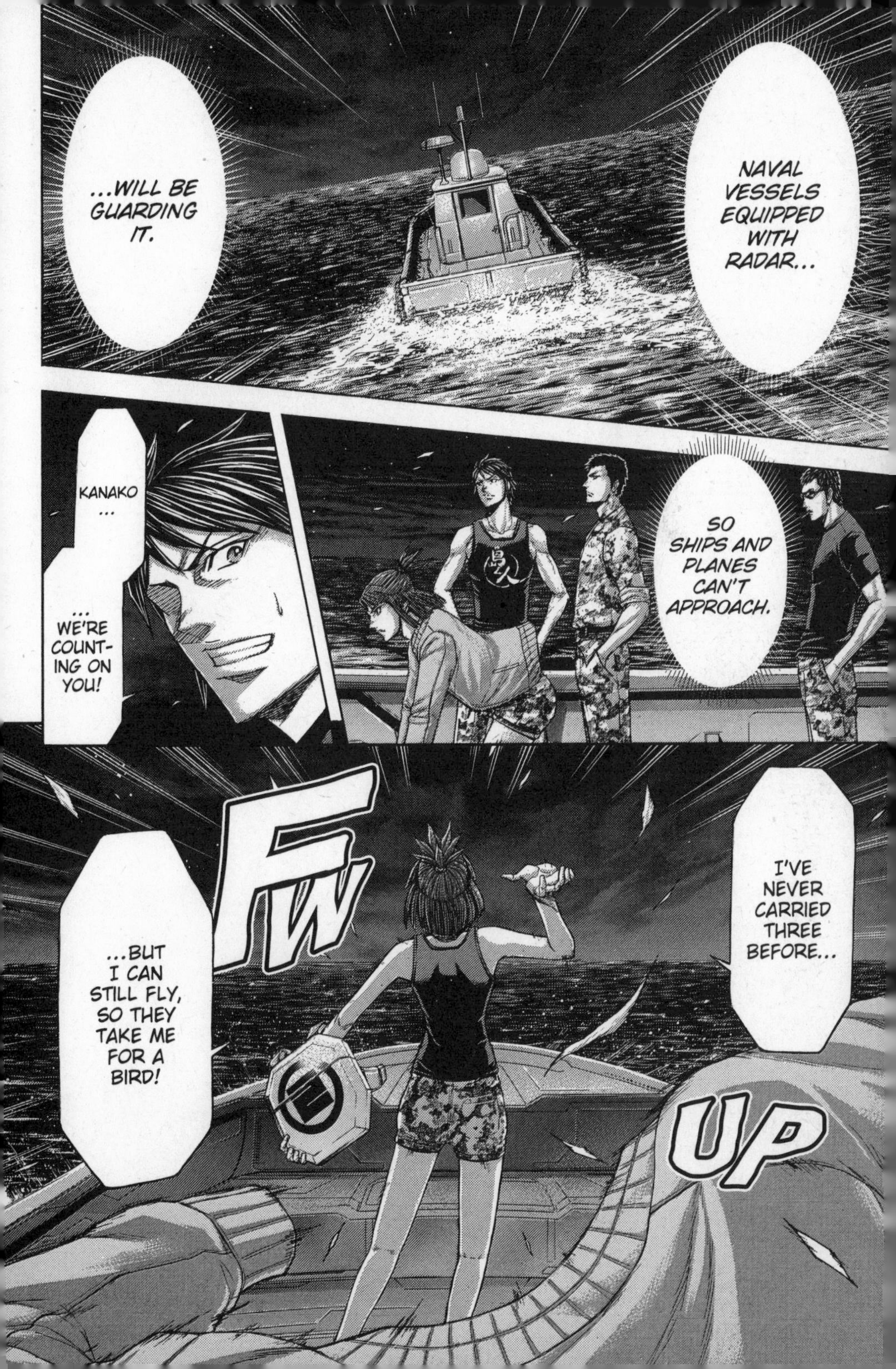
NAVAL VESSELS EQUIPPED WITH RADAR...
...WILL BE GUARDING IT.
SO SHIPS AND PLANES CAN'T APPROACH.
KANAKO...
...WE'RE COUNTING ON YOU!
I'VE NEVER CARRIED THREE BEFORE...
FW
UP
...BUT I CAN STILL FLY, SO THEY TAKE ME FOR A BIRD!

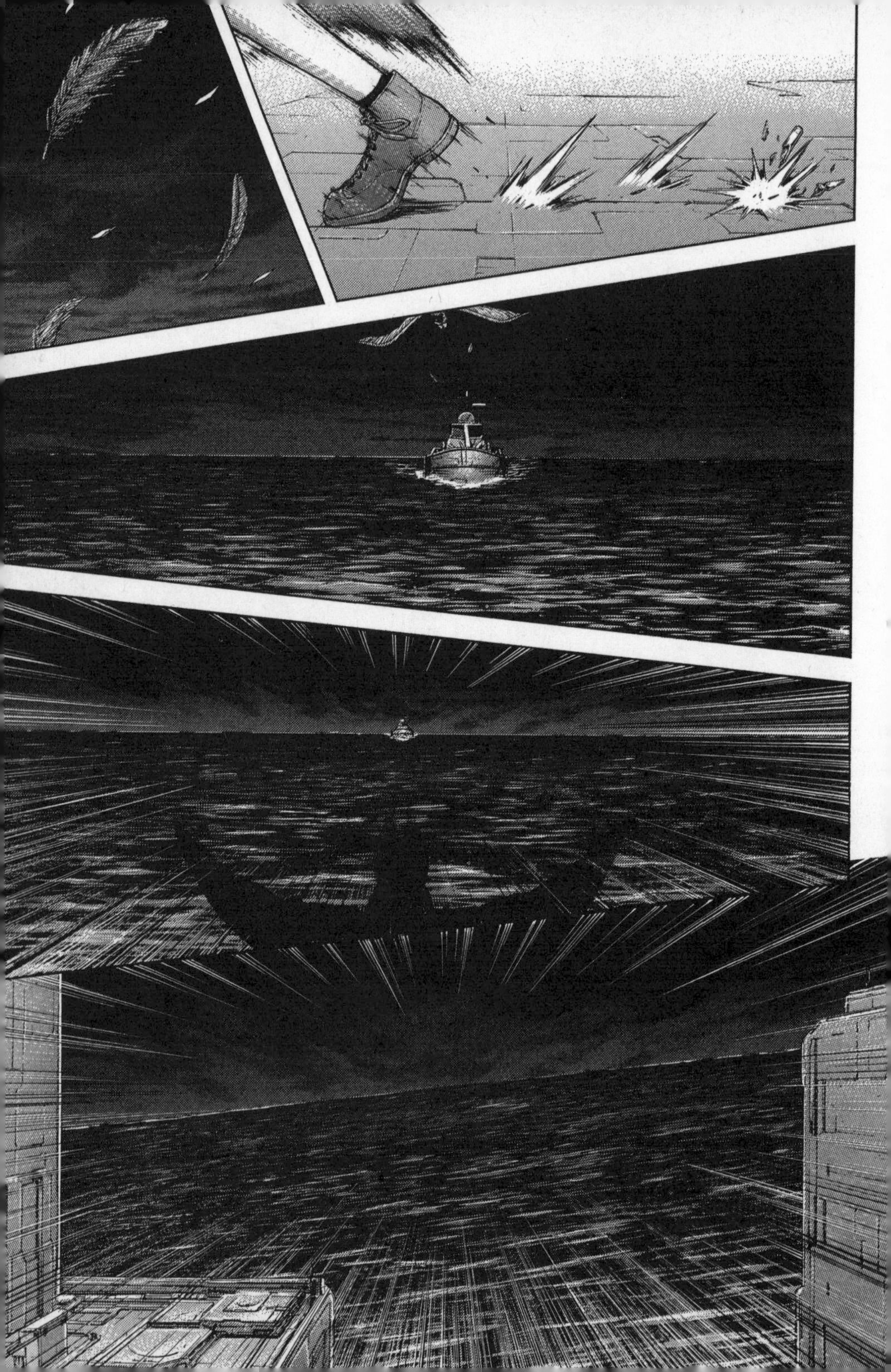

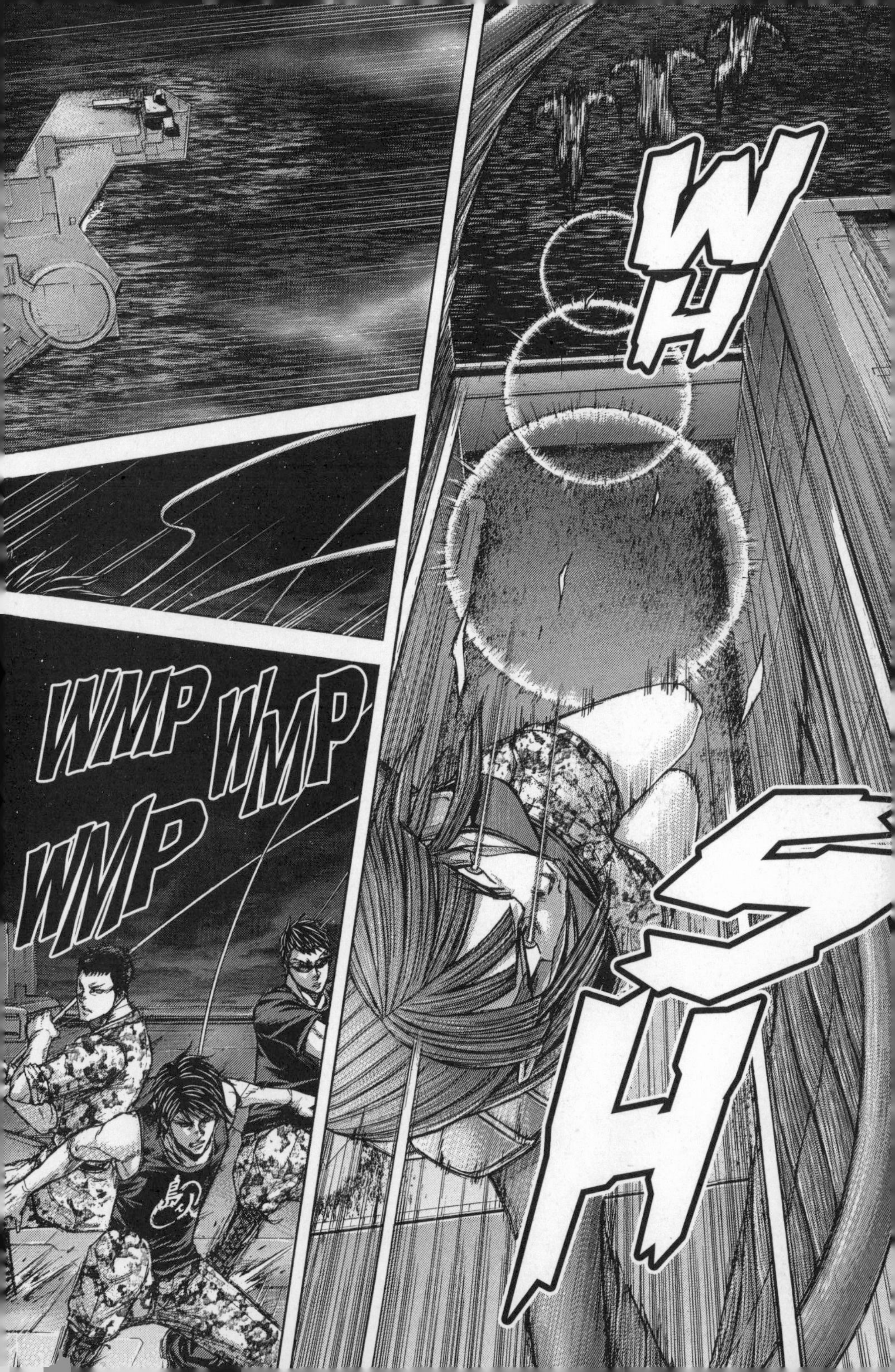
WH
SH
WMP WMP
WMP

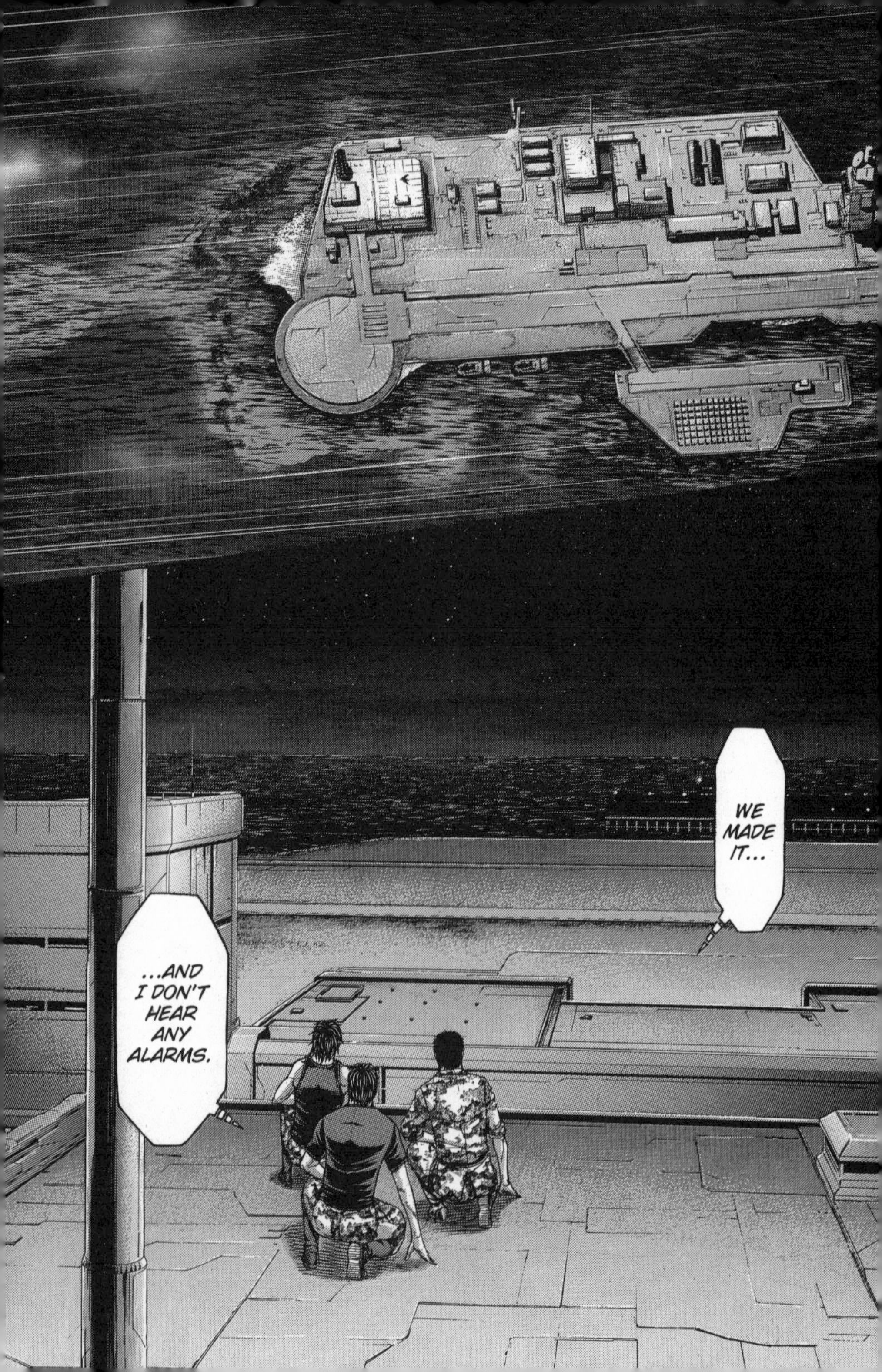
WE MADE IT...
...AND I DON'T HEAR ANY ALARMS.

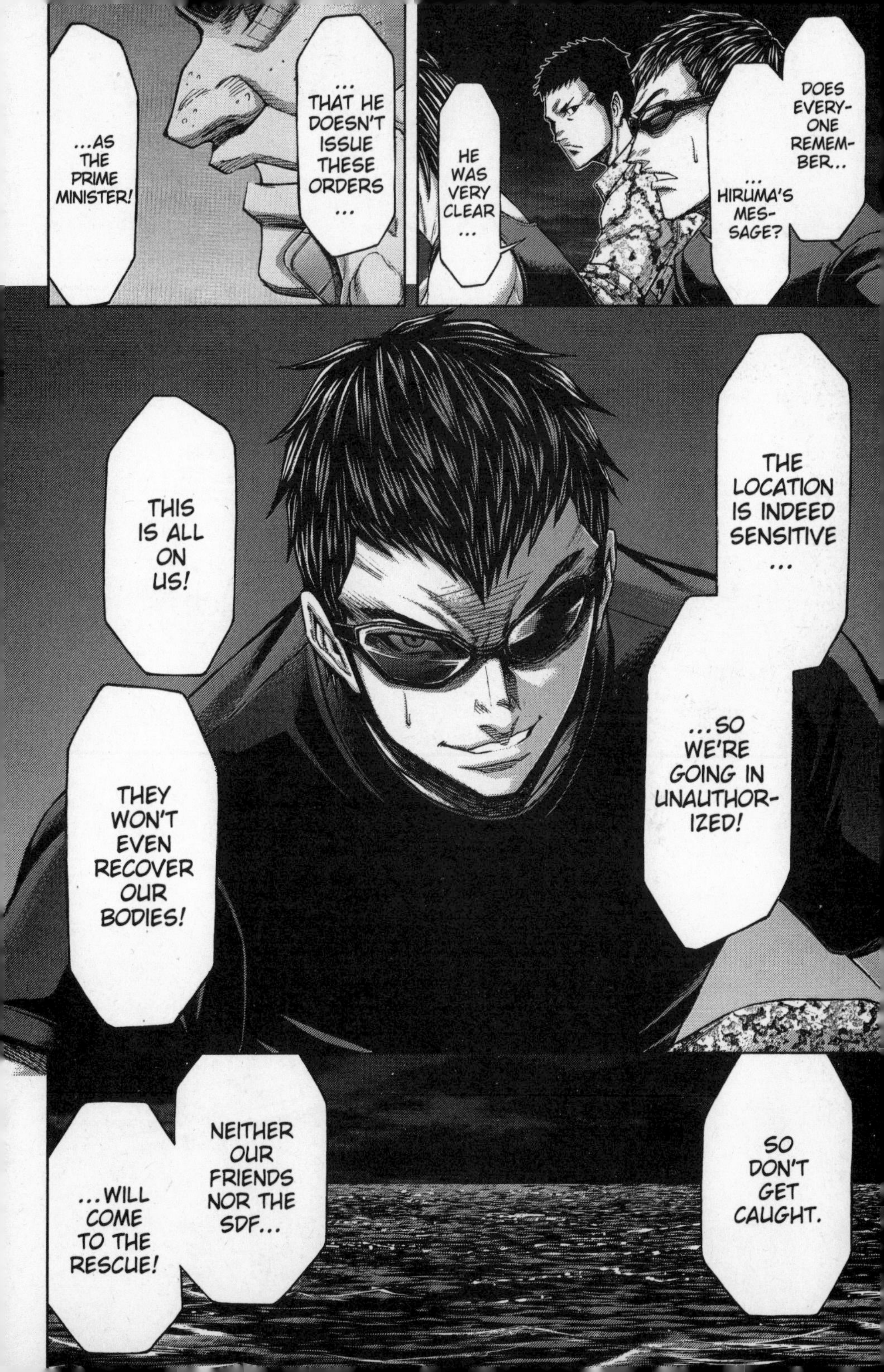
DOES EVERYONE REMEMBER...
...HIRUMA'S MESSAGE?
HE WAS VERY CLEAR...
...THAT HE DOESN'T ISSUE THESE ORDERS...
...AS THE PRIME MINISTER!
THE LOCATION IS INDEED SENSITIVE...
...SO WE'RE GOING IN UNAUTHORIZED!
THIS IS ALL ON US!
THEY WON'T EVEN RECOVER OUR BODIES!
SO DON'T GET CAUGHT.
NEITHER OUR FRIENDS NOR THE SDF...
...WILL COME TO THE RESCUE!

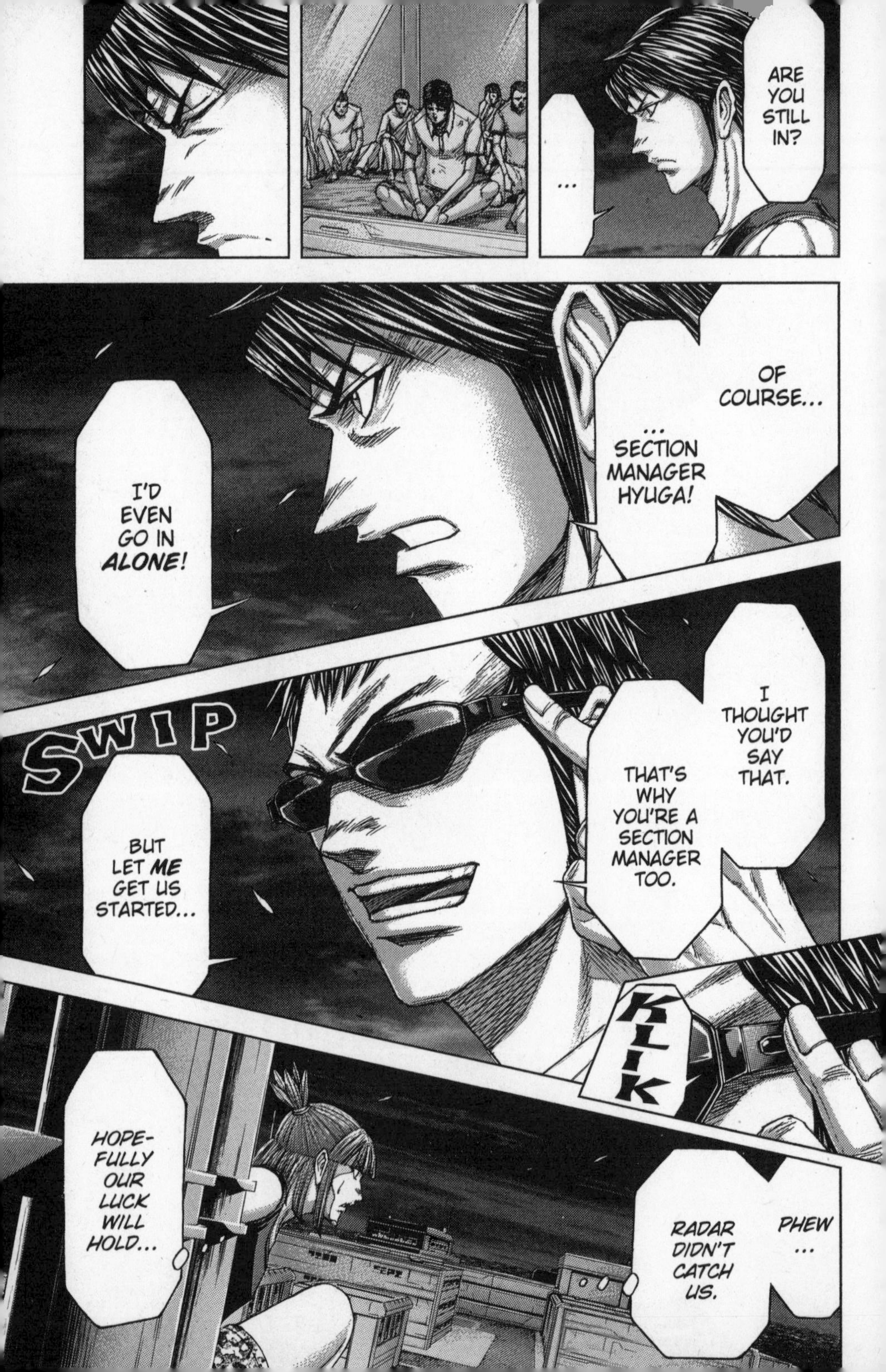
ARE YOU STILL IN?
...
OF COURSE...
...SECTION MANAGER HYUGA!
I'D EVEN GO IN ALONE!
I THOUGHT YOU'D SAY THAT.
THAT'S WHY YOU'RE A SECTION MANAGER TOO.
SWIP
BUT LET ME GET US STARTED...
KLIK
PHEW...
RADAR DIDN'T CATCH US.
HOPEFULLY OUR LUCK WILL HOLD...

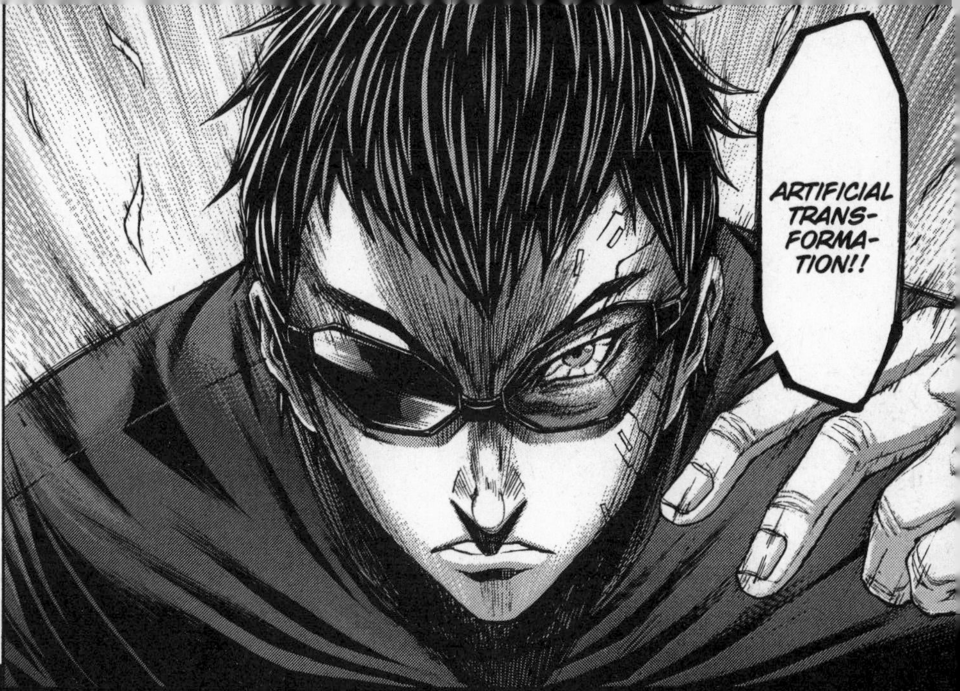
ARTIFICIAL TRANS-FORMA-TION!!
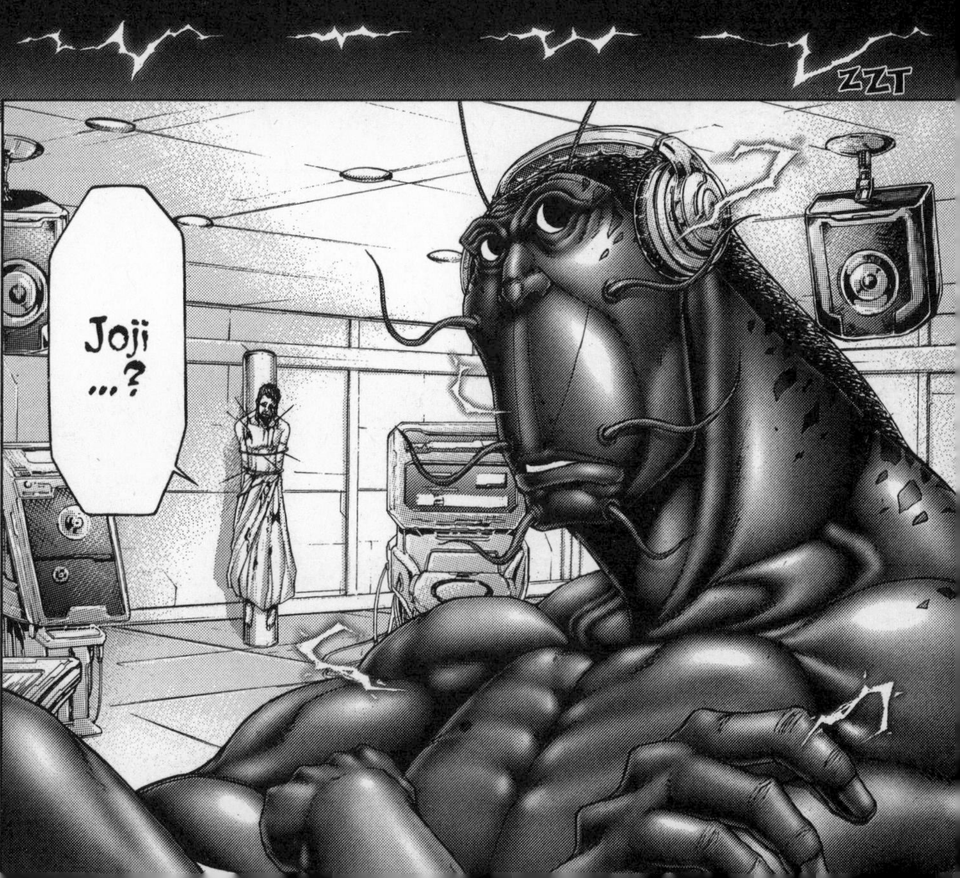
ZZT
Joji ...?

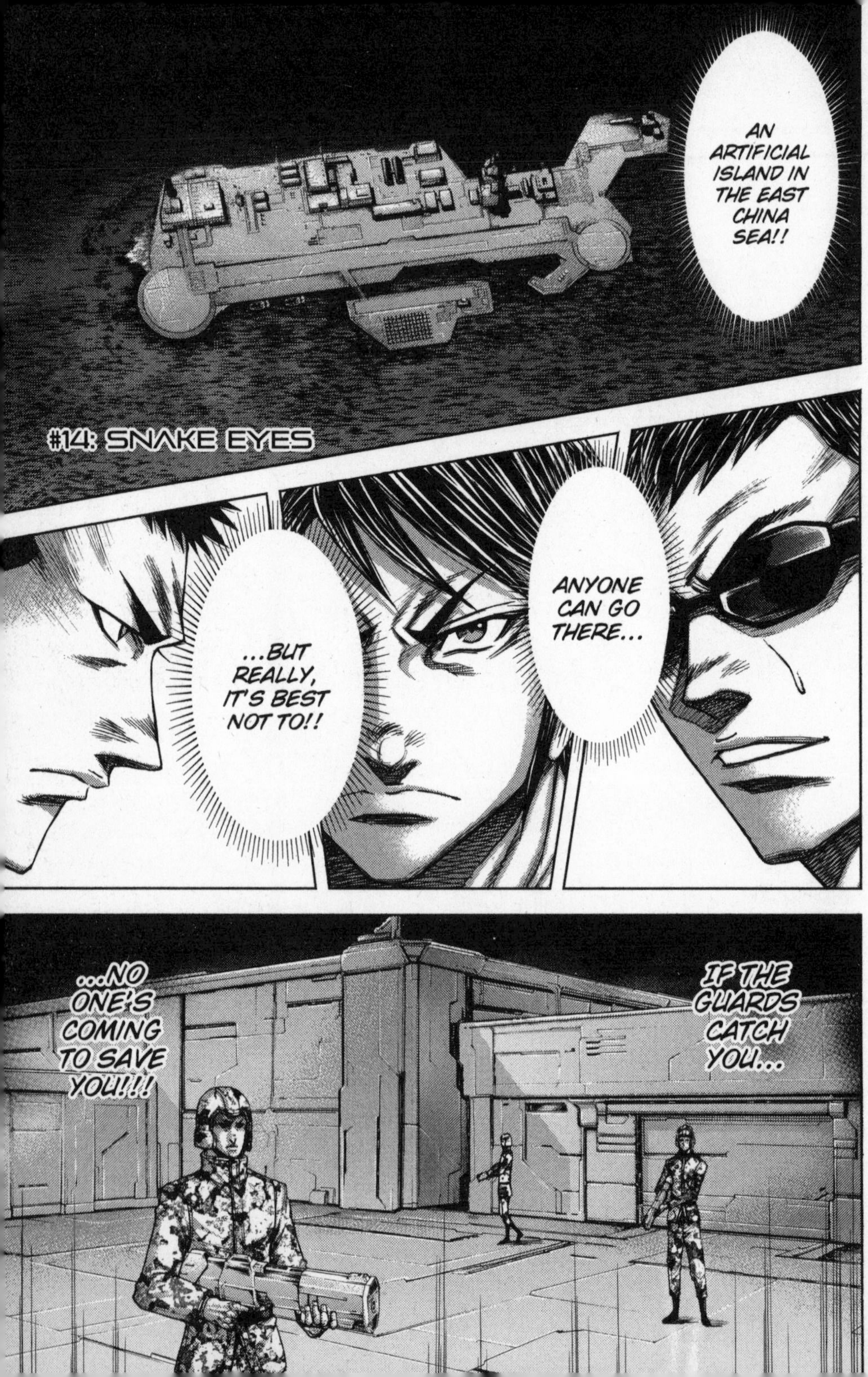
AN ARTIFICIAL ISLAND IN THE EAST CHINA SEA!!
#14: SNAKE EYES
ANYONE CAN GO THERE...
...BUT REALLY, IT'S BEST NOT TO!!
IF THE GUARDS CATCH YOU...
...NO ONE'S COMING TO SAVE YOU!!!

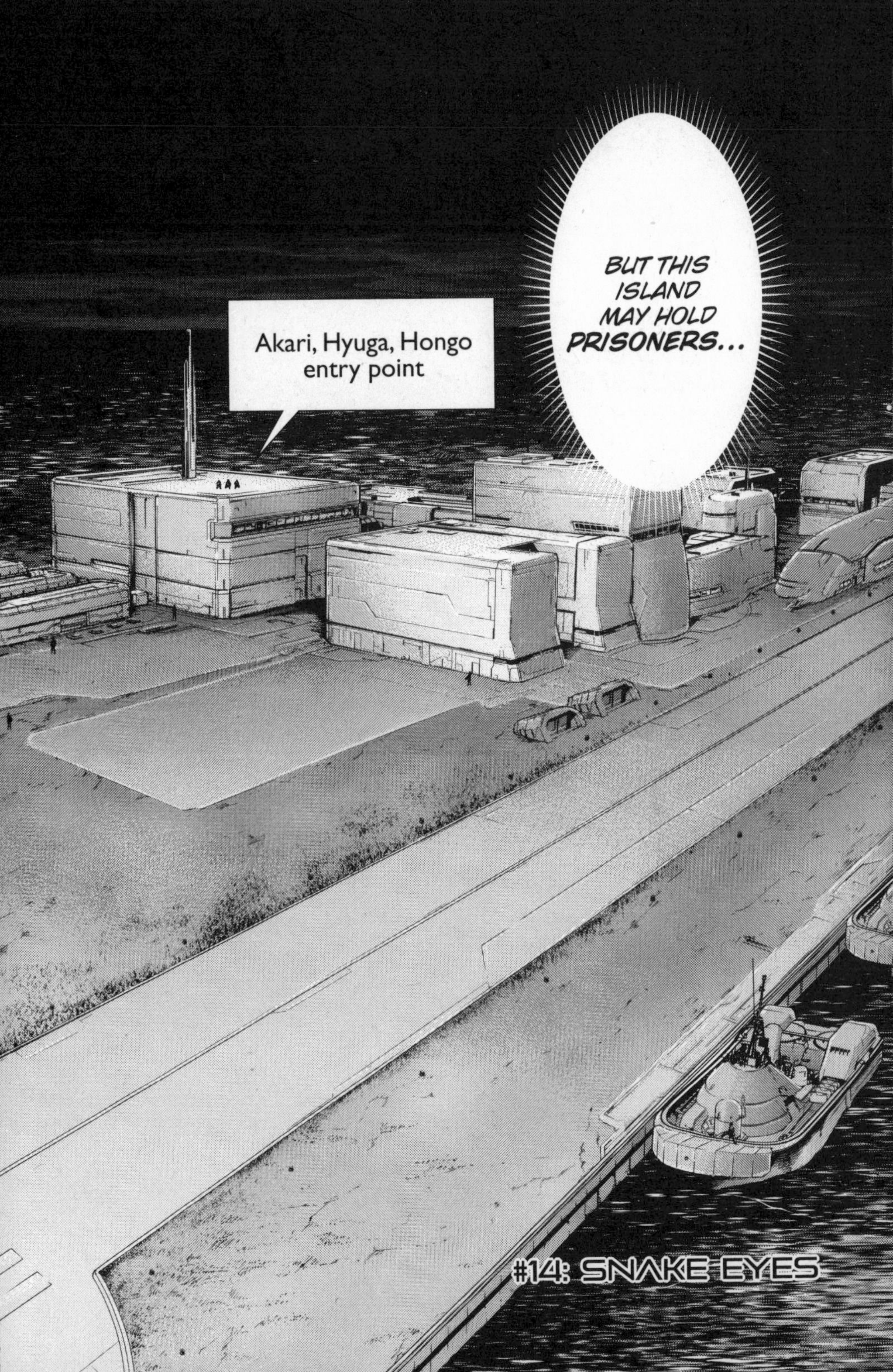
BUT THIS ISLAND MAY HOLD PRISONERS...
Akari, Hyuga, Hongo entry point
#14: SNAKE EYES

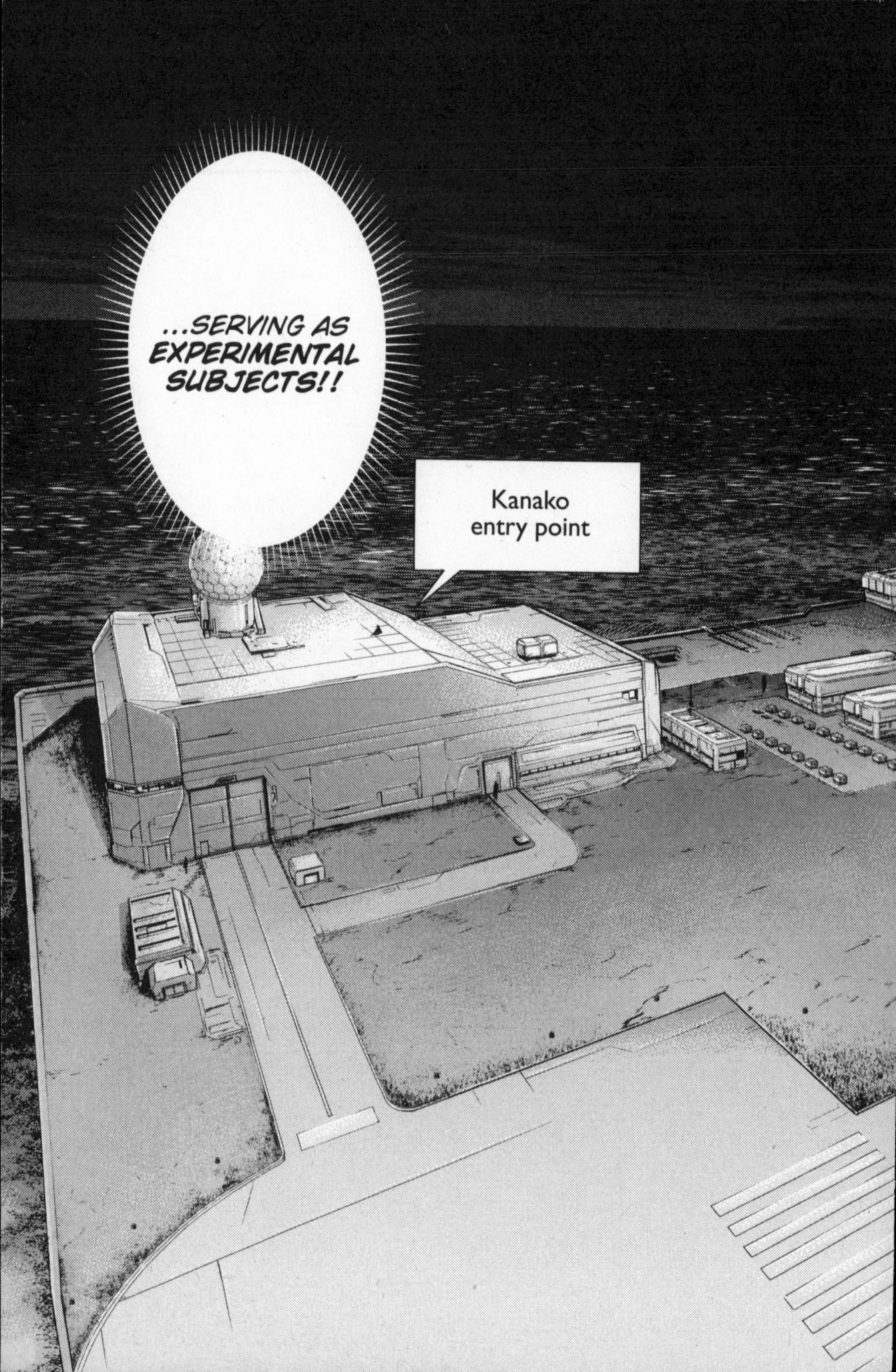
...SERVING AS EXPERIMENTAL SUBJECTS!!
Kanako entry point

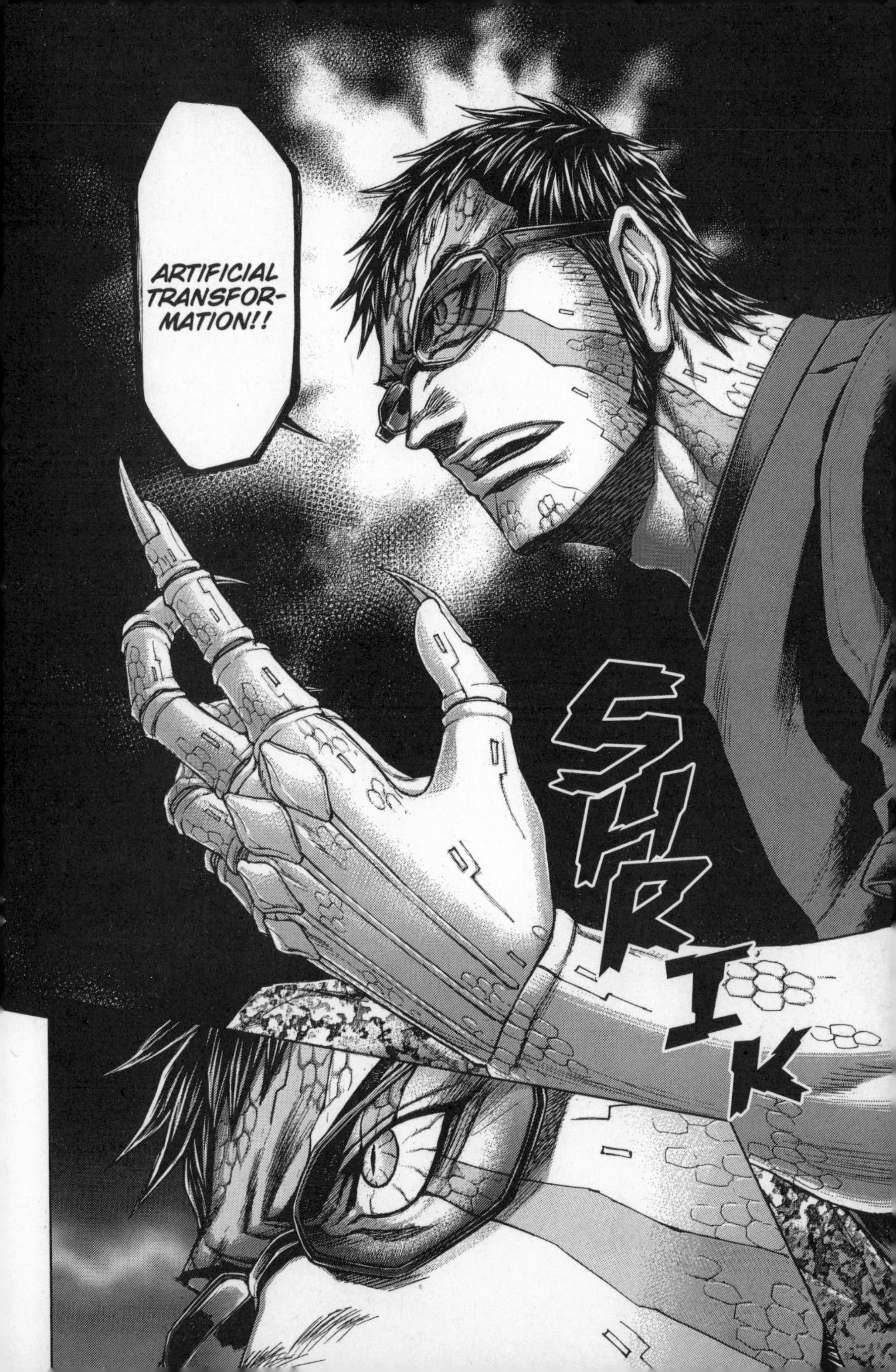
ARTIFICIAL TRANSFOR-MATION!!
SHRIK

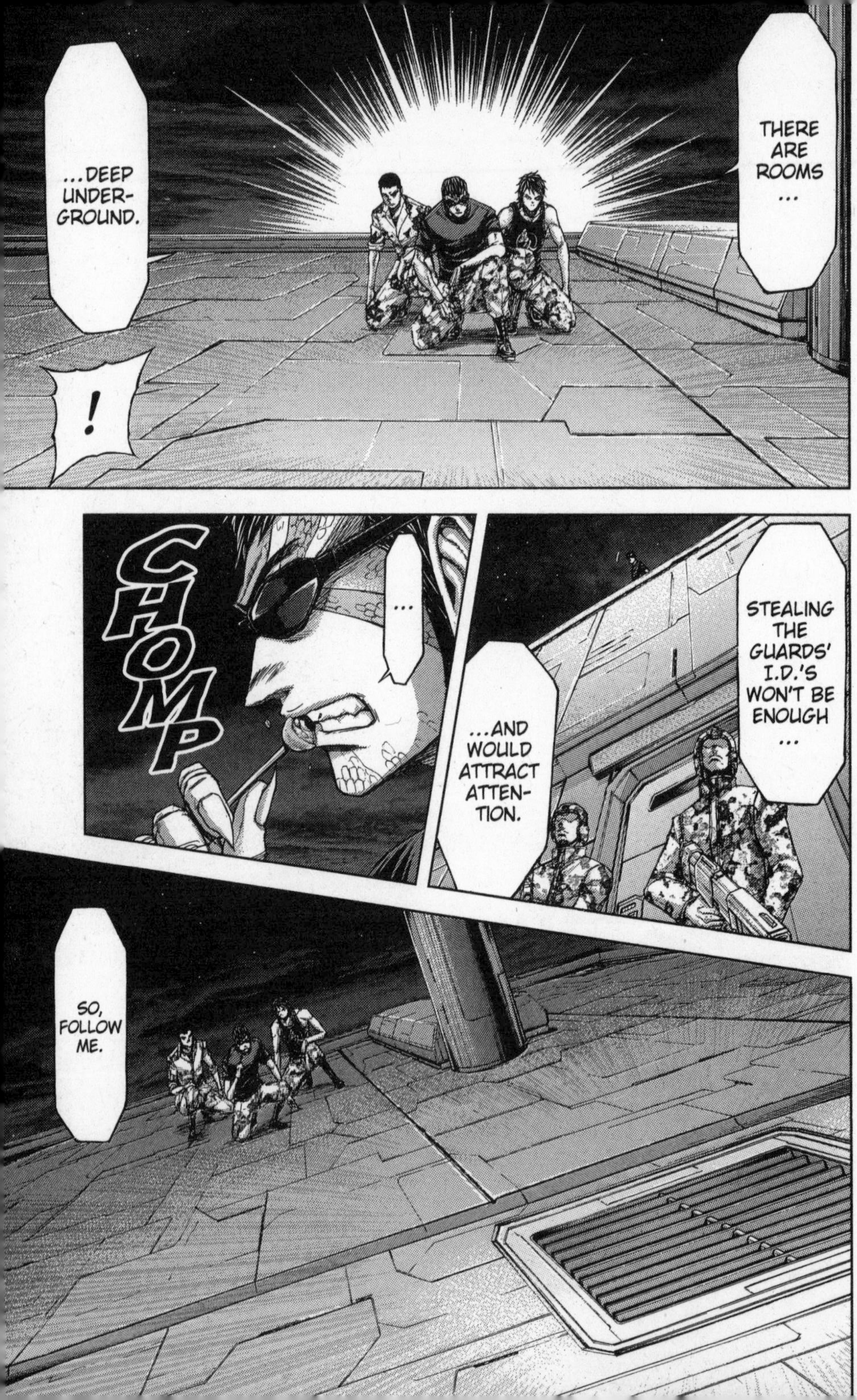
THERE ARE ROOMS ...
...DEEP UNDER-GROUND.
!
STEALING THE GUARDS' I.D.'S WON'T BE ENOUGH ...
...AND WOULD ATTRACT ATTEN-TION.
...
CHOMP
SO, FOLLOW ME.

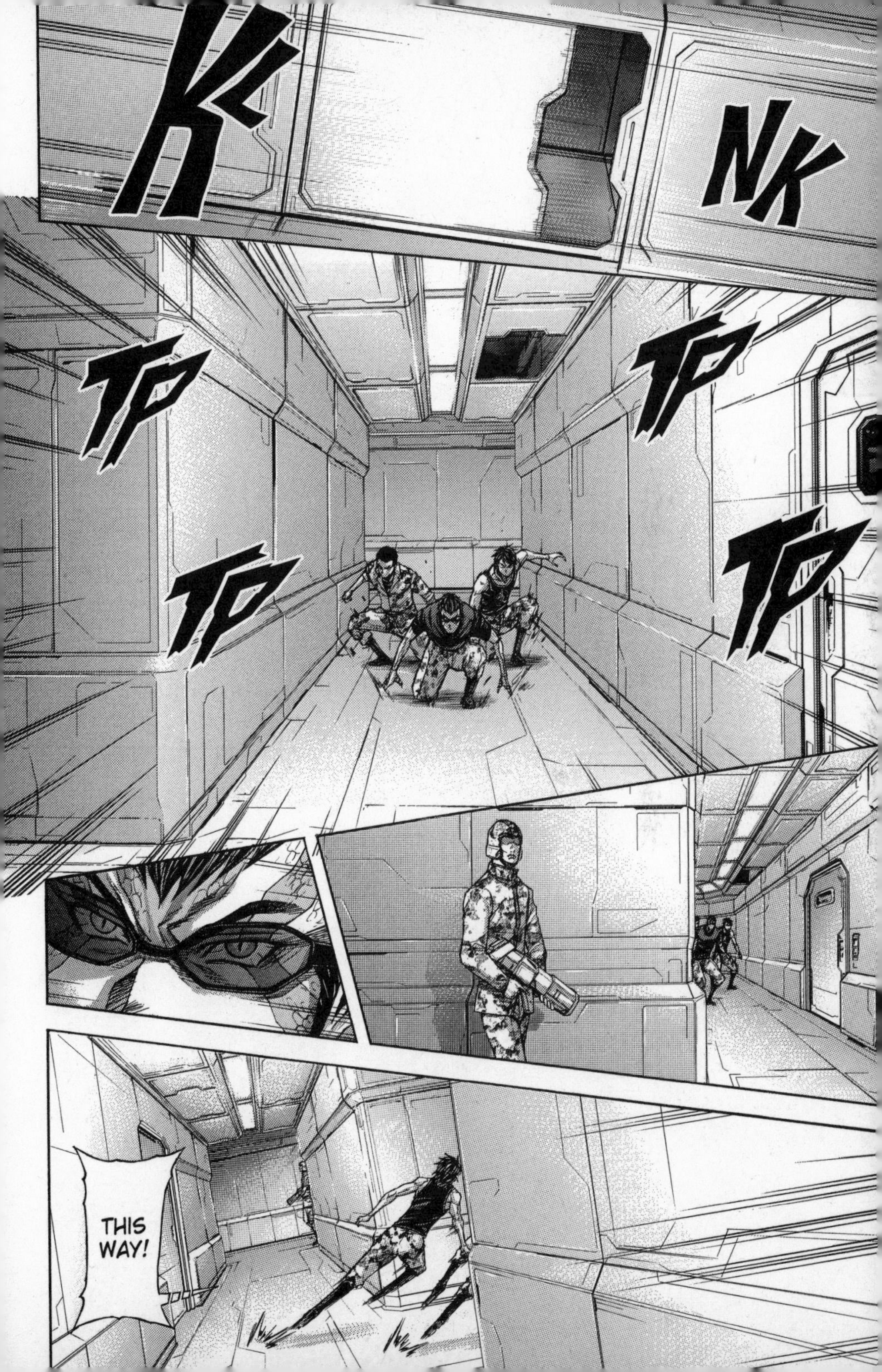
K
NK
TP
TP
TP
TP
THIS WAY!

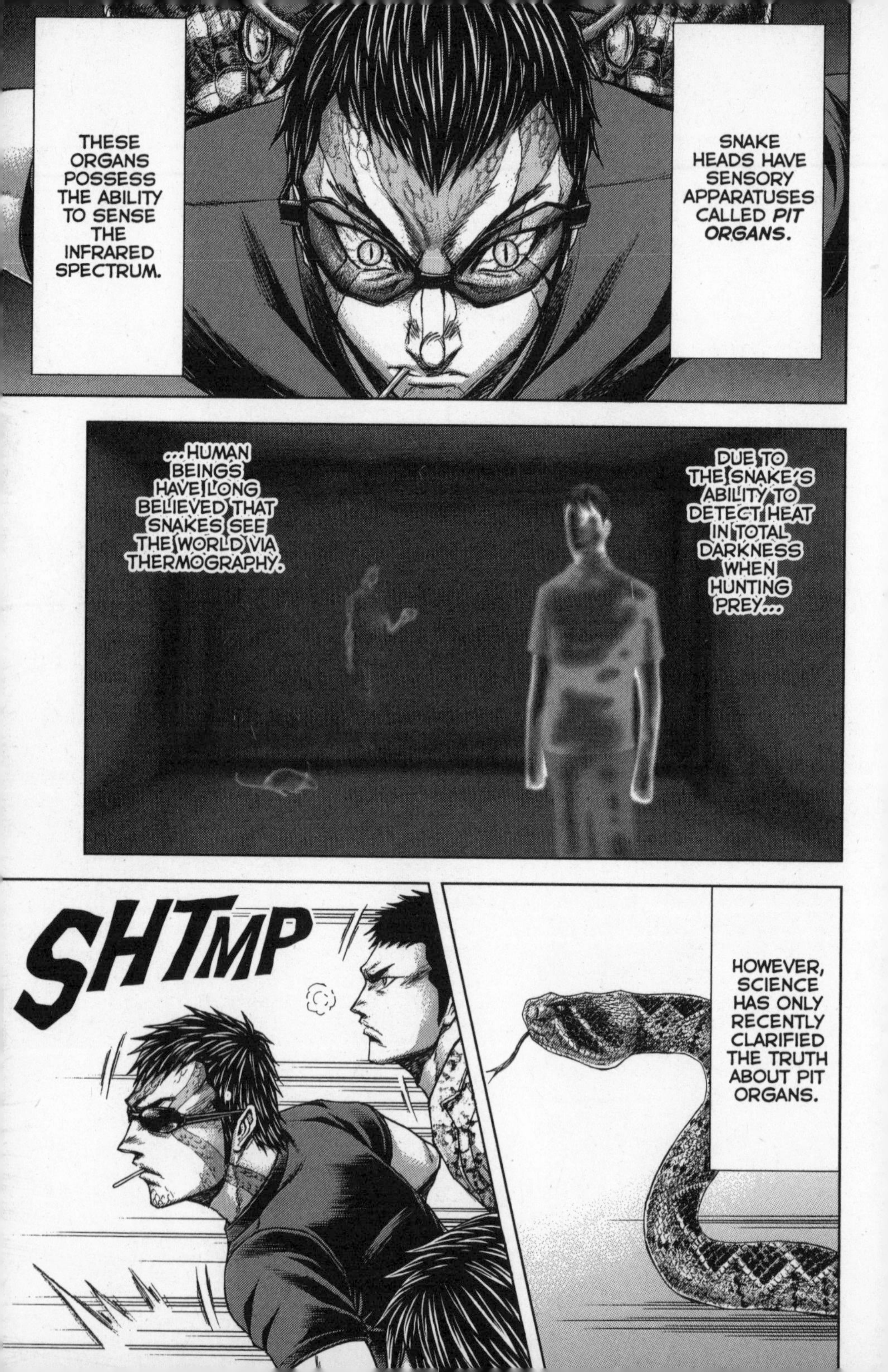
SNAKE HEADS HAVE SENSORY APPARATUSES CALLED *PIT ORGANS*.
THESE ORGANS POSSESS THE ABILITY TO SENSE THE INFRARED SPECTRUM.
DUE TO THE SNAKE'S ABILITY TO DETECT HEAT IN TOTAL DARKNESS WHEN HUNTING PREY...
...HUMAN BEINGS HAVE LONG BELIEVED THAT SNAKES SEE THE WORLD VIA THERMOGRAPHY.
HOWEVER, SCIENCE HAS ONLY RECENTLY CLARIFIED THE TRUTH ABOUT PIT ORGANS.
SHTMP

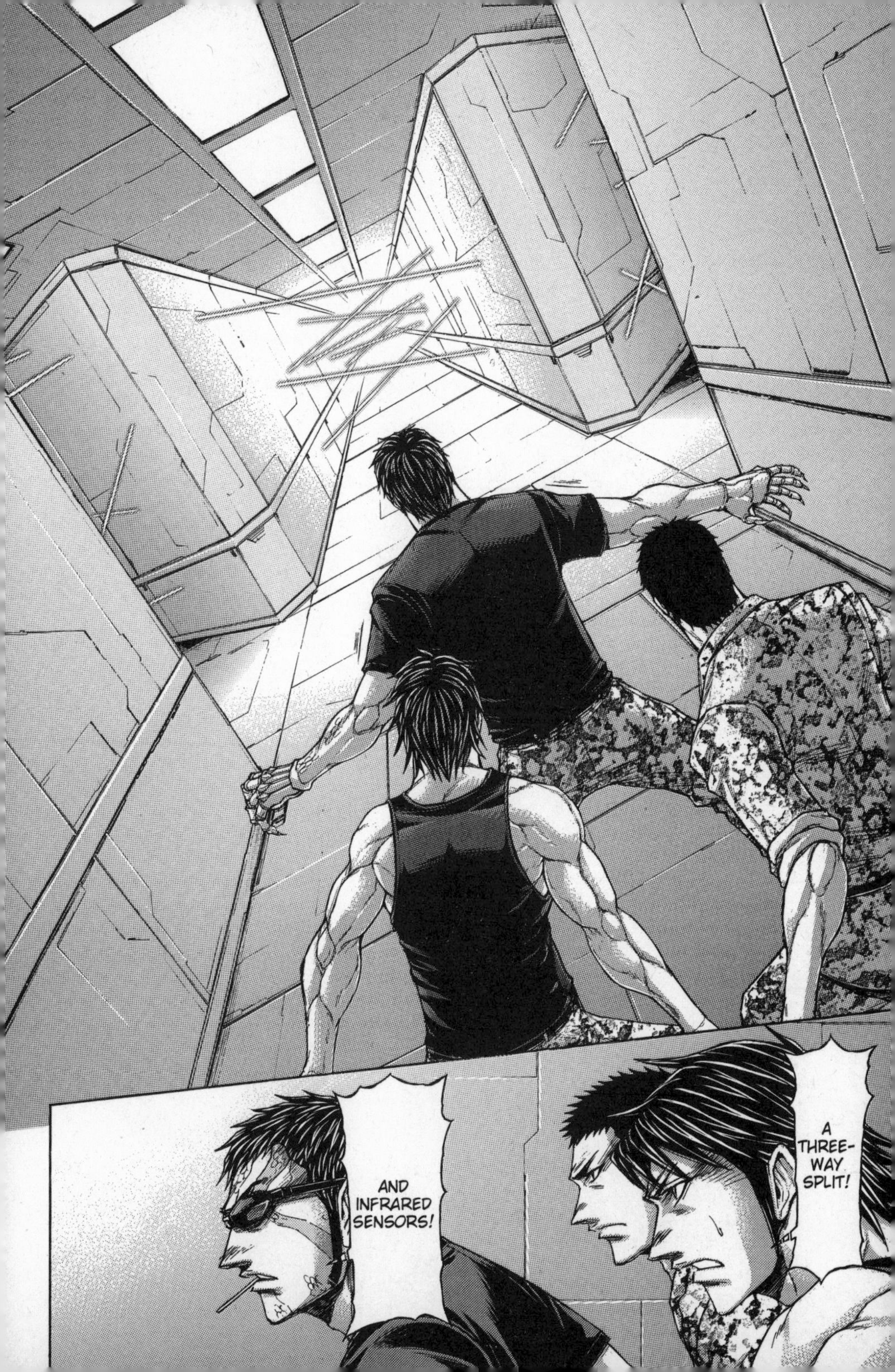
A THREE-WAY SPLIT!
AND INFRARED SENSORS!

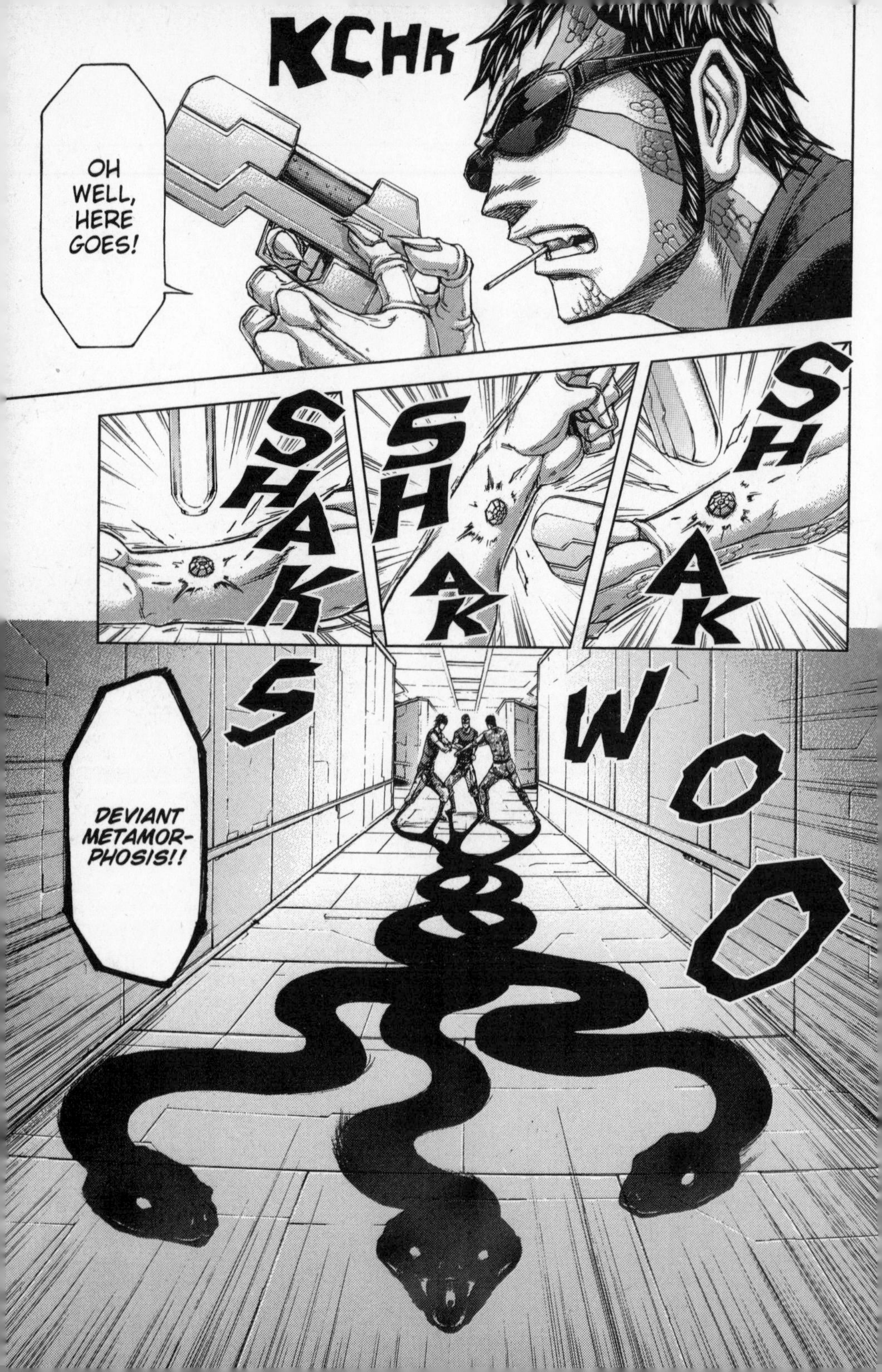
KCHK
OH WELL, HERE GOES!
SHAK
SHAK
SHAK
SWOOO
DEVIANT METAMORPHOSIS!!

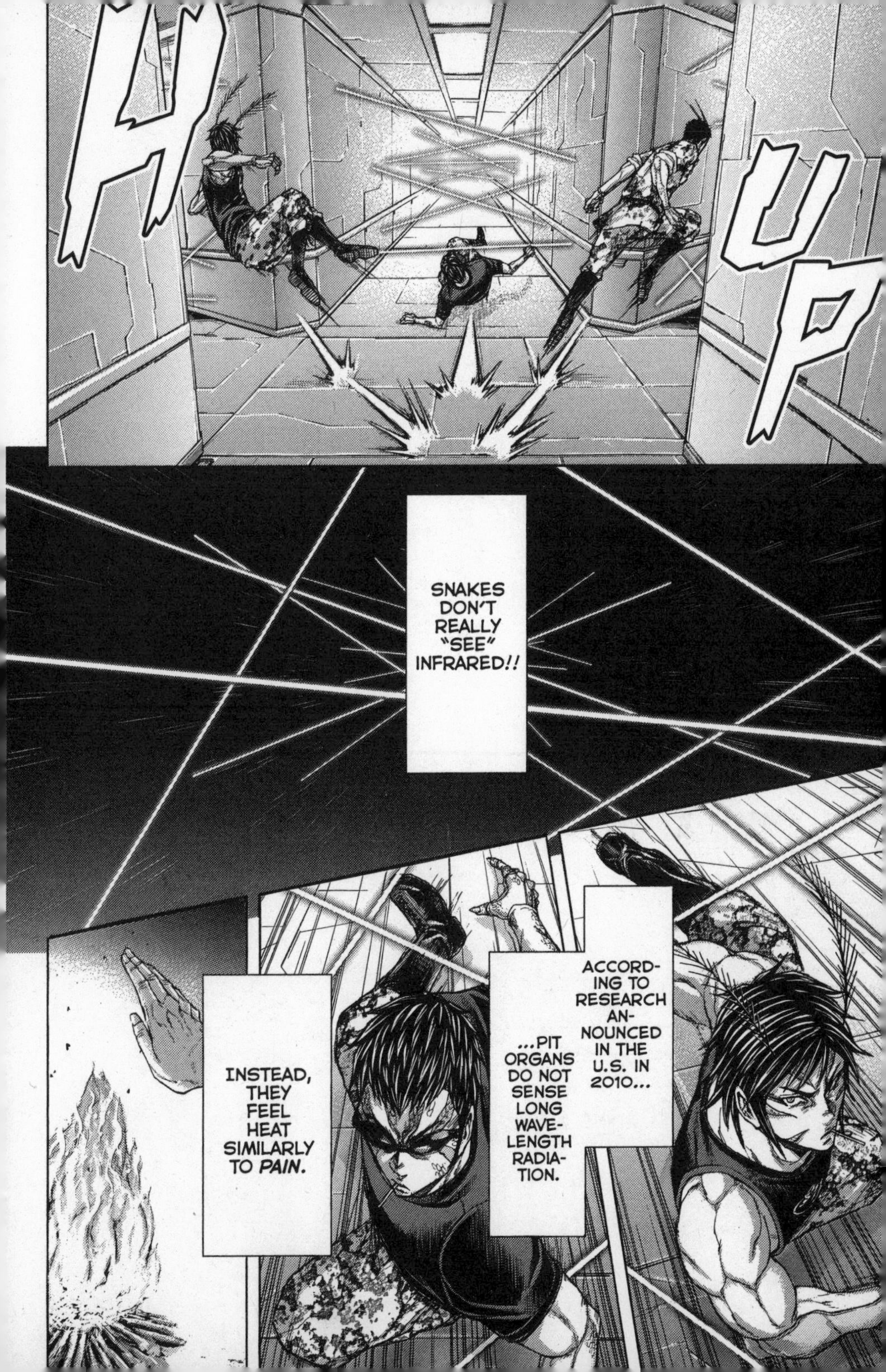
HUP
SNAKES DON'T REALLY "SEE" INFRARED!!
ACCORDING TO RESEARCH ANNOUNCED IN THE U.S. IN 2010...
...PIT ORGANS DO NOT SENSE LONG WAVELENGTH RADIATION.
INSTEAD, THEY FEEL HEAT SIMILARLY TO *PAIN*.

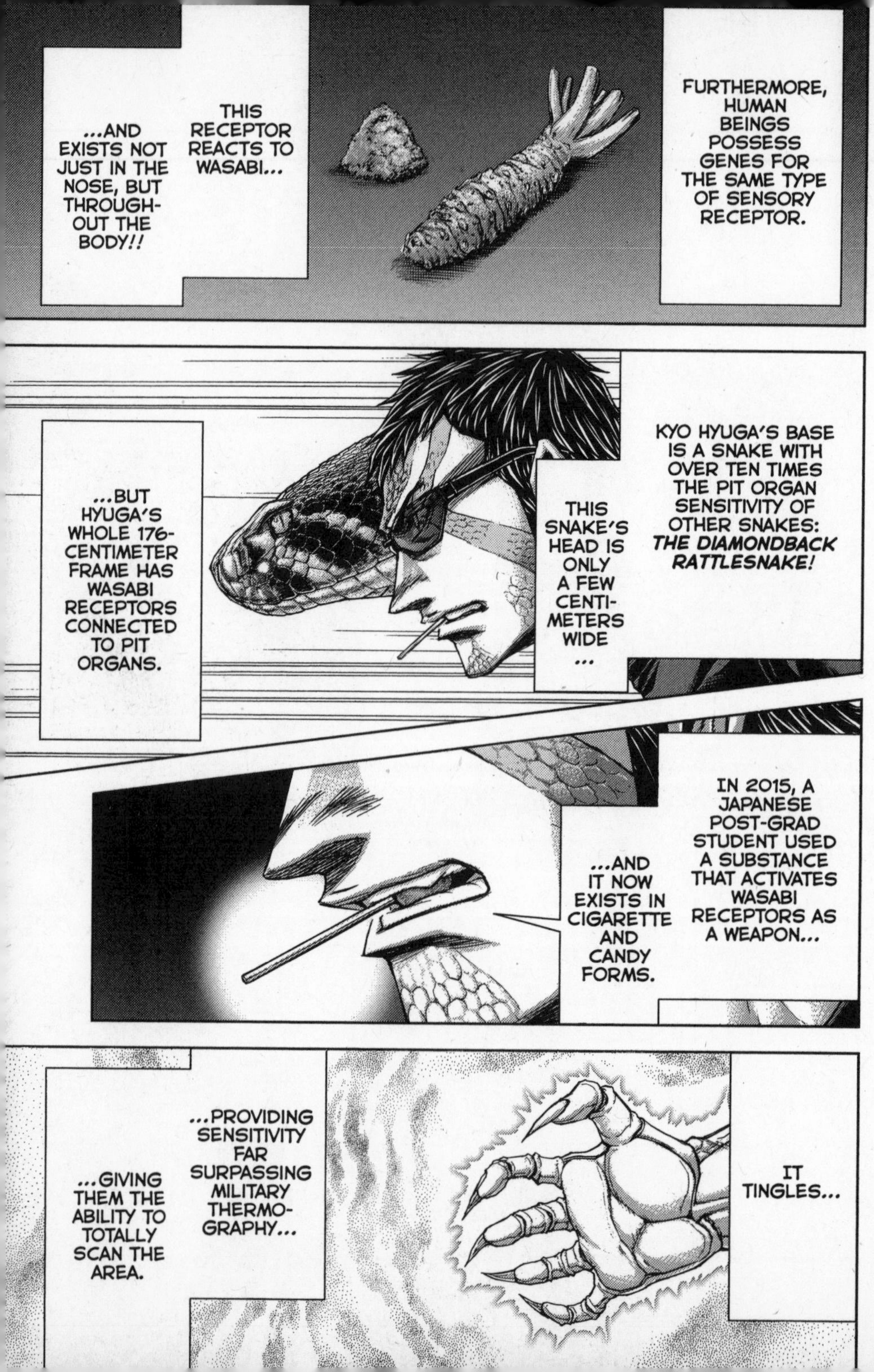

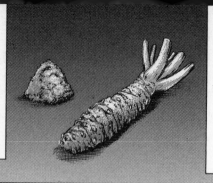

FURTHERMORE, HUMAN BEINGS POSSESS GENES FOR THE SAME TYPE OF SENSORY RECEPTOR.
THIS RECEPTOR REACTS TO WASABI...
...AND EXISTS NOT JUST IN THE NOSE, BUT THROUGH-OUT THE BODY!!
KYO HYUGA'S BASE IS A SNAKE WITH OVER TEN TIMES THE PIT ORGAN SENSITIVITY OF OTHER SNAKES: *THE DIAMONDBACK RATTLESNAKE!*
THIS SNAKE'S HEAD IS ONLY A FEW CENTI-METERS WIDE ...
...BUT HYUGA'S WHOLE 176-CENTIMETER FRAME HAS WASABI RECEPTORS CONNECTED TO PIT ORGANS.
IN 2015, A JAPANESE POST-GRAD STUDENT USED A SUBSTANCE THAT ACTIVATES WASABI RECEPTORS AS A WEAPON...
...AND IT NOW EXISTS IN CIGARETTE AND CANDY FORMS.
IT TINGLES...
...PROVIDING SENSITIVITY FAR SURPASSING MILITARY THERMO-GRAPHY...
...GIVING THEM THE ABILITY TO TOTALLY SCAN THE AREA.

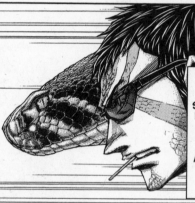

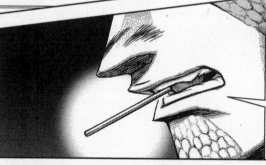

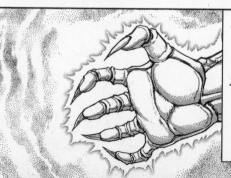

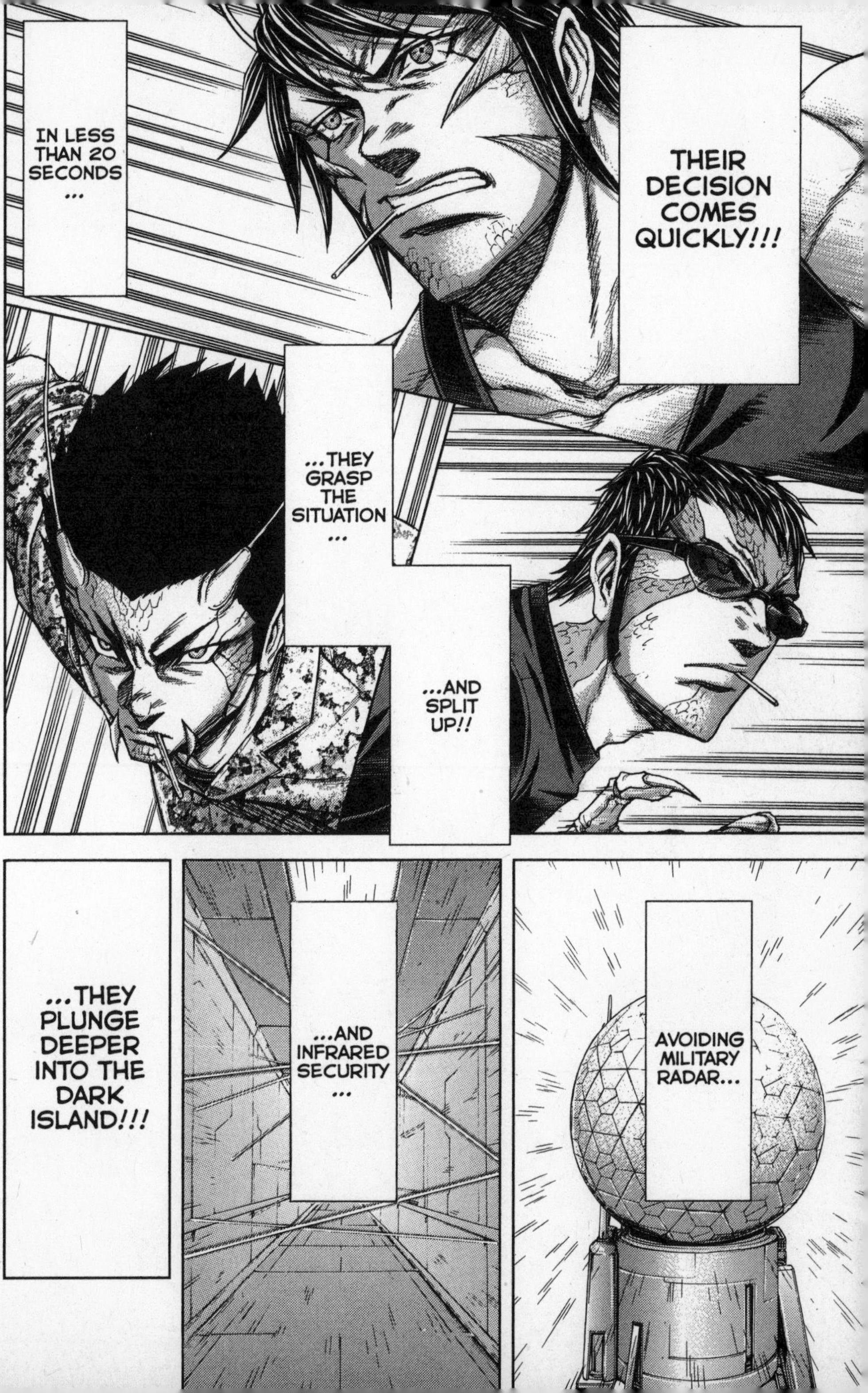
THEIR DECISION COMES QUICKLY!!!
IN LESS THAN 20 SECONDS ...
...THEY GRASP THE SITUATION ...
...AND SPLIT UP!!
AVOIDING MILITARY RADAR...
...AND INFRARED SECURITY ...
...THEY PLUNGE DEEPER INTO THE DARK ISLAND!!!

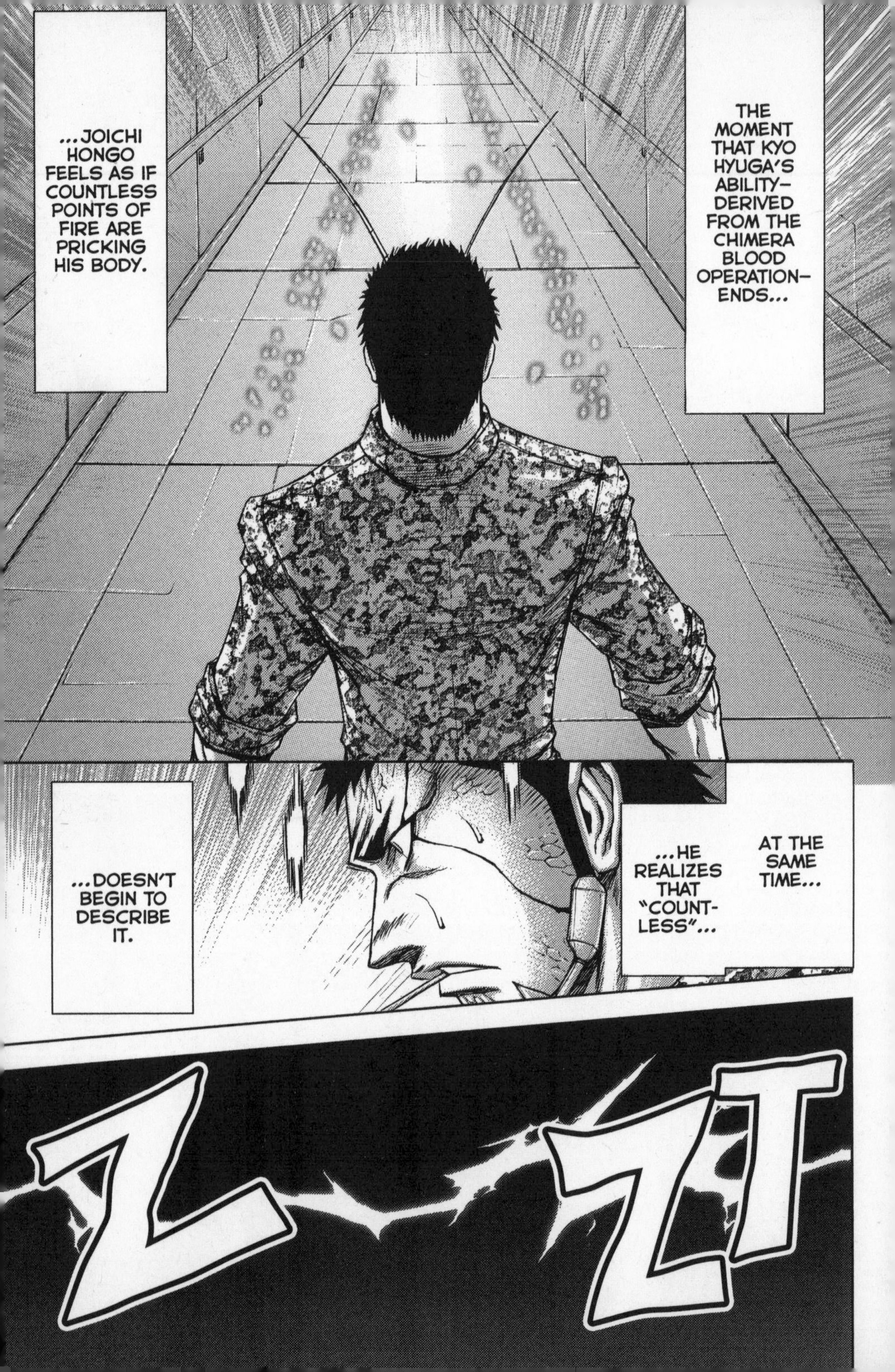
THE MOMENT THAT KYO HYUGA'S ABILITY—DERIVED FROM THE CHIMERA BLOOD OPERATION—ENDS...
...JOICHI HONGO FEELS AS IF COUNTLESS POINTS OF FIRE ARE PRICKING HIS BODY.
AT THE SAME TIME...
...HE REALIZES THAT "COUNT-LESS"...
...DOESN'T BEGIN TO DESCRIBE IT.
ZZT

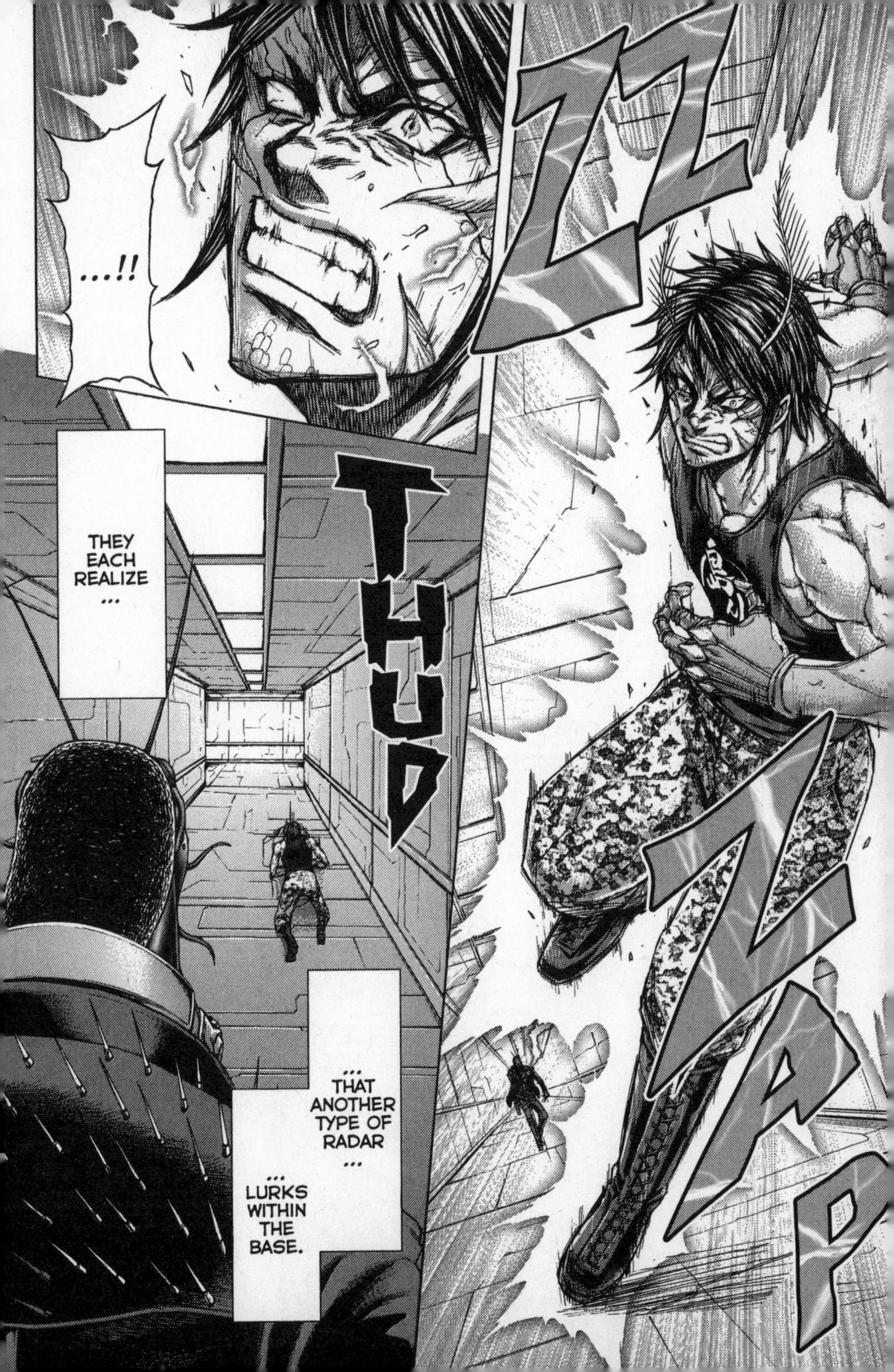
ZZZ
ZAP
...!!
THEY EACH REALIZE ...
THUD
... THAT ANOTHER TYPE OF RADAR ...
... LURKS WITHIN THE BASE.

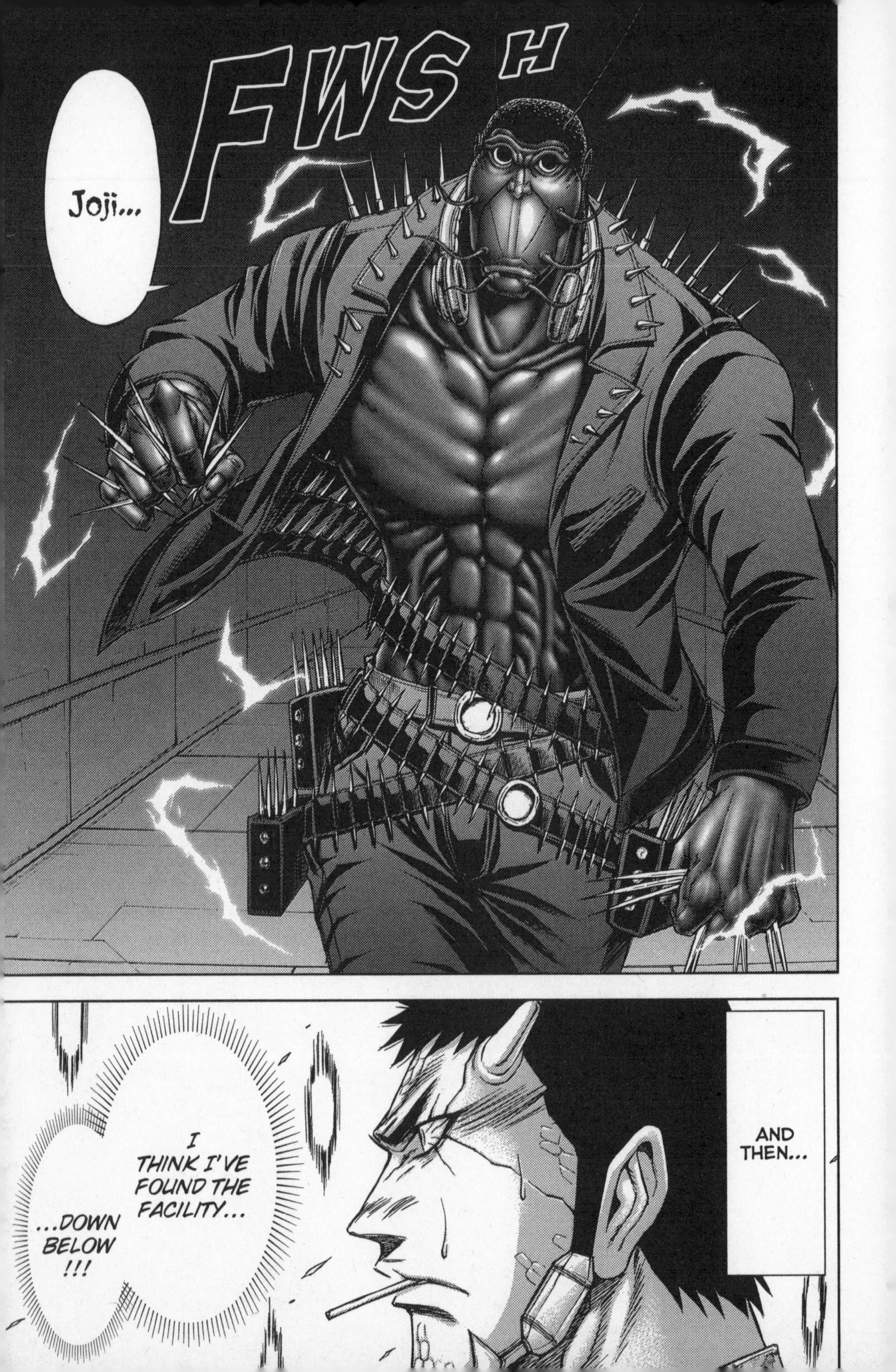
FWSH
Joji...
AND THEN...
I THINK I'VE FOUND THE FACILITY...
...DOWN BELOW!!!

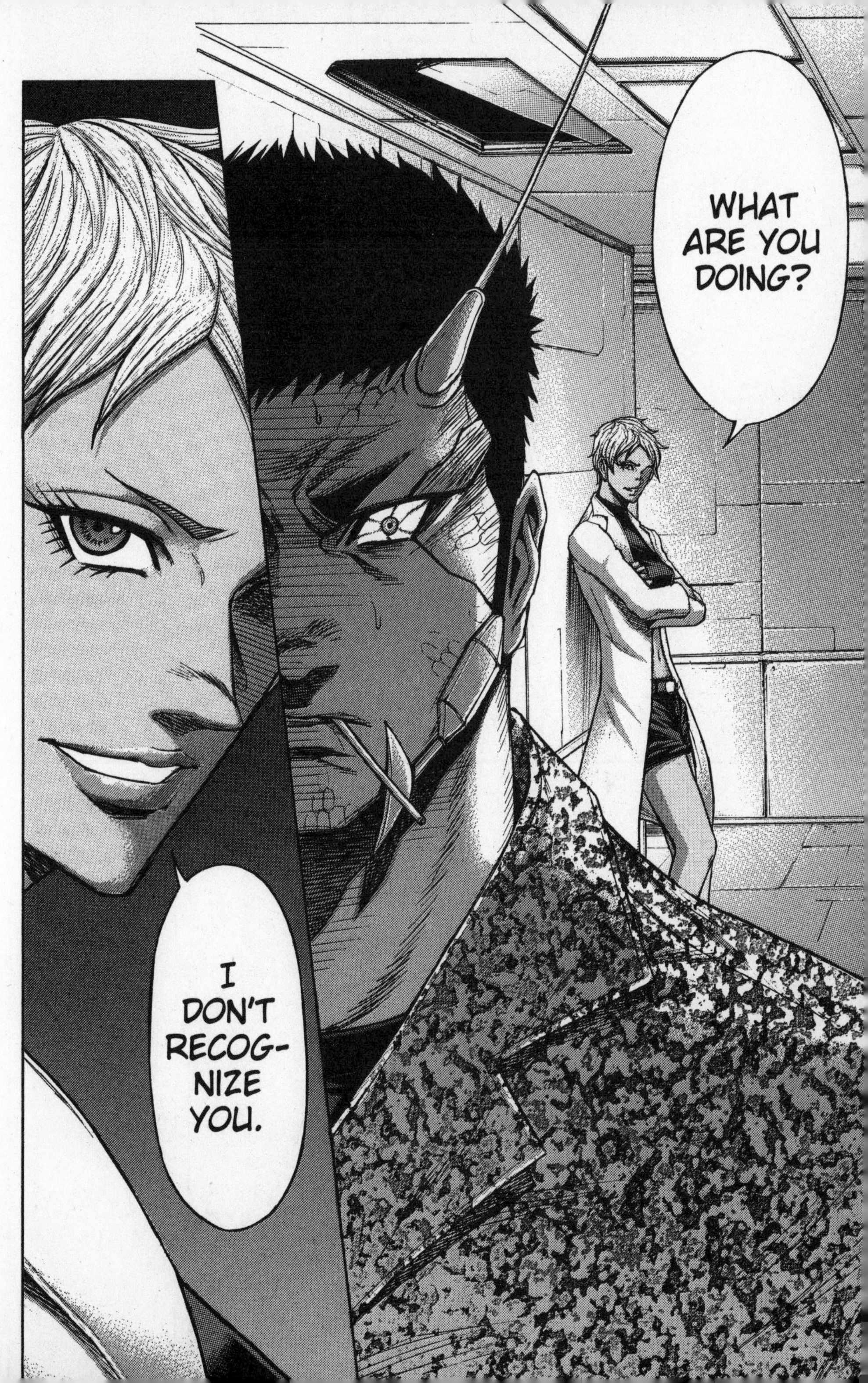
WHAT ARE YOU DOING?
I DON'T RECOG-NIZE YOU.

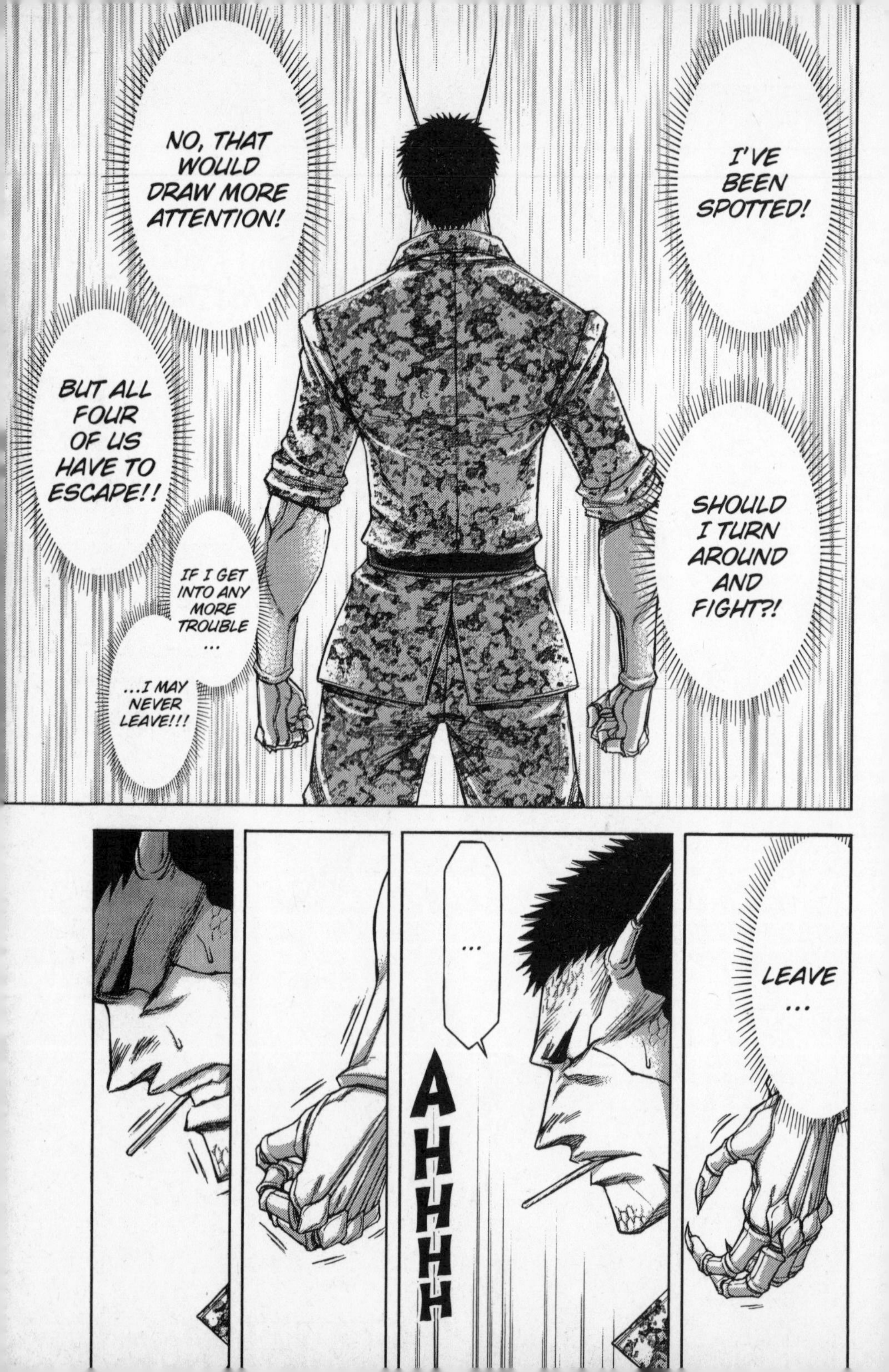
I'VE BEEN SPOTTED!
SHOULD I TURN AROUND AND FIGHT?!
NO, THAT WOULD DRAW MORE ATTENTION!
BUT ALL FOUR OF US HAVE TO ESCAPE!!
IF I GET INTO ANY MORE TROUBLE ...
...I MAY NEVER LEAVE!!!
LEAVE ...
...
AHHHHH

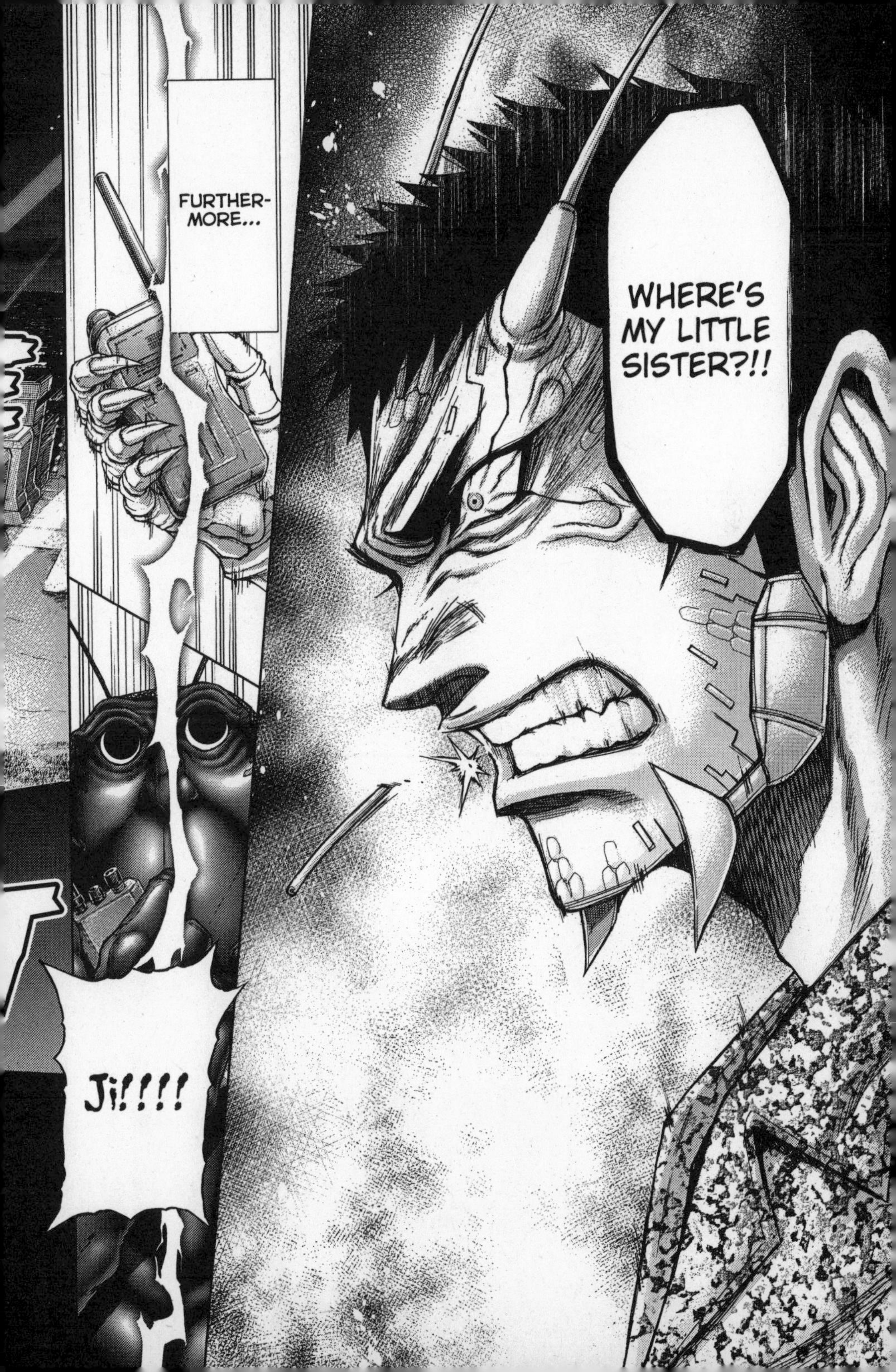
WHERE'S MY LITTLE SISTER?!!
FURTHER-MORE...
Ji!!!!

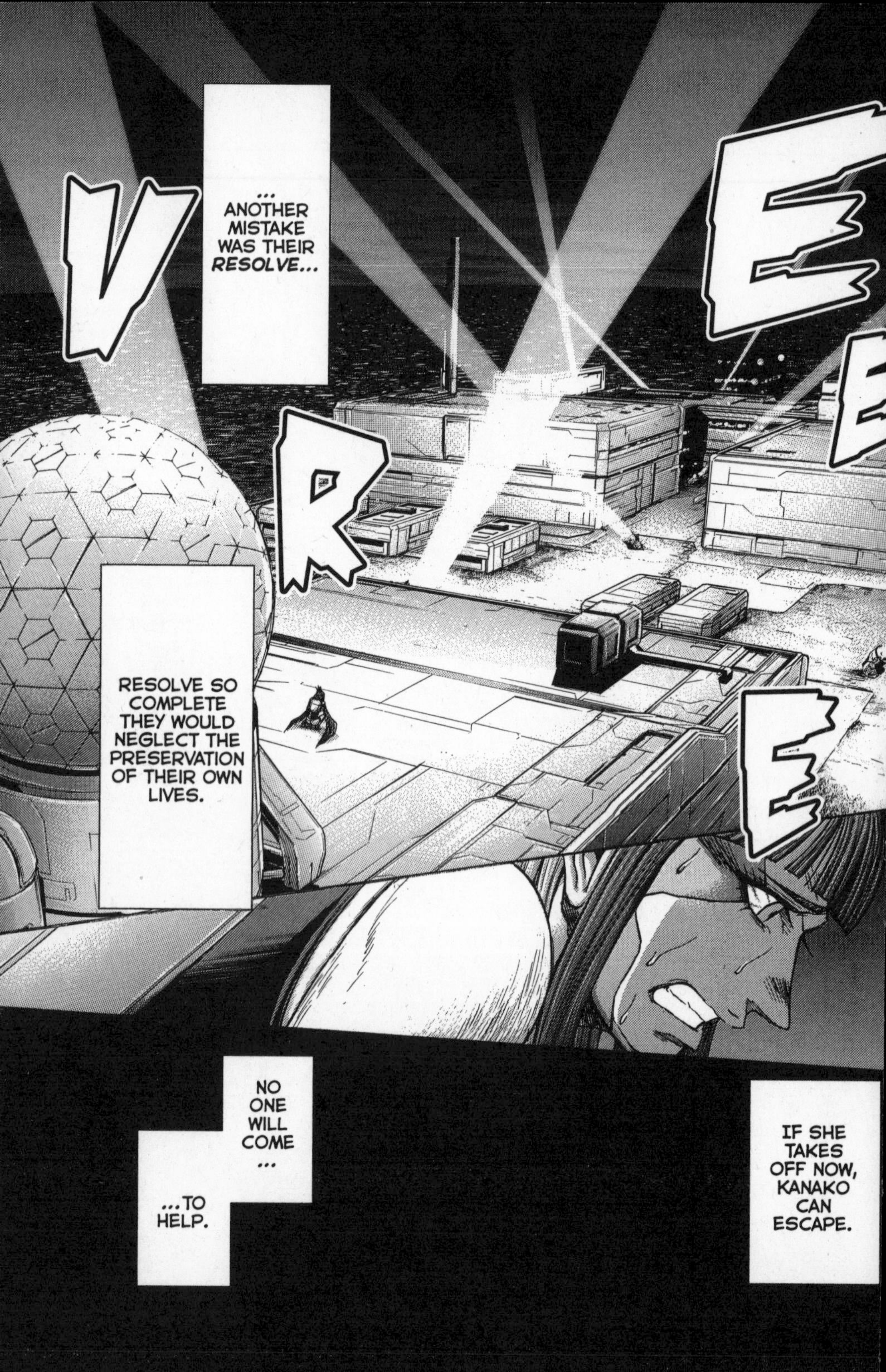
VREEE
...ANOTHER MISTAKE WAS THEIR *RESOLVE*...
RESOLVE SO COMPLETE THEY WOULD NEGLECT THE PRESERVATION OF THEIR OWN LIVES.
IF SHE TAKES OFF NOW, KANAKO CAN ESCAPE.
NO ONE WILL COME...
...TO HELP.

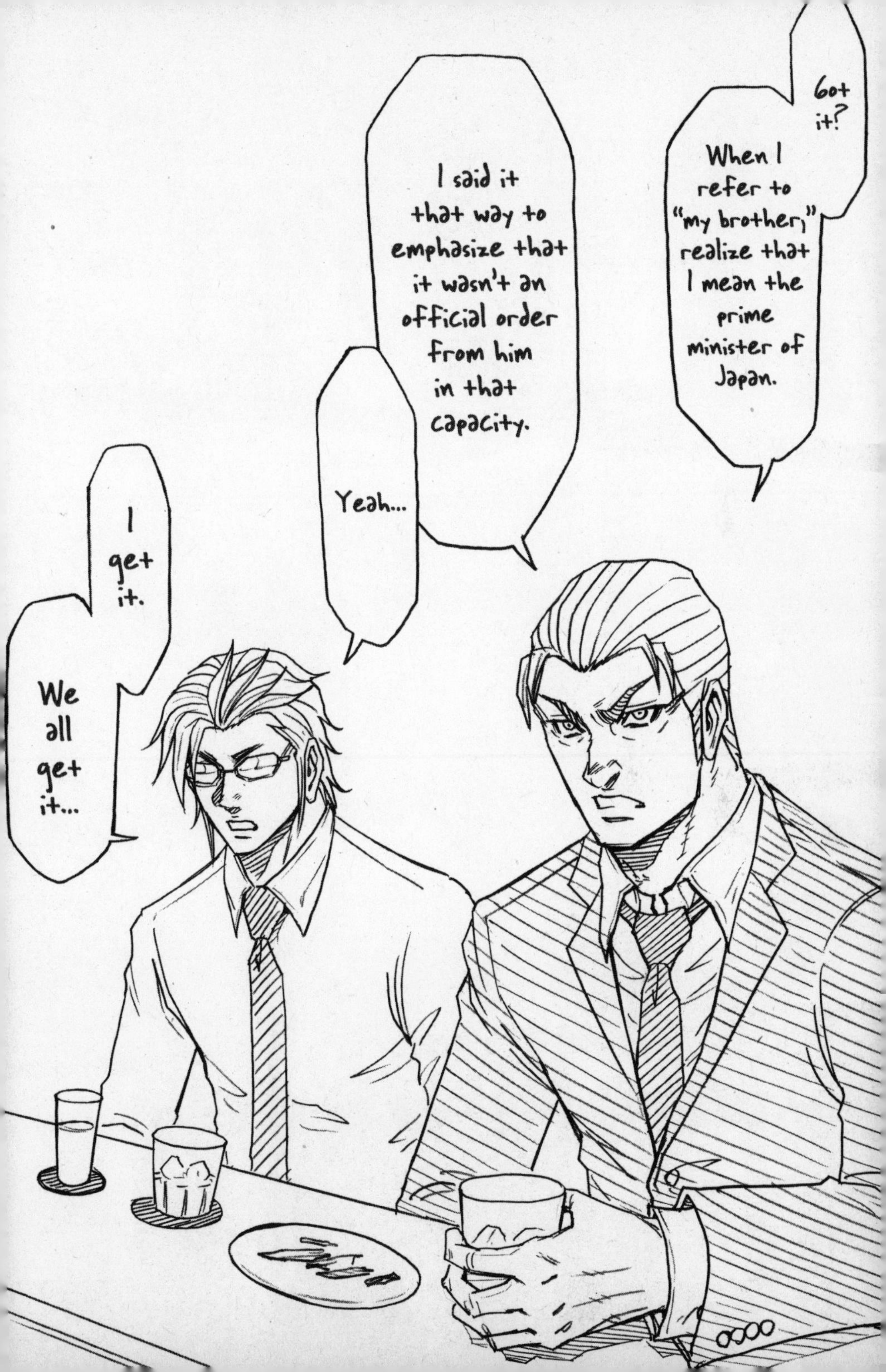
Got it?
When I refer to "my brother," realize that I mean the prime minister of Japan.
I said it that way to emphasize that it wasn't an official order from him in that capacity.
Yeah...
I get it.
We all get it...

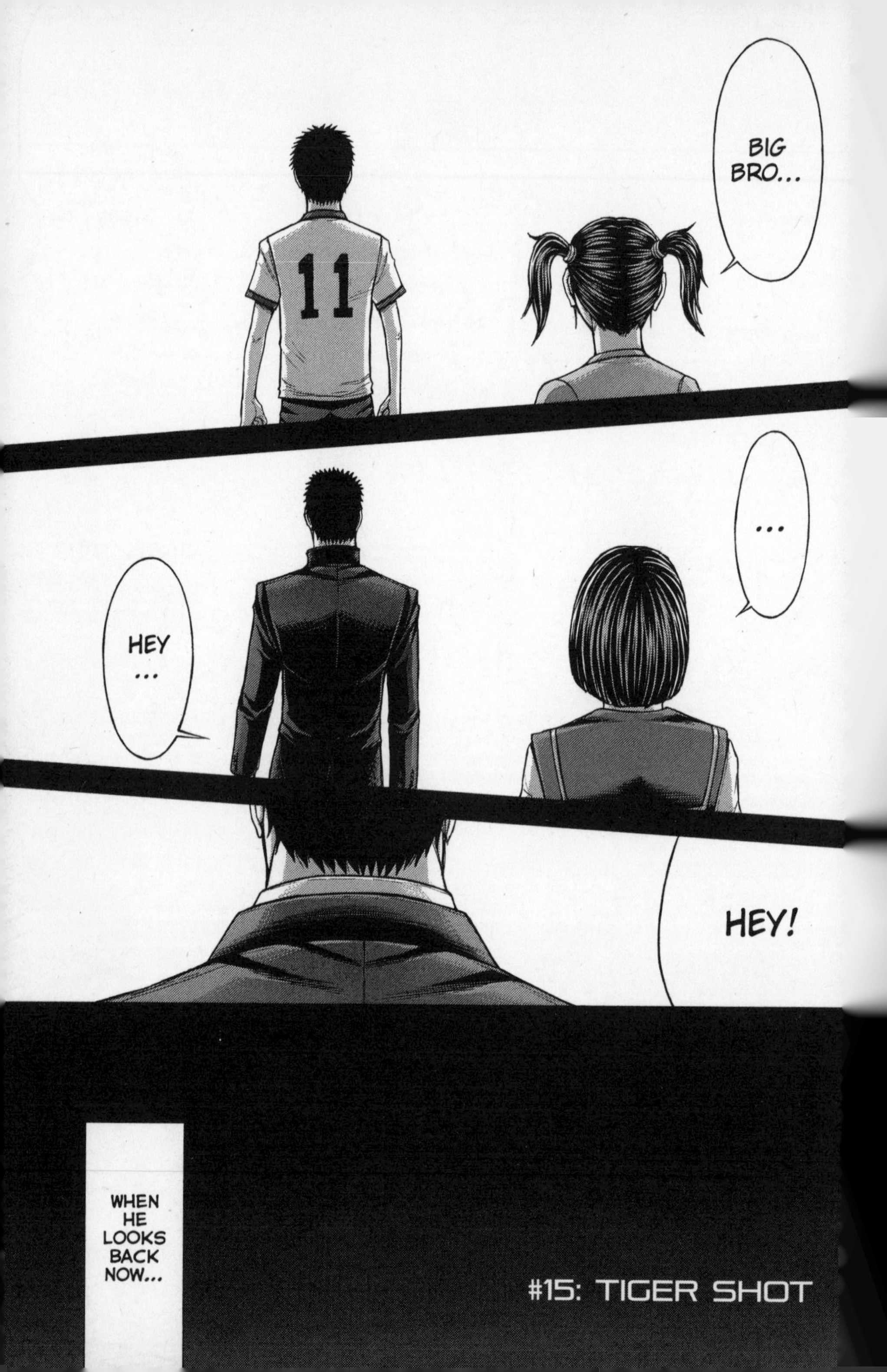
BIG BRO...
...
HEY ...
HEY!
WHEN HE LOOKS BACK NOW...
#15: TIGER SHOT

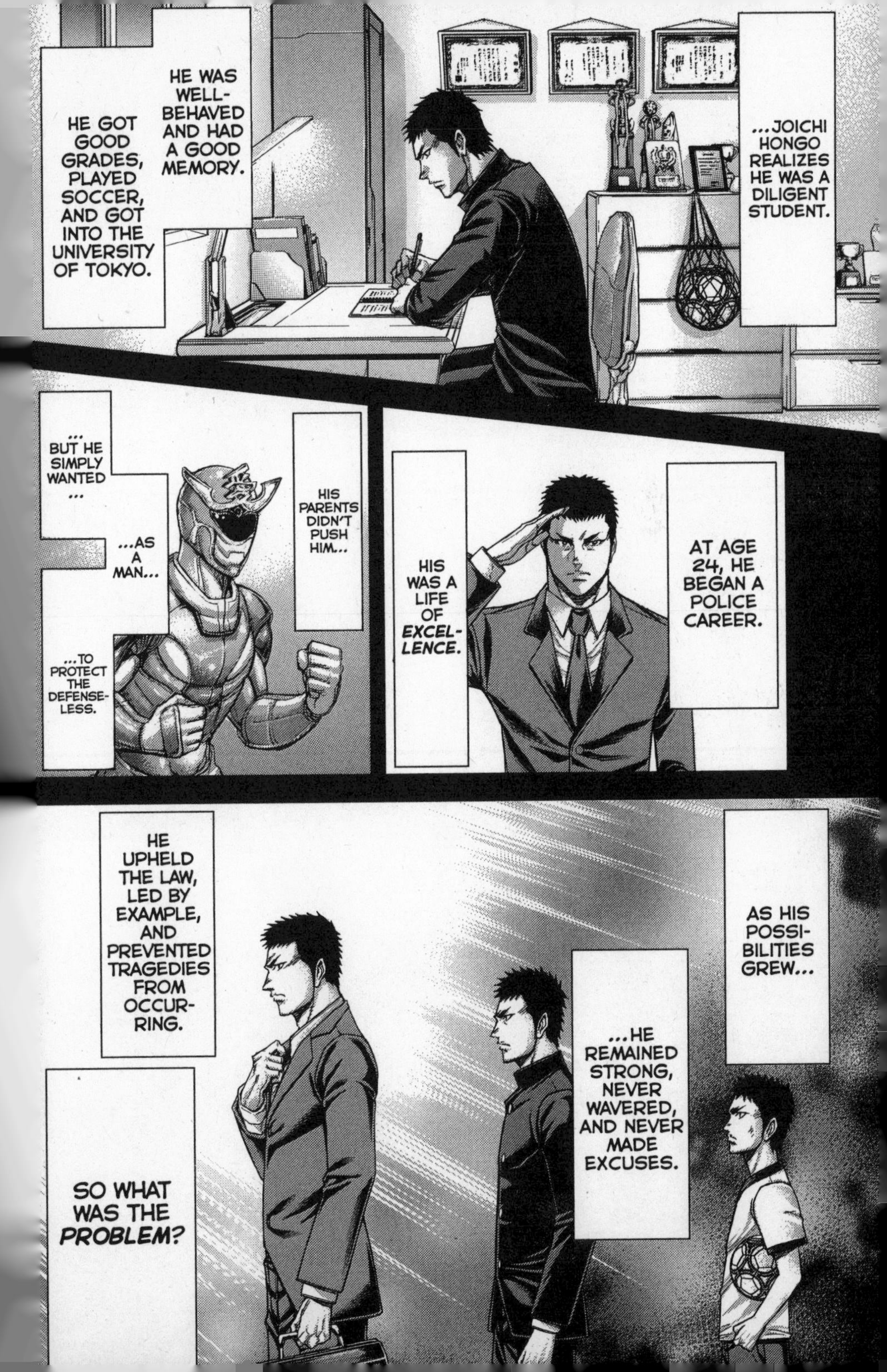
...JOICHI HONGO REALIZES HE WAS A DILIGENT STUDENT.
HE WAS WELL-BEHAVED AND HAD A GOOD MEMORY.
HE GOT GOOD GRADES, PLAYED SOCCER, AND GOT INTO THE UNIVERSITY OF TOKYO.
AT AGE 24, HE BEGAN A POLICE CAREER.
HIS WAS A LIFE OF *EXCELLENCE.*
HIS PARENTS DIDN'T PUSH HIM...
...BUT HE SIMPLY WANTED...
...AS A MAN...
...TO PROTECT THE DEFENSELESS.
AS HIS POSSIBILITIES GREW...
...HE REMAINED STRONG, NEVER WAVERED, AND NEVER MADE EXCUSES.
HE UPHELD THE LAW, LED BY EXAMPLE, AND PREVENTED TRAGEDIES FROM OCCURRING.
SO WHAT WAS THE *PROBLEM?*

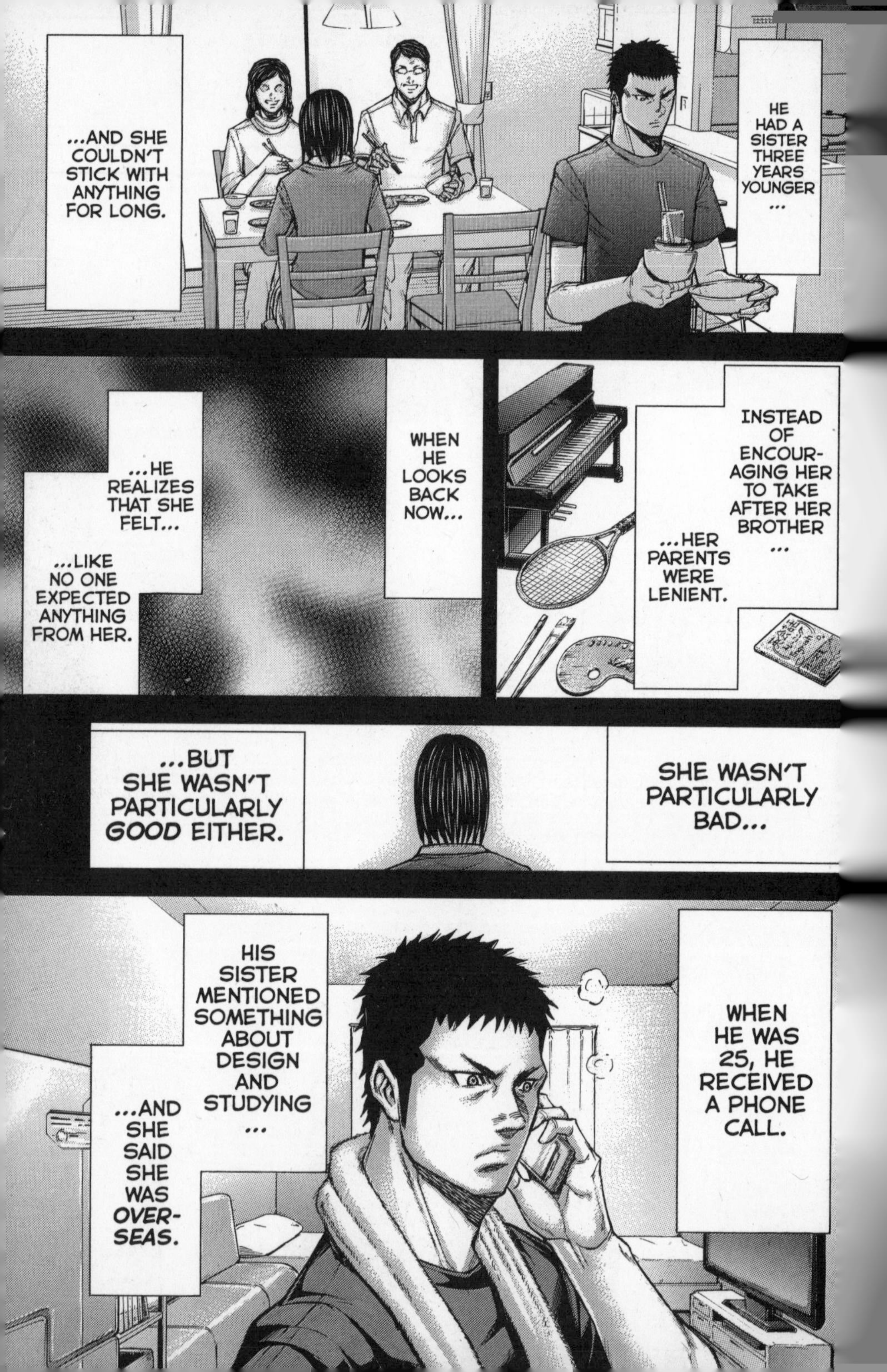
HE HAD A SISTER THREE YEARS YOUNGER...
...AND SHE COULDN'T STICK WITH ANYTHING FOR LONG.
INSTEAD OF ENCOURAGING HER TO TAKE AFTER HER BROTHER...
...HER PARENTS WERE LENIENT.
WHEN HE LOOKS BACK NOW...
...HE REALIZES THAT SHE FELT...
...LIKE NO ONE EXPECTED ANYTHING FROM HER.
SHE WASN'T PARTICULARLY BAD...
...BUT SHE WASN'T PARTICULARLY *GOOD* EITHER.
WHEN HE WAS 25, HE RECEIVED A PHONE CALL.
HIS SISTER MENTIONED SOMETHING ABOUT DESIGN AND STUDYING...
...AND SHE SAID SHE WAS *OVERSEAS*.

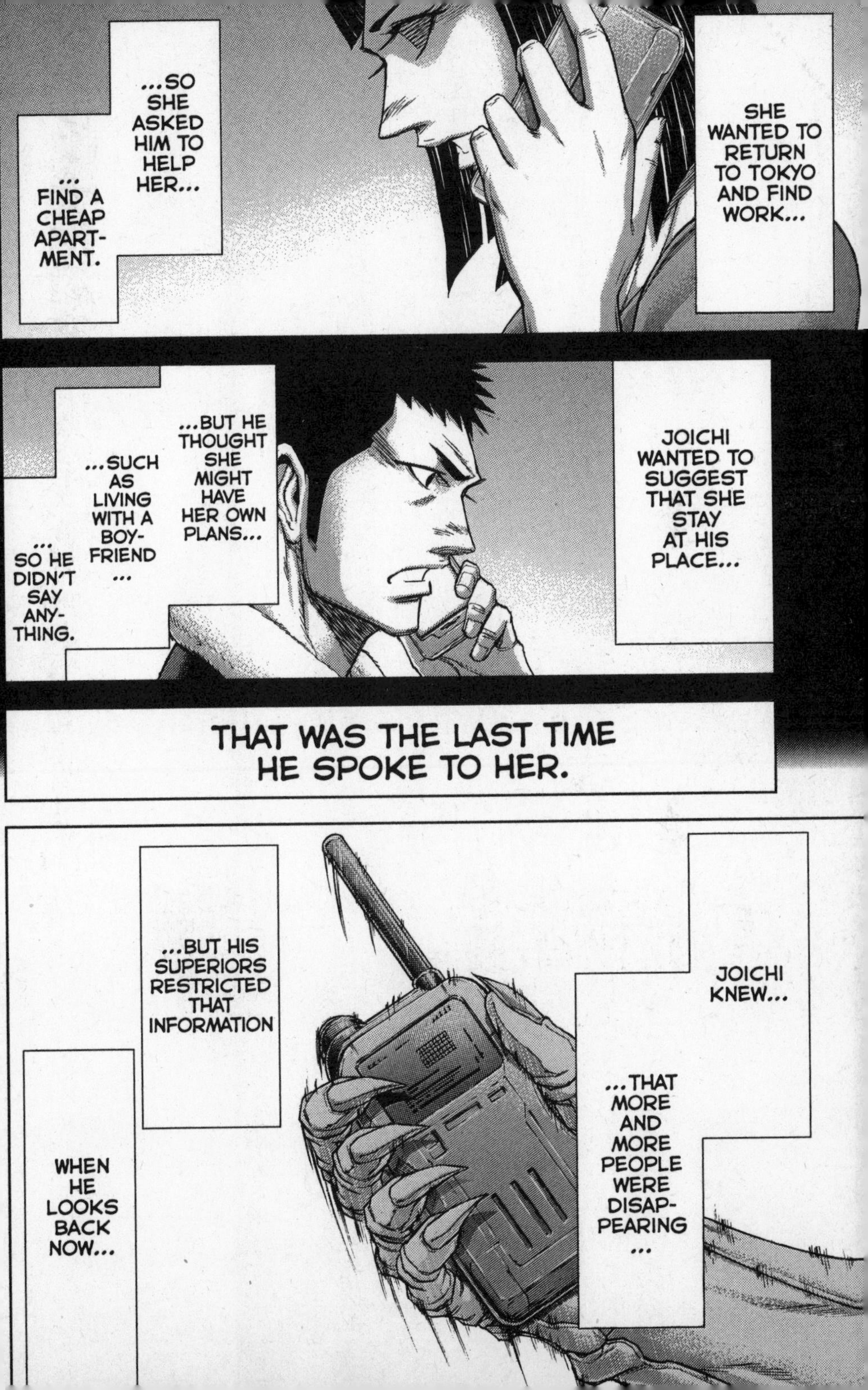
SHE WANTED TO RETURN TO TOKYO AND FIND WORK...
...SO SHE ASKED HIM TO HELP HER...
... FIND A CHEAP APARTMENT.
JOICHI WANTED TO SUGGEST THAT SHE STAY AT HIS PLACE...
...BUT HE THOUGHT SHE MIGHT HAVE HER OWN PLANS...
...SUCH AS LIVING WITH A BOYFRIEND...
... SO HE DIDN'T SAY ANYTHING.
THAT WAS THE LAST TIME HE SPOKE TO HER.
JOICHI KNEW...
...THAT MORE AND MORE PEOPLE WERE DISAPPEARING...
...BUT HIS SUPERIORS RESTRICTED THAT INFORMATION
WHEN HE LOOKS BACK NOW...

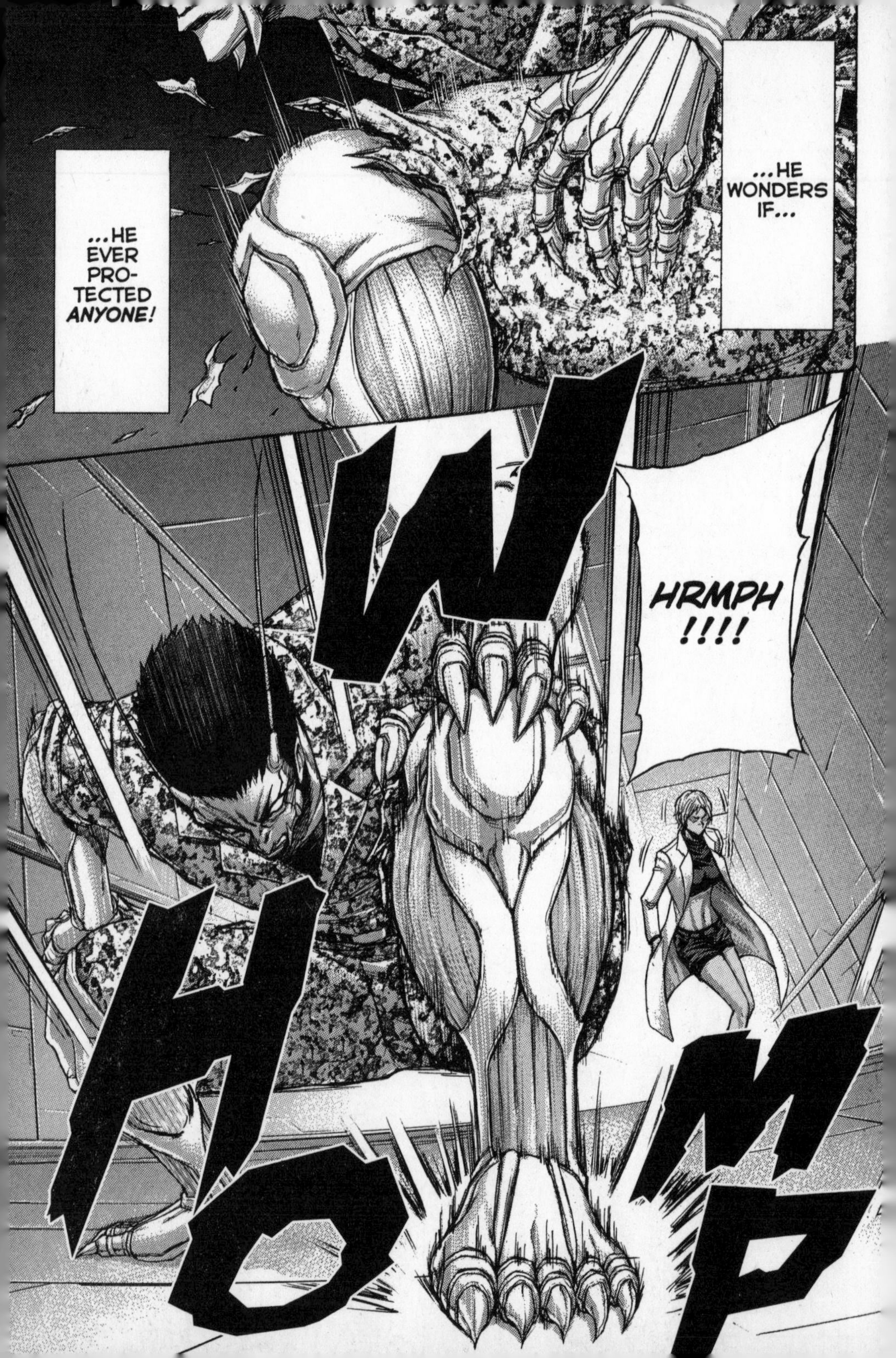
...HE WONDERS IF...
...HE EVER PROTECTED ANYONE!
HRMPH !!!!
WHOMP

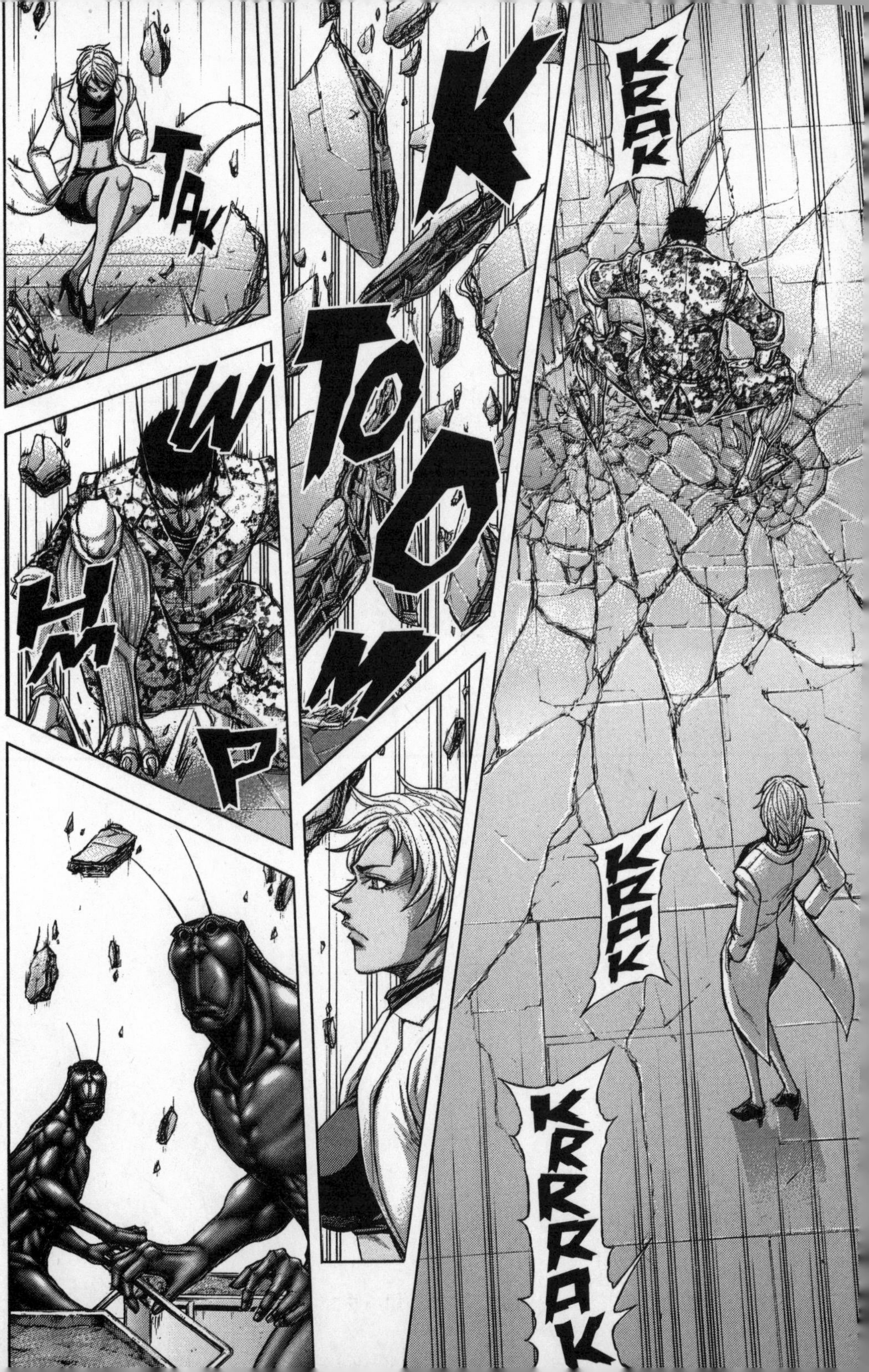
KRAK
KRAK
KRRRAK
KTOOM
TAK
WHMP

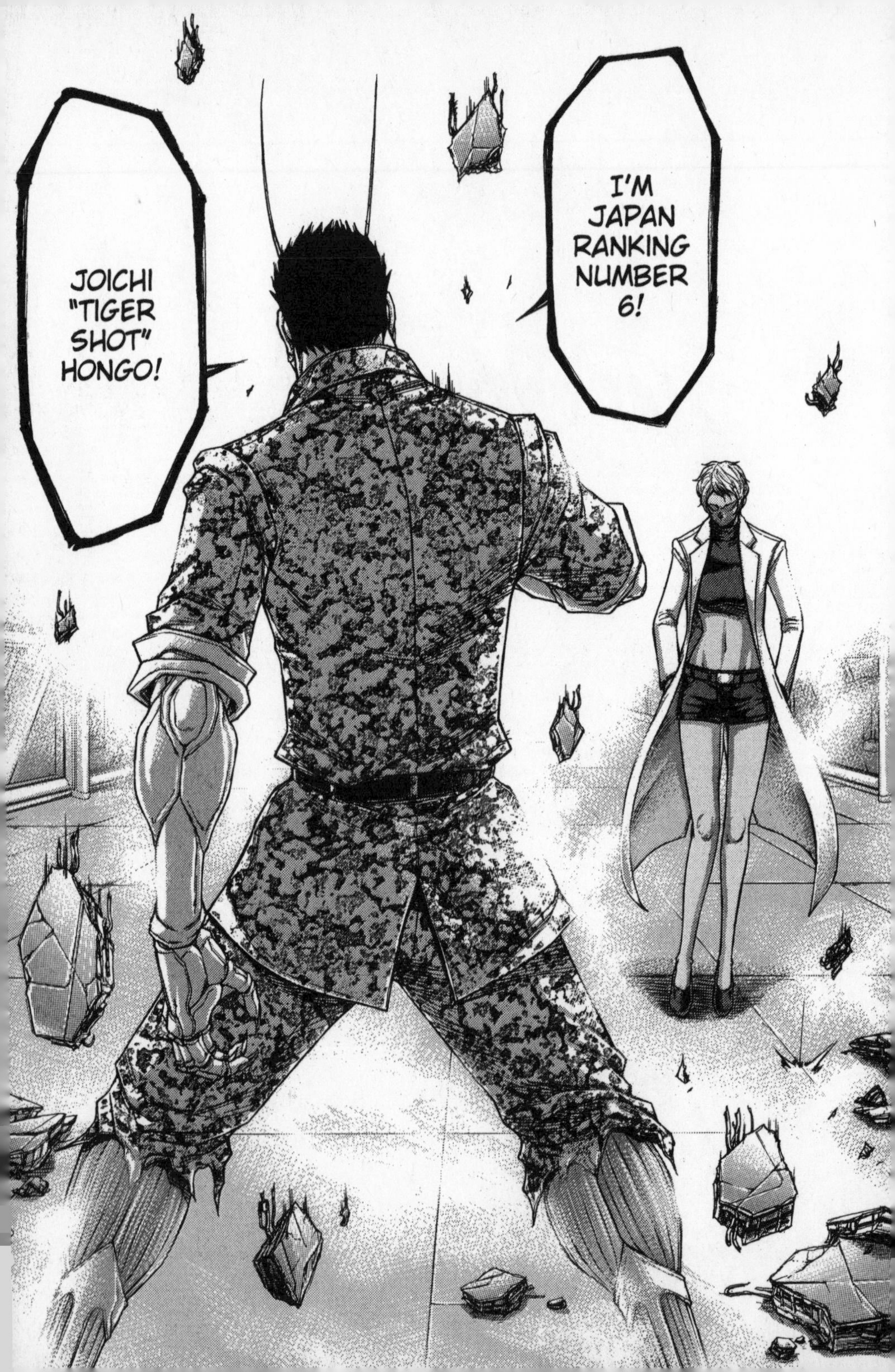
I'M JAPAN RANKING NUMBER 6!
JOICHI "TIGER SHOT" HONGO!

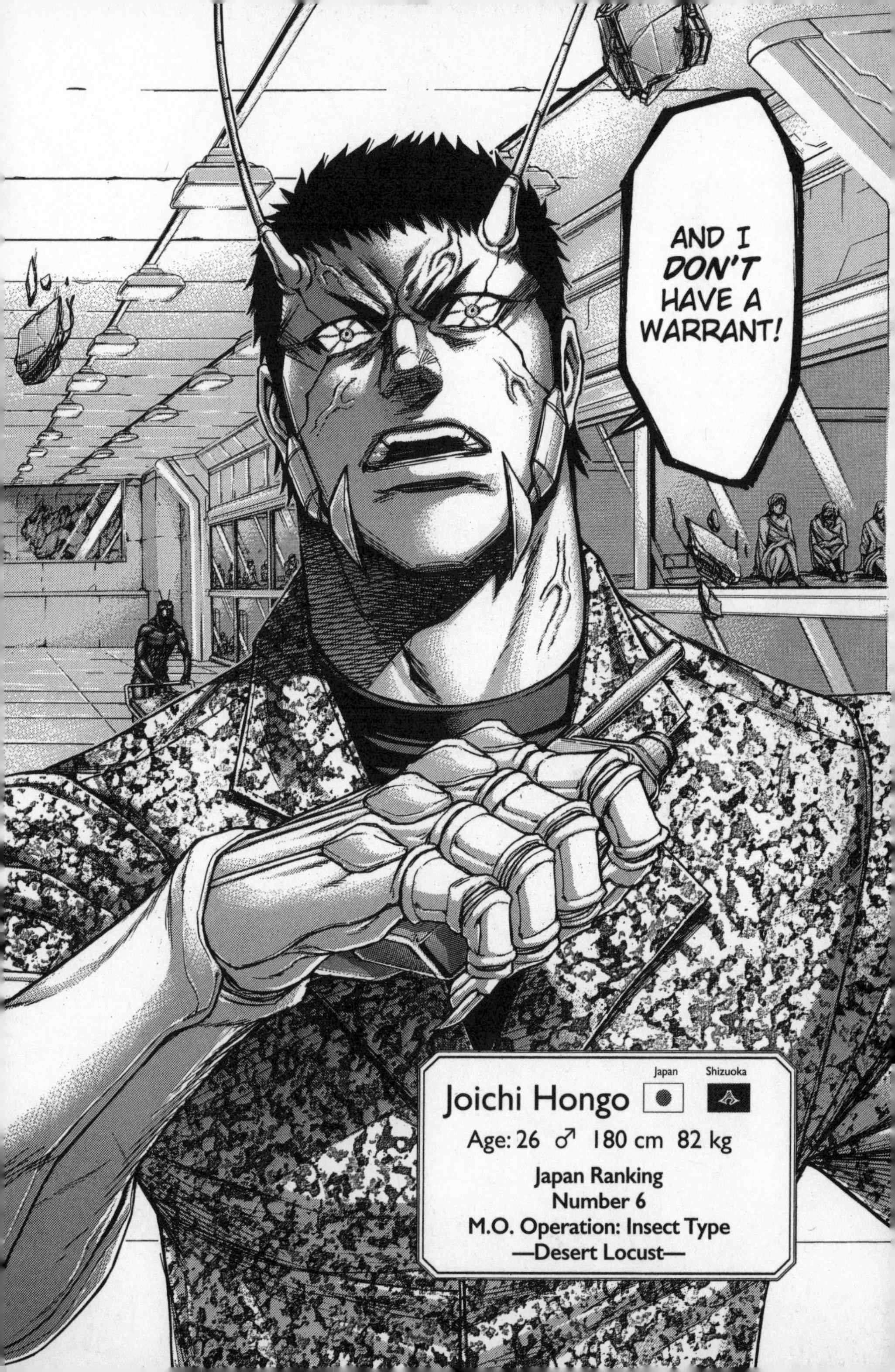
AND I DON'T HAVE A WARRANT!
Japan
Shizuoka
Joichi Hongo
Age: 26 ♂ 180 cm 82 kg
Japan Ranking
Number 6
M.O. Operation: Insect Type
—Desert Locust—

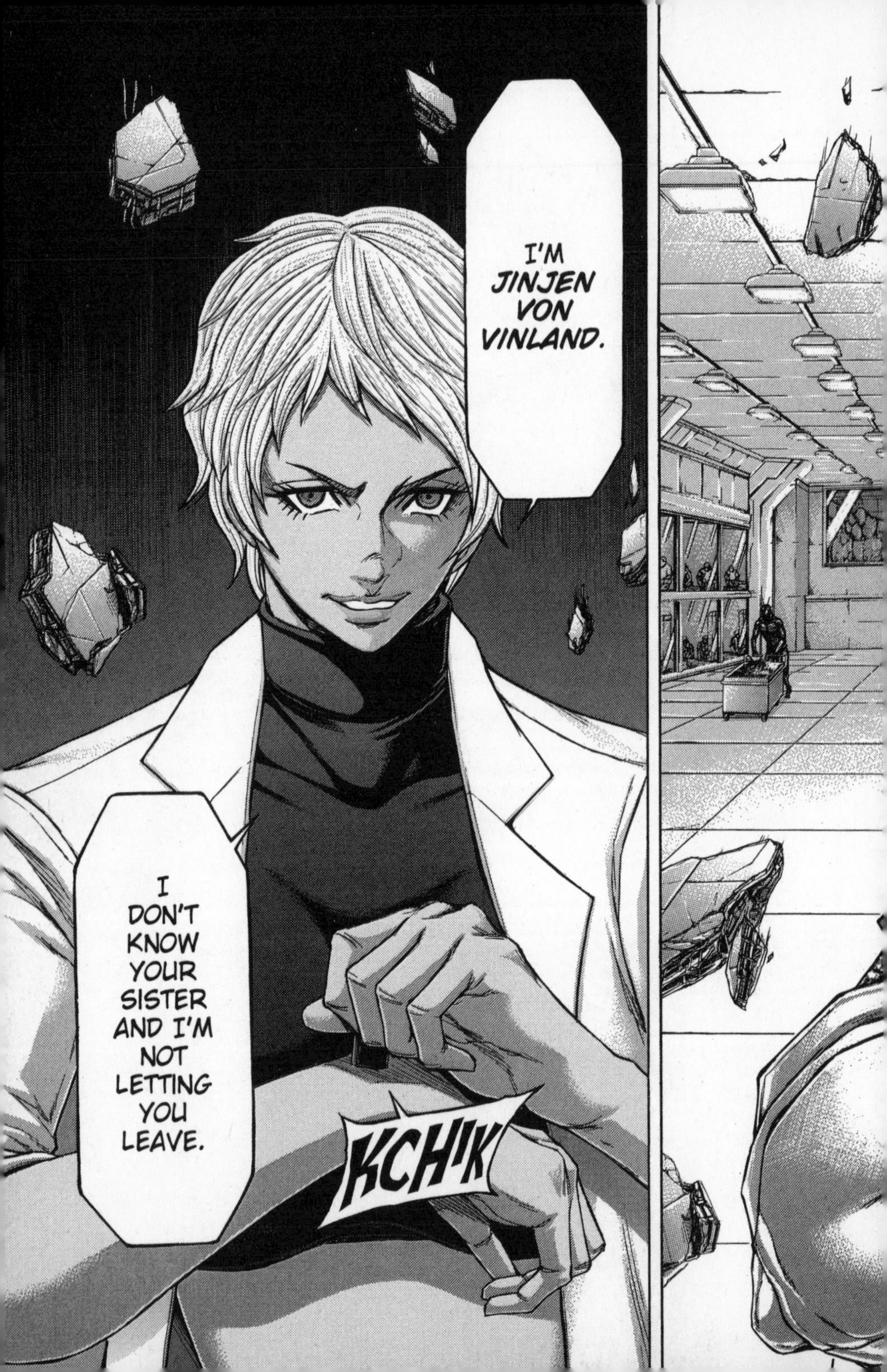
I'M JINJEN VON VINLAND.
I DON'T KNOW YOUR SISTER AND I'M NOT LETTING YOU LEAVE.
KCHIK

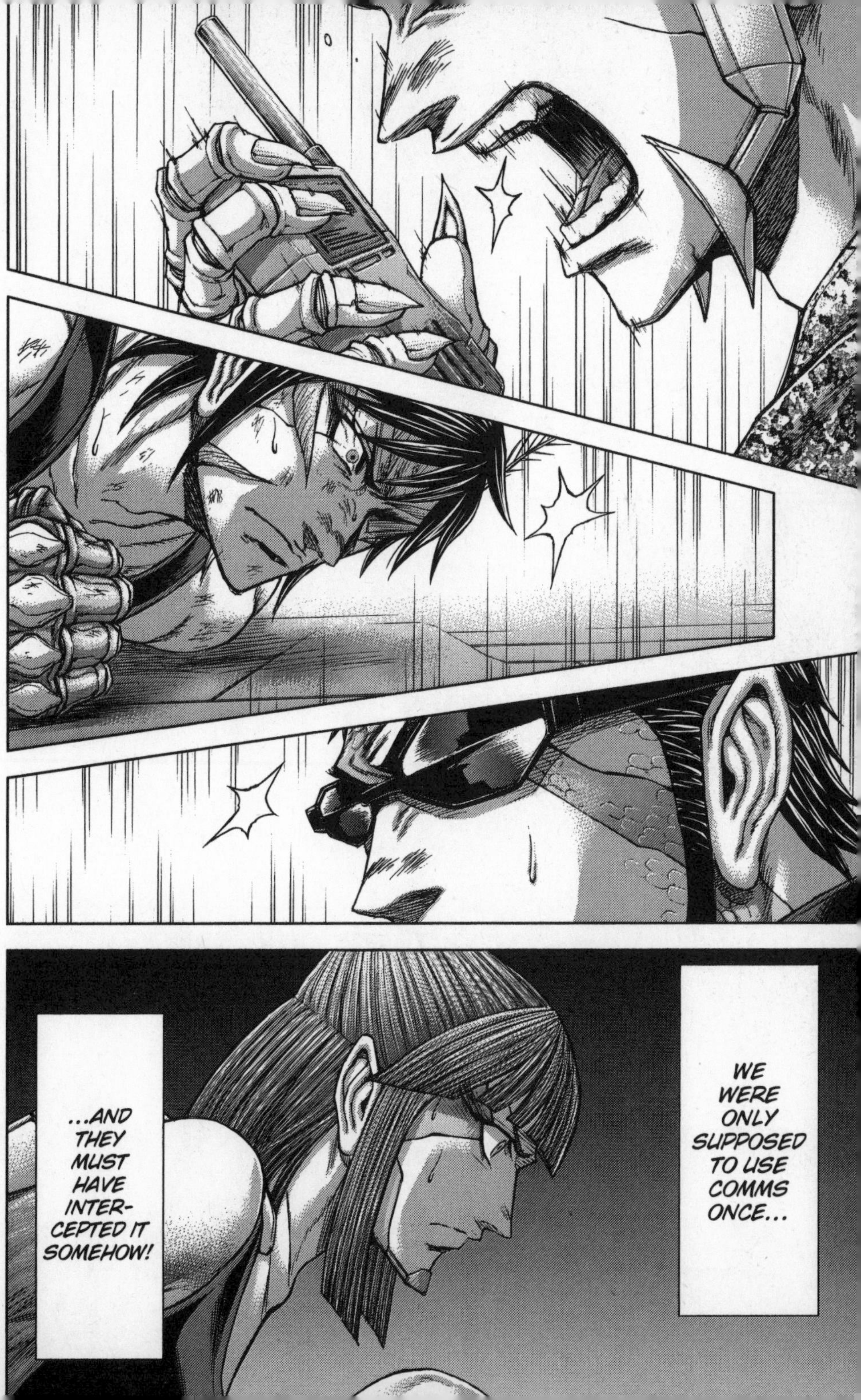
WE WERE ONLY SUPPOSED TO USE COMMS ONCE...
...AND THEY MUST HAVE INTER-CEPTED IT SOMEHOW!

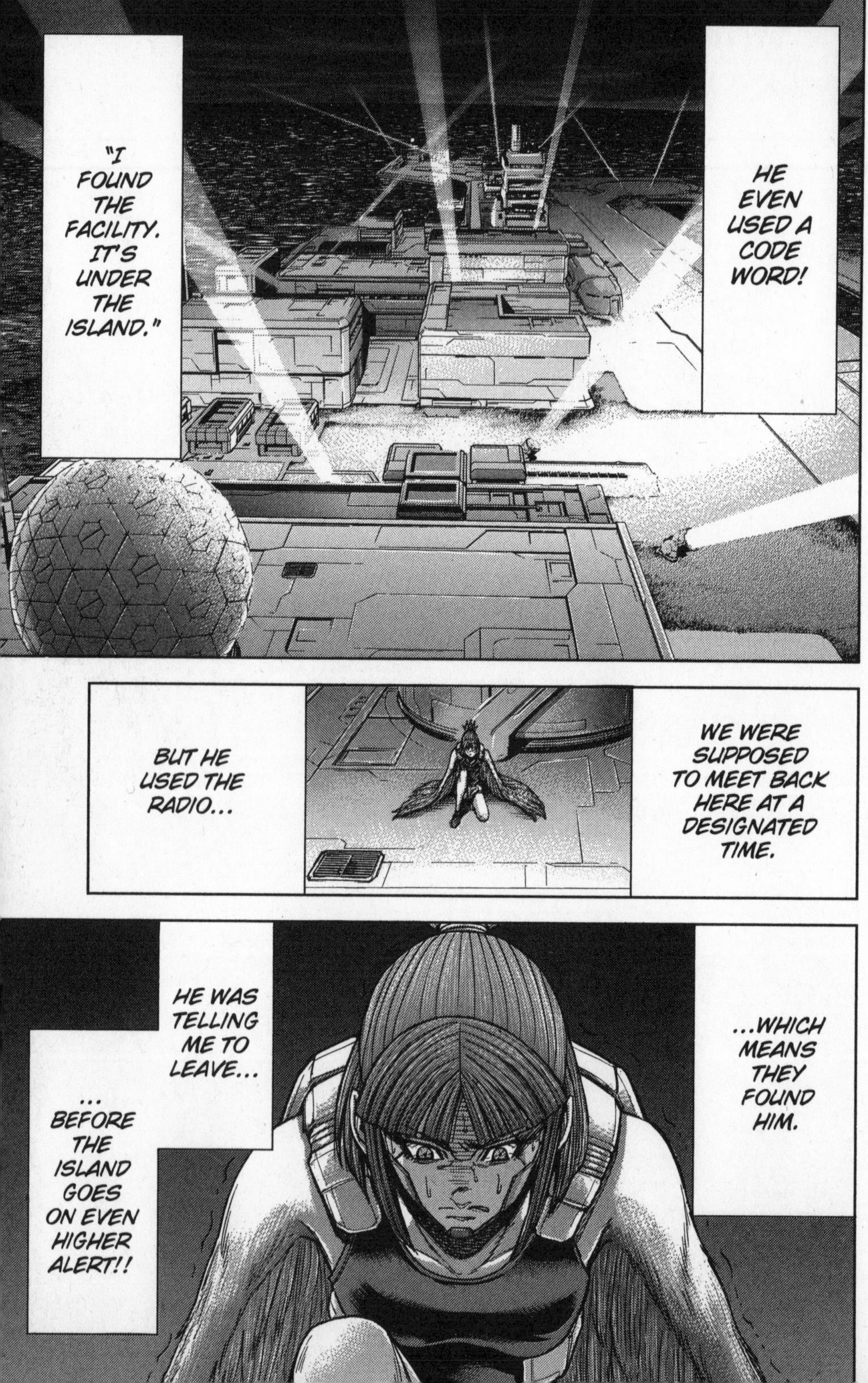
HE EVEN USED A CODE WORD!
"I FOUND THE FACILITY. IT'S UNDER THE ISLAND."
WE WERE SUPPOSED TO MEET BACK HERE AT A DESIGNATED TIME.
BUT HE USED THE RADIO...
...WHICH MEANS THEY FOUND HIM.
HE WAS TELLING ME TO LEAVE...
...BEFORE THE ISLAND GOES ON EVEN HIGHER ALERT!!

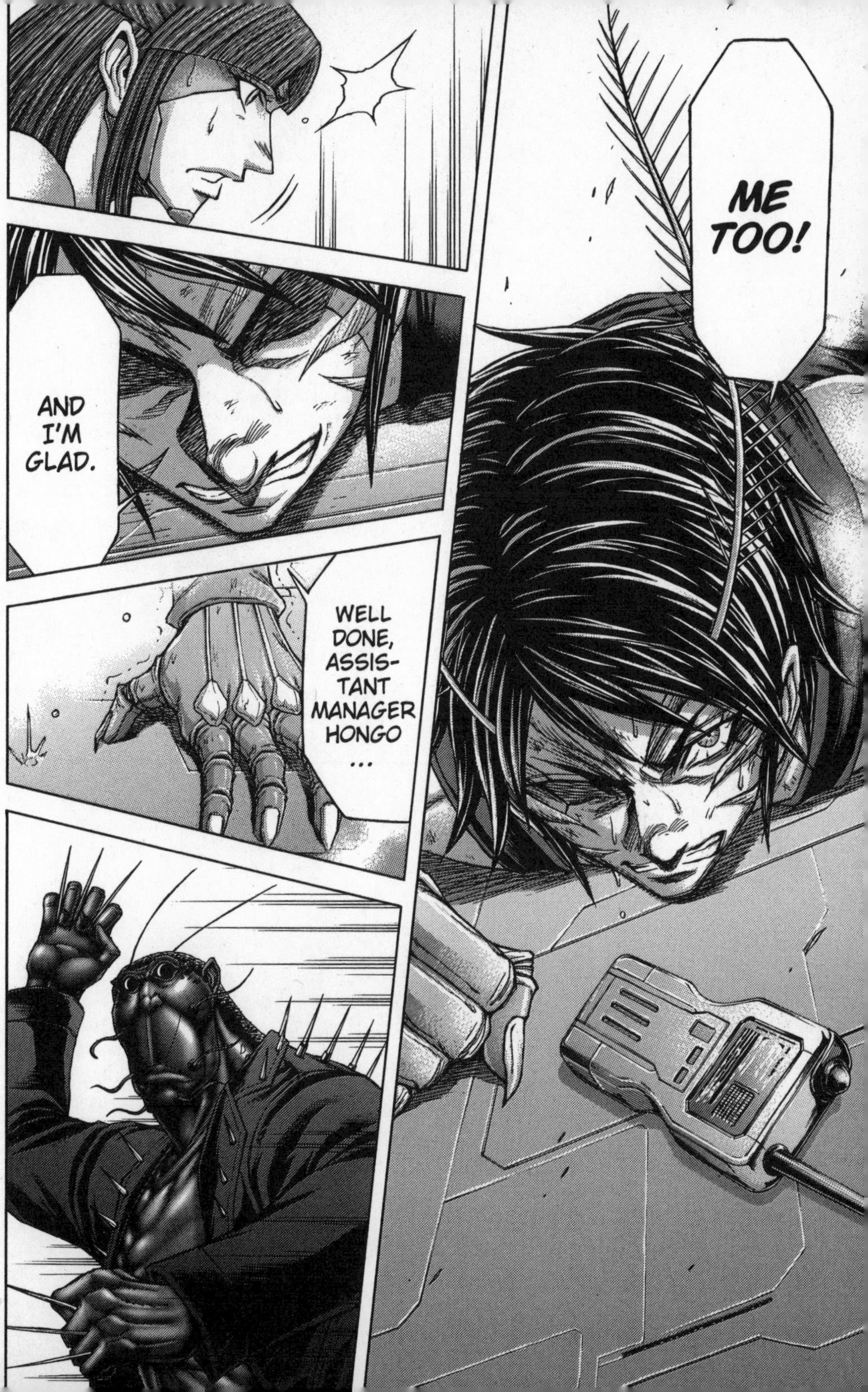
ME TOO!
AND I'M GLAD.
WELL DONE, ASSIS- TANT MANAGER HONGO ...

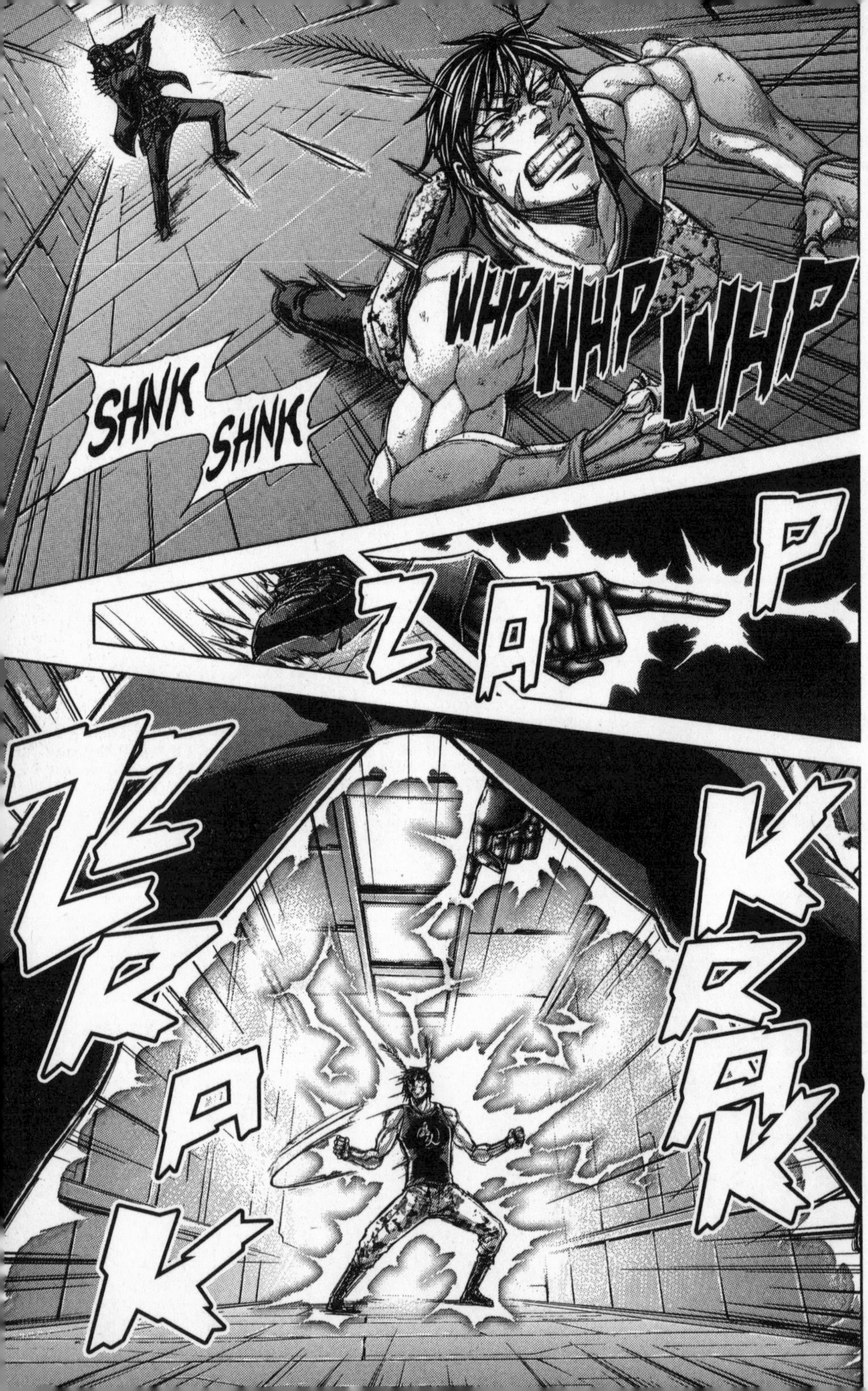
WHP WHP WHP
SHNK SHNK
ZAP
KRAK
ZZRAK

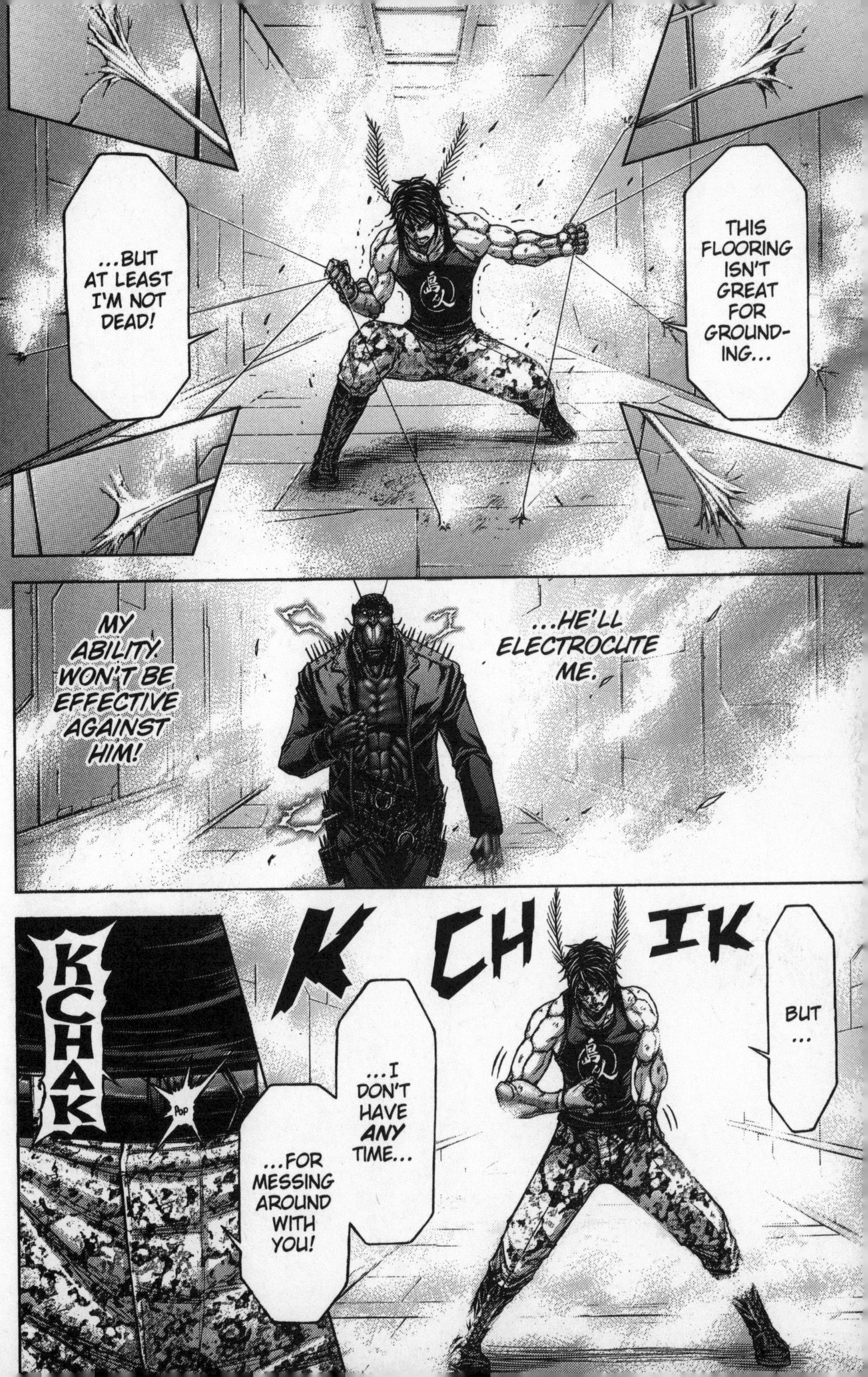
THIS FLOORING ISN'T GREAT FOR GROUNDING...
...BUT AT LEAST I'M NOT DEAD!
...HE'LL ELECTROCUTE ME.
MY ABILITY WON'T BE EFFECTIVE AGAINST HIM!
BUT...
K CH IK
...I DON'T HAVE ANY TIME...
...FOR MESSING AROUND WITH YOU!
POP
KCHAK

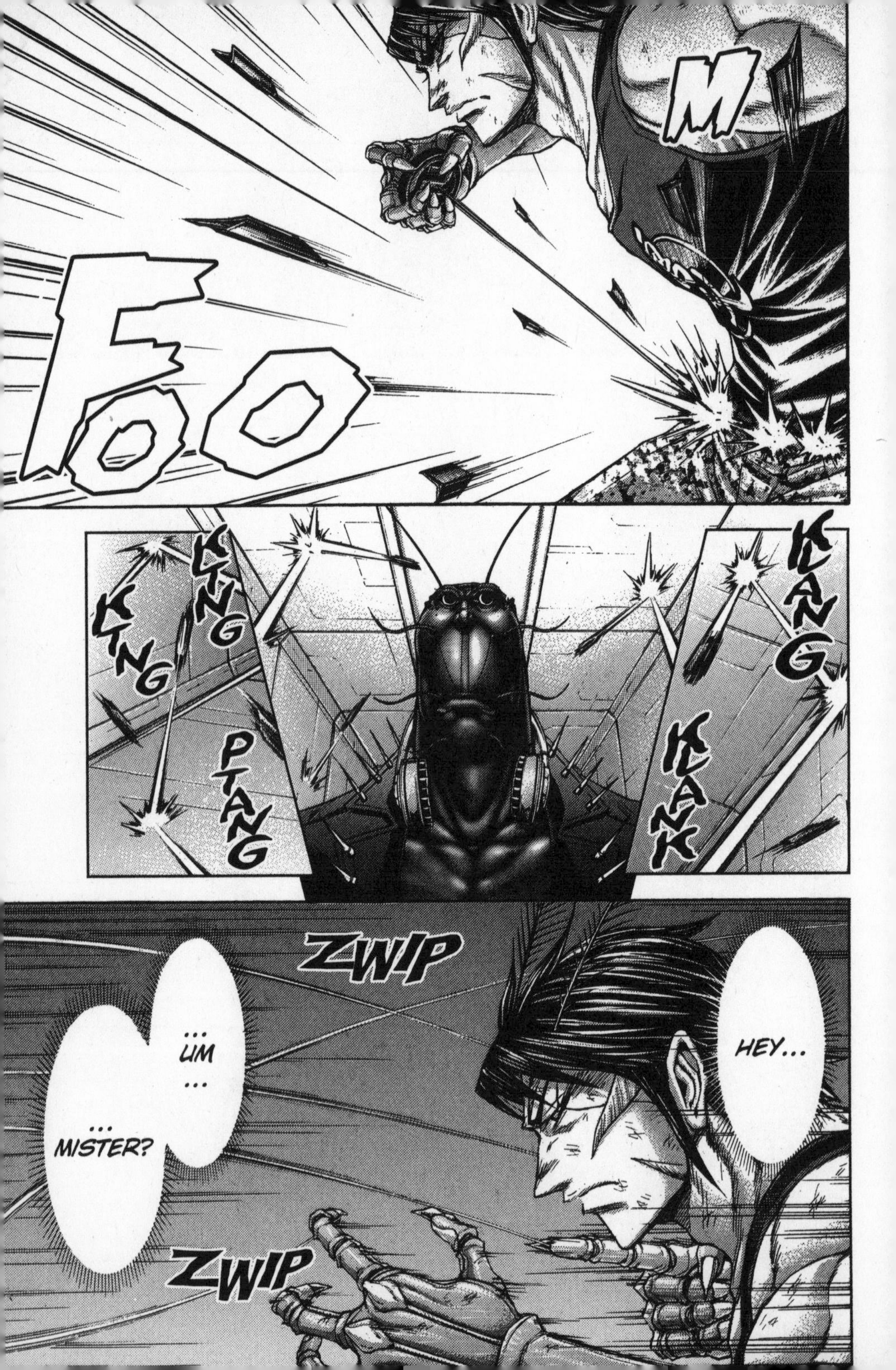

M
FOO
KLANG
KLING
KLING
KLANK
PTANG
ZWIP
HEY...
...UM... ...MISTER?
ZWIP

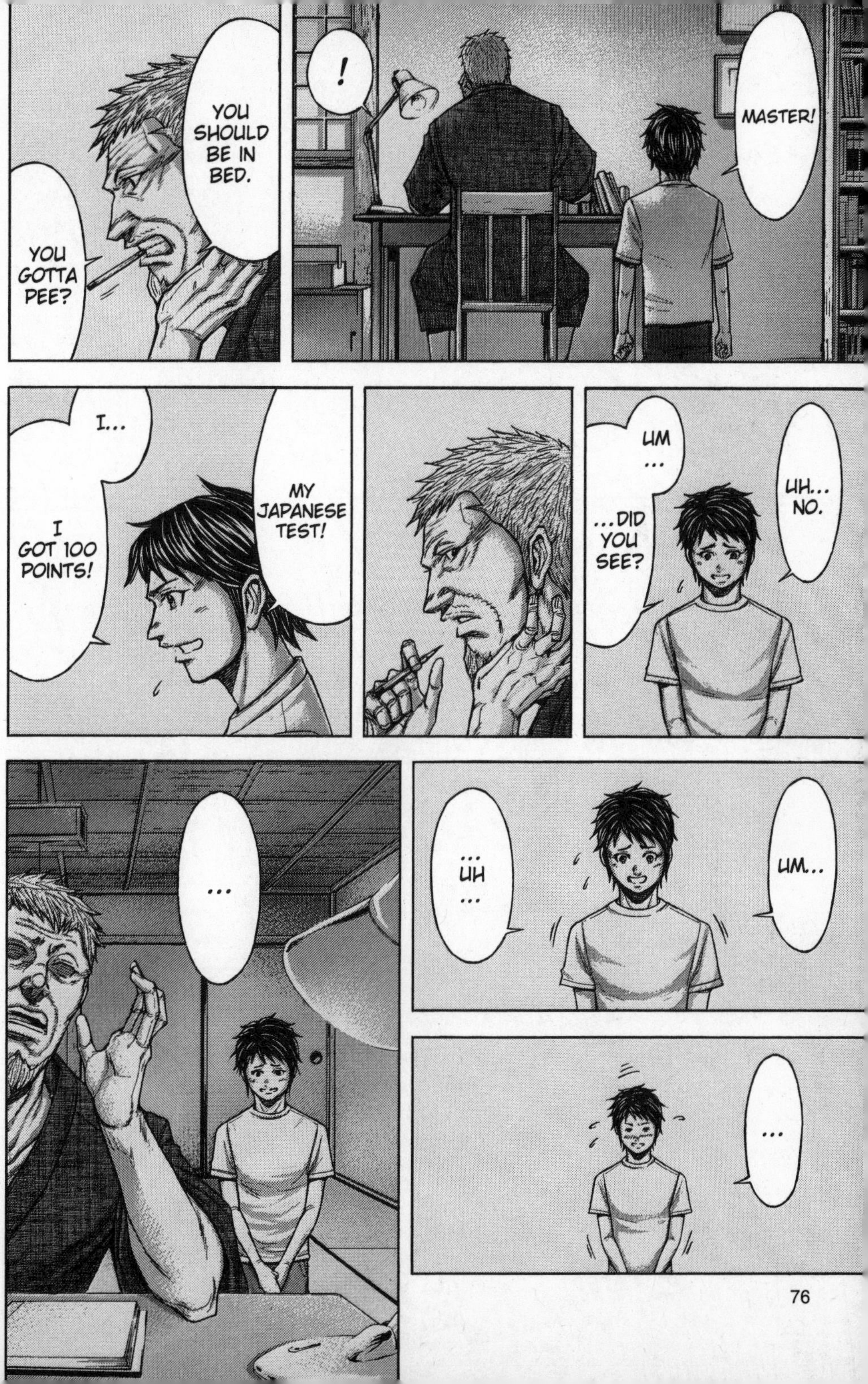
MASTER!
!
YOU SHOULD BE IN BED.
YOU GOTTA PEE?
UH... NO.
UM ...
...DID YOU SEE?
MY JAPANESE TEST!
I...
I GOT 100 POINTS!
UM...
... UH ...
...
...

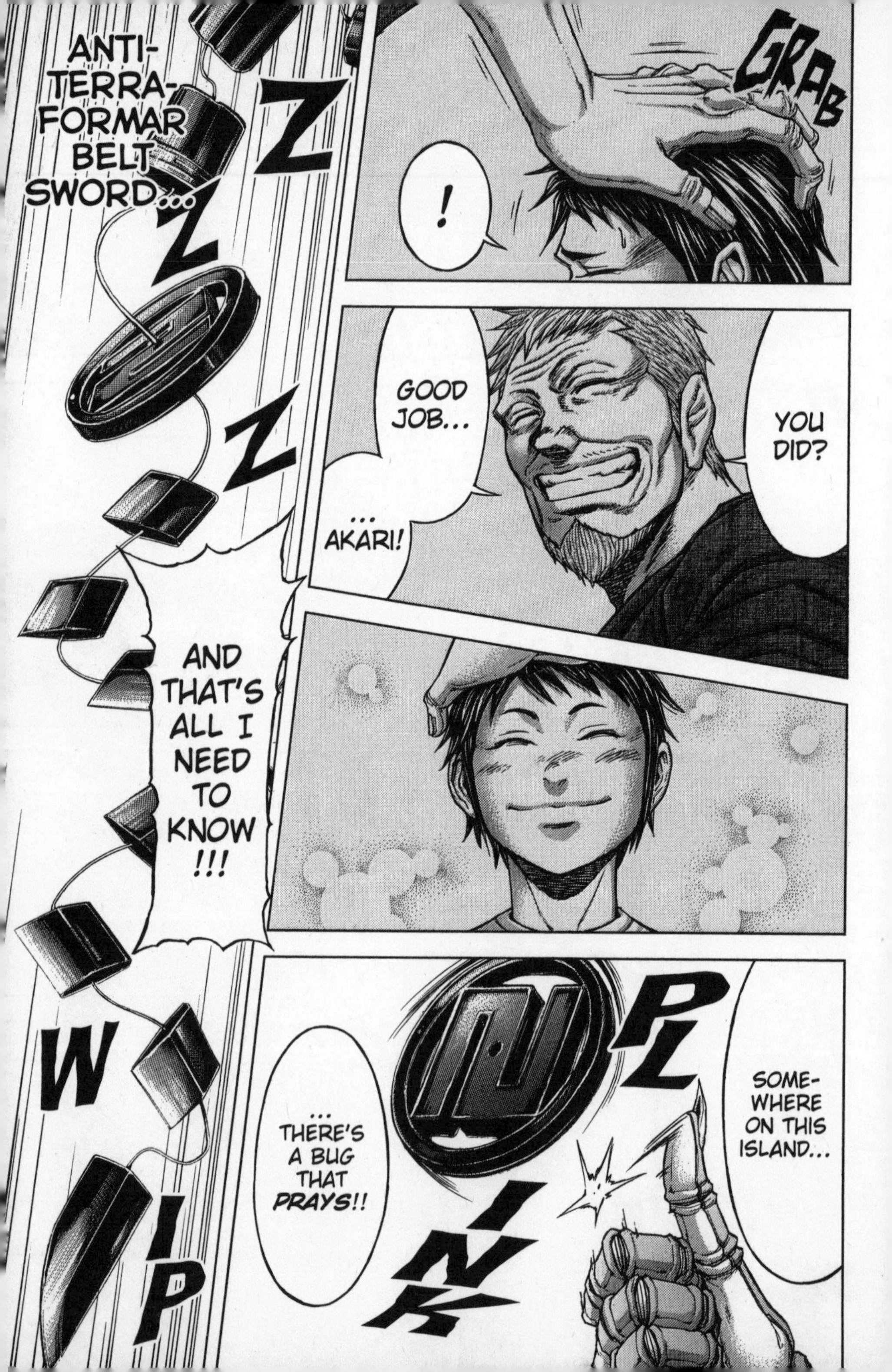
GRAB
!
YOU DID?
GOOD JOB...
...AKARI!
SOME-WHERE ON THIS ISLAND...
...THERE'S A BUG THAT *PRAYS*!!
PLINK
ANTI-TERRA-FORMAR BELT SWORD...
ZZZ
AND THAT'S ALL I NEED TO KNOW!!!
WHIP

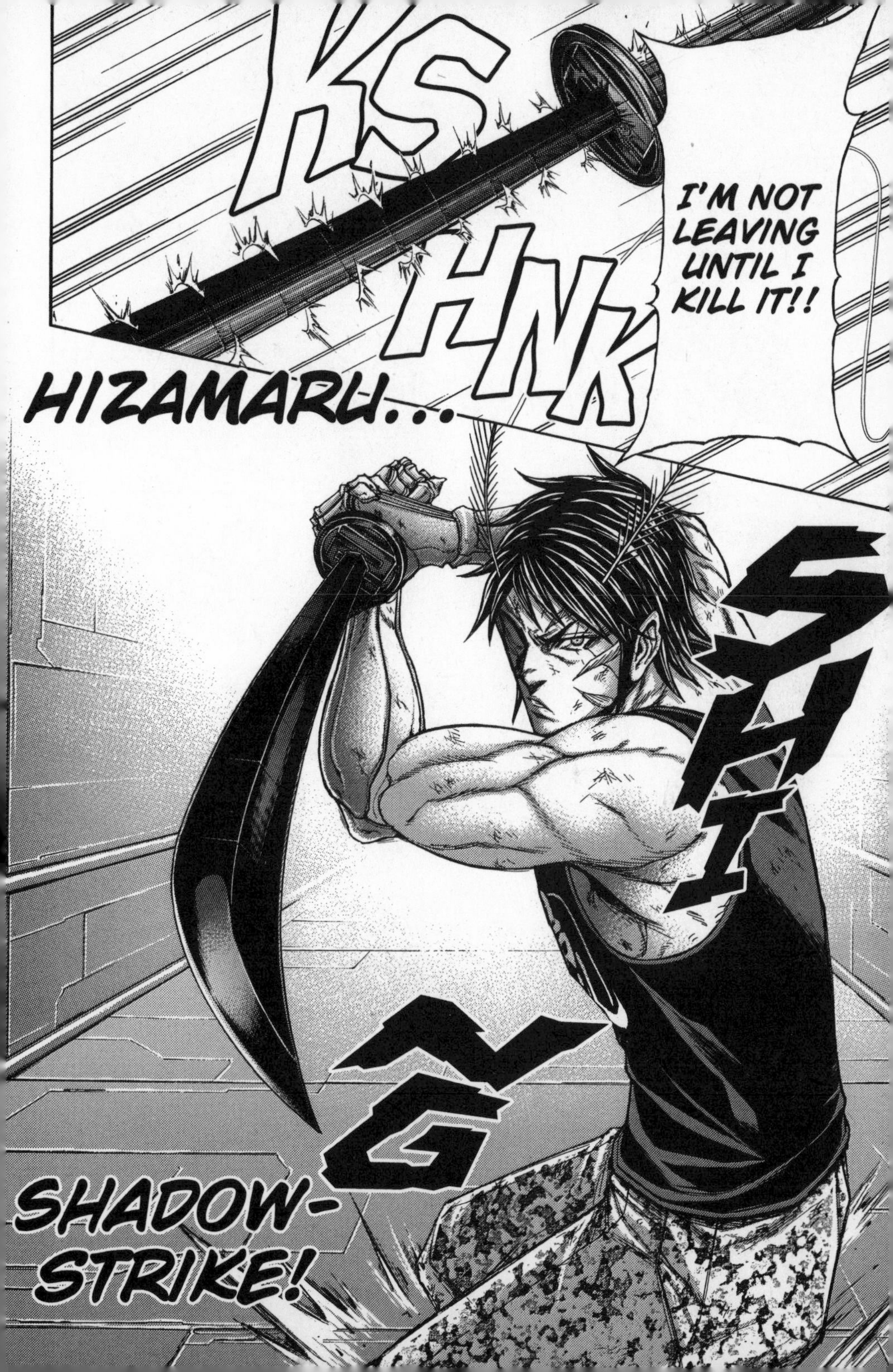
I'M NOT LEAVING UNTIL I KILL IT!!
KS
HNK
HIZAMARU...
SHING
SHADOW-STRIKE!

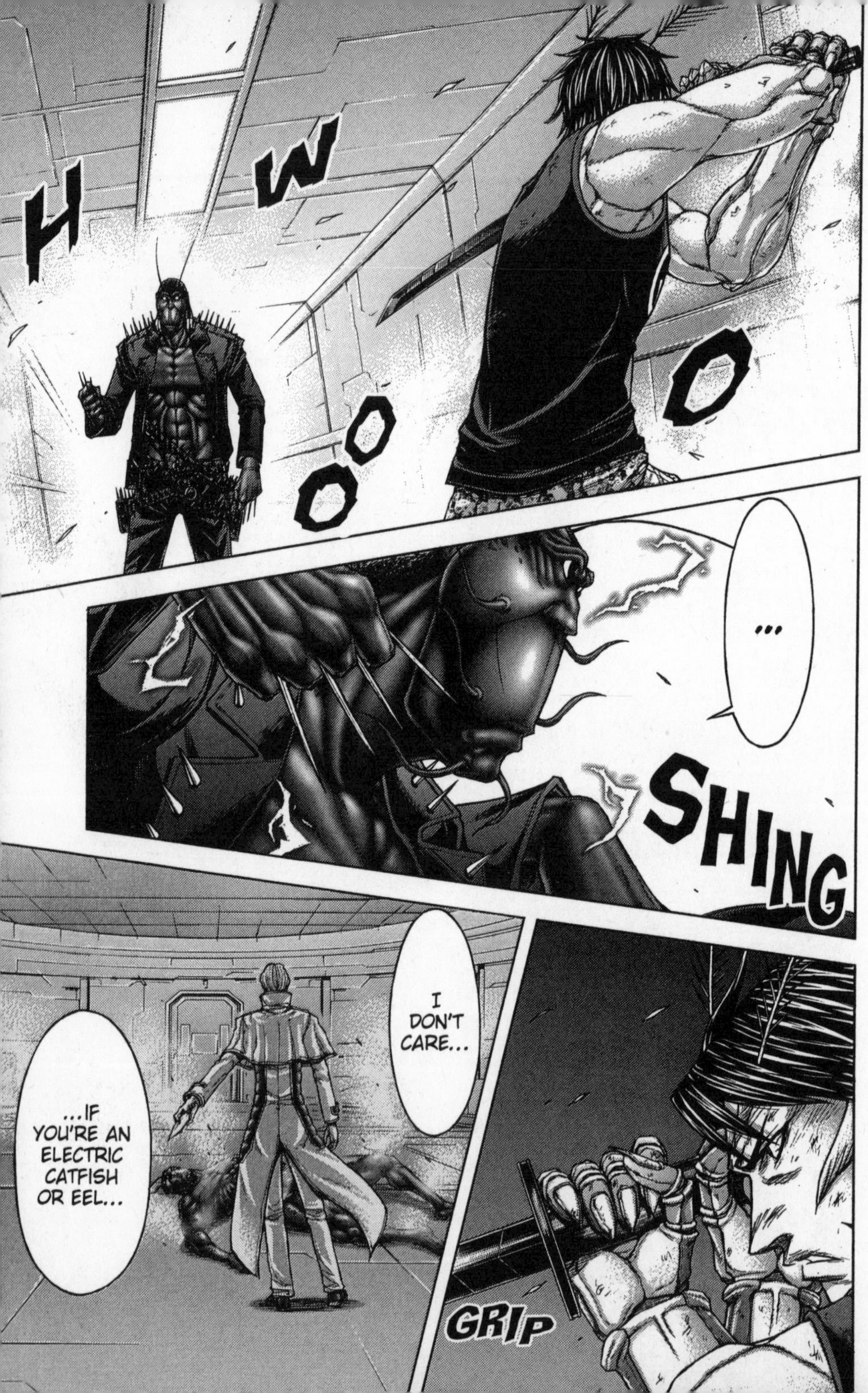
HWOOOO
...
SHING
GRIP
I DON'T CARE...
...IF YOU'RE AN ELECTRIC CATFISH OR EEL...

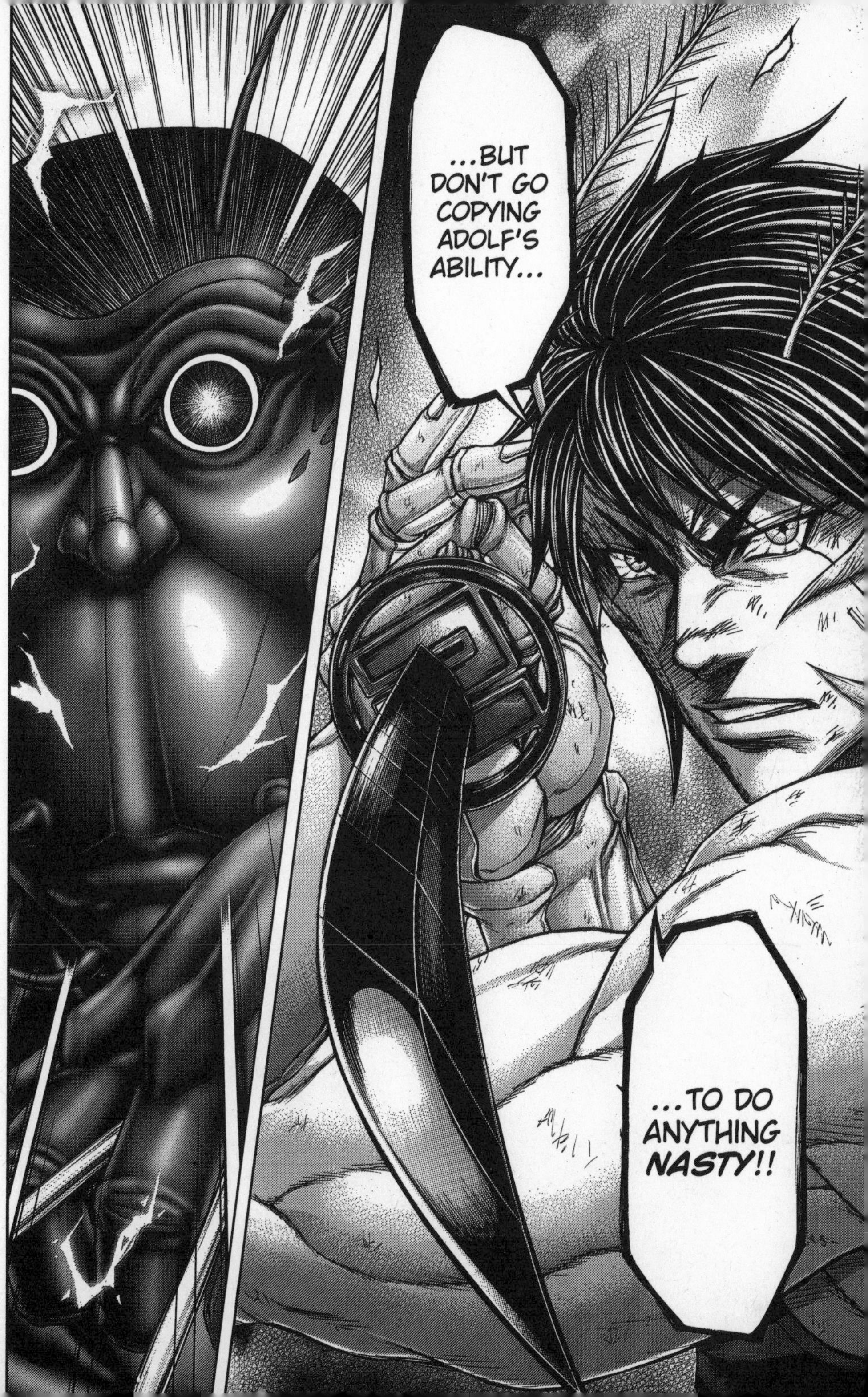
...BUT DON'T GO COPYING ADOLF'S ABILITY...
...TO DO ANYTHING NASTY!!

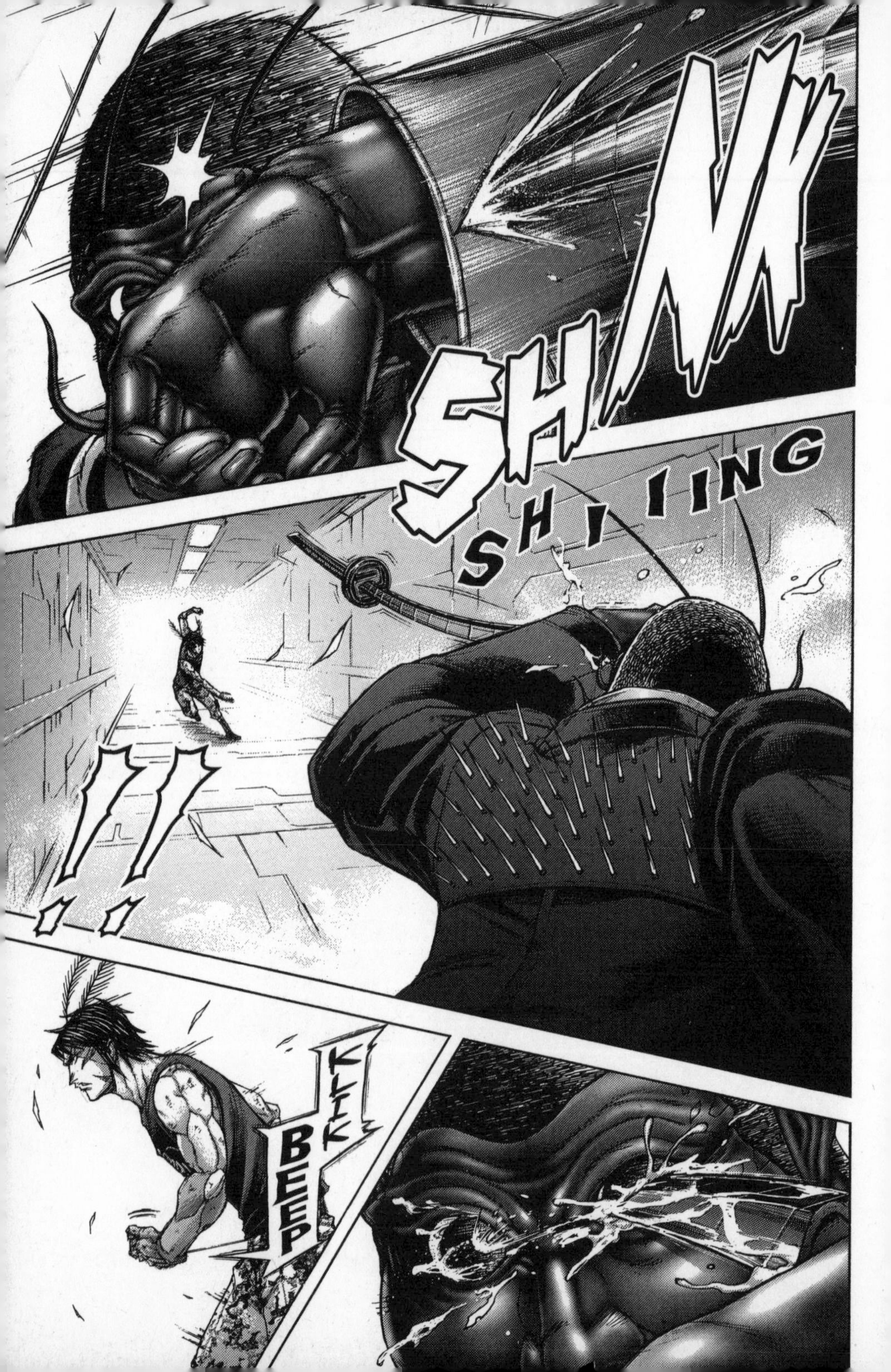
SHIIING
!!
KLIK
BEEP

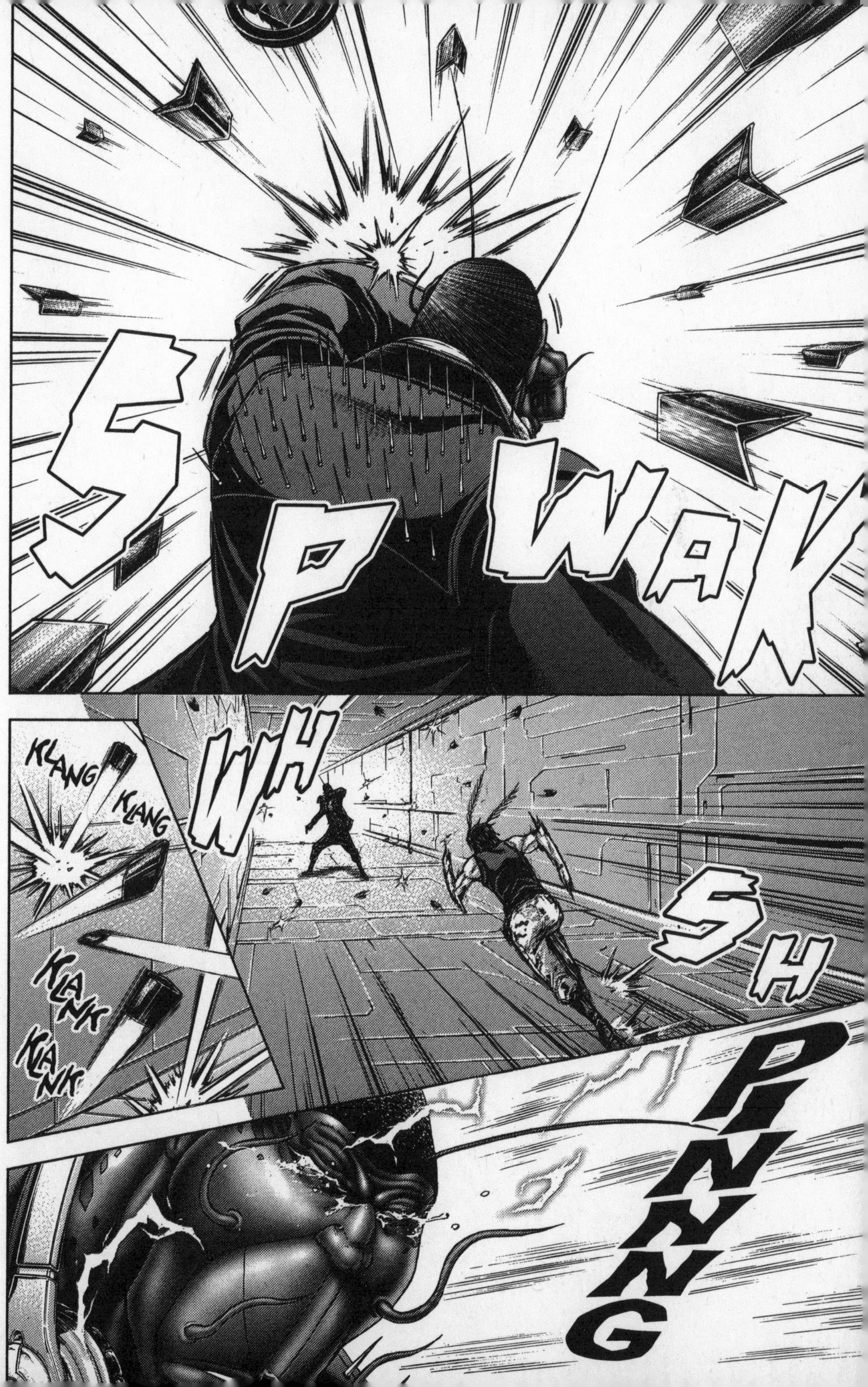
SPWAK
WHW
SH
KLANG
KLANG
KLANK
KLANK
PINNNG

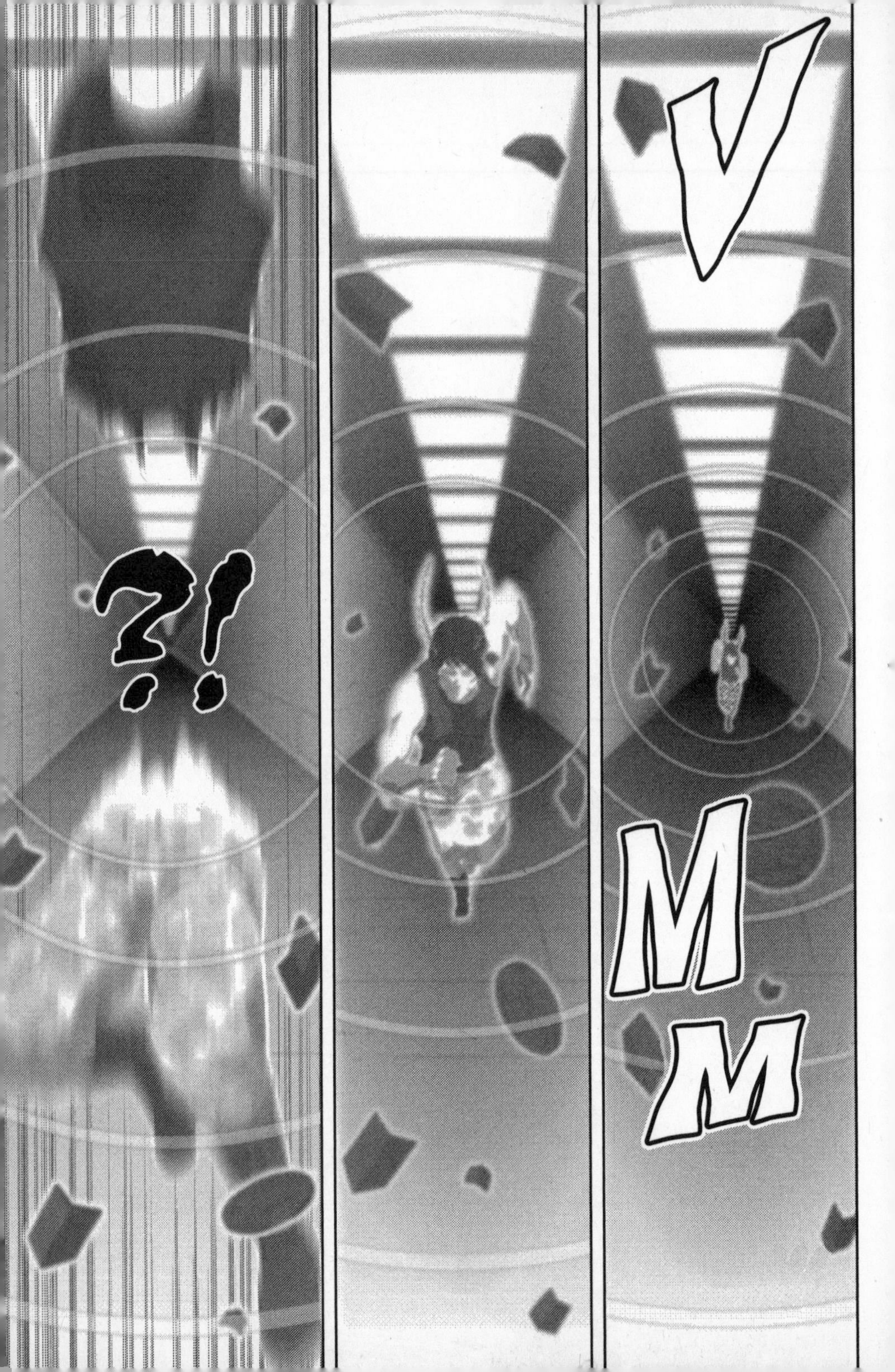
VMM
?!

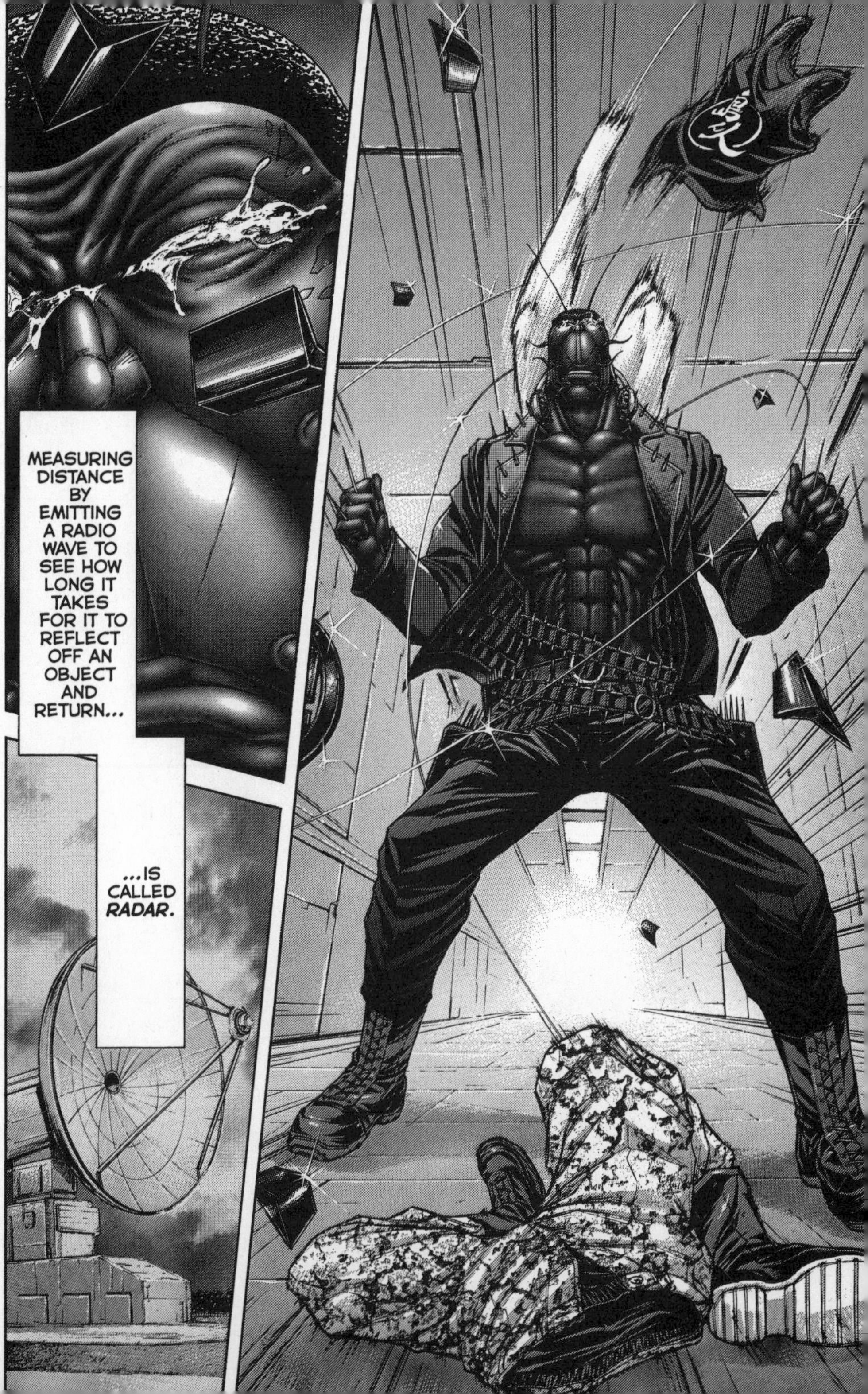
MEASURING DISTANCE BY EMITTING A RADIO WAVE TO SEE HOW LONG IT TAKES FOR IT TO REFLECT OFF AN OBJECT AND RETURN...
...IS CALLED *RADAR*.

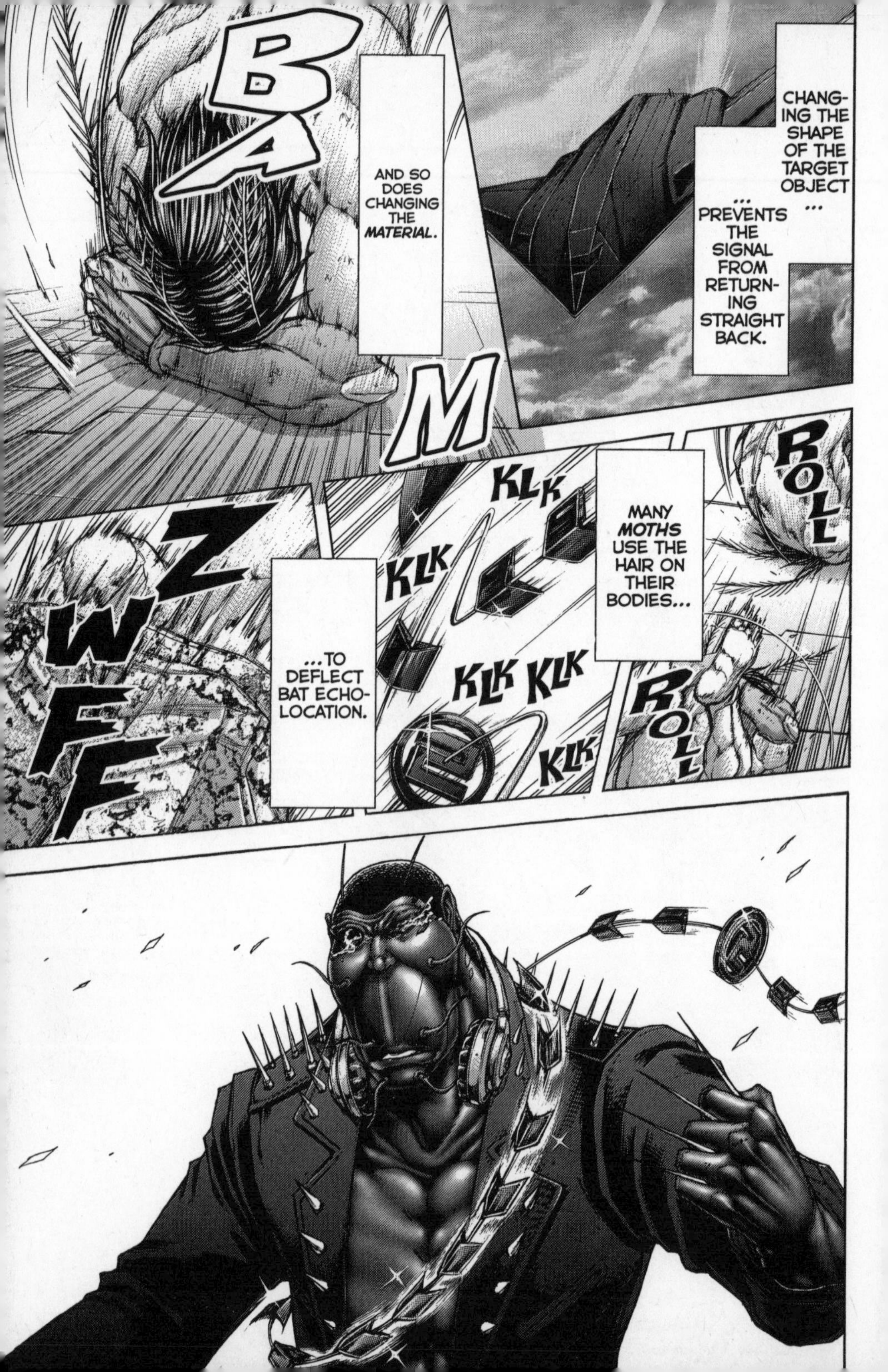

CHANGING THE SHAPE OF THE TARGET OBJECT...
...PREVENTS THE SIGNAL FROM RETURNING STRAIGHT BACK.
AND SO DOES CHANGING THE *MATERIAL*.
BAM
ROLL
ROLL
MANY *MOTHS* USE THE HAIR ON THEIR BODIES...
KLK
KLK
KLK KLK
KLK
...TO DEFLECT BAT ECHOLOCATION.
FFWZ

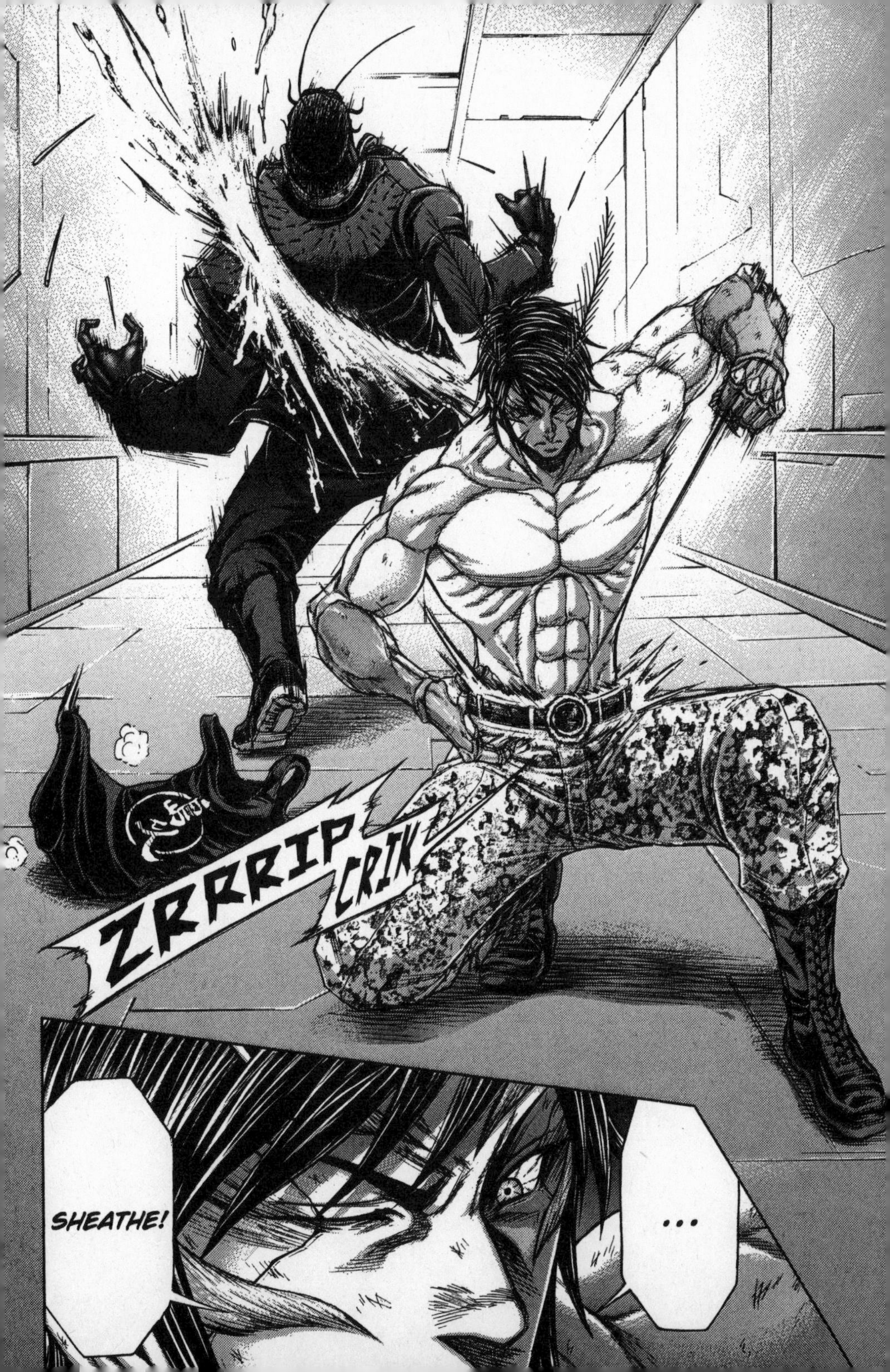
CRIK
ZRRRIP
...
SHEATHE!

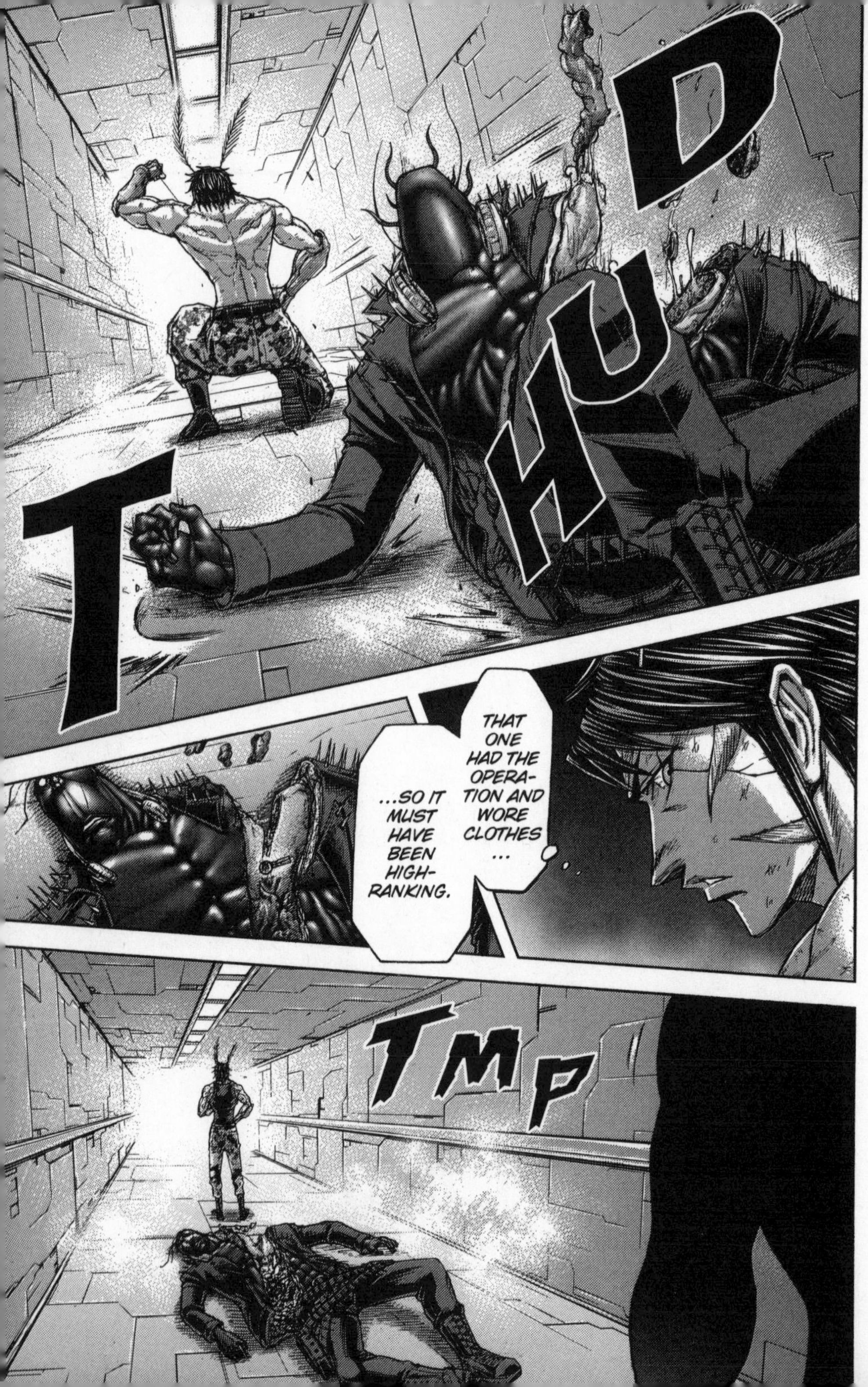
THUD
THAT ONE HAD THE OPERATION AND WORE CLOTHES...
...SO IT MUST HAVE BEEN HIGH-RANKING.
TMP

TERRA FORMARS

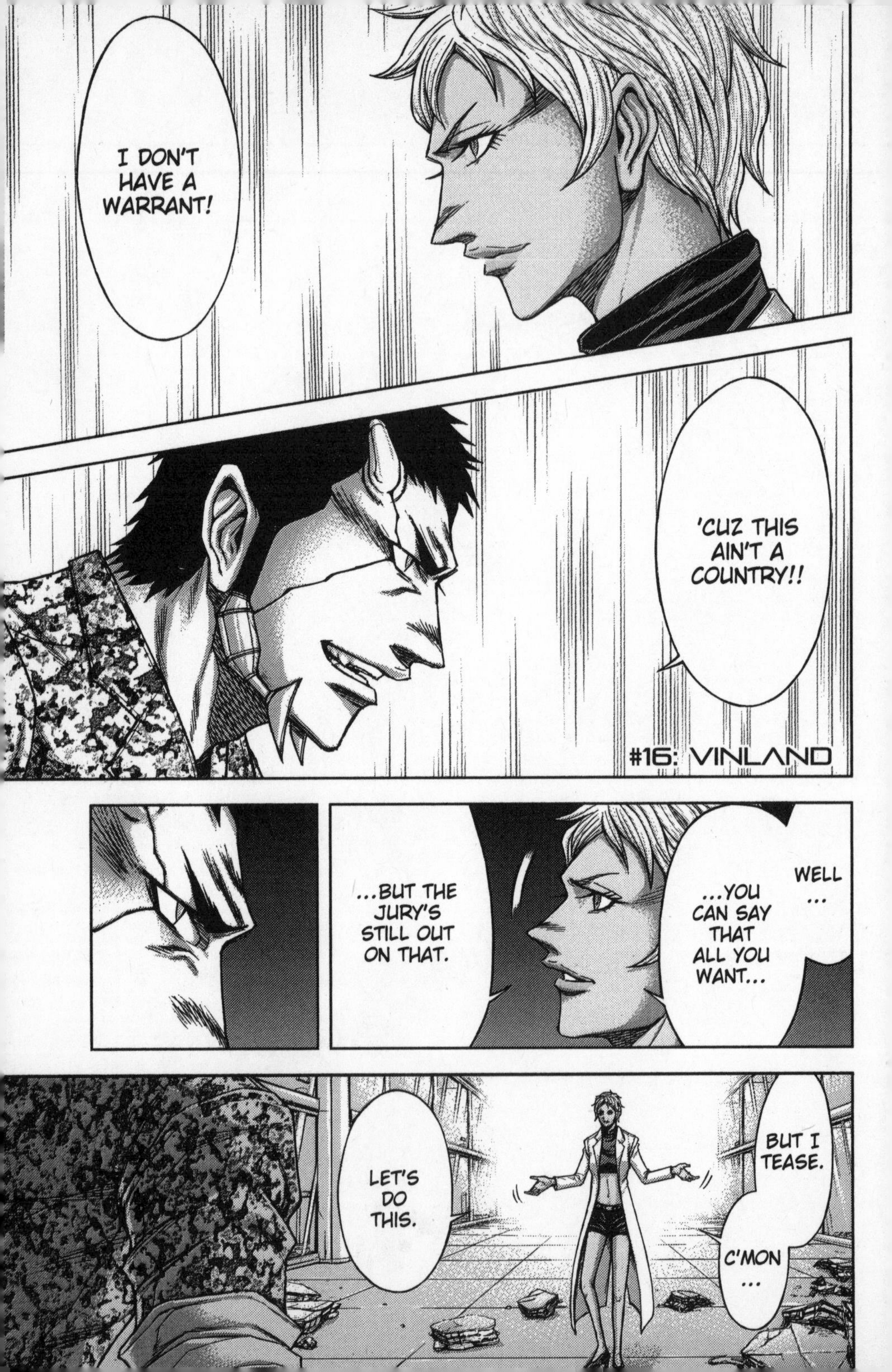
I DON'T HAVE A WARRANT!
'CUZ THIS AIN'T A COUNTRY!!
#16: VINLAND
WELL ...
...YOU CAN SAY THAT ALL YOU WANT...
...BUT THE JURY'S STILL OUT ON THAT.
BUT I TEASE.
C'MON ...
LET'S DO THIS.

#16: VINLAND

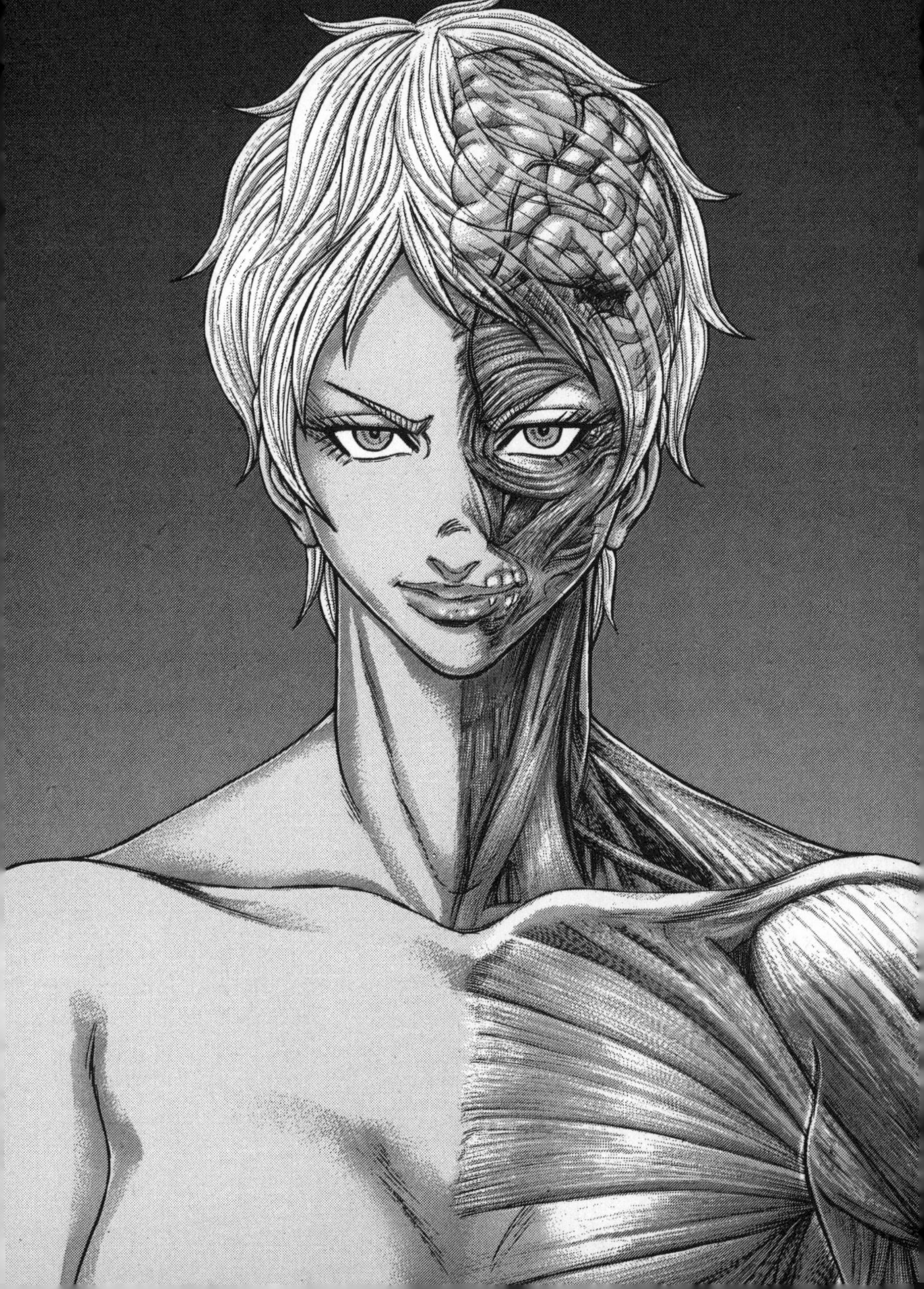

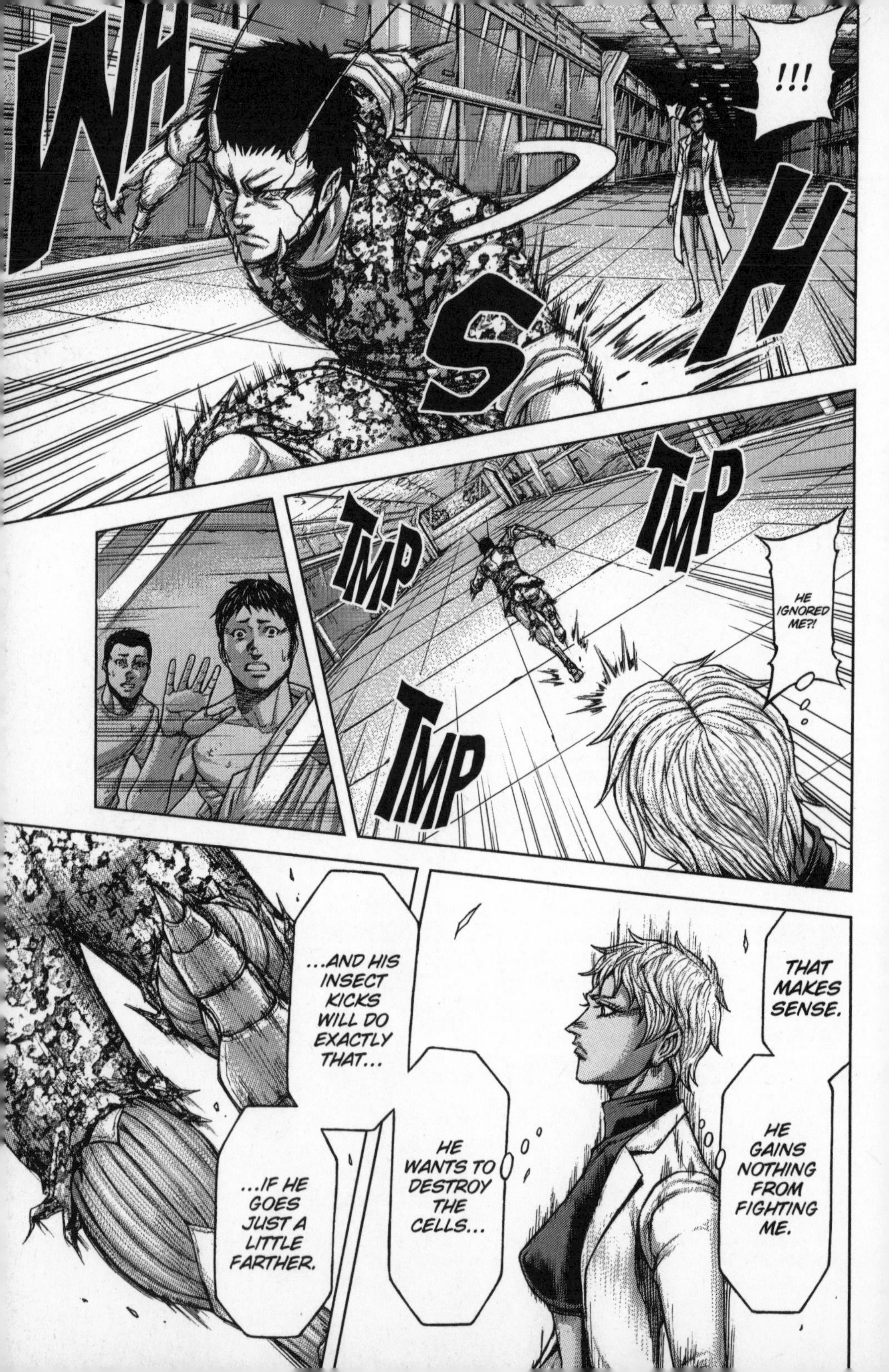
!!!
WH
S
H
TMP
TMP
TMP
HE IGNORED ME?!
THAT MAKES SENSE.
HE GAINS NOTHING FROM FIGHTING ME.
HE WANTS TO DESTROY THE CELLS...
...AND HIS INSECT KICKS WILL DO EXACTLY THAT...
...IF HE GOES JUST A LITTLE FARTHER.

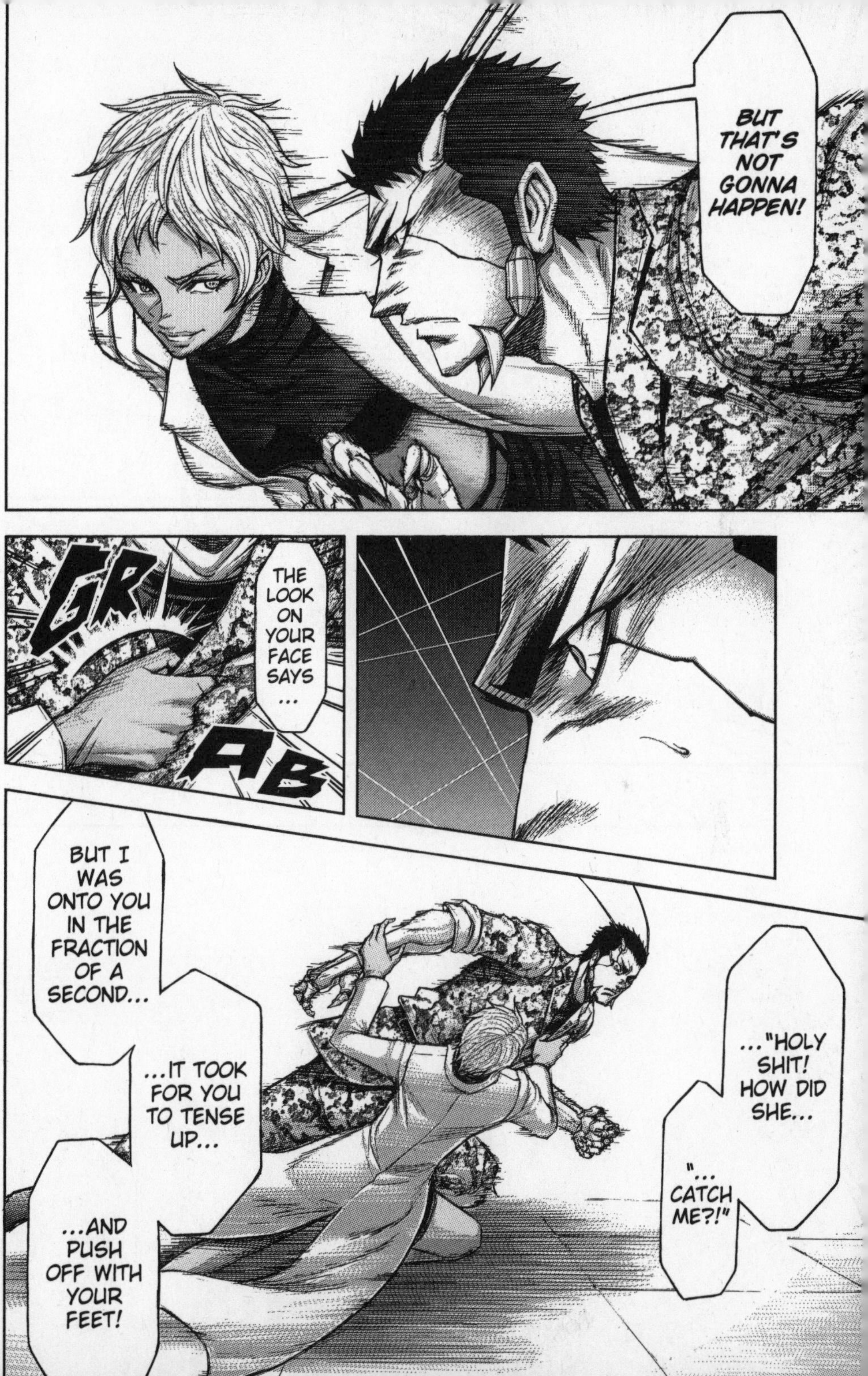
BUT THAT'S NOT GONNA HAPPEN!
GR
AB
THE LOOK ON YOUR FACE SAYS...
..."HOLY SHIT! HOW DID SHE...
"...CATCH ME?!"
BUT I WAS ONTO YOU IN THE FRACTION OF A SECOND...
...IT TOOK FOR YOU TO TENSE UP...
...AND PUSH OFF WITH YOUR FEET!

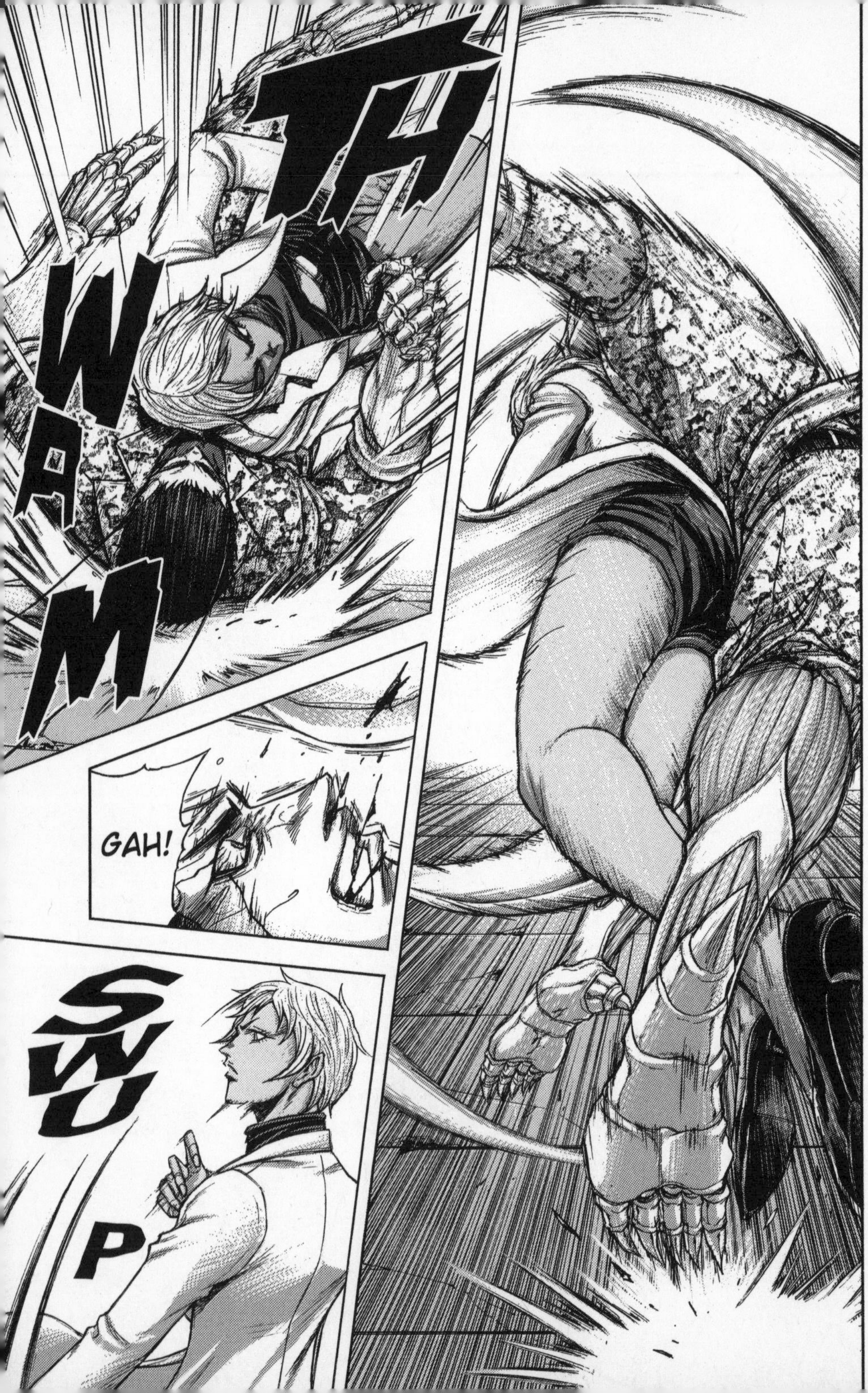
THWAM
GAH!
SWUP

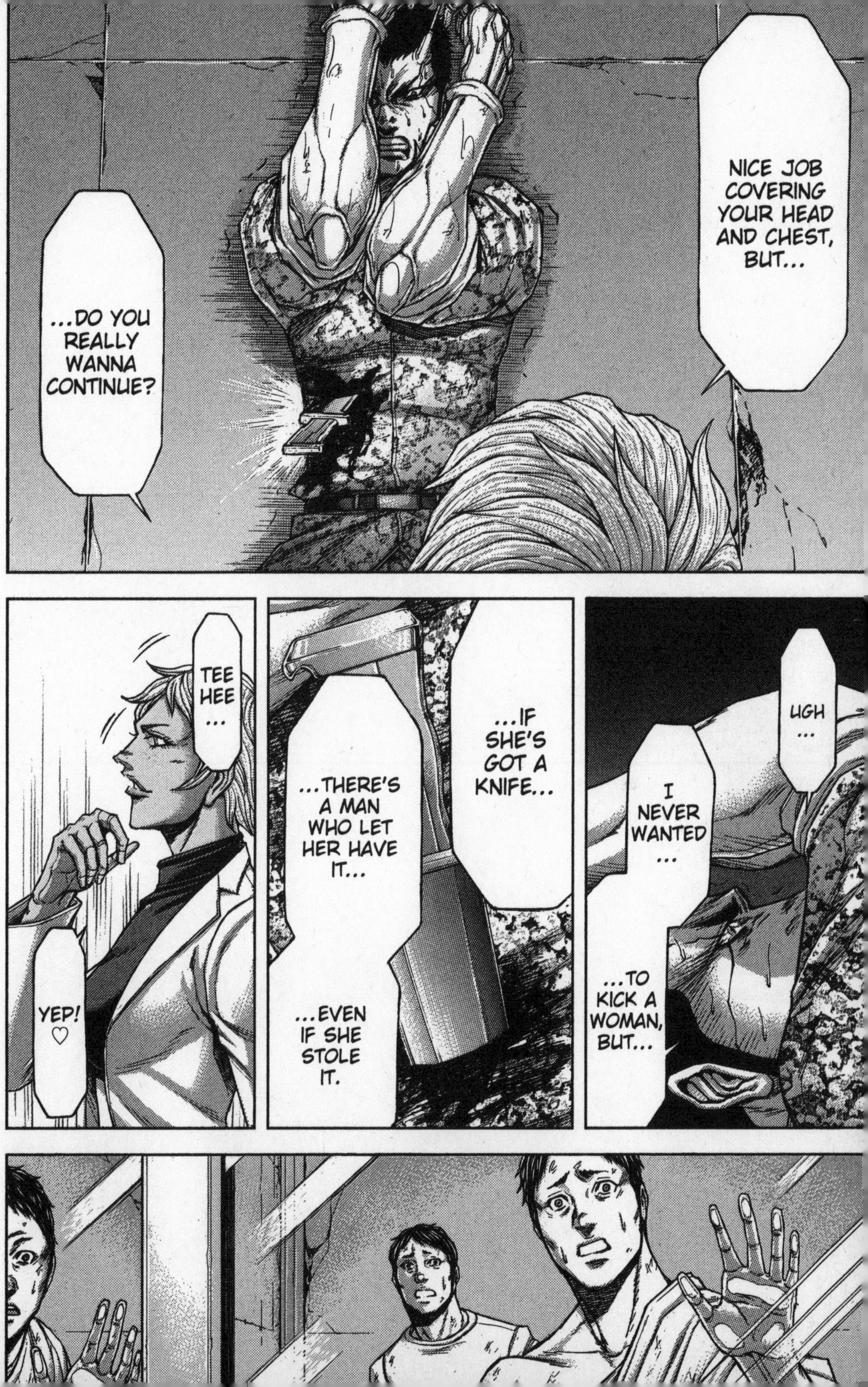
NICE JOB COVERING YOUR HEAD AND CHEST, BUT...
...DO YOU REALLY WANNA CONTINUE?
UGH...
I NEVER WANTED...
...TO KICK A WOMAN, BUT...
...IF SHE'S GOT A KNIFE...
...THERE'S A MAN WHO LET HER HAVE IT...
...EVEN IF SHE STOLE IT.
TEE HEE...
YEP! ♡

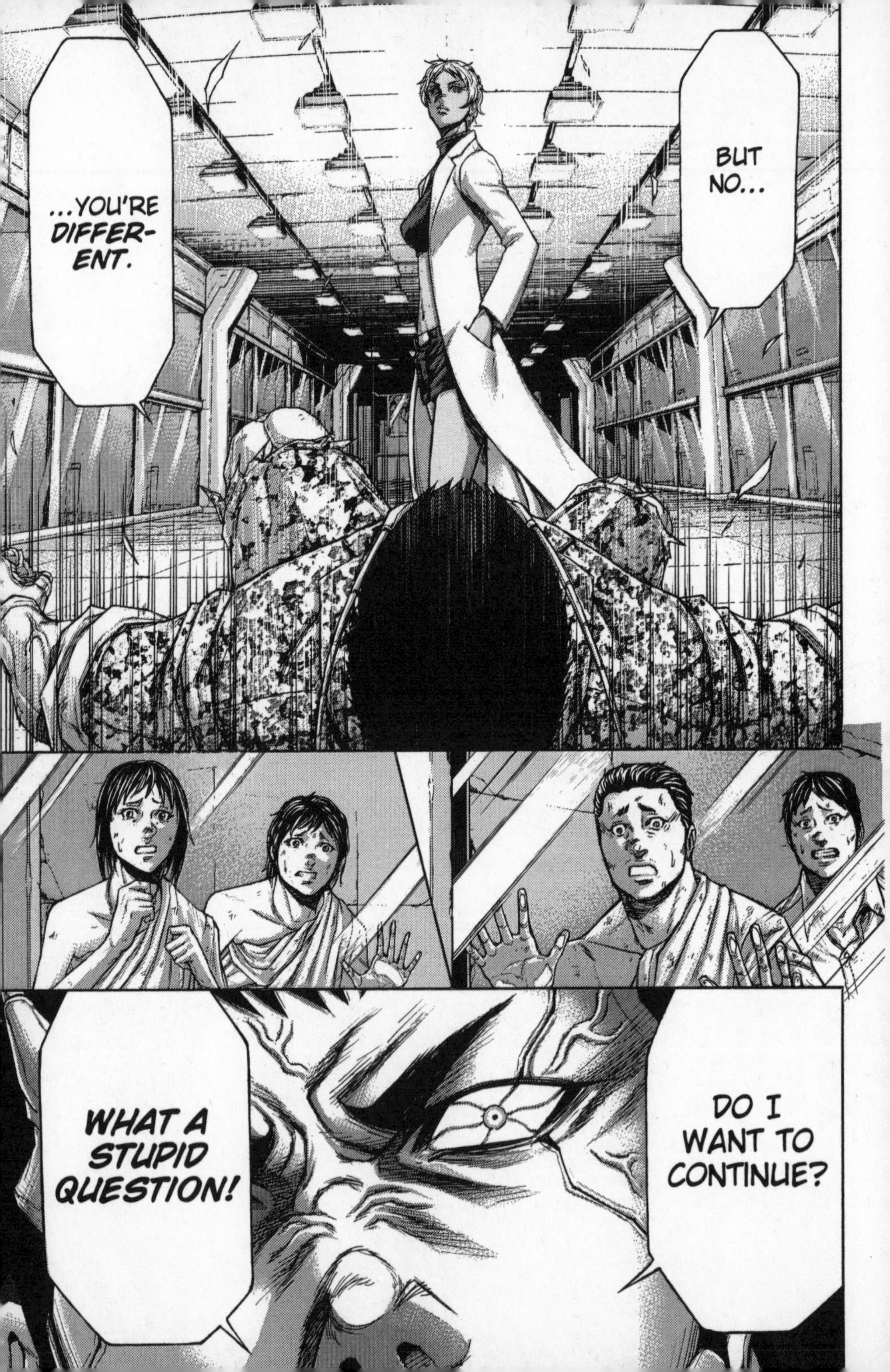
BUT NO...
...YOU'RE DIFFER-ENT.
DO I WANT TO CONTINUE?
WHAT A STUPID QUESTION!

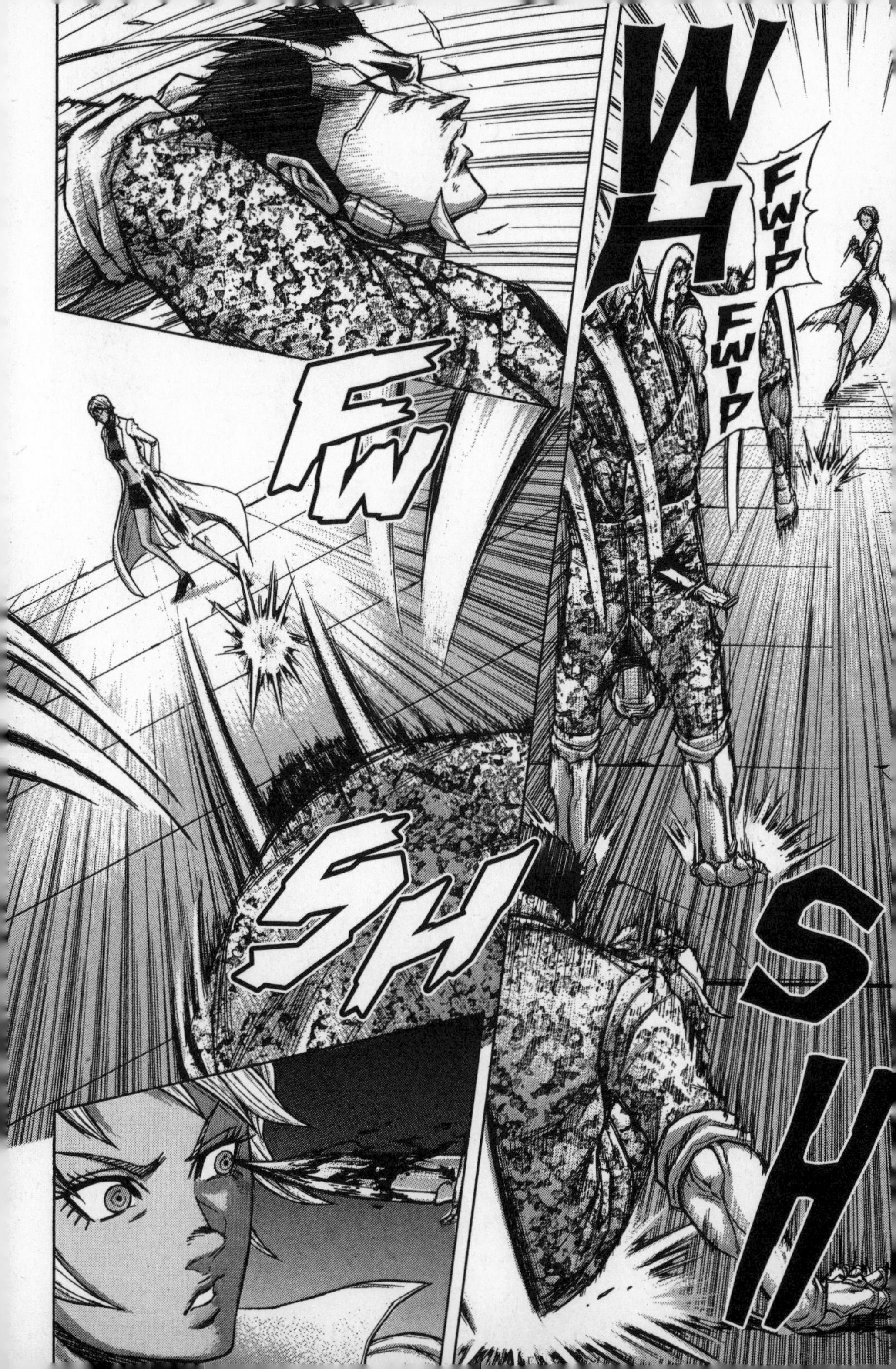
WH
FWIP
FWIP
SH
FW
SH

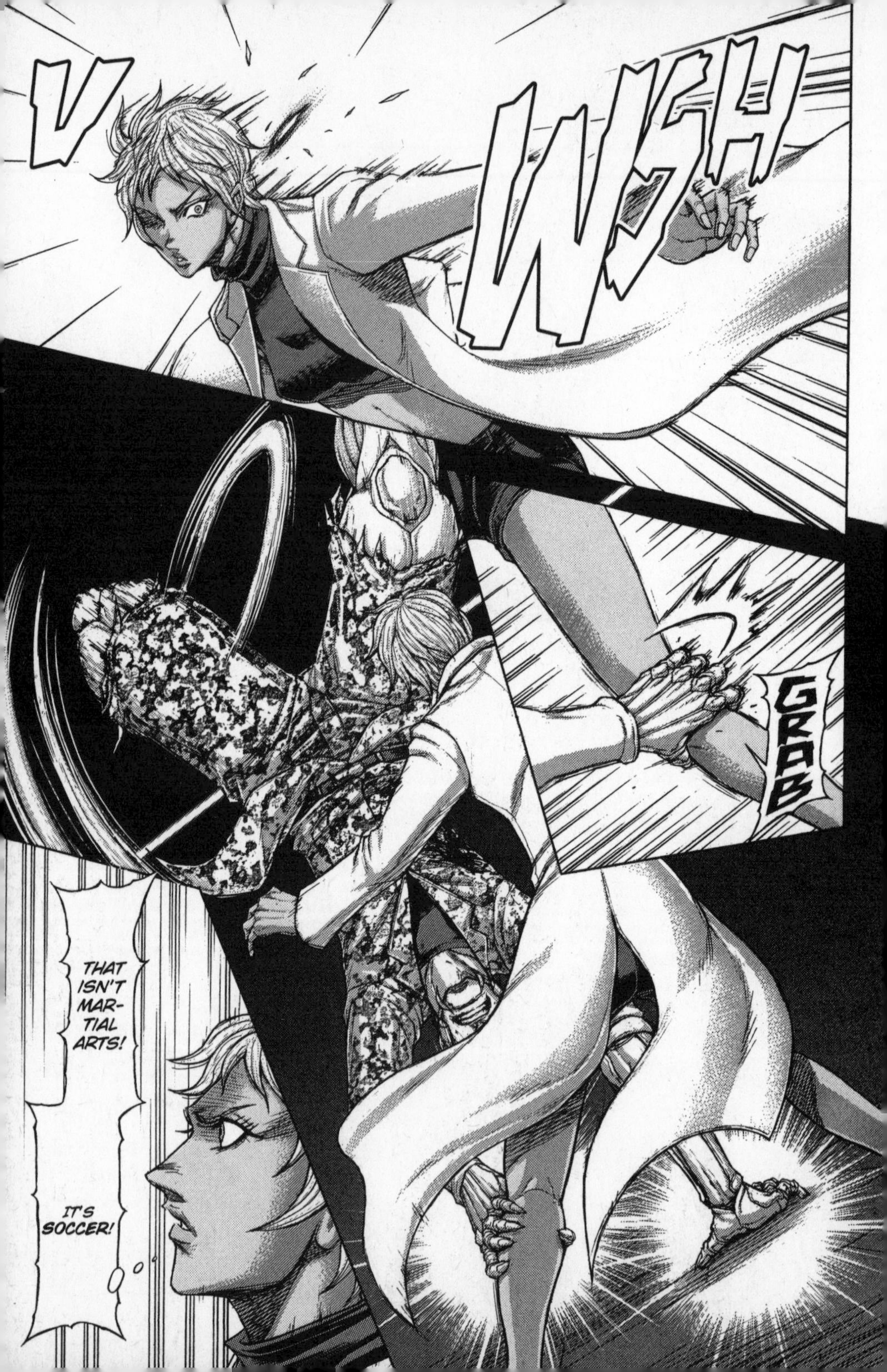
VWISH
GRAB
THAT ISN'T MAR-TIAL ARTS!
IT'S SOCCER!

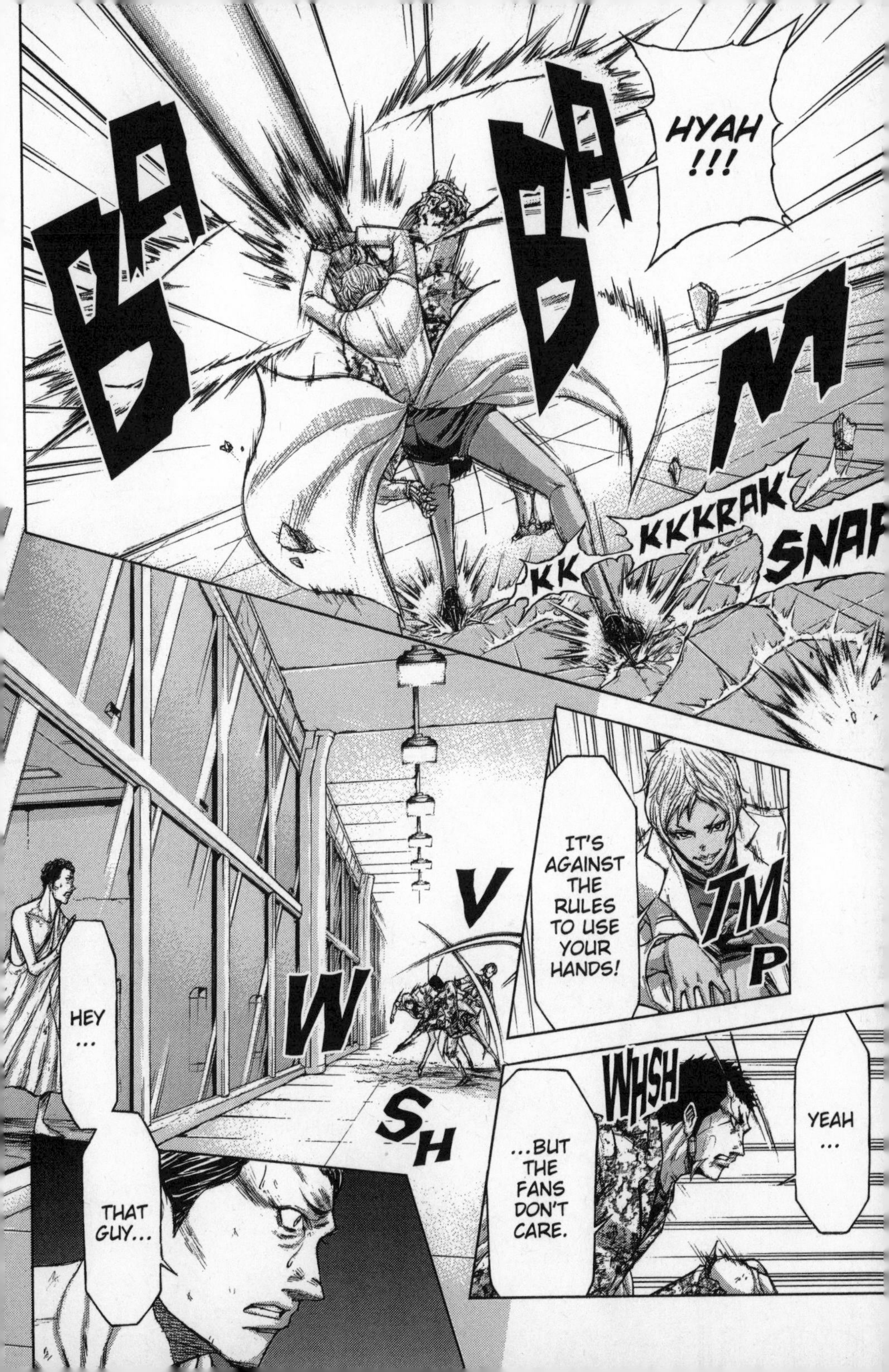
HYAH !!!
BA BA BAM
KK KKKRAK
SNAP
IT'S AGAINST THE RULES TO USE YOUR HANDS!
TMP
YEAH ...
WHSH
...BUT THE FANS DON'T CARE.
V
W
SH
HEY ...
THAT GUY...

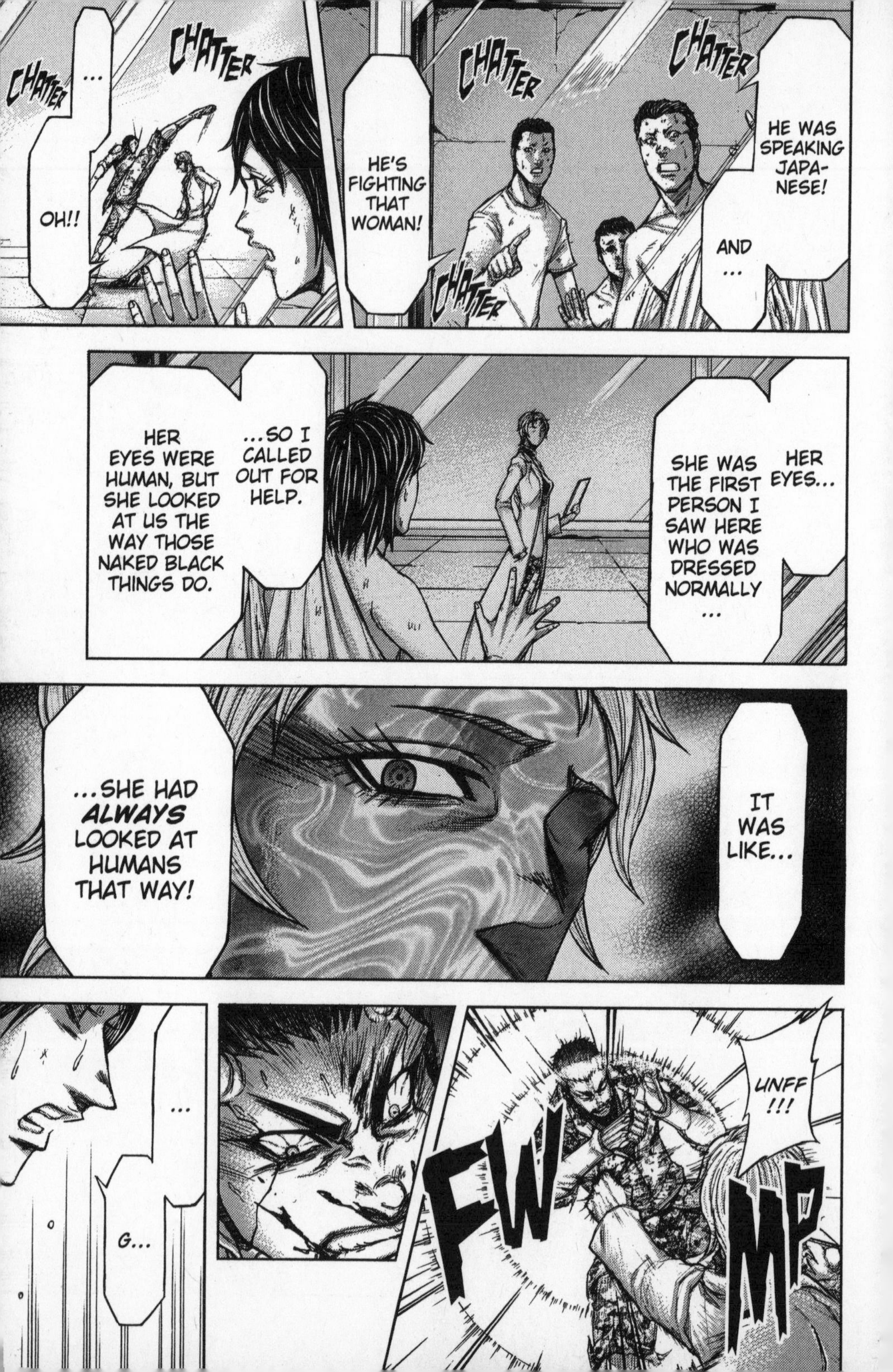
CHATTER
HE WAS SPEAKING JAPA-NESE!
AND ...
CHATTER
CHATTER
HE'S FIGHTING THAT WOMAN!
CHATTER
CHATTER
...
OH!!
HER EYES...
SHE WAS THE FIRST PERSON I SAW HERE WHO WAS DRESSED NORMALLY ...
...SO I CALLED OUT FOR HELP.
HER EYES WERE HUMAN, BUT SHE LOOKED AT US THE WAY THOSE NAKED BLACK THINGS DO.
IT WAS LIKE...
...SHE HAD ALWAYS LOOKED AT HUMANS THAT WAY!
UNFF !!!
FWMP
...
G...

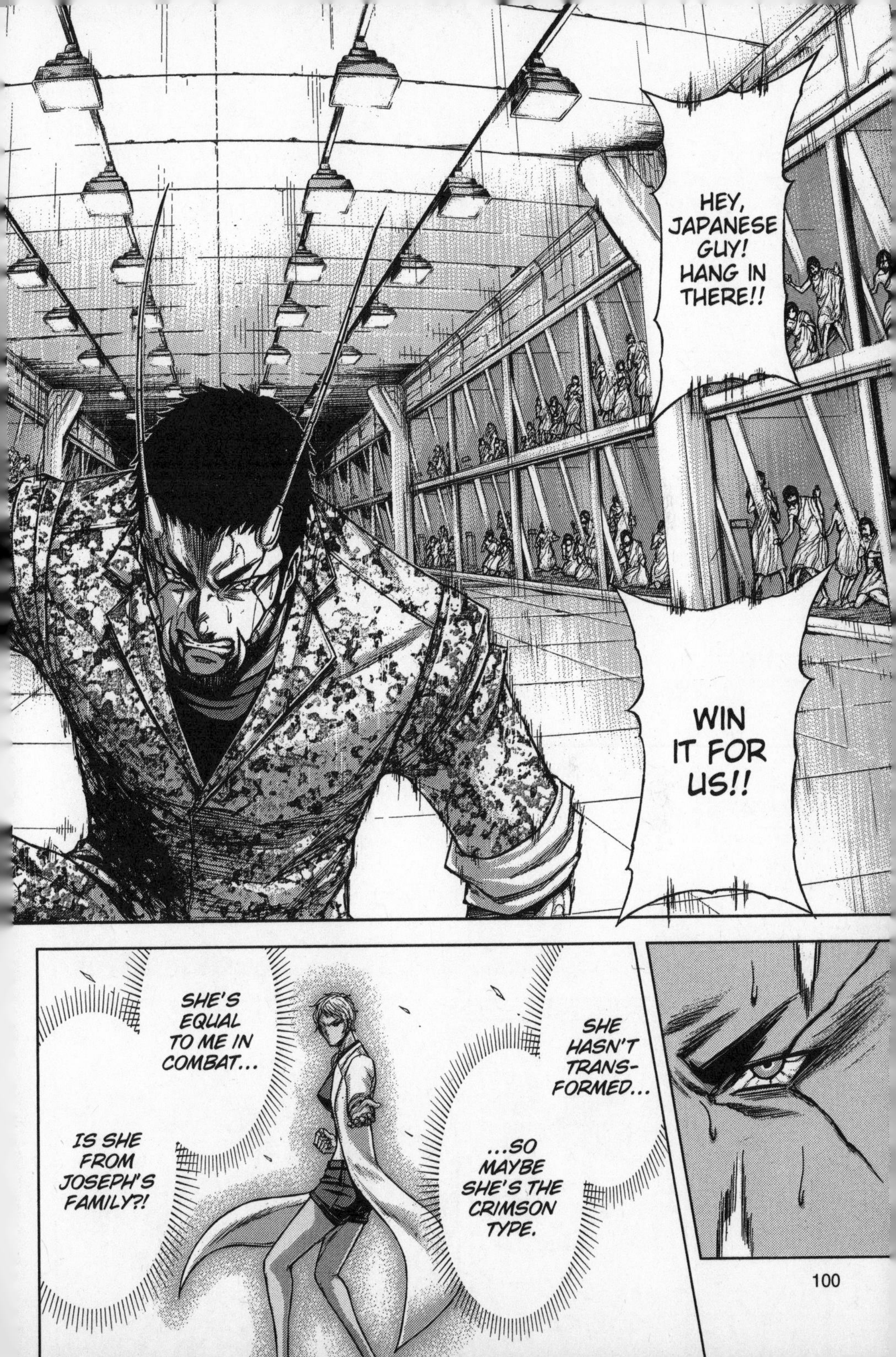
HEY, JAPANESE GUY! HANG IN THERE!!
WIN IT FOR US!!
SHE HASN'T TRANS-FORMED...
...SO MAYBE SHE'S THE CRIMSON TYPE.
SHE'S EQUAL TO ME IN COMBAT...
IS SHE FROM JOSEPH'S FAMILY?!

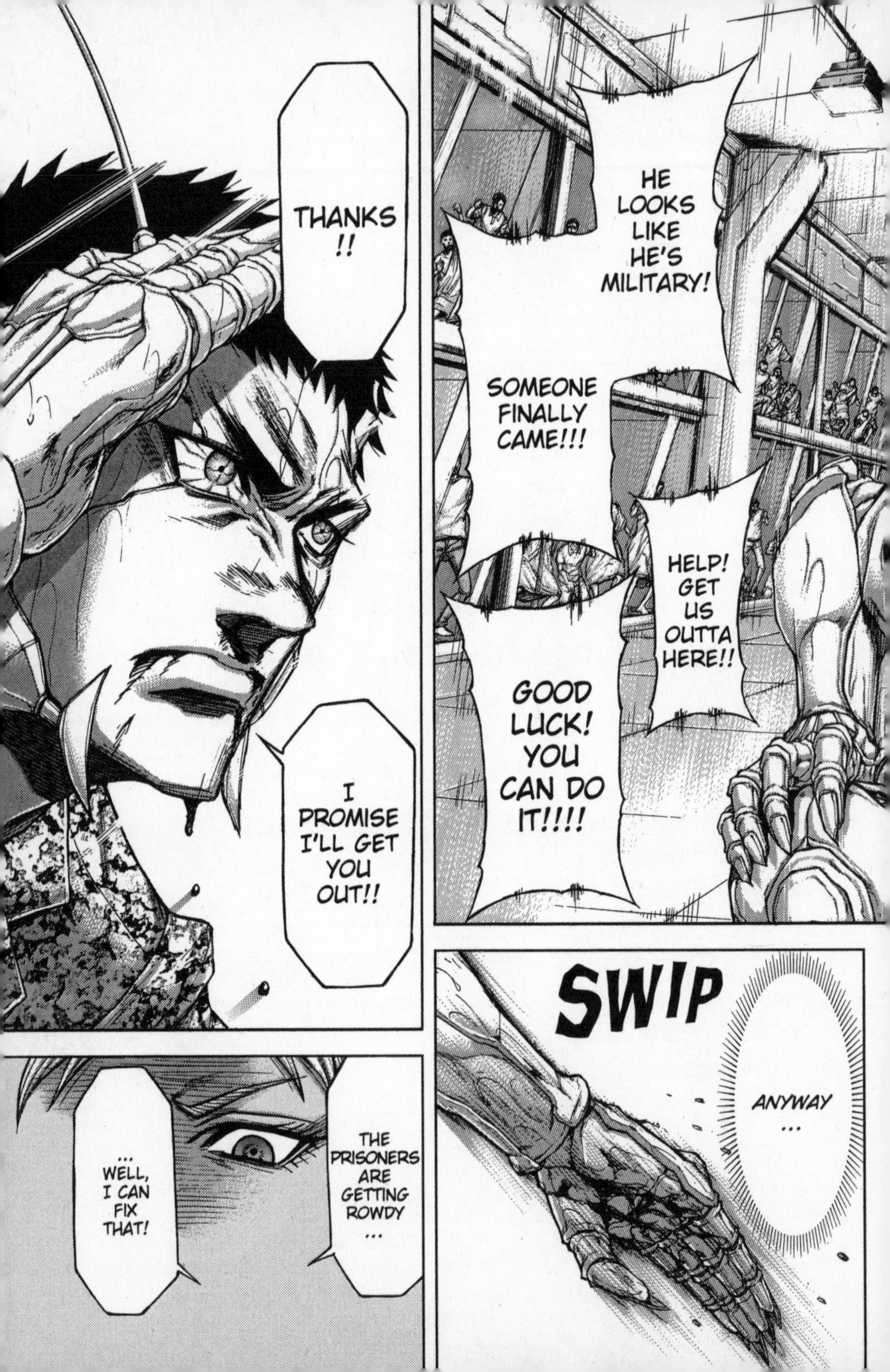
HE LOOKS LIKE HE'S MILITARY!
SOMEONE FINALLY CAME!!!
HELP! GET US OUTTA HERE!!
GOOD LUCK! YOU CAN DO IT!!!!
THANKS!!
I PROMISE I'LL GET YOU OUT!!
THE PRISONERS ARE GETTING ROWDY ...
... WELL, I CAN FIX THAT!
SWIP
ANYWAY ...

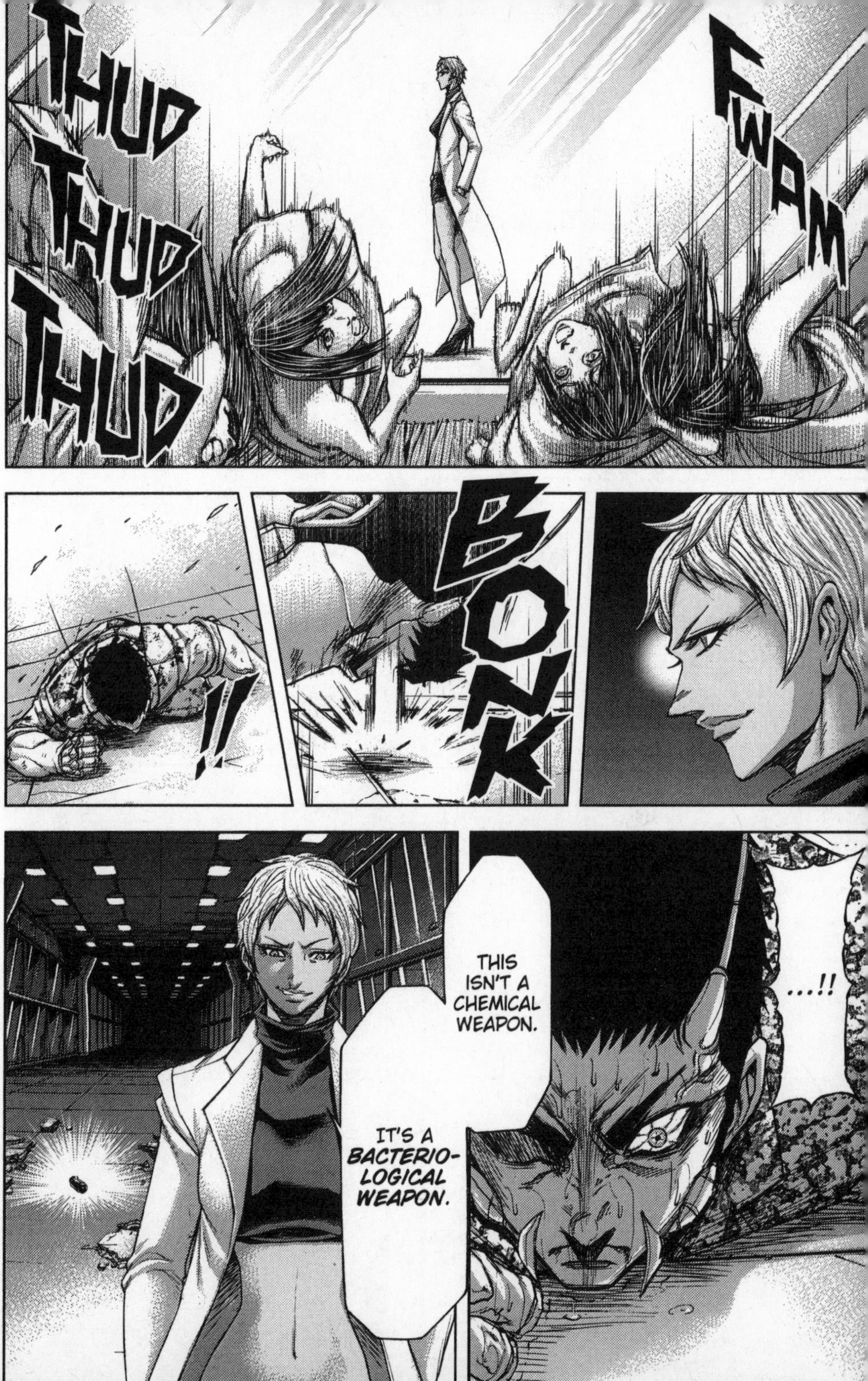
FWAM
THUD THUD THUD
BONK
!!
...!!
THIS ISN'T A CHEMICAL WEAPON.
IT'S A BACTERIO-LOGICAL WEAPON.

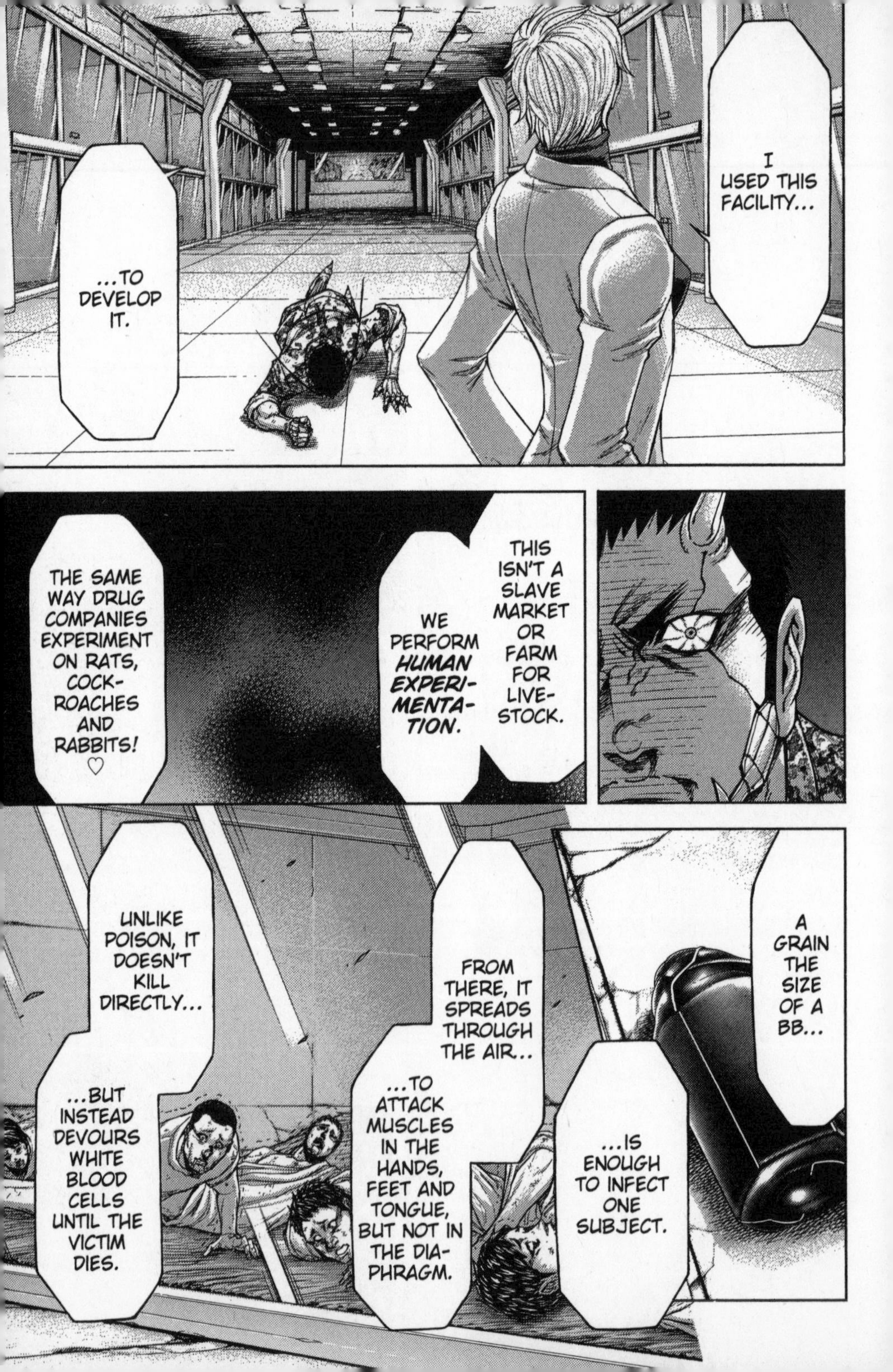
I USED THIS FACILITY...
...TO DEVELOP IT.
THIS ISN'T A SLAVE MARKET OR FARM FOR LIVE-STOCK.
WE PERFORM ***HUMAN EXPERI-MENTA-TION***.
THE SAME WAY DRUG COMPANIES EXPERIMENT ON RATS, COCK-ROACHES AND RABBITS! ♡
A GRAIN THE SIZE OF A BB...
...IS ENOUGH TO INFECT ONE SUBJECT.
FROM THERE, IT SPREADS THROUGH THE AIR...
...TO ATTACK MUSCLES IN THE HANDS, FEET AND TONGUE, BUT NOT IN THE DIA-PHRAGM.
UNLIKE POISON, IT DOESN'T KILL DIRECTLY...
...BUT INSTEAD DEVOURS WHITE BLOOD CELLS UNTIL THE VICTIM DIES.

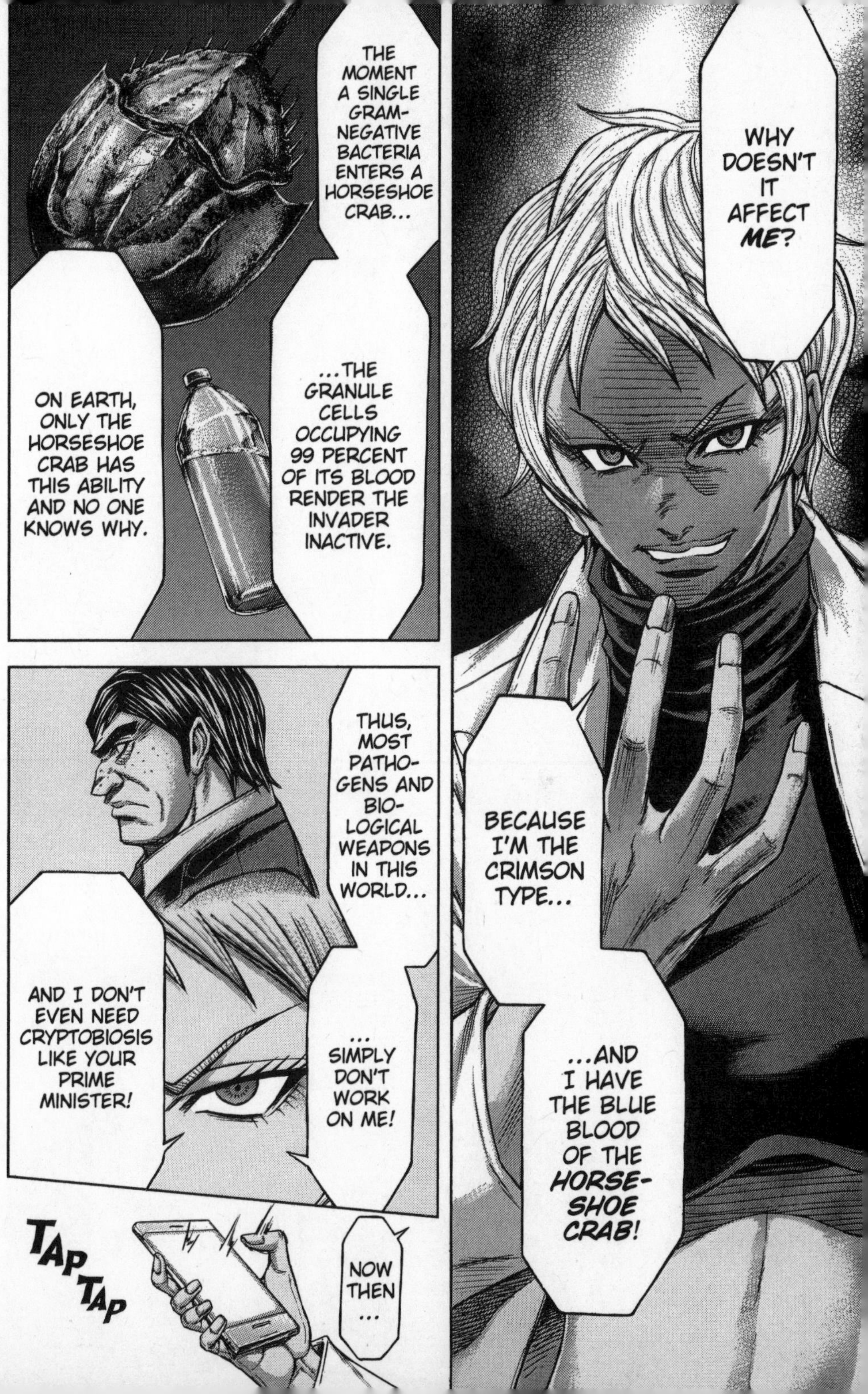
WHY DOESN'T IT AFFECT ME?
BECAUSE I'M THE CRIMSON TYPE...
...AND I HAVE THE BLUE BLOOD OF THE HORSE-SHOE CRAB!
THE MOMENT A SINGLE GRAM-NEGATIVE BACTERIA ENTERS A HORSESHOE CRAB...
...THE GRANULE CELLS OCCUPYING 99 PERCENT OF ITS BLOOD RENDER THE INVADER INACTIVE.
ON EARTH, ONLY THE HORSESHOE CRAB HAS THIS ABILITY AND NO ONE KNOWS WHY.
THUS, MOST PATHO-GENS AND BIO-LOGICAL WEAPONS IN THIS WORLD...
...SIMPLY DON'T WORK ON ME!
AND I DON'T EVEN NEED CRYPTOBIOSIS LIKE YOUR PRIME MINISTER!
NOW THEN...
TAP TAP

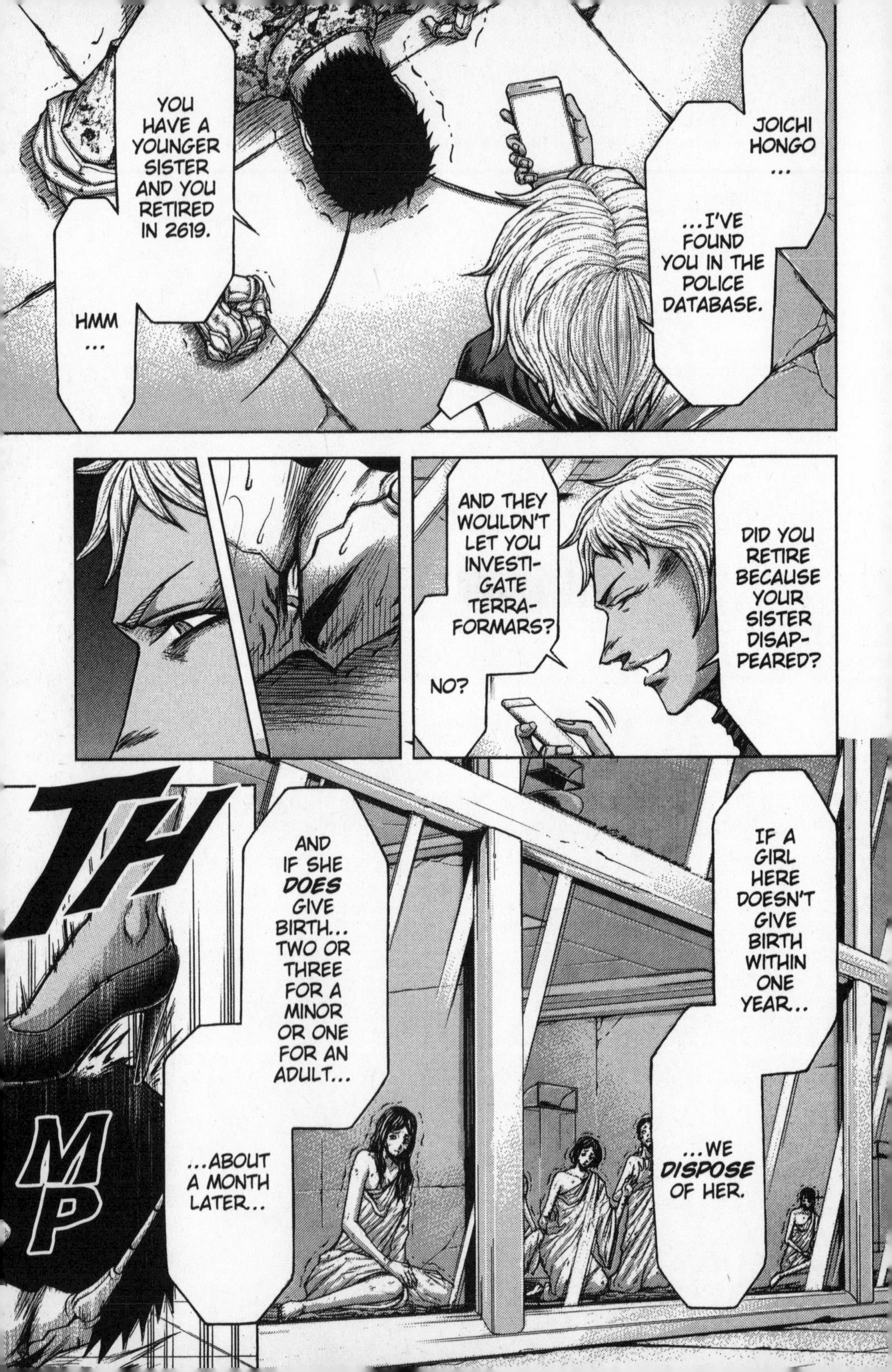
JOICHI HONGO...
...I'VE FOUND YOU IN THE POLICE DATABASE.
YOU HAVE A YOUNGER SISTER AND YOU RETIRED IN 2619.
HMM...
DID YOU RETIRE BECAUSE YOUR SISTER DISAPPEARED?
AND THEY WOULDN'T LET YOU INVESTIGATE TERRAFORMARS?
NO?
IF A GIRL HERE DOESN'T GIVE BIRTH WITHIN ONE YEAR...
...WE *DISPOSE* OF HER.
AND IF SHE *DOES* GIVE BIRTH... TWO OR THREE FOR A MINOR OR ONE FOR AN ADULT...
...ABOUT A MONTH LATER...
THMP

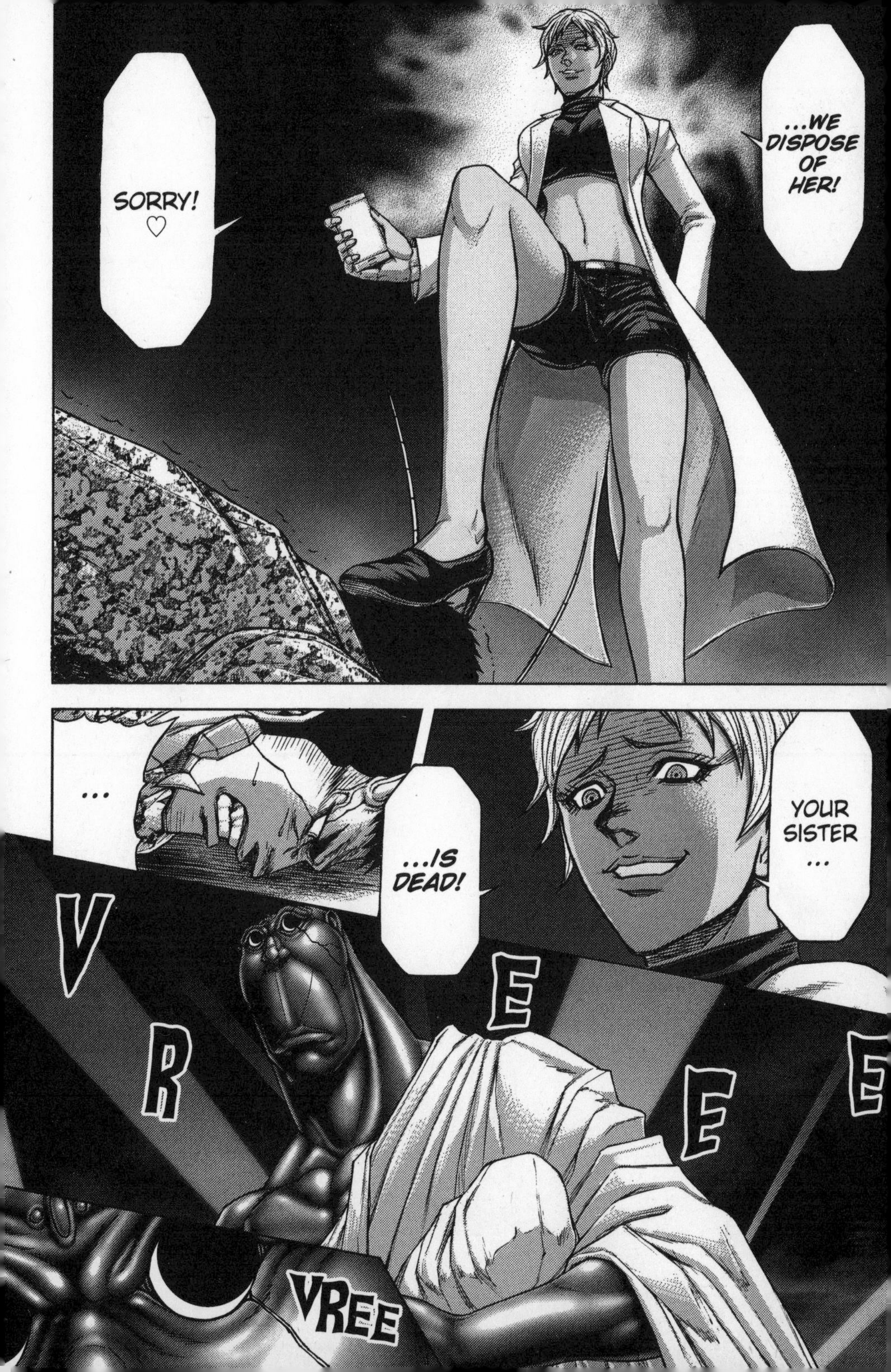
...WE DISPOSE OF HER!
SORRY! ♡
YOUR SISTER ...
...IS DEAD!
...
VREEE
VREE

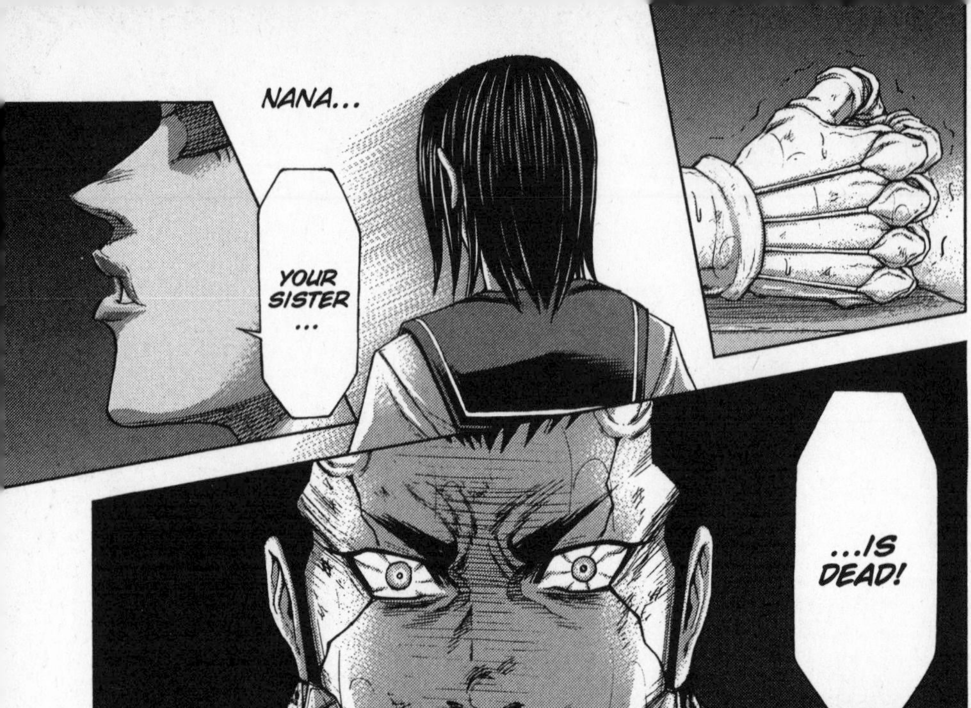
NANA...
YOUR SISTER ...
...IS DEAD!
I CAN'T REMEMBER HER FACE.
HER HAIR AND CLOTHES ALWAYS CHANGED.
WHAT DID SHE LOOK LIKE THE LAST TIME WE SPOKE...
...ON THE PHONE?

#17: FLY, BRO, FLY!

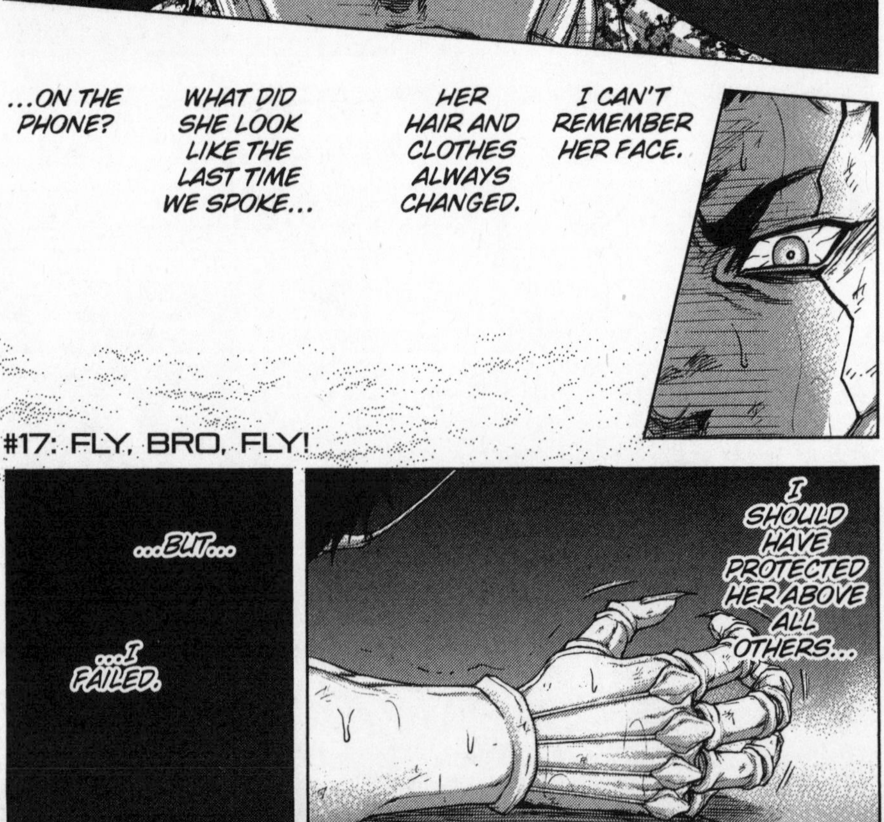
I SHOULD HAVE PROTECTED HER ABOVE ALL OTHERS...
...BUT...
...I FAILED.

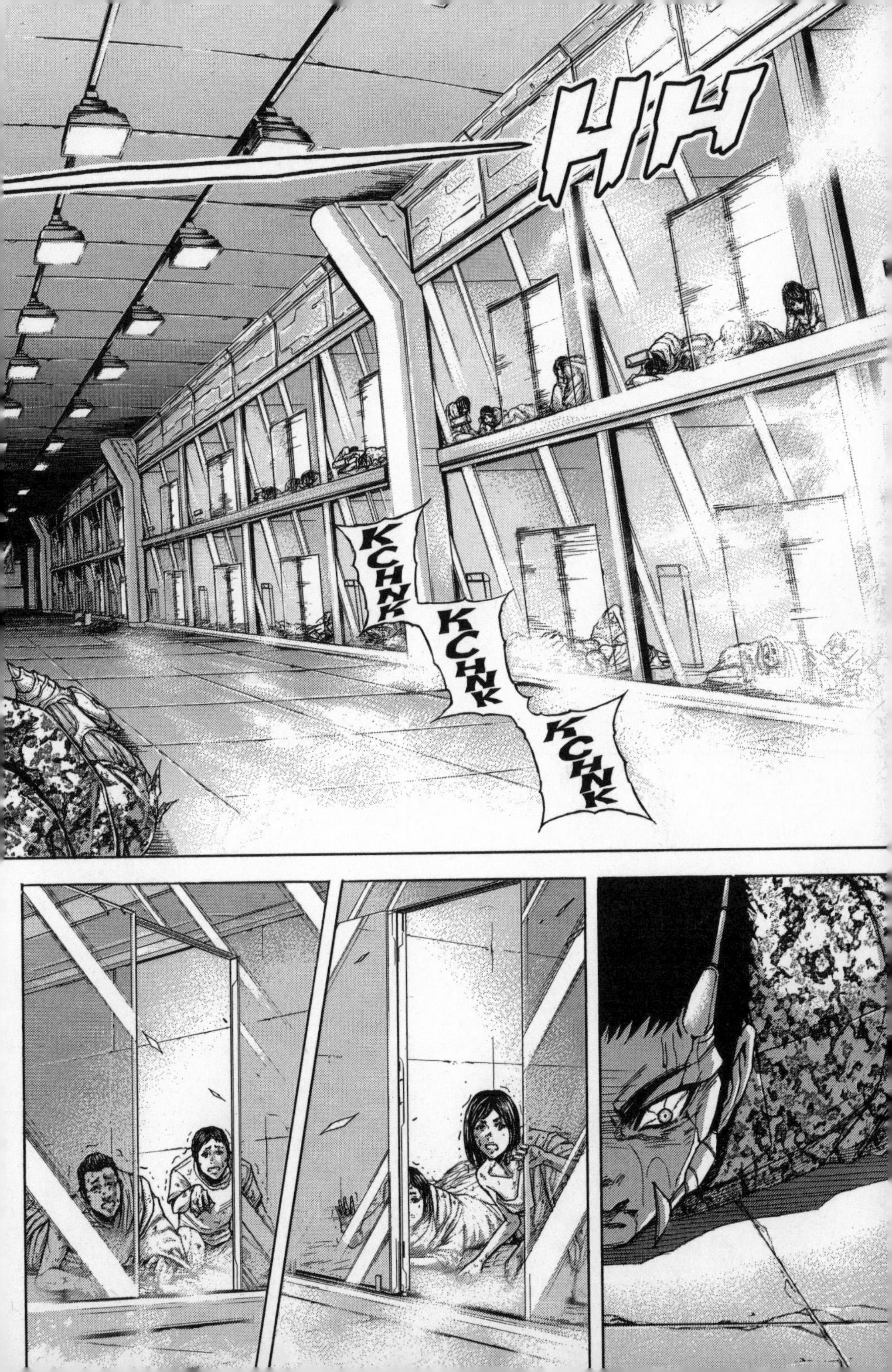
HH
KCHNK
KCHNK
KCHNK

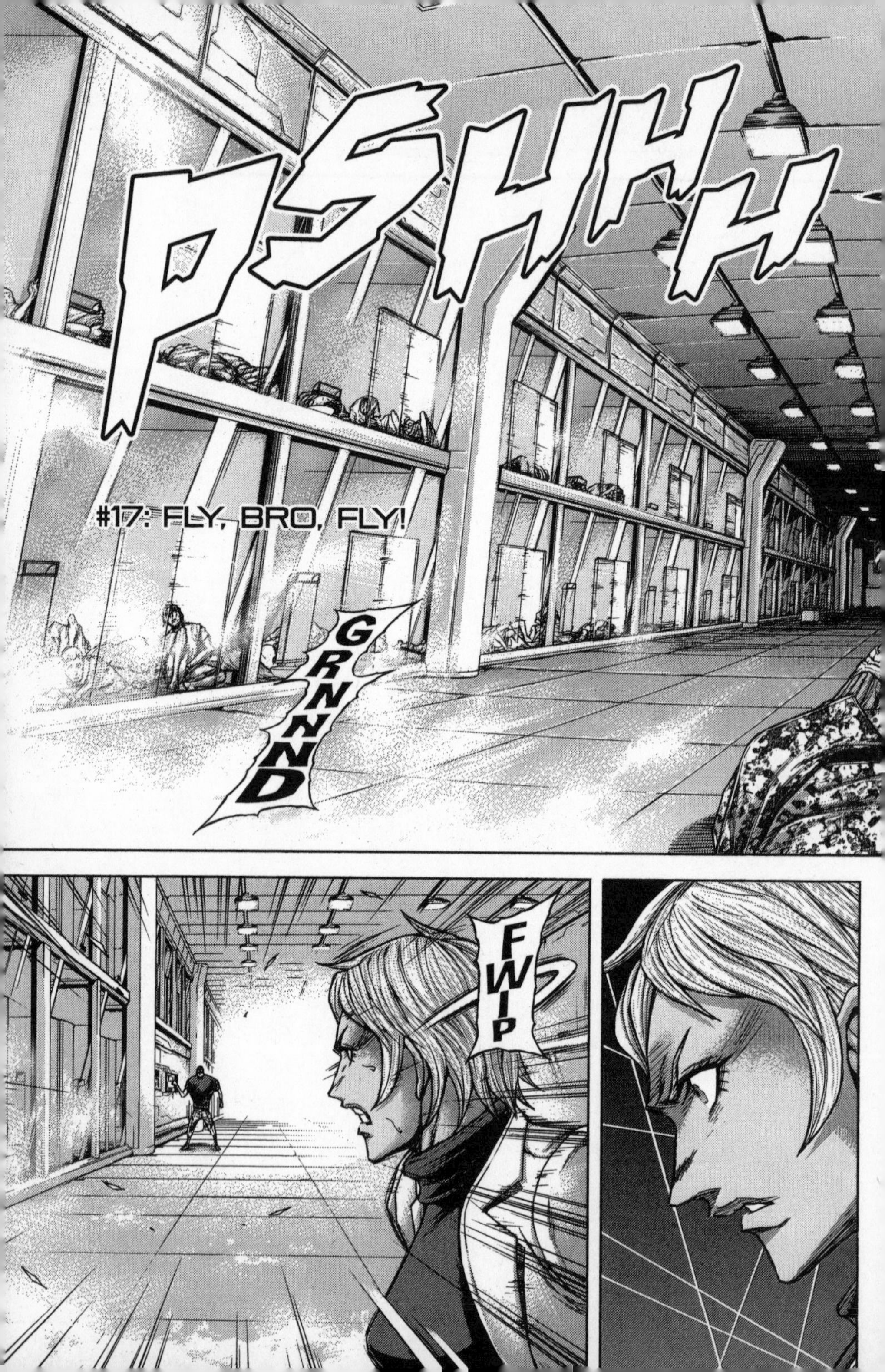
PSHHH
#17: FLY, BRO, FLY!
GRNNND
FWIP

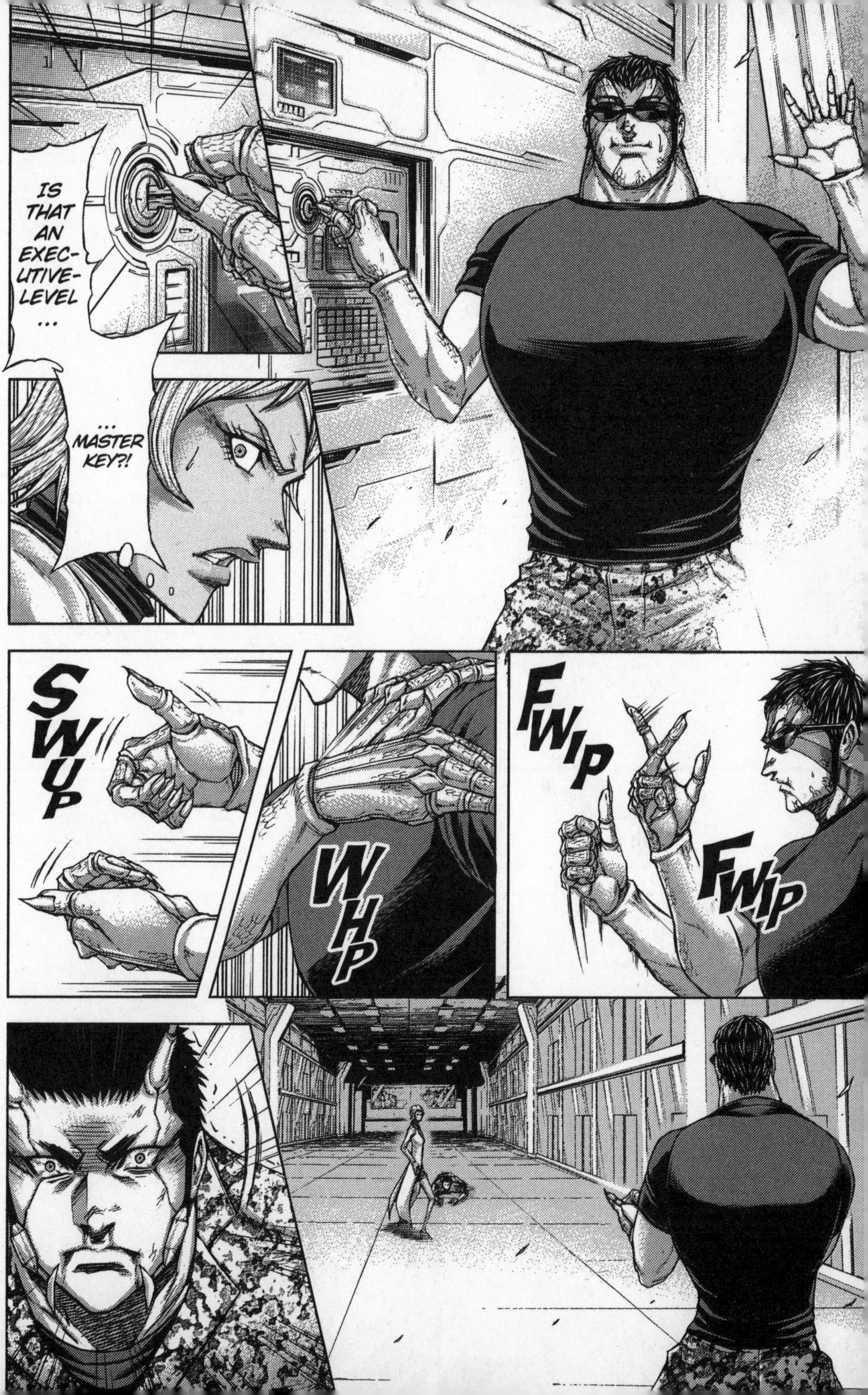
IS THAT AN EXECUTIVE-LEVEL...
...MASTER KEY?!
FWIP
FWIP
WHP
SWUP

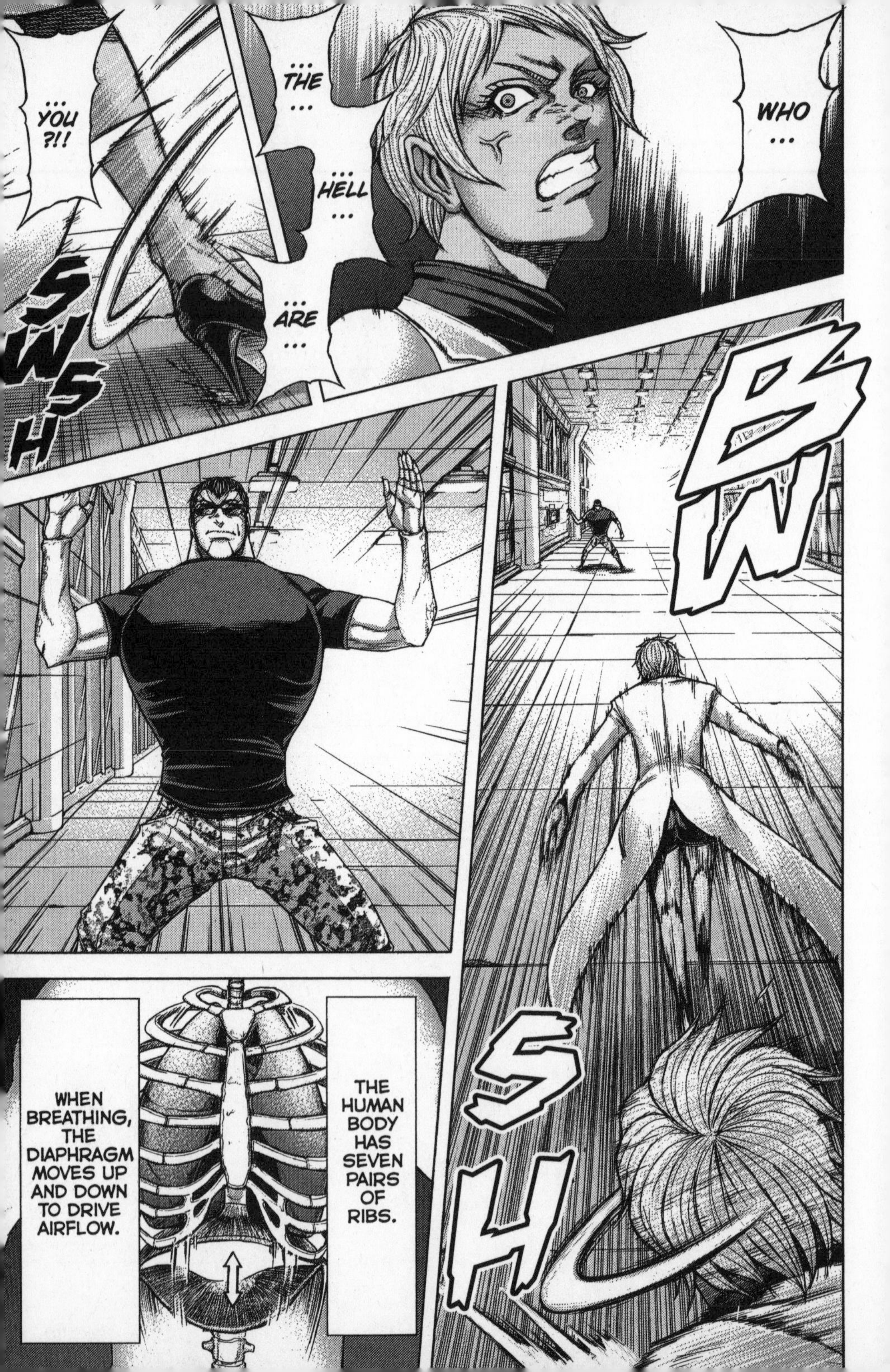
WHO ...
... THE ...
... HELL ...
... ARE ...
... YOU ?!!
SWSH
BW
SH
THE HUMAN BODY HAS SEVEN PAIRS OF RIBS.
WHEN BREATHING, THE DIAPHRAGM MOVES UP AND DOWN TO DRIVE AIRFLOW.

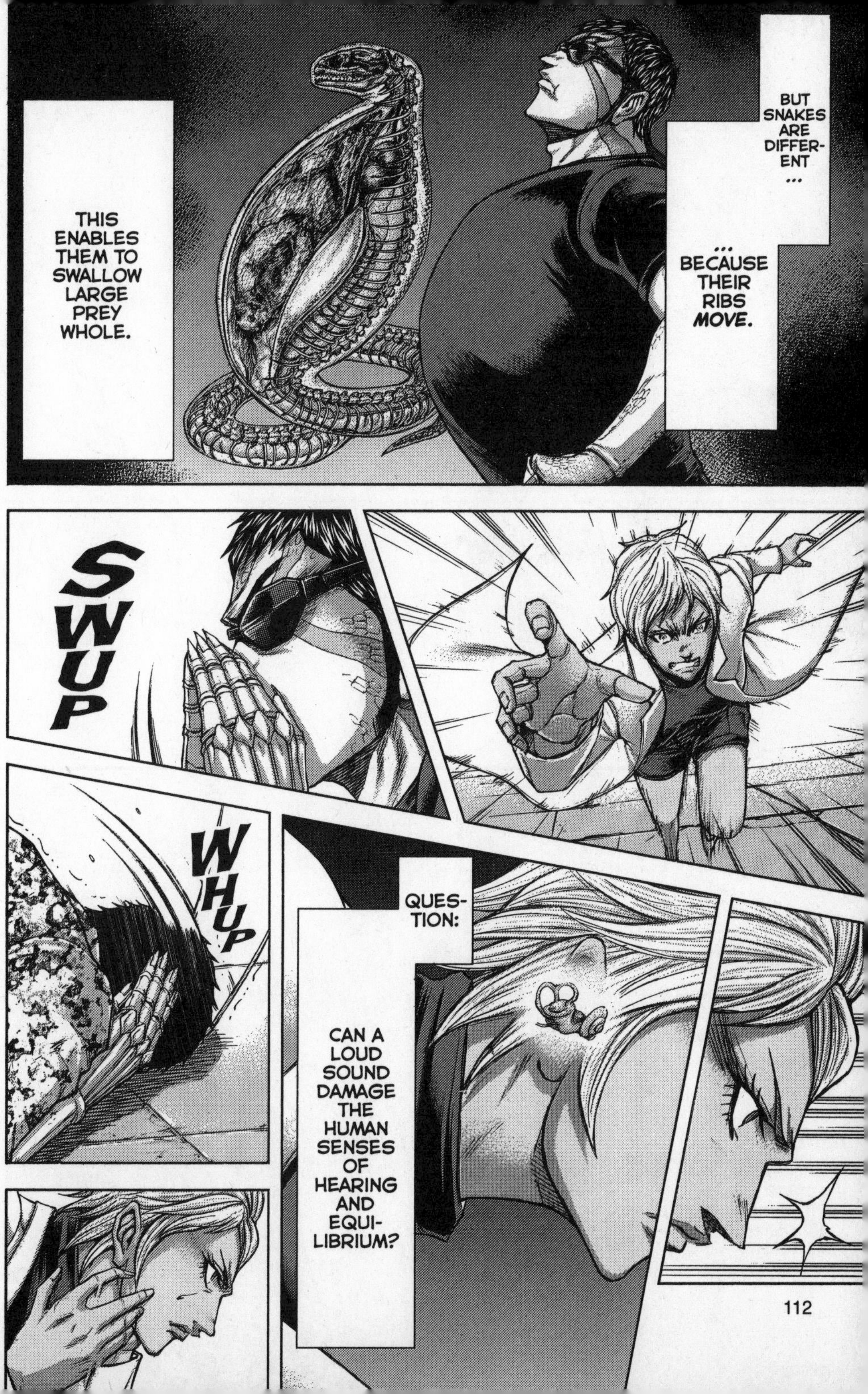
BUT SNAKES ARE DIFFERENT...
...BECAUSE THEIR RIBS MOVE.
THIS ENABLES THEM TO SWALLOW LARGE PREY WHOLE.
SWUP
QUESTION:
CAN A LOUD SOUND DAMAGE THE HUMAN SENSES OF HEARING AND EQUILIBRIUM?
WHUP

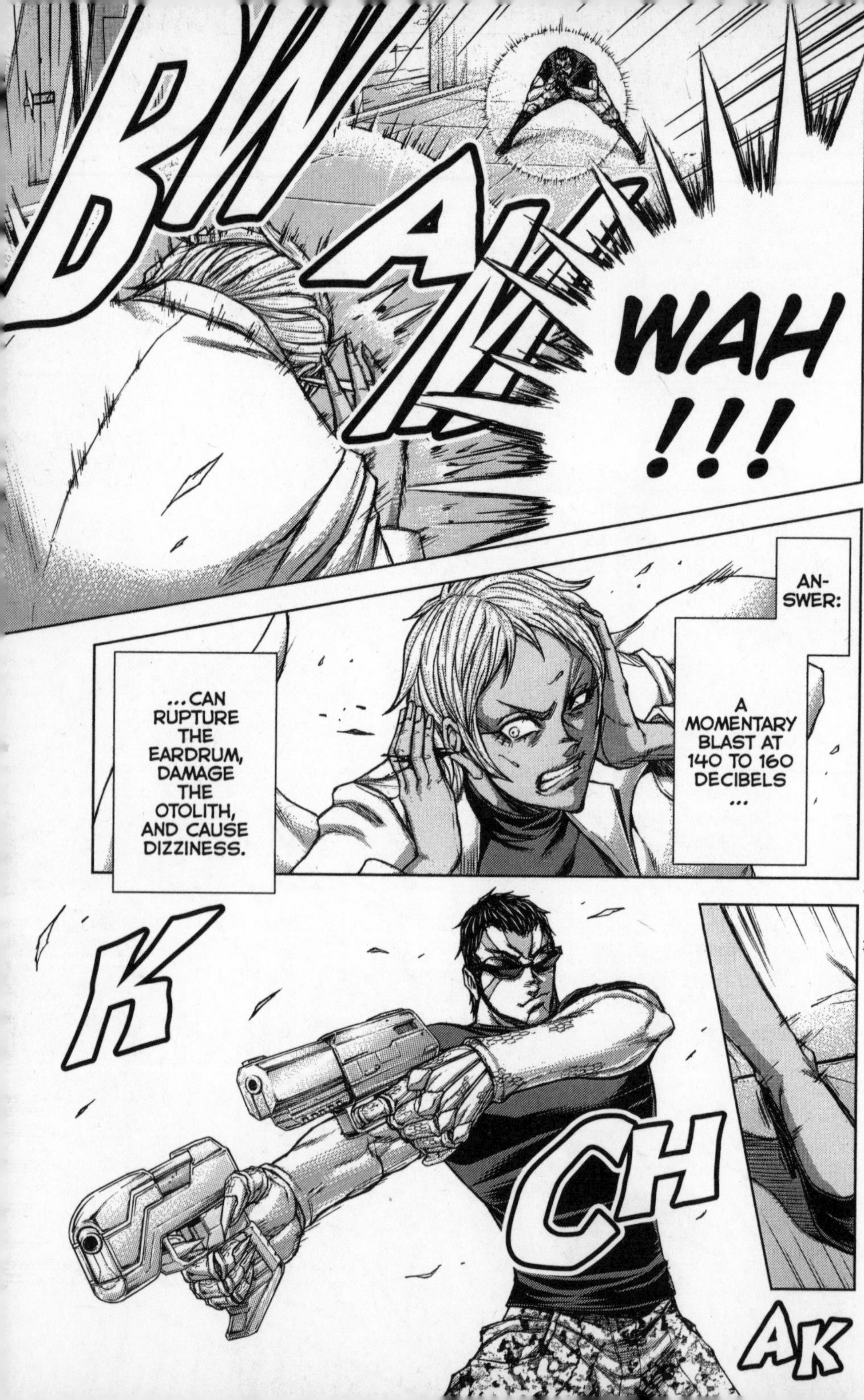
BWAAAWAH!!!
ANSWER:
A MOMENTARY BLAST AT 140 TO 160 DECIBELS ...
...CAN RUPTURE THE EARDRUM, DAMAGE THE OTOLITH, AND CAUSE DIZZINESS.
KCHAK

*A normal conversation is 60 dB, and a rock concert is about 120-130 dB.

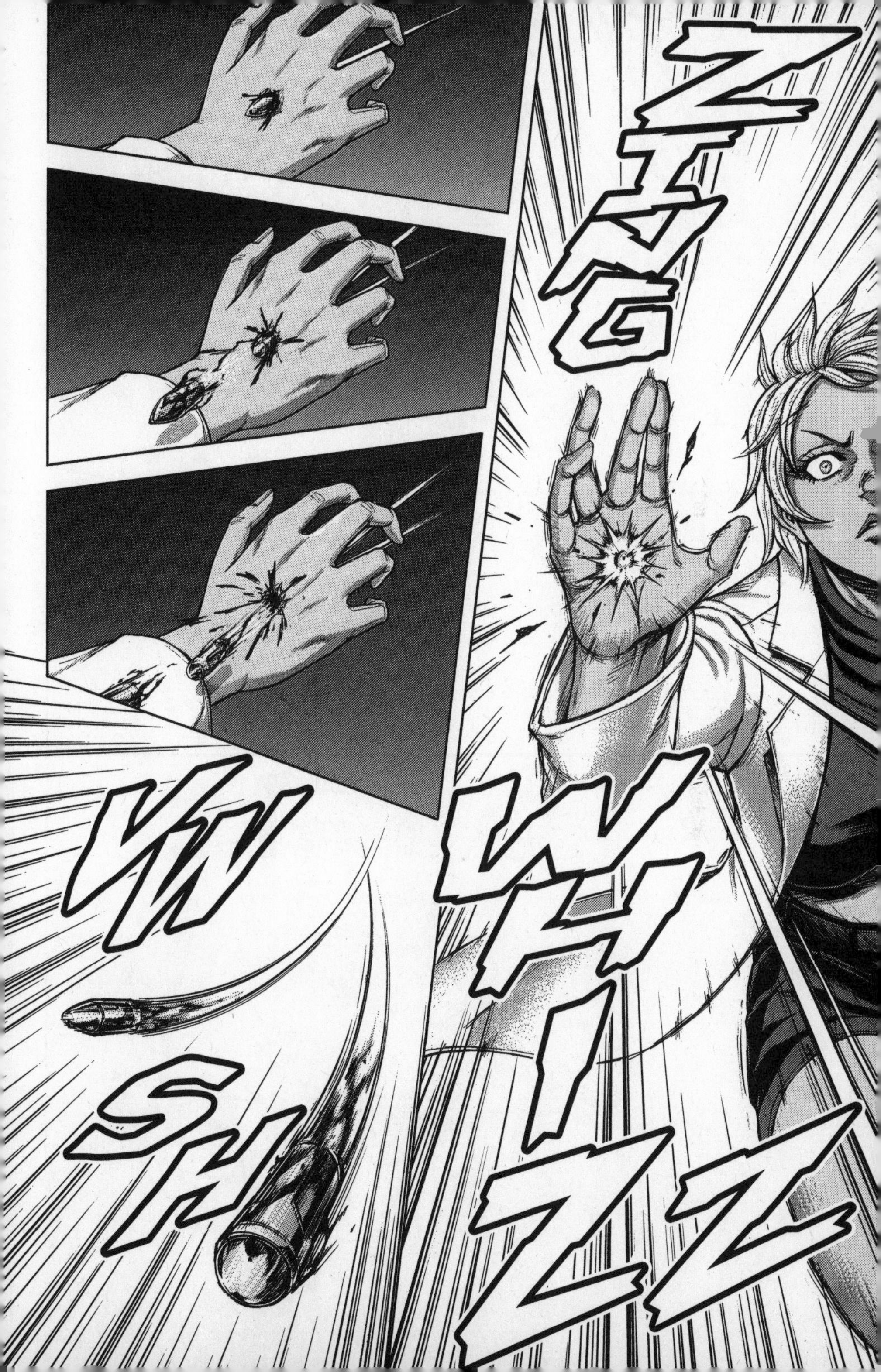
ZING
WHIZZ
VWSH

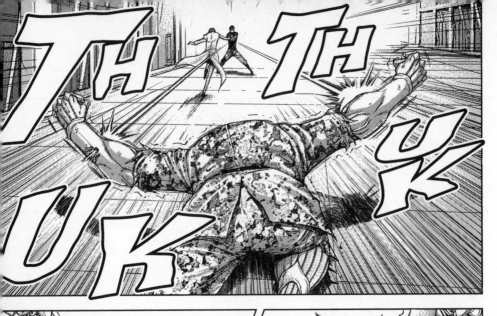

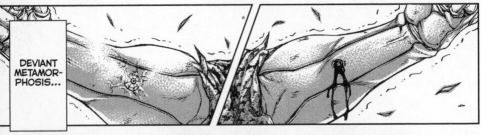

THUK
THUK
DEVIANT METAMORPHOSIS...
...REQUIRES AN INJECTOR GUN FOR THE UNIVERSAL METAMORPHOSIS DRUG.
INJECTION INTO THE SKIN OF SOMEONE WHO HAS UNDERGONE THE BUGS PROCEDURE OR M.O. OPERATION...
...CAUSES A THERMUS AQUATICUS C.B. STIMULATION UNIT TO AFFIX ITSELF TO BLOOD VESSELS.
USUALLY UNITS WOULD PAIR...
...LIKE THIS.

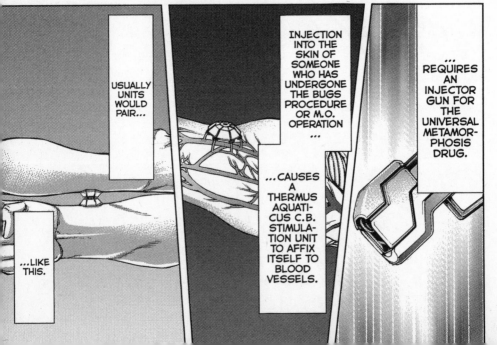

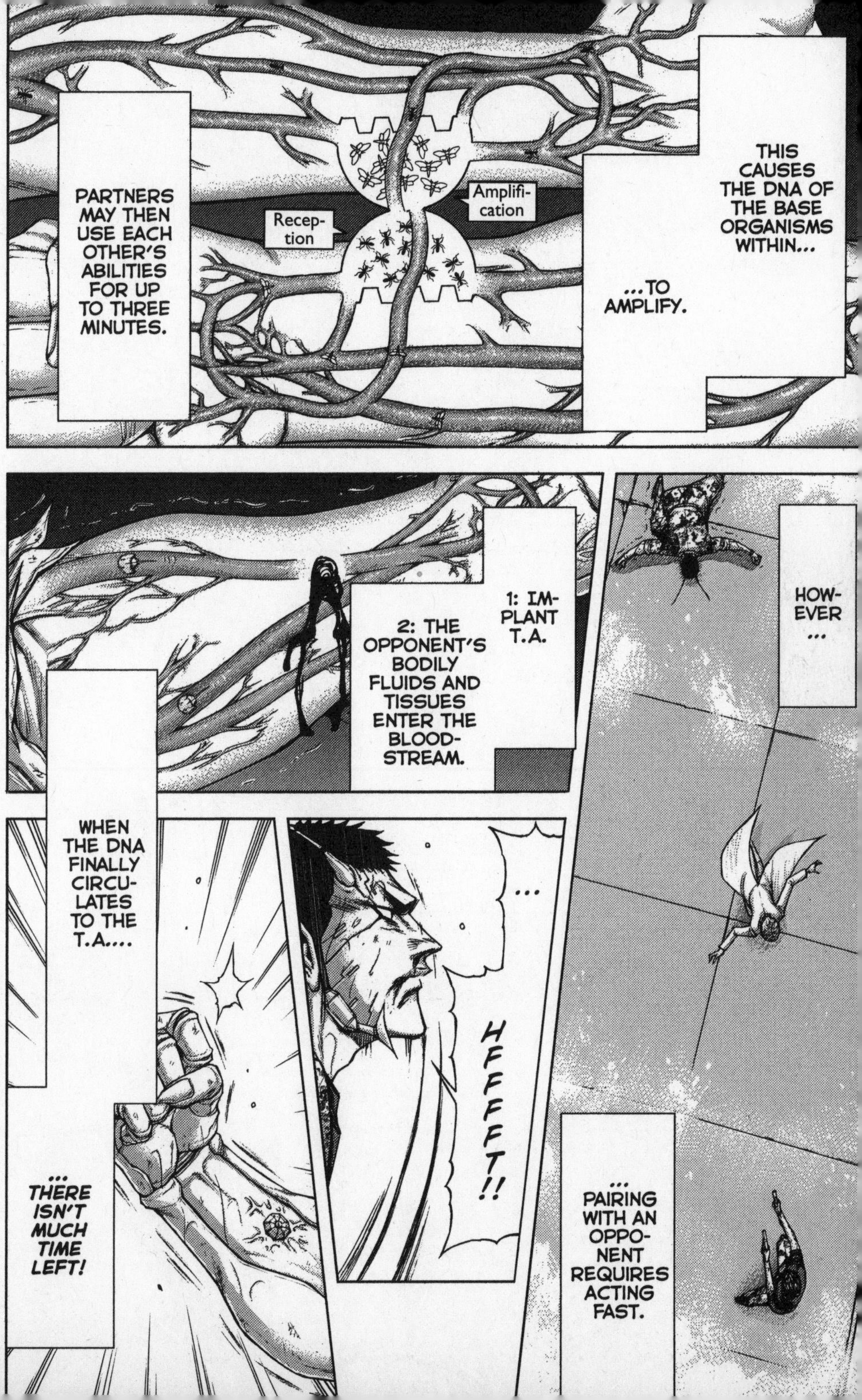
THIS CAUSES THE DNA OF THE BASE ORGANISMS WITHIN...
...TO AMPLIFY.
Amplifi-cation
Recep-tion
PARTNERS MAY THEN USE EACH OTHER'S ABILITIES FOR UP TO THREE MINUTES.
HOW-EVER...
...PAIRING WITH AN OPPO-NENT REQUIRES ACTING FAST.
1: IM-PLANT T.A.
2: THE OPPONENT'S BODILY FLUIDS AND TISSUES ENTER THE BLOOD-STREAM.
...
HFFFFT!!
WHEN THE DNA FINALLY CIRCU-LATES TO THE T.A....
...THERE ISN'T MUCH TIME LEFT!

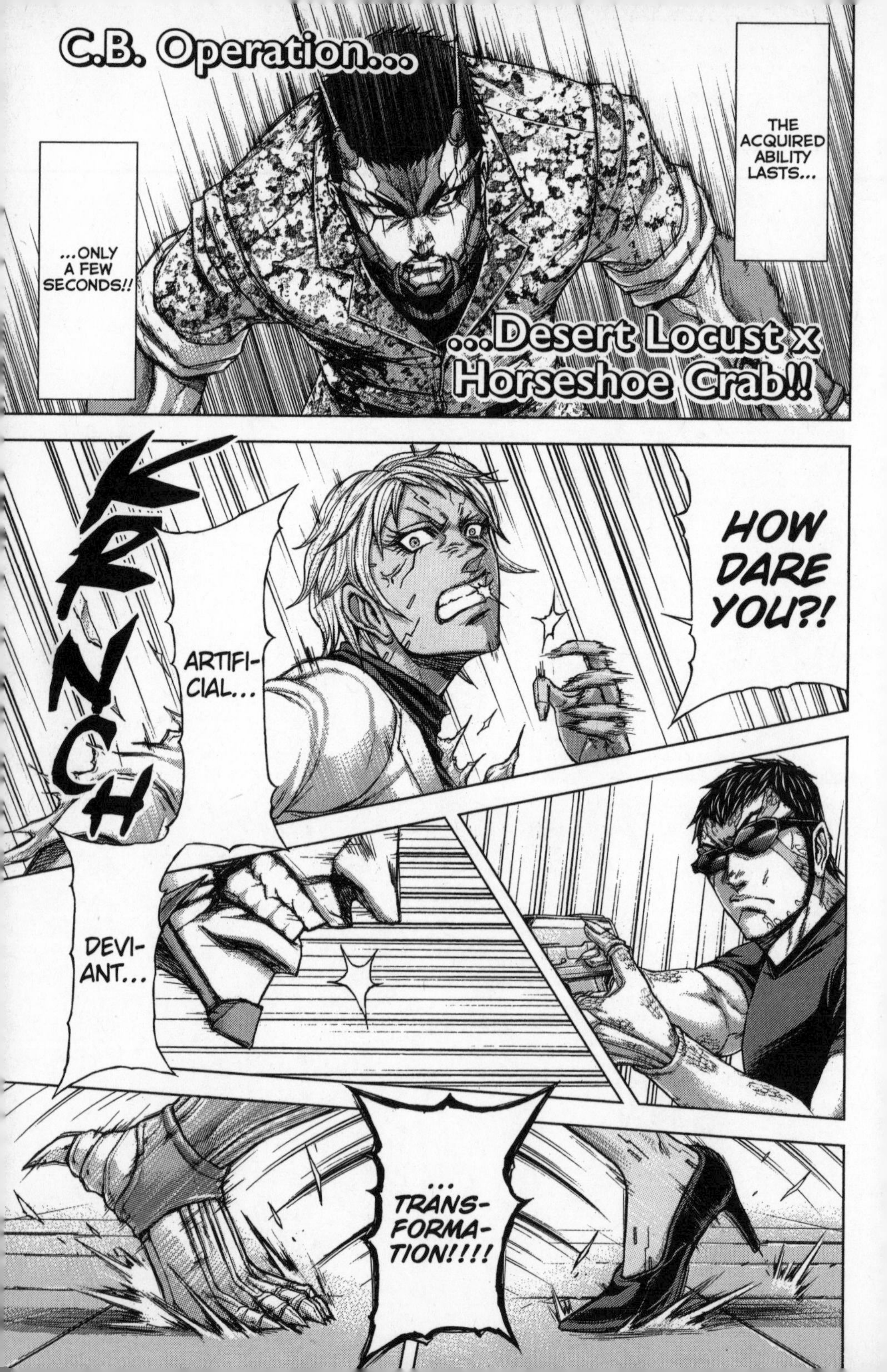
C.B. Operation...
...Desert Locust x Horseshoe Crab!!
THE ACQUIRED ABILITY LASTS...
...ONLY A FEW SECONDS!!
HOW DARE YOU?!
ARTIFICIAL...
KRNCH
DEVIANT...
...TRANSFORMATION!!!!

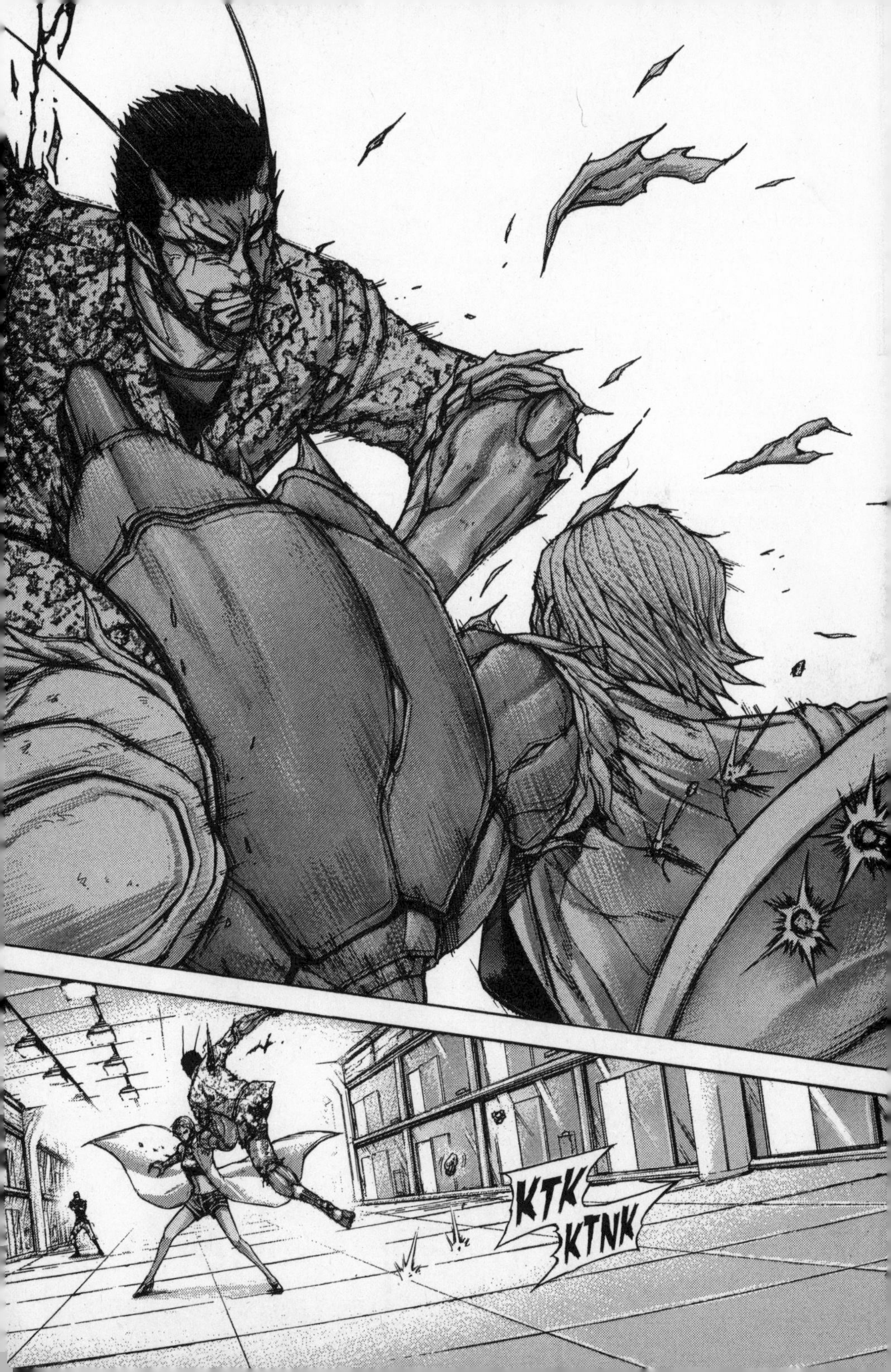
KTK KTNK

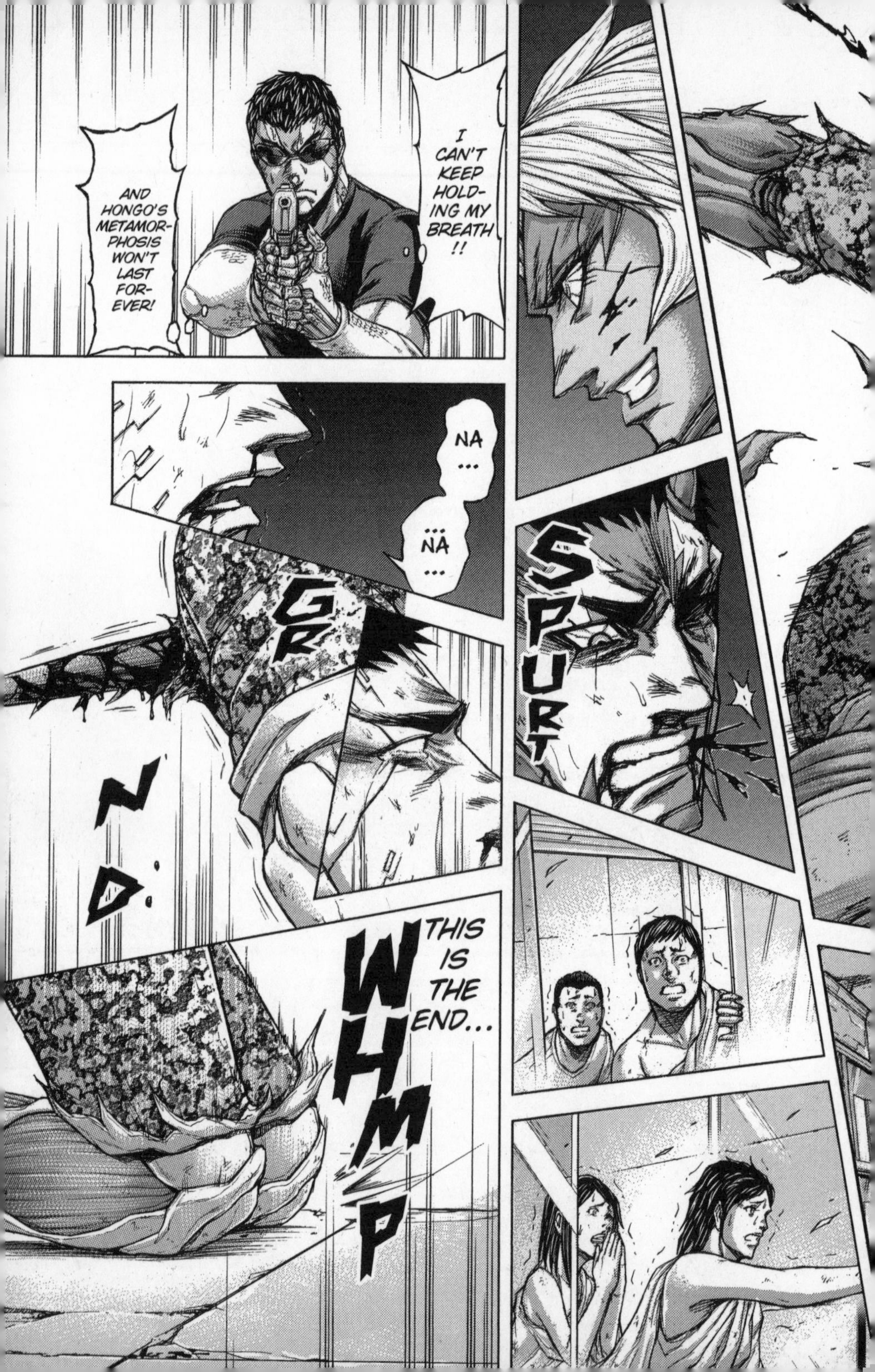
I CAN'T KEEP HOLDING MY BREATH!!
AND HONGO'S METAMORPHOSIS WON'T LAST FOREVER!
SPURT
NA...
...NÄ...
GR
ND
THIS IS THE END...
WHMP

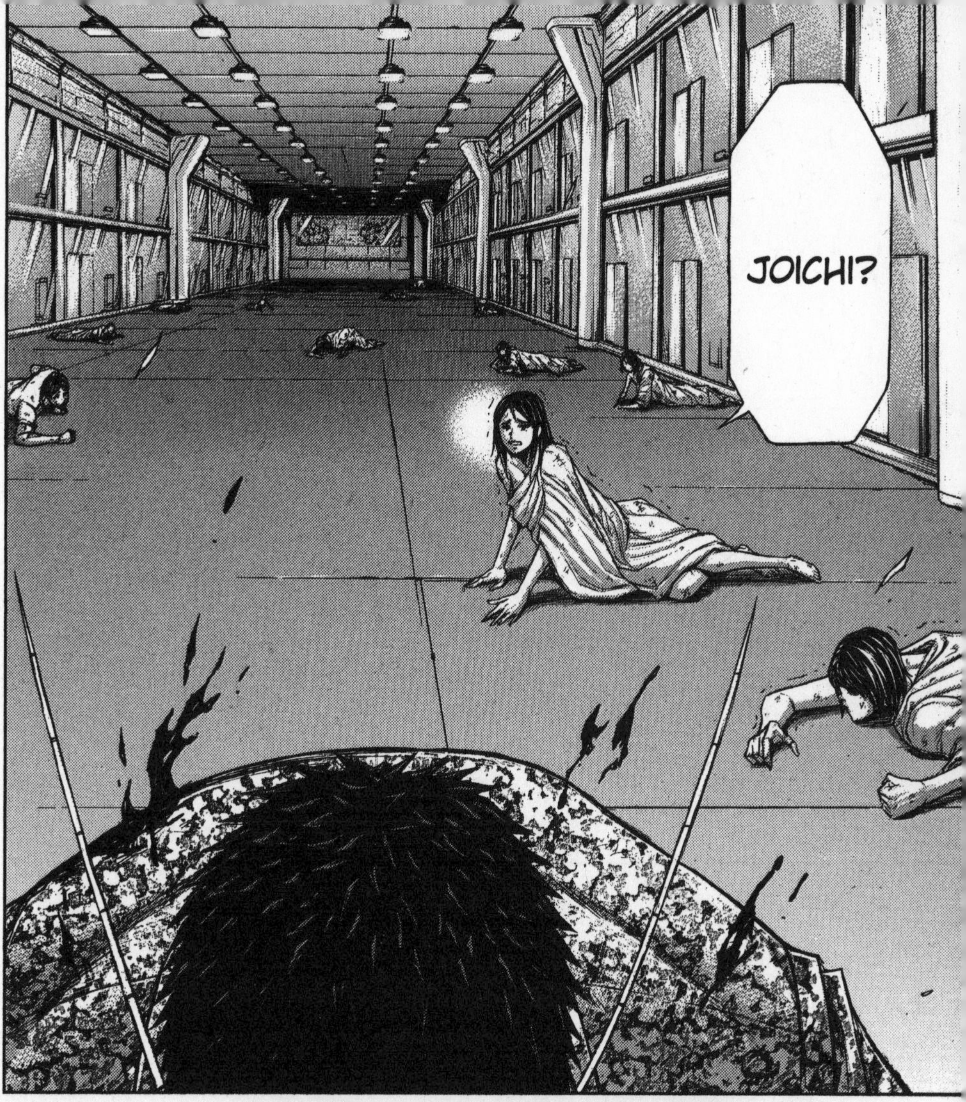
JOICHI?
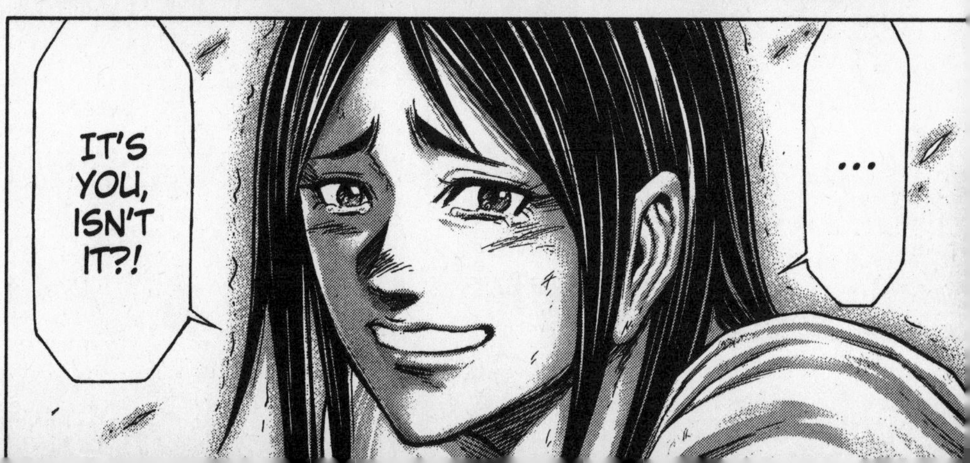
...
IT'S YOU, ISN'T IT?!

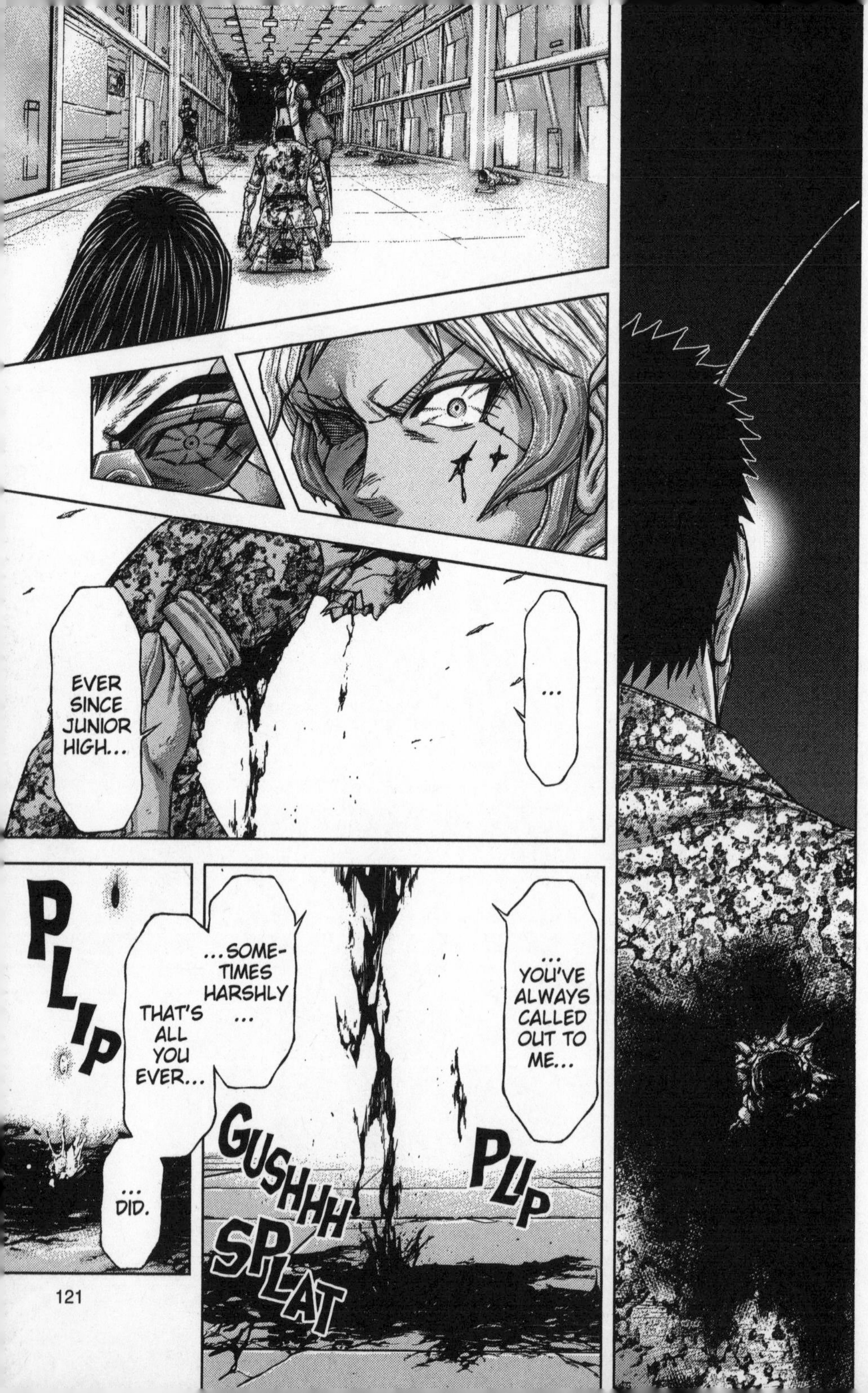
...
EVER SINCE JUNIOR HIGH...
... YOU'VE ALWAYS CALLED OUT TO ME...
PLIP
GUSHHH
SPLAT
...SOME-TIMES HARSHLY...
THAT'S ALL YOU EVER...
... DID.
PLIP

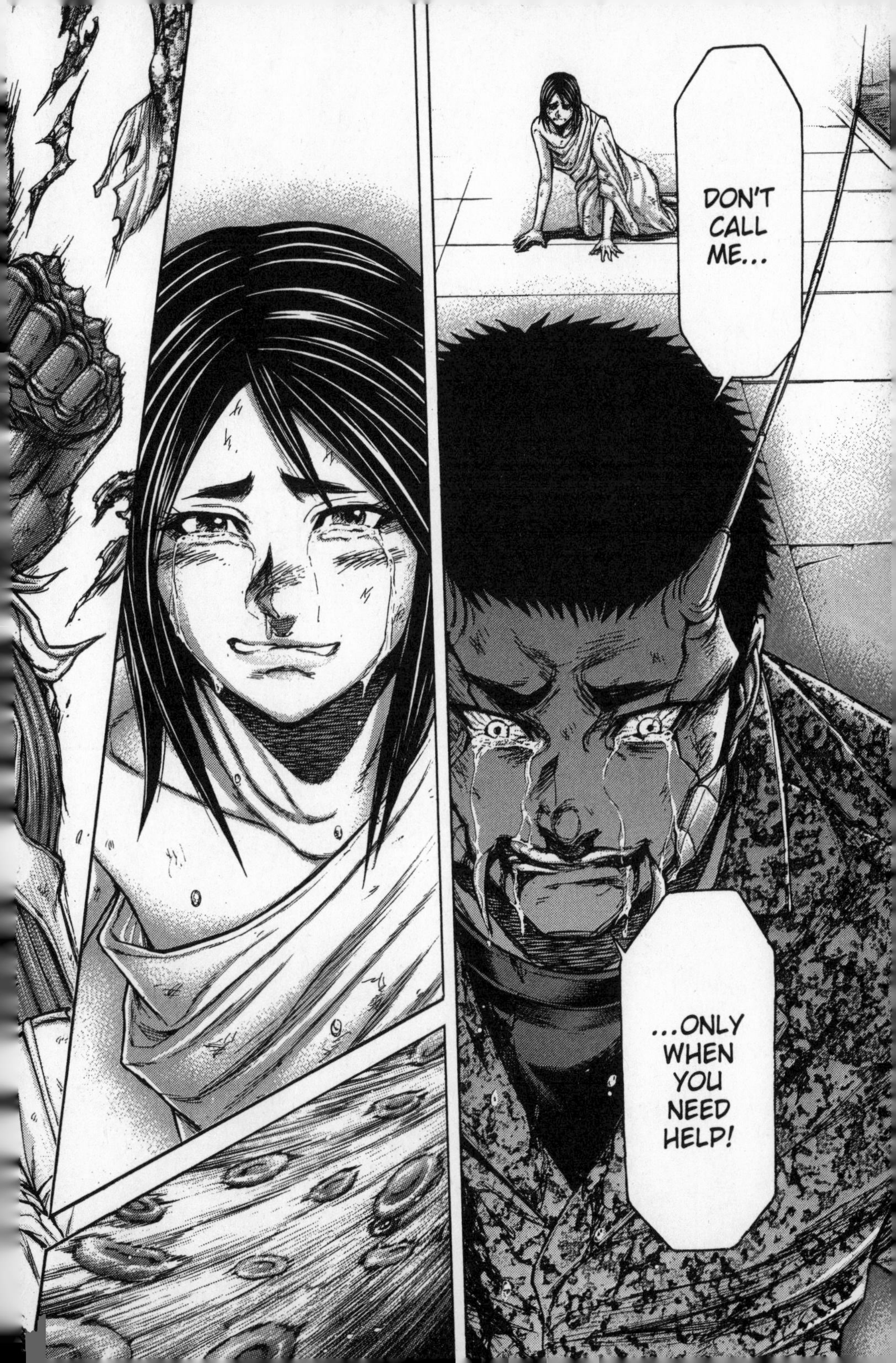
DON'T CALL ME...
...ONLY WHEN YOU NEED HELP!

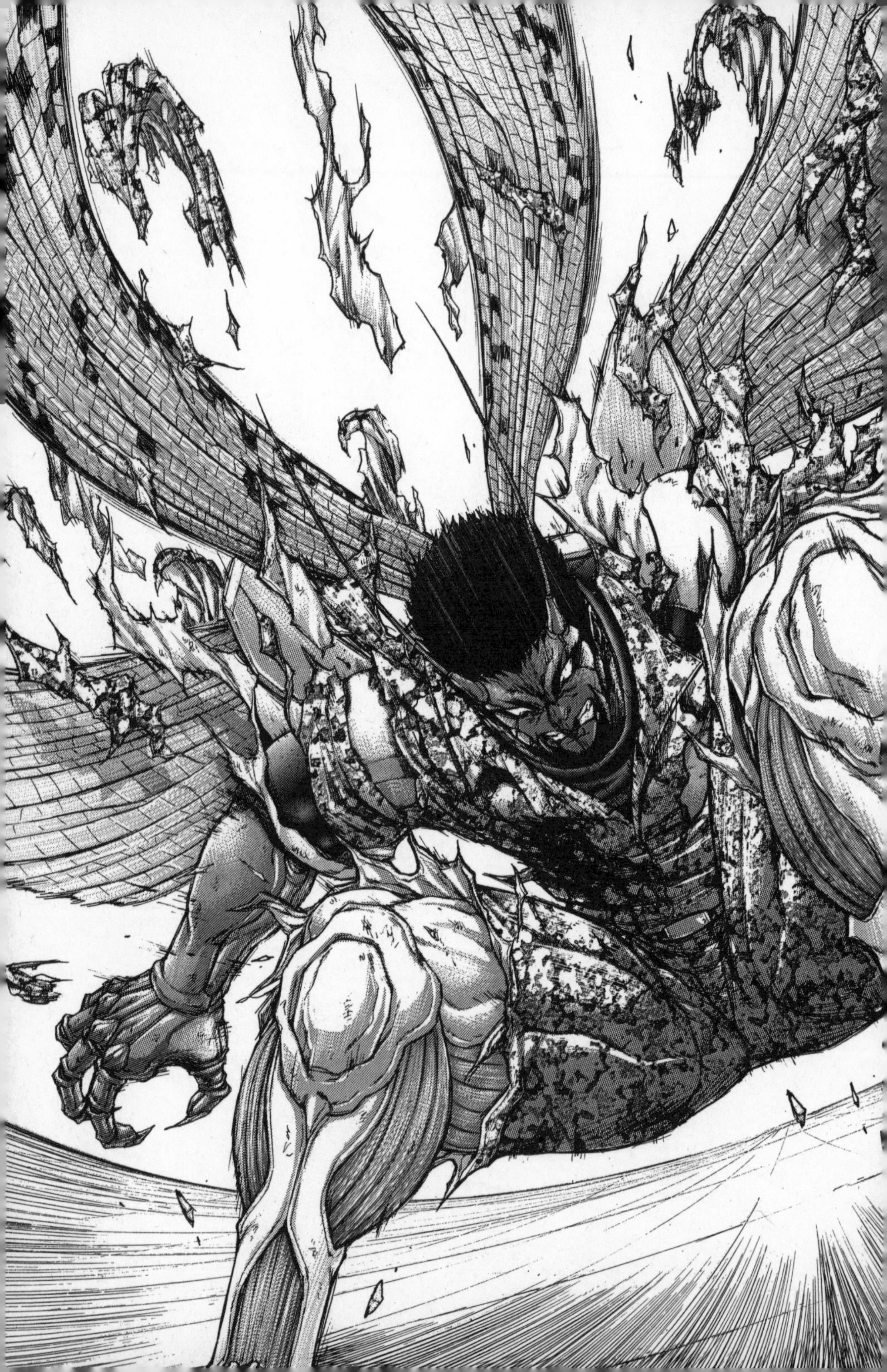

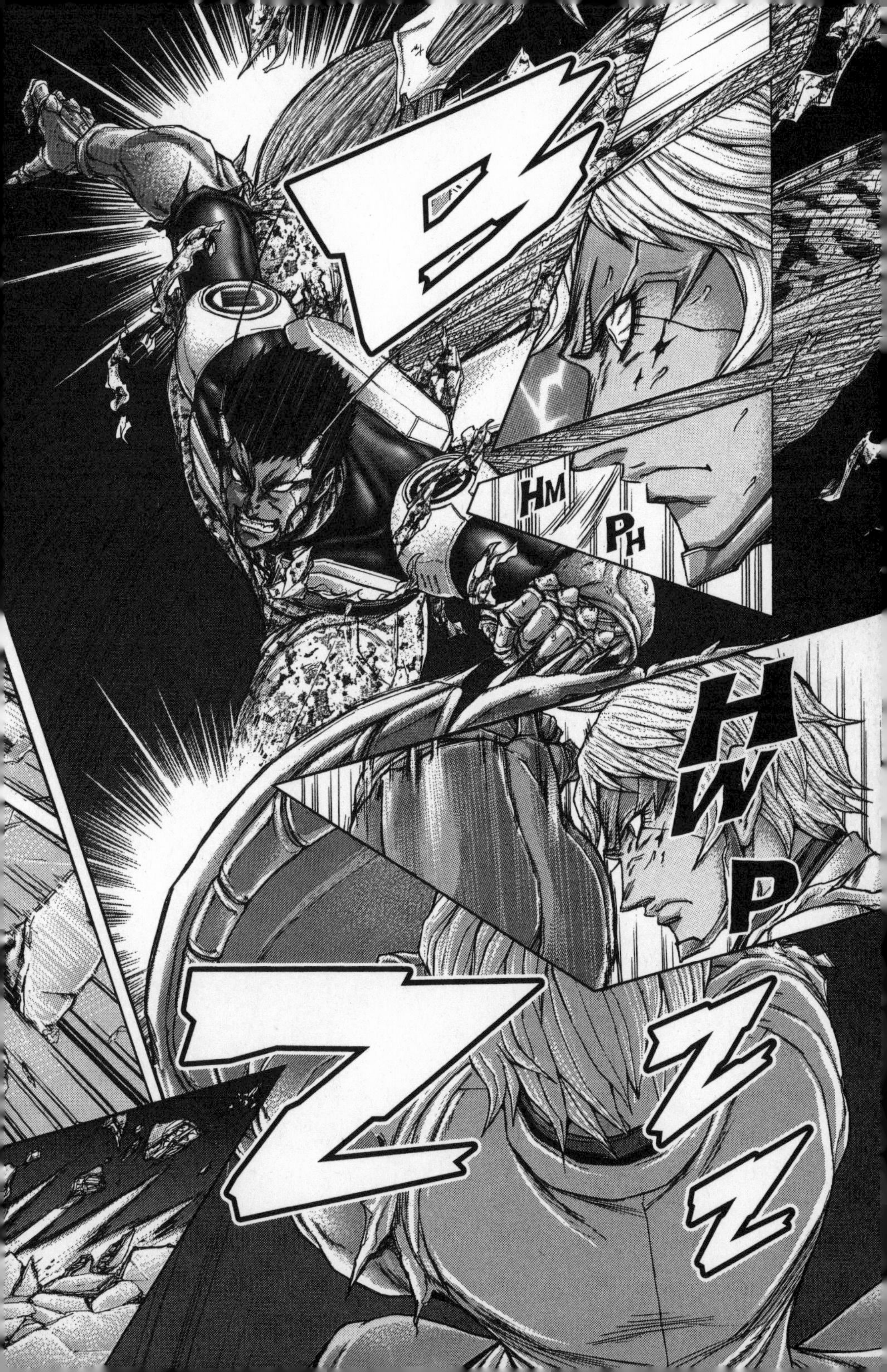
Z
HMPH
HWP
ZZ
Z

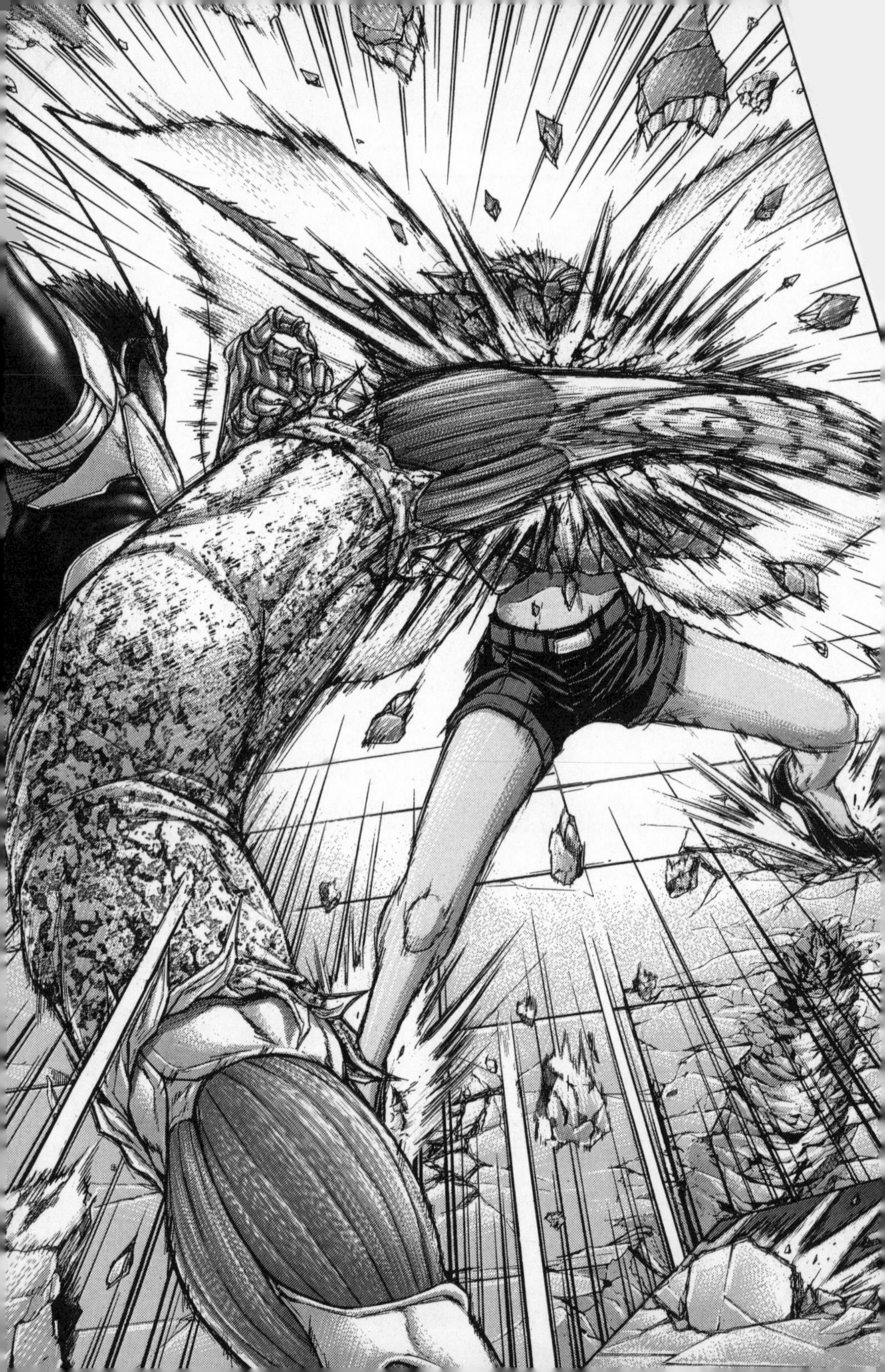

TERRA FORMARS

Character

Kyo Hyuga ♂

Saitama 20 yrs. 176 cm 75 kg

Operation Base:

Diamondback Rattlesnake

Favorite Foods: Pickled plum, anything good
with white rice
Dislikes: Erotic manga with orgasms that come too soon.
Eye Color: Black Blood Type: A
DOB: September 21 (Virgo)
Favorite thing about aquariums: How the director will
sometimes walk along and explain things.

His father was a bureaucrat and his mother was a
university professor who gave their son an education for
gifted children. In high school, after-school activities were
compulsory, so he was scrum-half for the rugby team.
However, he didn't get along well with his teammates
and the team wasn't very good anyway. He secured a
recommendation to university but suddenly joined Ichi
Security with Tatsuhiro. Prefers AM radio.

Tatsuhiro Someya ♂

Saitama 20 yrs. 194 cm 165 kg

Japan Ranking: ? → 2

Favorite Foods: Barbecue, lightly grilled offal
Dislikes: Convenience stores that don't
carry *Champion* (manga magazine)
Eye Color: Light Brown Blood Type: B
DOB: August 8 (Leo)
Favorite thing about aquariums: Worrying about seals
staying underwater too long.

His father was Fijian and his mother was Chinese-Russian.
They both refused Japanese citizenship and wouldn't raise
Tatsuhiro, so he ended up the foster child of an elderly
couple in Saitama. In China, his rugby skills set him on
course to a high school with a powerhouse team, but he
was surprisingly prone to sickness. When his asthma
worsened, he quit rugby and entered a public school. He
prefers FM radio and dislikes AM radio's focus on political
elections. He straightens his hair. Position: Number 8.

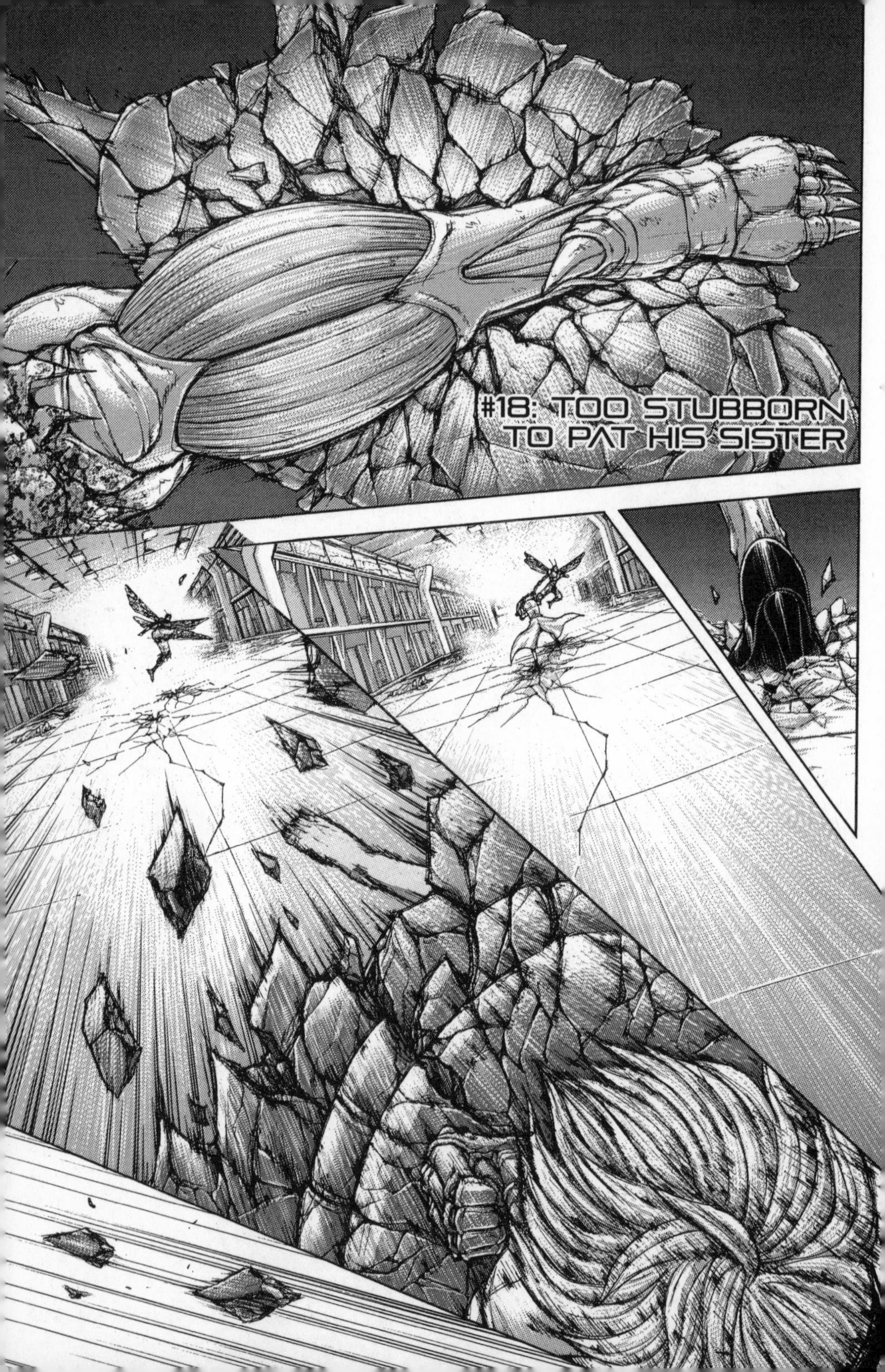
#18: TOO STUBBORN
TO PAT HIS SISTER

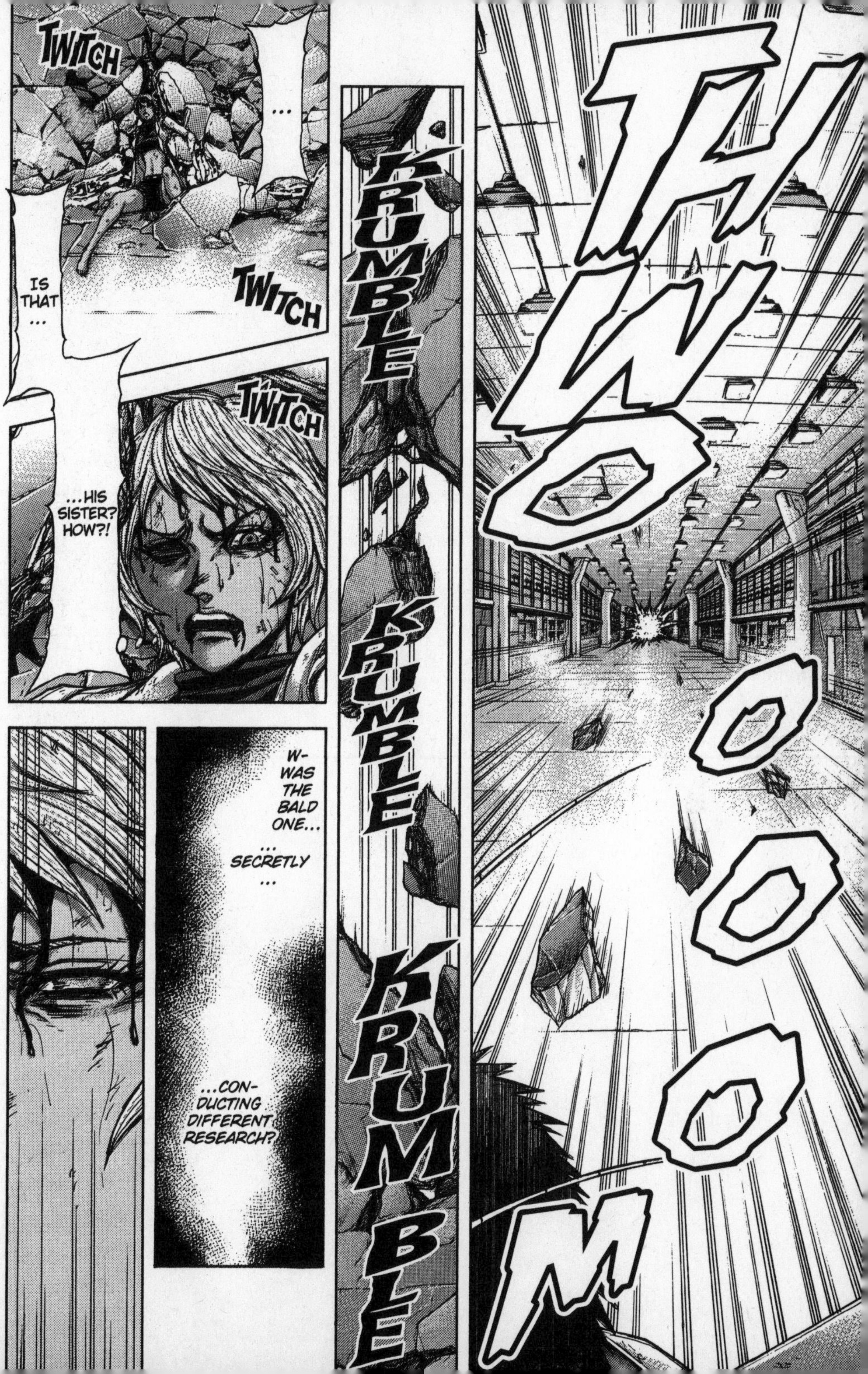
THWOOOOM
KRUMBLE
KRUMBLE
KRUMBLE
TWITCH
...
IS THAT ...
TWITCH
TWITCH
...HIS SISTER? HOW?!
W-WAS THE BALD ONE...
... SECRETLY ...
...CON-DUCTING DIFFERENT RESEARCH?

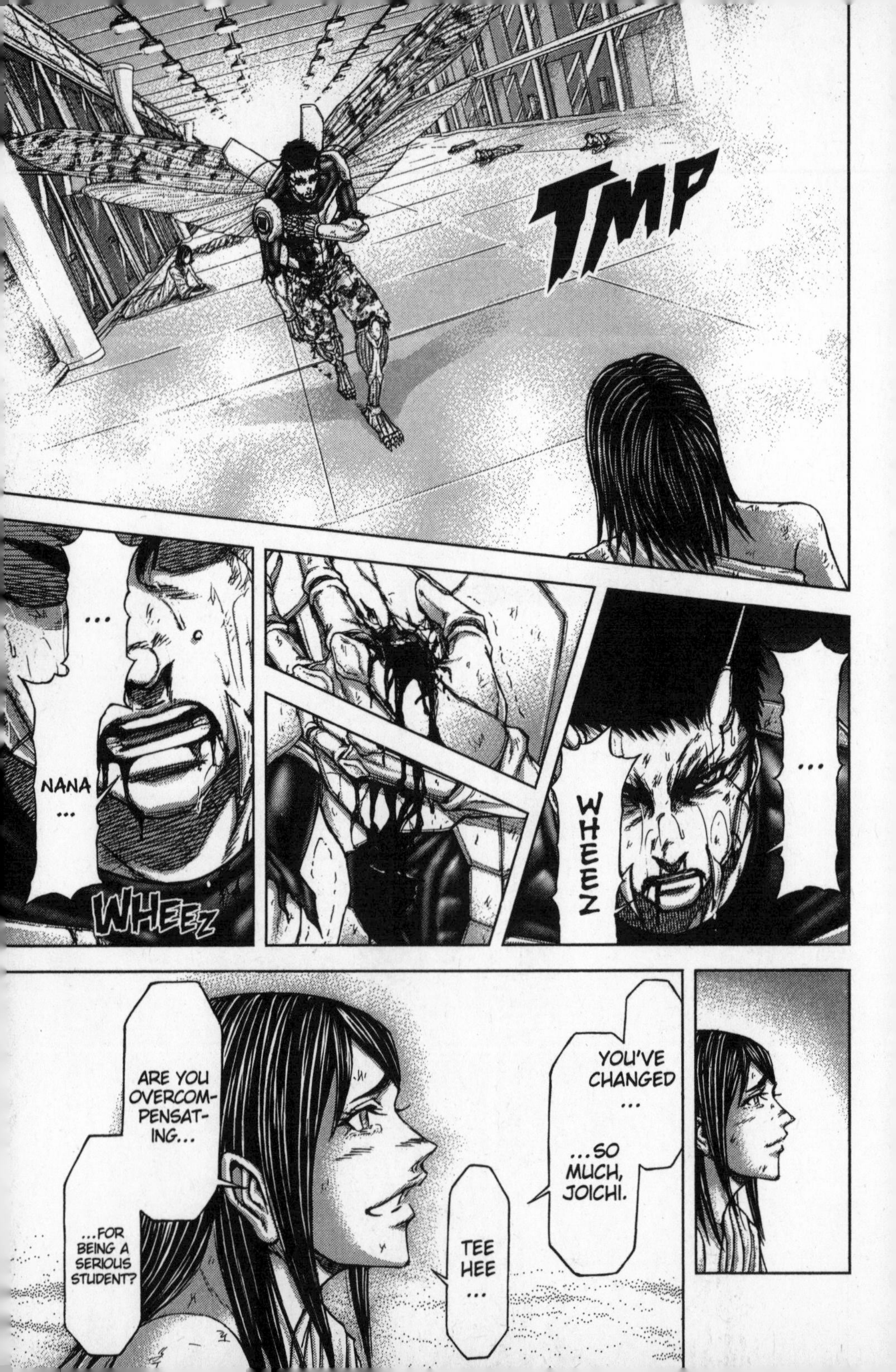
TMP
...
WHEEZ
...
NANA ...
WHEEZ
YOU'VE CHANGED ...
...SO MUCH, JOICHI.
TEE HEE ...
ARE YOU OVERCOMPENSATING...
...FOR BEING A SERIOUS STUDENT?

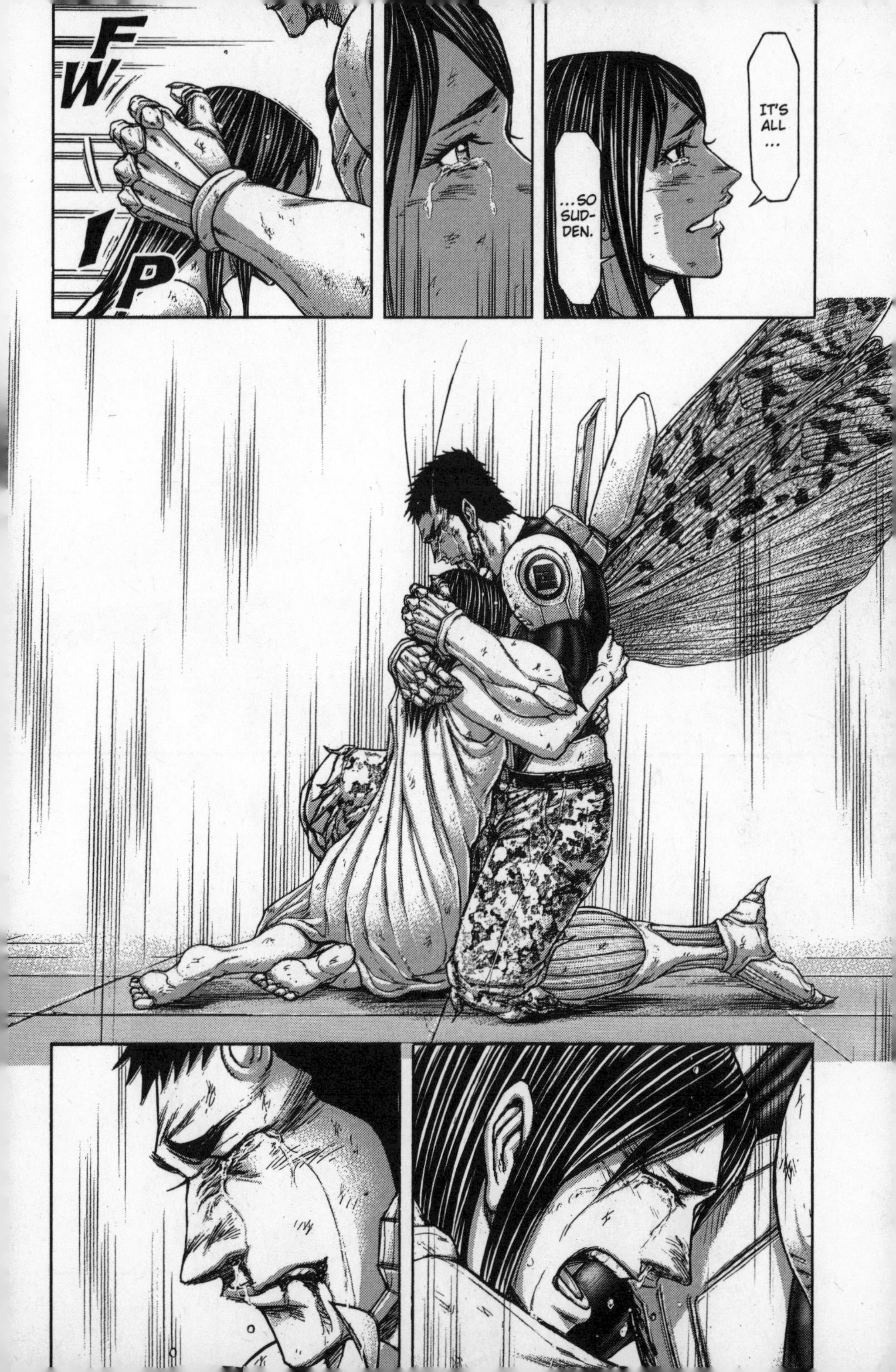
IT'S ALL ...
...SO SUD-DEN.
FWIP

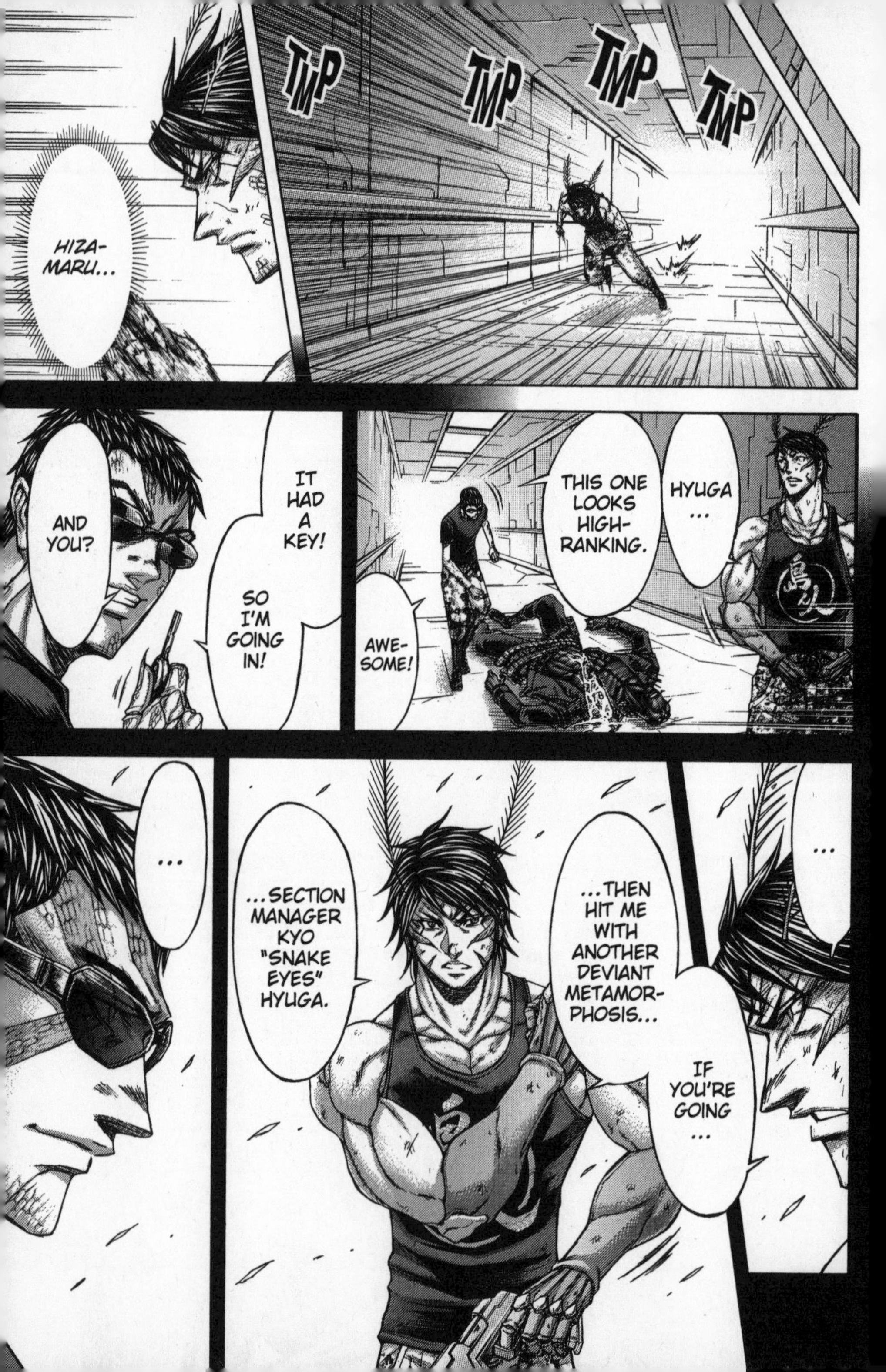
TMP
TMP
TMP
TMP
HIZA-MARU...
HYUGA...
THIS ONE LOOKS HIGH-RANKING.
AWE-SOME!
IT HAD A KEY!
SO I'M GOING IN!
AND YOU?
...
IF YOU'RE GOING...
...THEN HIT ME WITH ANOTHER DEVIANT METAMORPHOSIS...
...SECTION MANAGER KYO "SNAKE EYES" HYUGA.
...

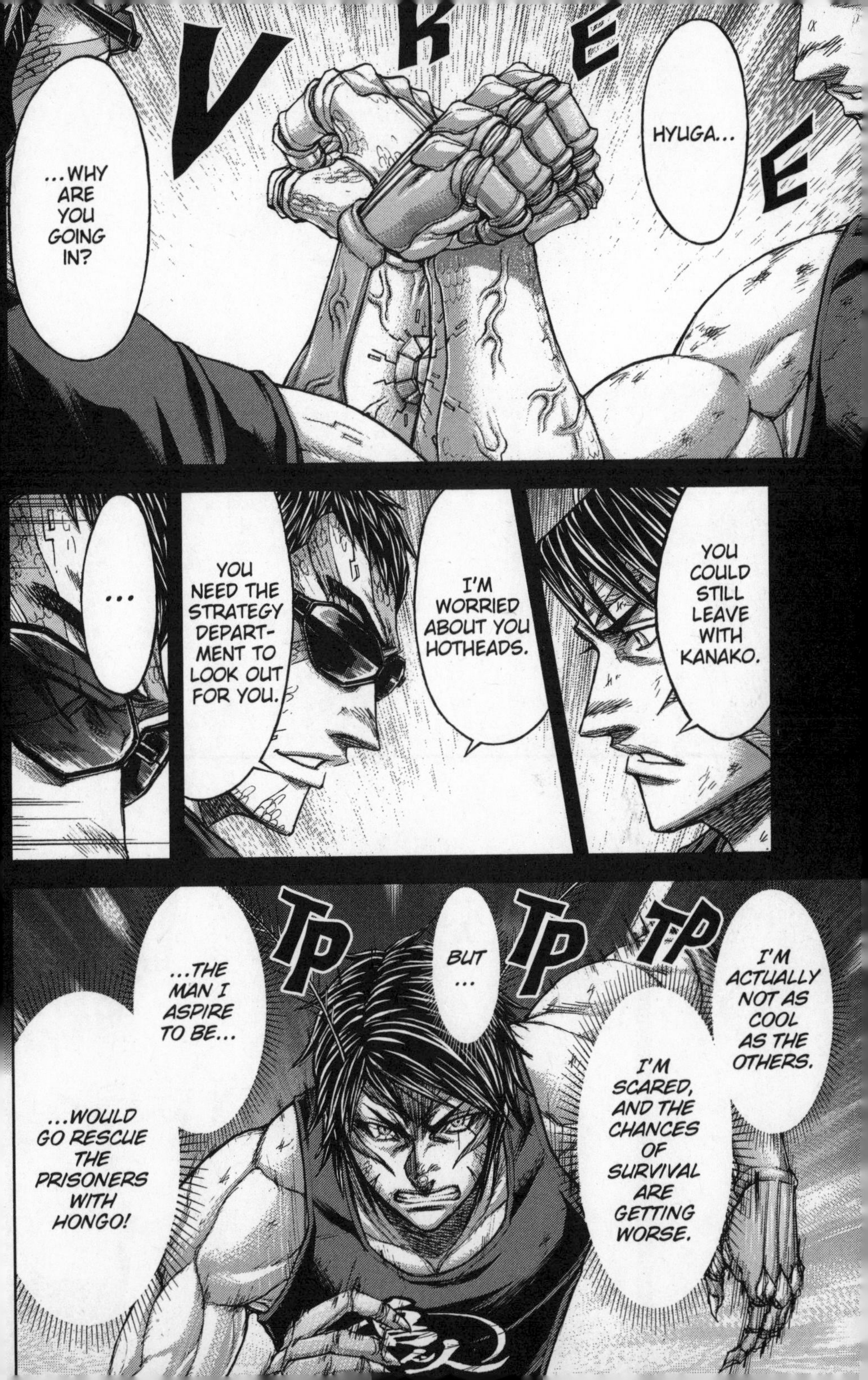
HYUGA...
VKEE
...WHY ARE YOU GOING IN?
YOU COULD STILL LEAVE WITH KANAKO.
I'M WORRIED ABOUT YOU HOTHEADS.
YOU NEED THE STRATEGY DEPART-MENT TO LOOK OUT FOR YOU.
...
TP TP TP
I'M ACTUALLY NOT AS COOL AS THE OTHERS.
I'M SCARED, AND THE CHANCES OF SURVIVAL ARE GETTING WORSE.
BUT...
...THE MAN I ASPIRE TO BE...
...WOULD GO RESCUE THE PRISONERS WITH HONGO!

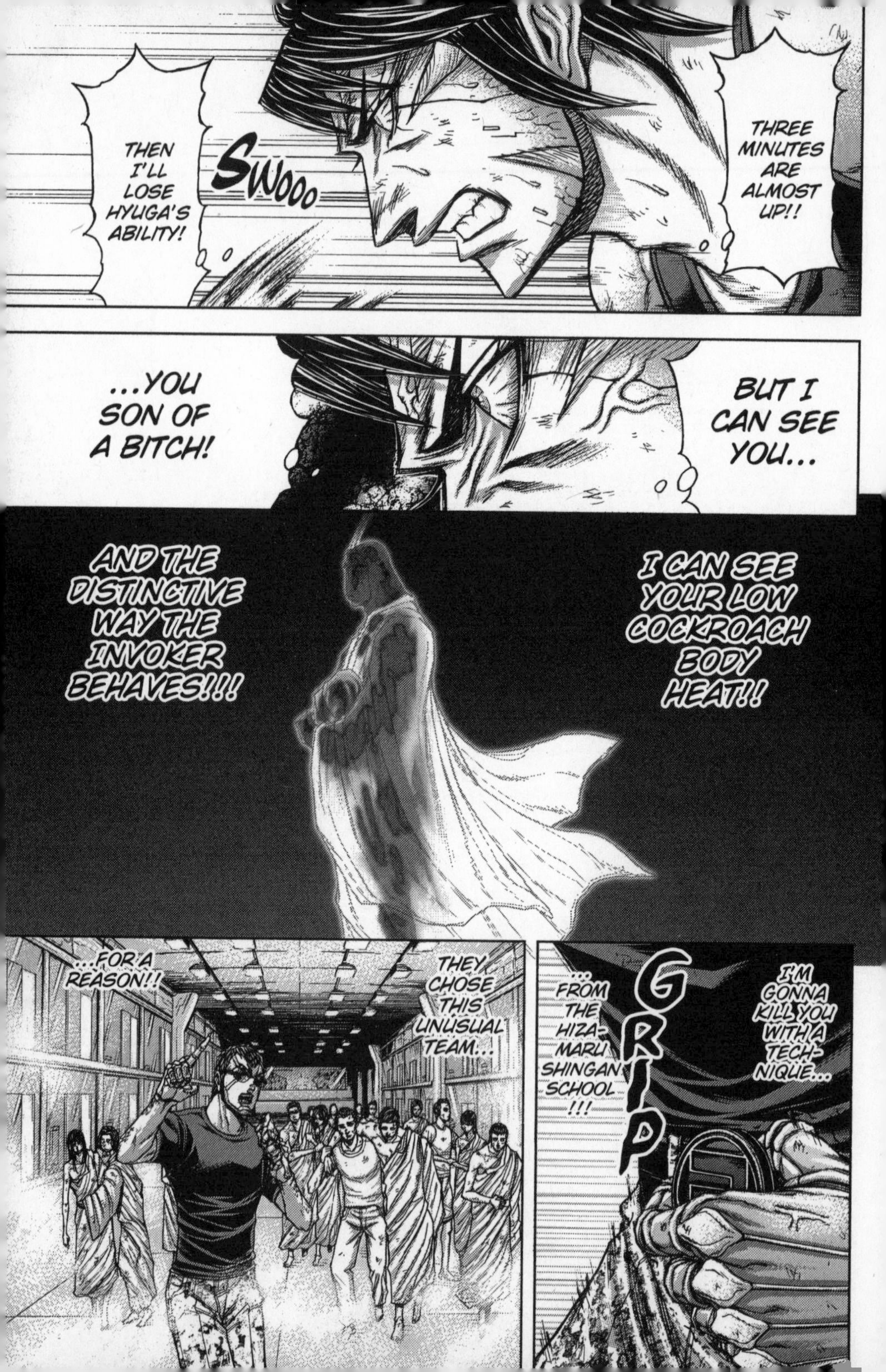
THREE MINUTES ARE ALMOST UP!!
SWOOO
THEN I'LL LOSE HYUGA'S ABILITY!
BUT I CAN SEE YOU...
...YOU SON OF A BITCH!
I CAN SEE YOUR LOW COCKROACH BODY HEAT!!
AND THE DISTINCTIVE WAY THE INVOKER BEHAVES!!!
I'M GONNA KILL YOU WITH A TECH-NIQUE...
GRIP
...FROM THE HIZA-MARU SHINGAN SCHOOL!!!
THEY CHOSE THIS UNUSUAL TEAM...
...FOR A REASON!!

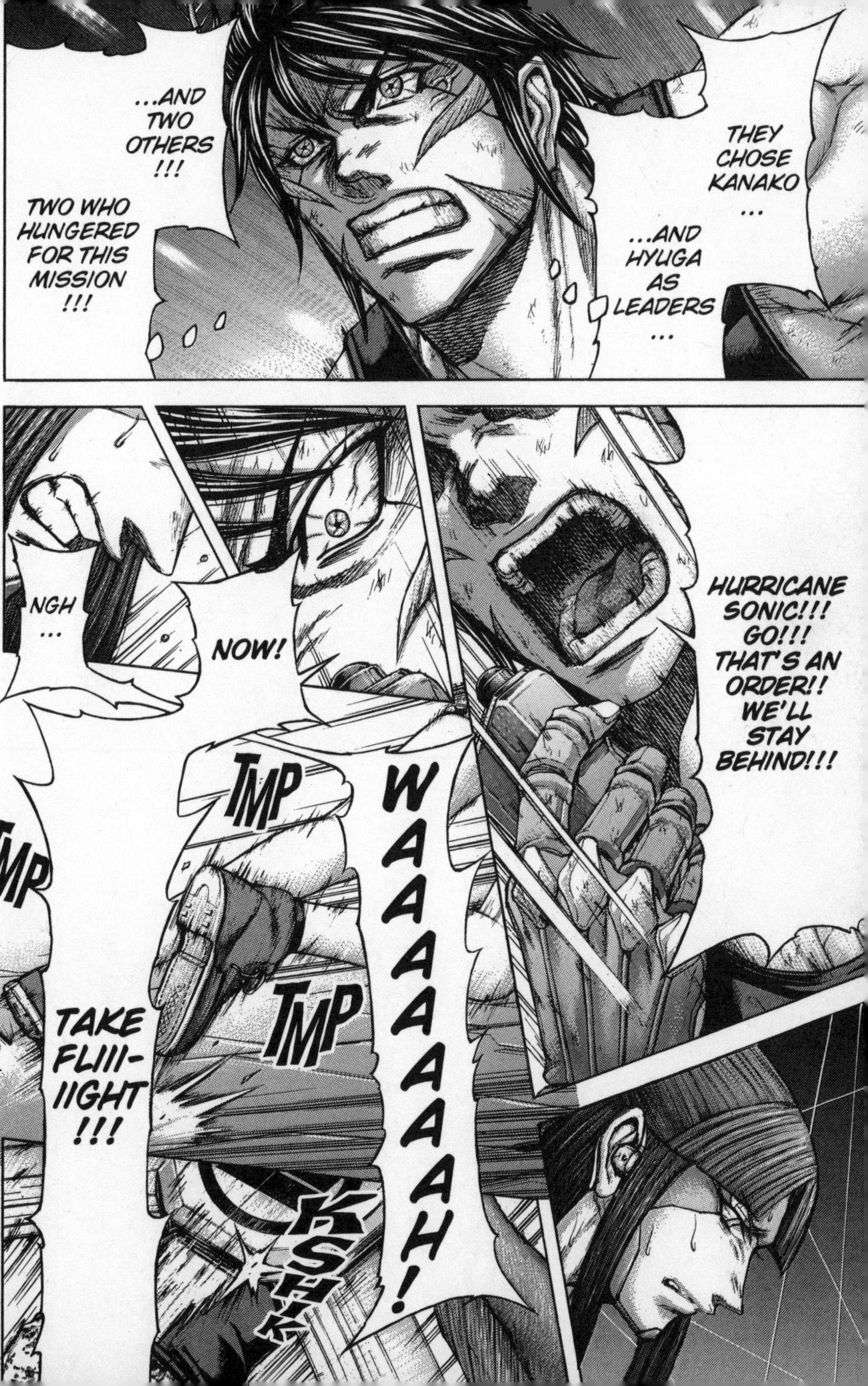
THEY CHOSE KANAKO ...
...AND HYUGA AS LEADERS ...
...AND TWO OTHERS !!!
TWO WHO HUNGERED FOR THIS MISSION !!!
HURRICANE SONIC!!! GO!!! THAT'S AN ORDER!! WE'LL STAY BEHIND!!!
NOW!
NGH ...
WAAAAAAAAH!
TMP
TMP
TMP
TAKE FLIII-IIGHT !!!
KSHIK

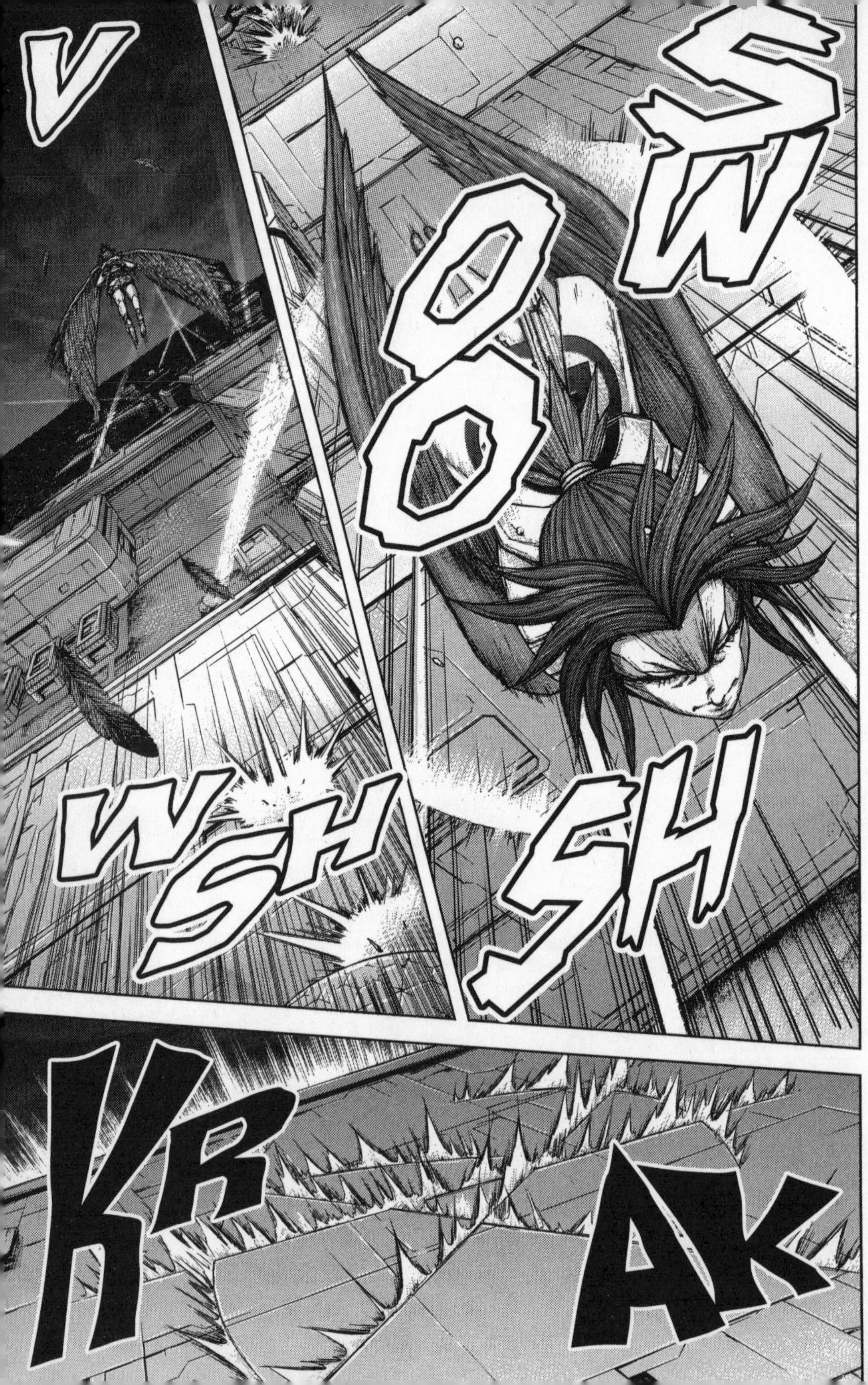

SWOOSH
V
WSH
KRAK

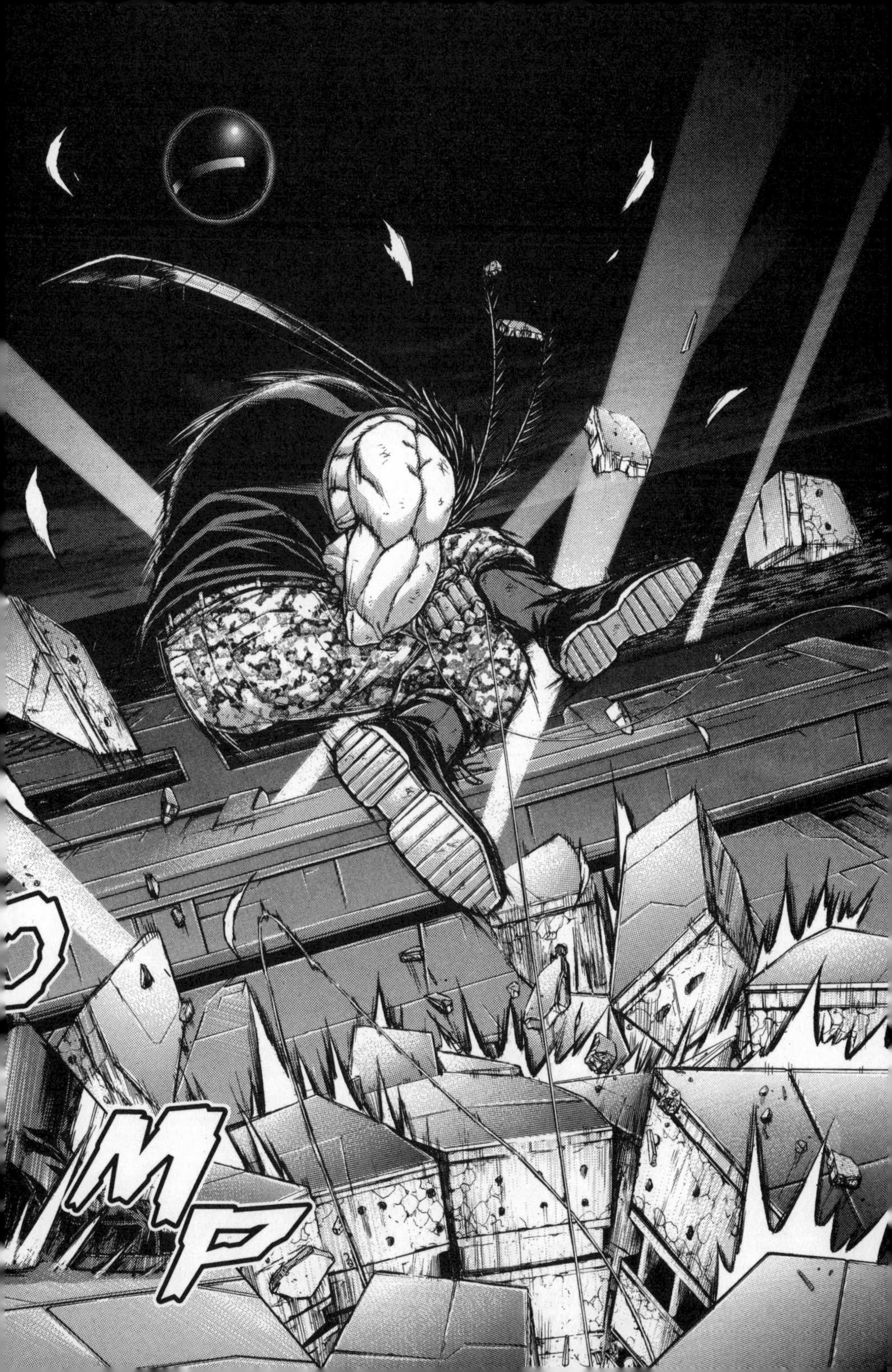
MP

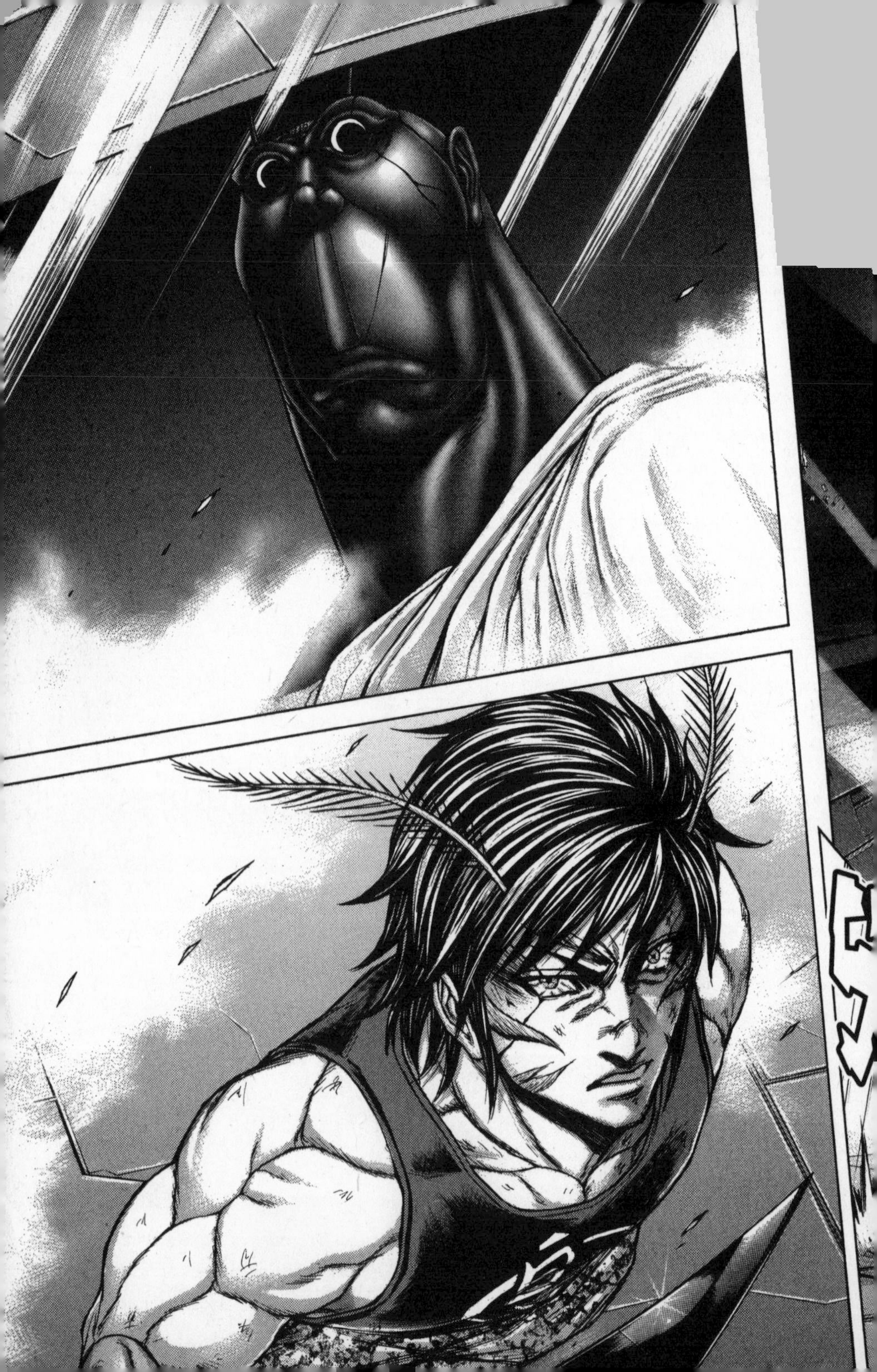

U-NASA PRELIMINARY FILE 7 - HORSESHOE CRAB

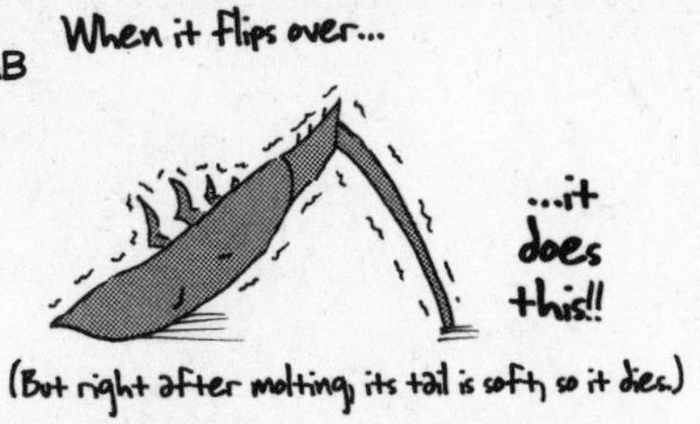
When it flips over...
...it does this!!
(But right after molting, its tail is soft, so it dies.)

●SEVERAL ORGANISMS ARE CONSIDERED LIVING FOSSILS, BUT AMONG THEM, THE HORSESHOE CRAB RETAINS THE MOST TRAITS FROM THE PAST. ACCORDING TO SOME THEORIES, IT IS OVER 400 MILLION YEARS OLD.

●ONE REASON FOR THIS IS THE SIMPLICITY OF ITS IMMUNE SYSTEM. VERTEBRATES DEMONSTRATE SEVERAL TYPES OF IMMUNE SYSTEMS, BUT THE CELLS IN A HORSESHOE CRAB'S BLOOD PLASMA ARE THE GRANULE CELLS MENTIONED IN THIS VOLUME.

●BACTERIA EXIST AS GRAM-NEGATIVE AND GRAM-POSITIVE BACTERIA. HORSESHOE CRAB BLOOD RESPONDS IMMEDIATELY TO A SUBSTANCE IN THE CELL WALLS OF GRAM-NEGATIVE BACTERIA. IT ALSO REACTS TO GRAM-POSITIVE BACTERIA AND FUNGI, BUT IT TAKES A LITTLE MORE TIME.

●RESEARCHERS USE THIS BLOOD TO DETERMINE WHETHER BACTERIA EXIST IN DRUGS FOR ADMINISTRATION TO HUMANS. PREVIOUSLY, THEY HAD TO WAIT A FEW DAYS UNTIL RABBITS DEVELOPED A FEVER, BUT WITH HORSESHOE CRABS IT ONLY TAKES ABOUT 40 MINUTES.

●RESEARCHERS ALSO EXPECT TO USE THIS BLOOD TO TEST FOR ORGANISMS (BACTERIA) ON MARS AND IN SPACE. WHEREAS THE PREVIOUS METHOD TOOK THREE DAYS, NOW RESULTS ARE POSSIBLE IN TEN MINUTES.

●TO ACQUIRE THIS BLOOD, AMERICAN CORPORATIONS INSERT NEEDLES INTO THE HEARTS OF HORSESHOE CRABS. AFTER DRAWING 25 PERCENT OF A CRAB'S BLOOD, THEY RELEASE IT. THREE PERCENT OF THE CRABS DIE AFTERWARD, WHILE THE REST SUPPOSEDLY RECOVER AFTER TWO MONTHS, BUT THE METHOD HAS BEEN THE SUBJECT OF CRITICISM.

●IN JAPAN, THE HORSESHOE CRAB IS A NATIONAL TREASURE, BUT IN TAIWAN, PEOPLE HAVE USED ITS SHELL FOR TABLEWARE AND MASKS FOR DISPELLING EVIL SINCE ANCIENT TIMES.

●IN SOME COUNTRIES, PEOPLE EAT THE EGGS, AND THE AUTHOR HAS TRIED THEM. IT LOOKS LIKE WHITE CAVIAR AND IS SORT OF CRUNCHY AND HARD WITHOUT ANY FLAVOR, SO IT WASN'T TASTY AT ALL. LATER, I LEARNED PEOPLE USUALLY MIX IT WITH SOME OTHER FOOD.

-WHAT DO YOU THINK ABOUT THIS?

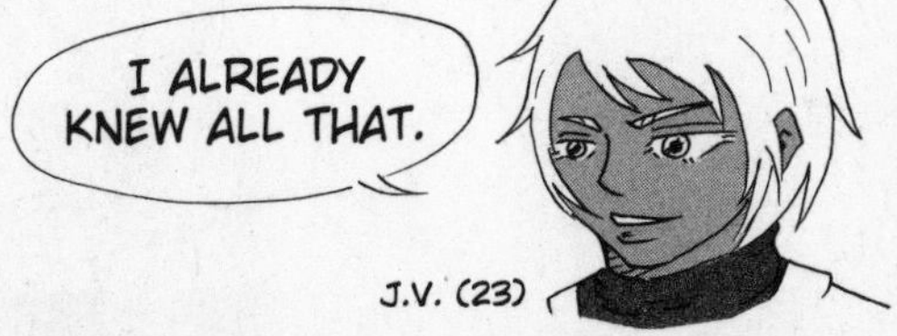
I ALREADY KNEW ALL THAT.
J.V. (23)

REFERENCES:

SURVIVORS: THE ANIMALS AND PLANTS THAT TIME HAS LEFT BEHIND, RICHARD FORTEY (AUTHOR), MACHIKO YANO (TRANSLATOR), CHIKUMASHOBO, 2014.
STUDIES ON THE MOLECULAR OF MECHANISM C3B DEPOSITION ON MICROBES IN THE HORSESHOE CRAB COMPLEMENT SYSTEM, 2013 DOCTORAL DISSERTATION BY KEISUKE TAGAWA STUDYING CHEMISTRY AT KYUSHU UNIVERSITY.
THE 400-MILLION-YEAR-OLD LIVING FOSSIL: SECRETS OF THE HORSESHOE CRAB, NATIONAL GEOGRAPHIC CHANNEL, DON WEN BIN (DIRECTOR), 2007.

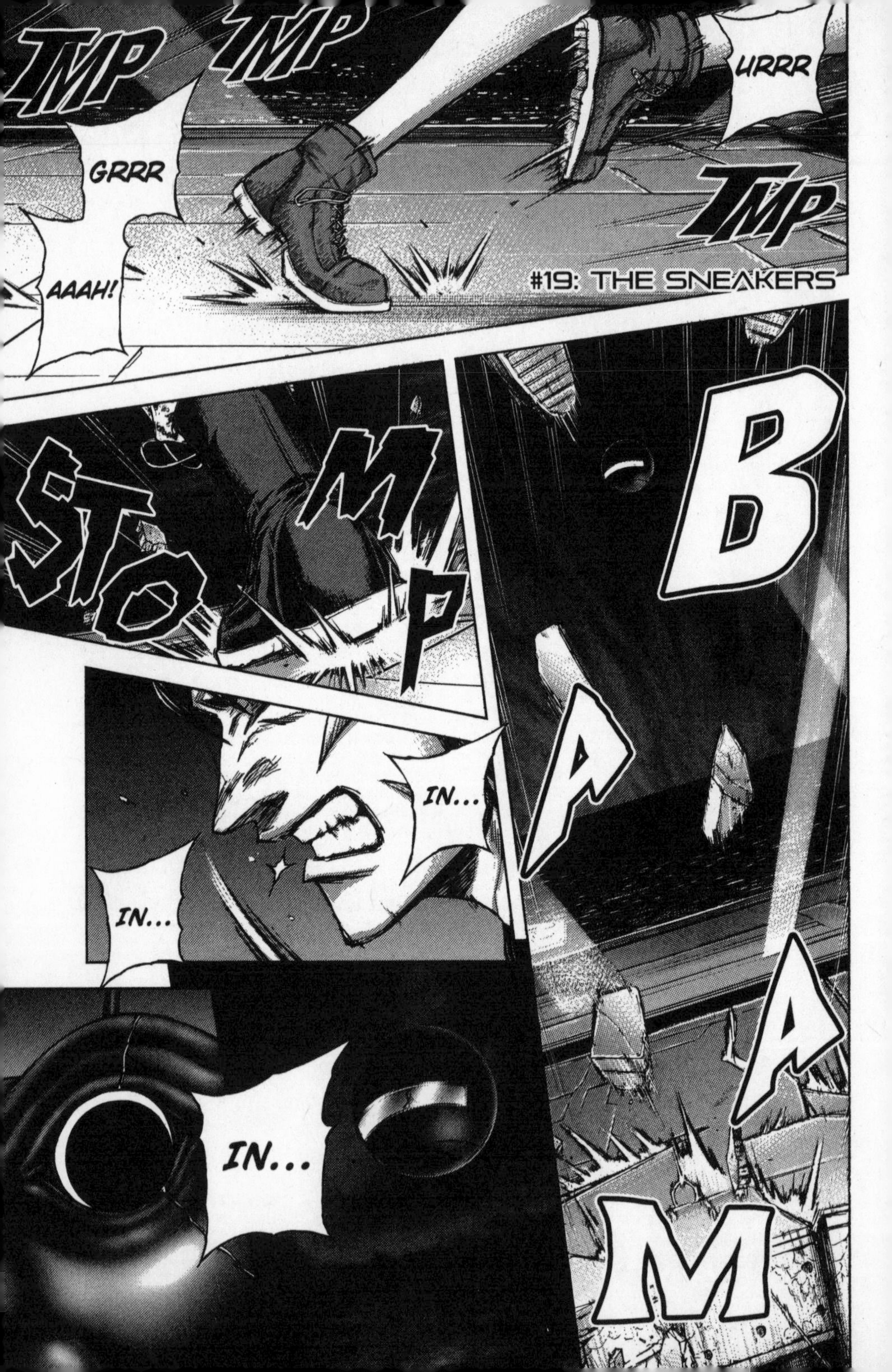
URRR
TMP
TMP
TMP
GRRR
AAAH!
#19: THE SNEAKERS
BAAM
STOMP
IN...
IN...
IN...

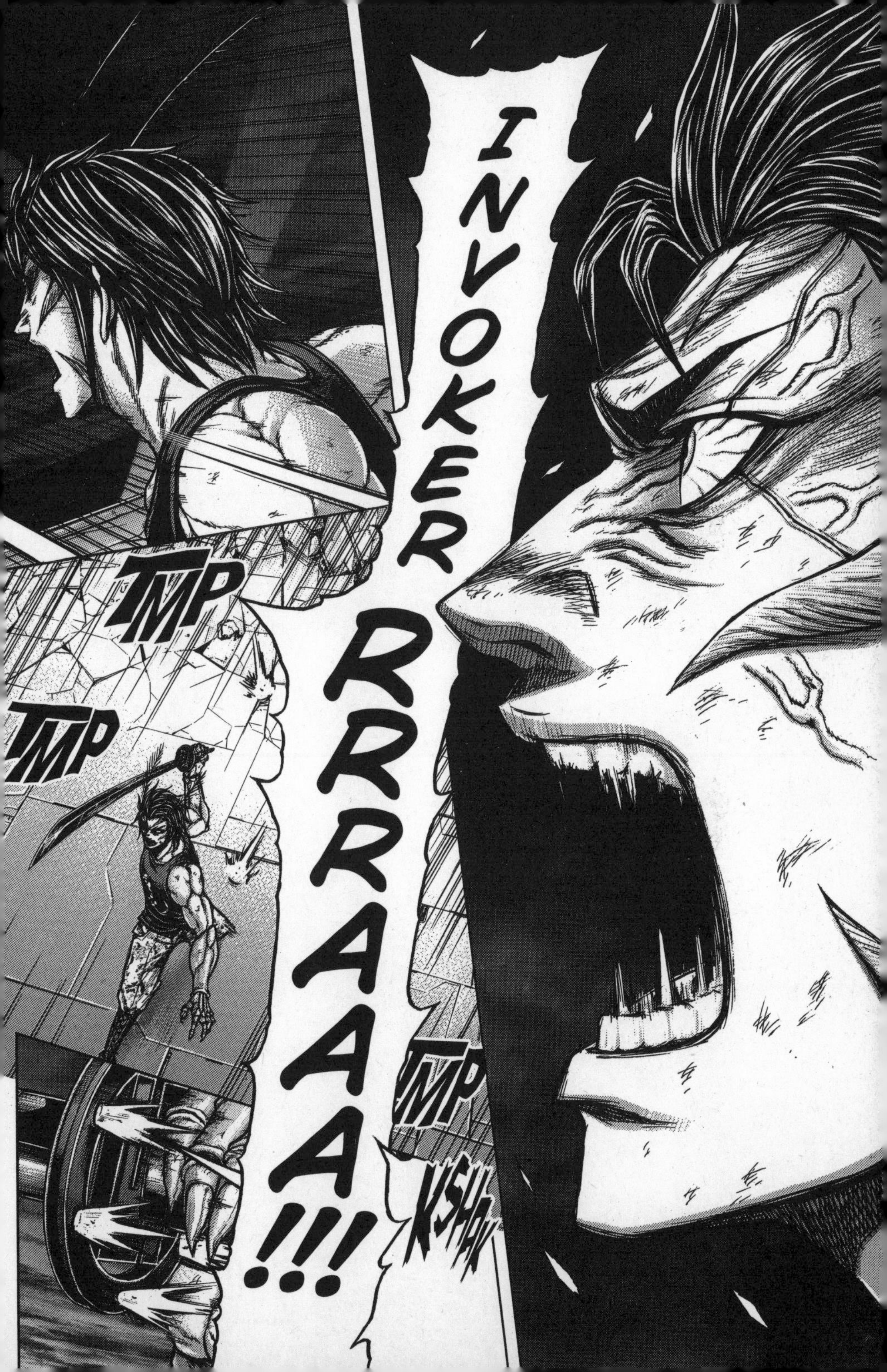
INVOKER
RRRAAA!!!
TMP
TMP
TMP
KSHH

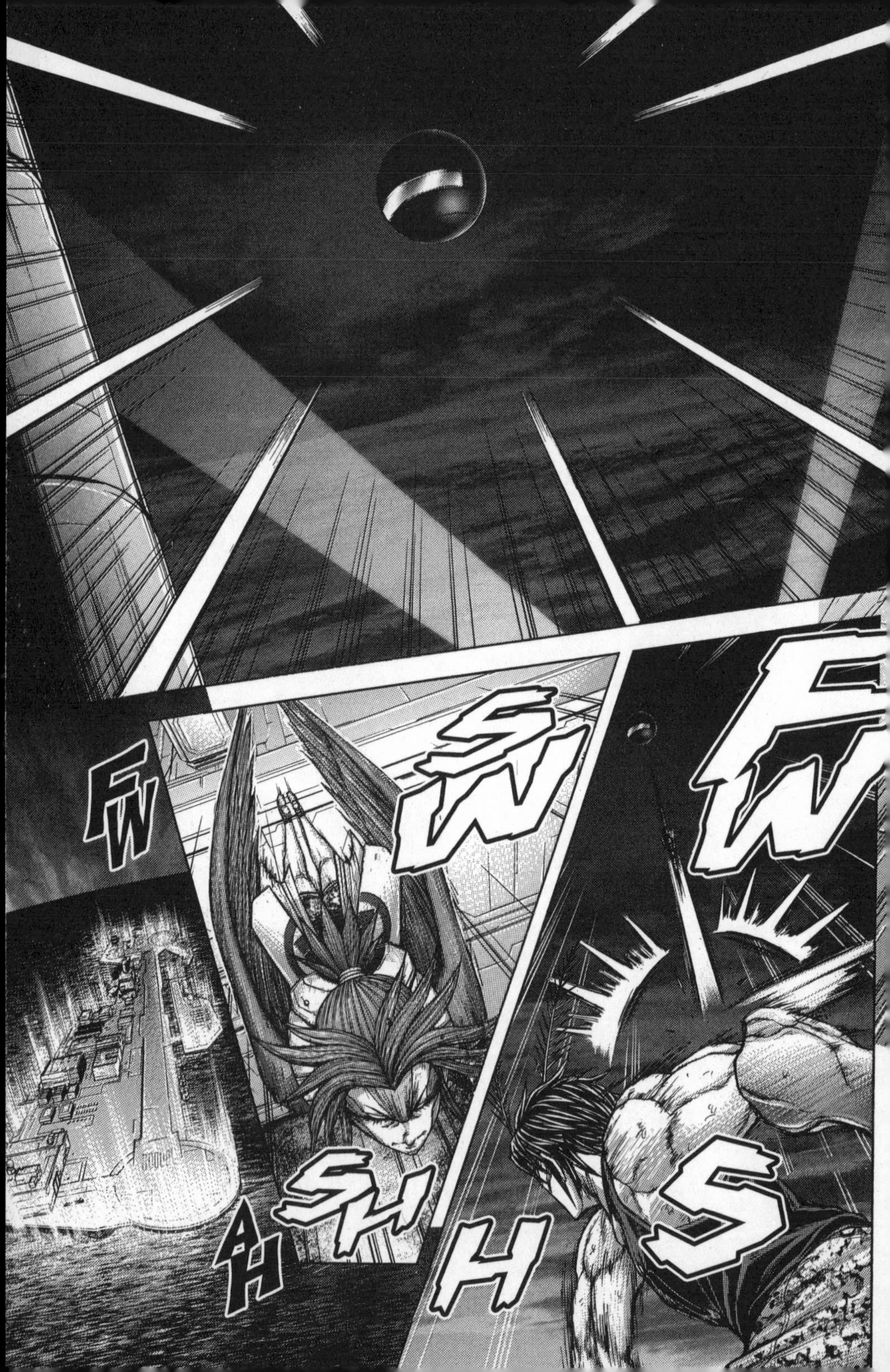
FW
SH
SW
SH
FW
AH

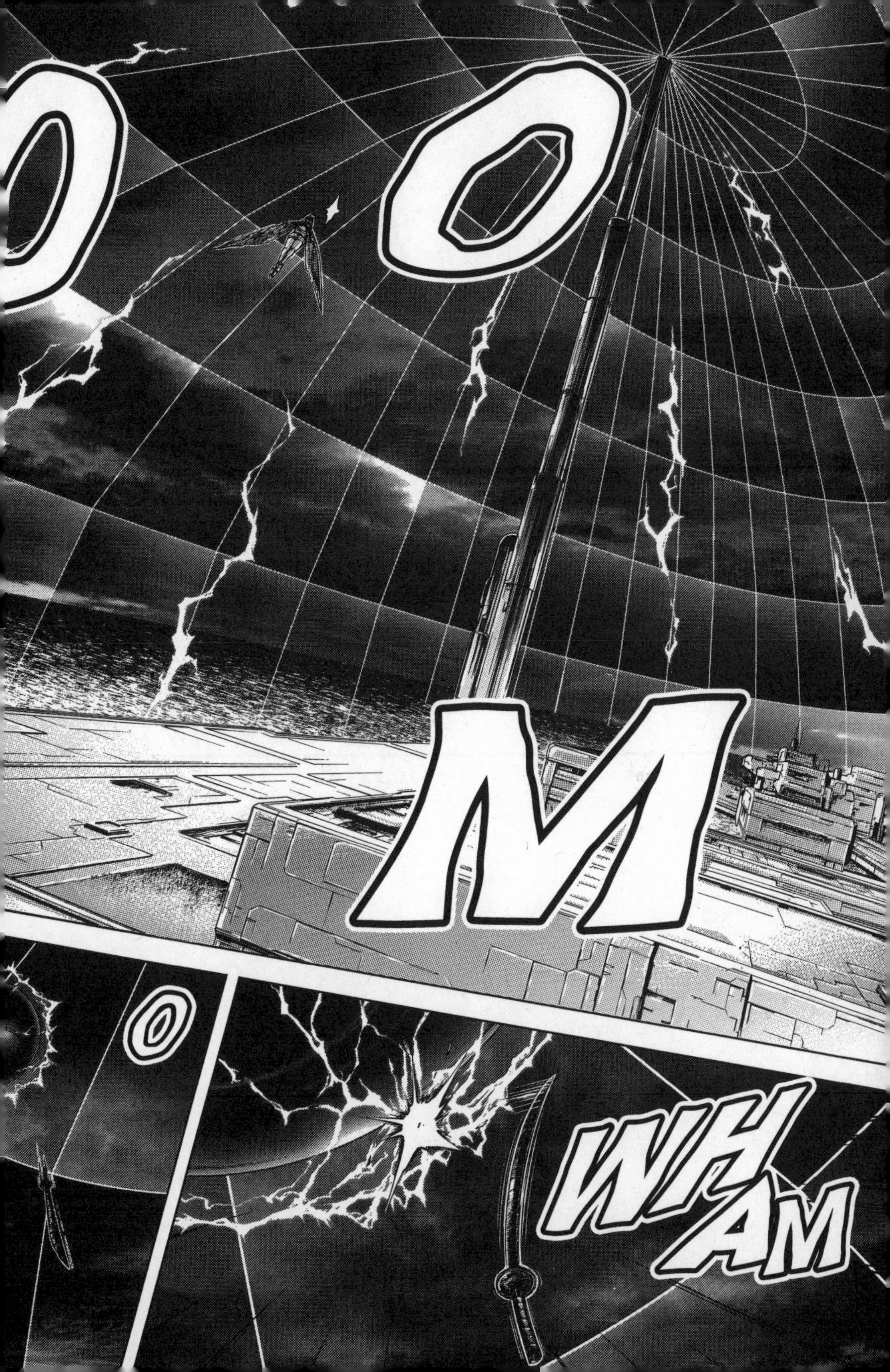
OOM
WHAM
O

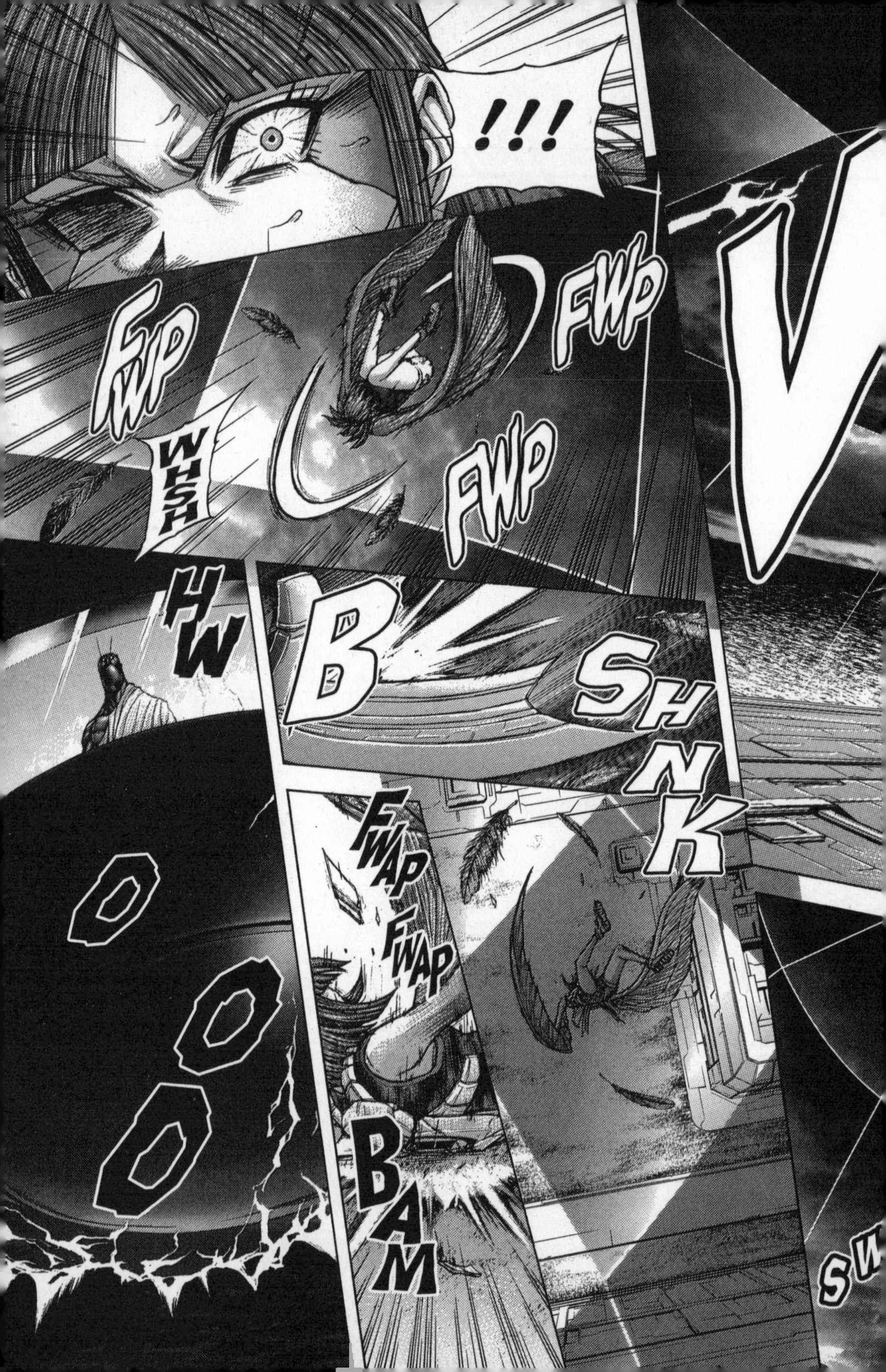

!!!
V
FWP
FWP
FWP
WHSH
SHNK
B
HW
FWAP
FWAP
BAM
OOO
SW

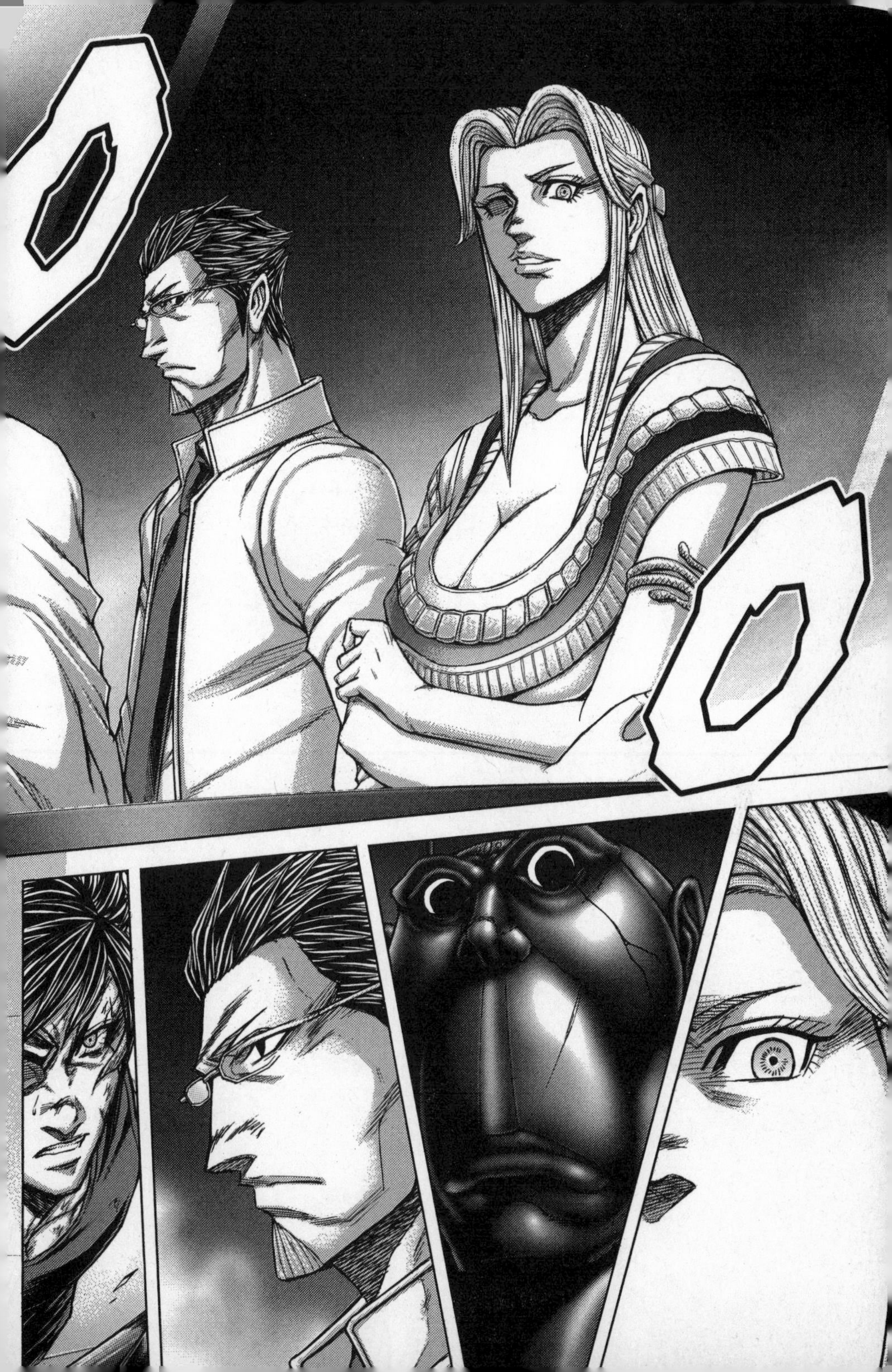

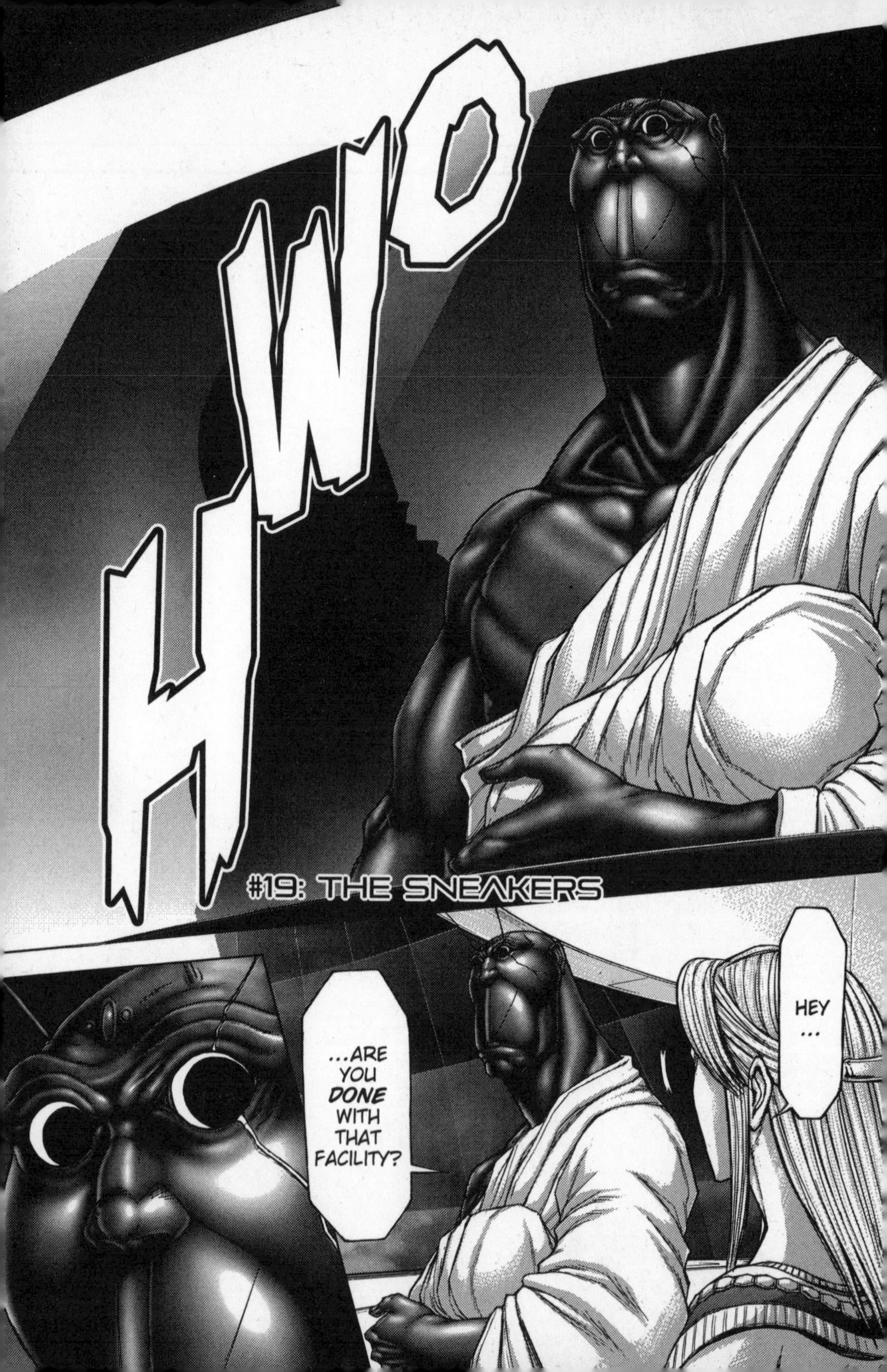
HWO
#19: THE SNEAKERS
HEY ...
...ARE YOU *DONE* WITH THAT FACILITY?

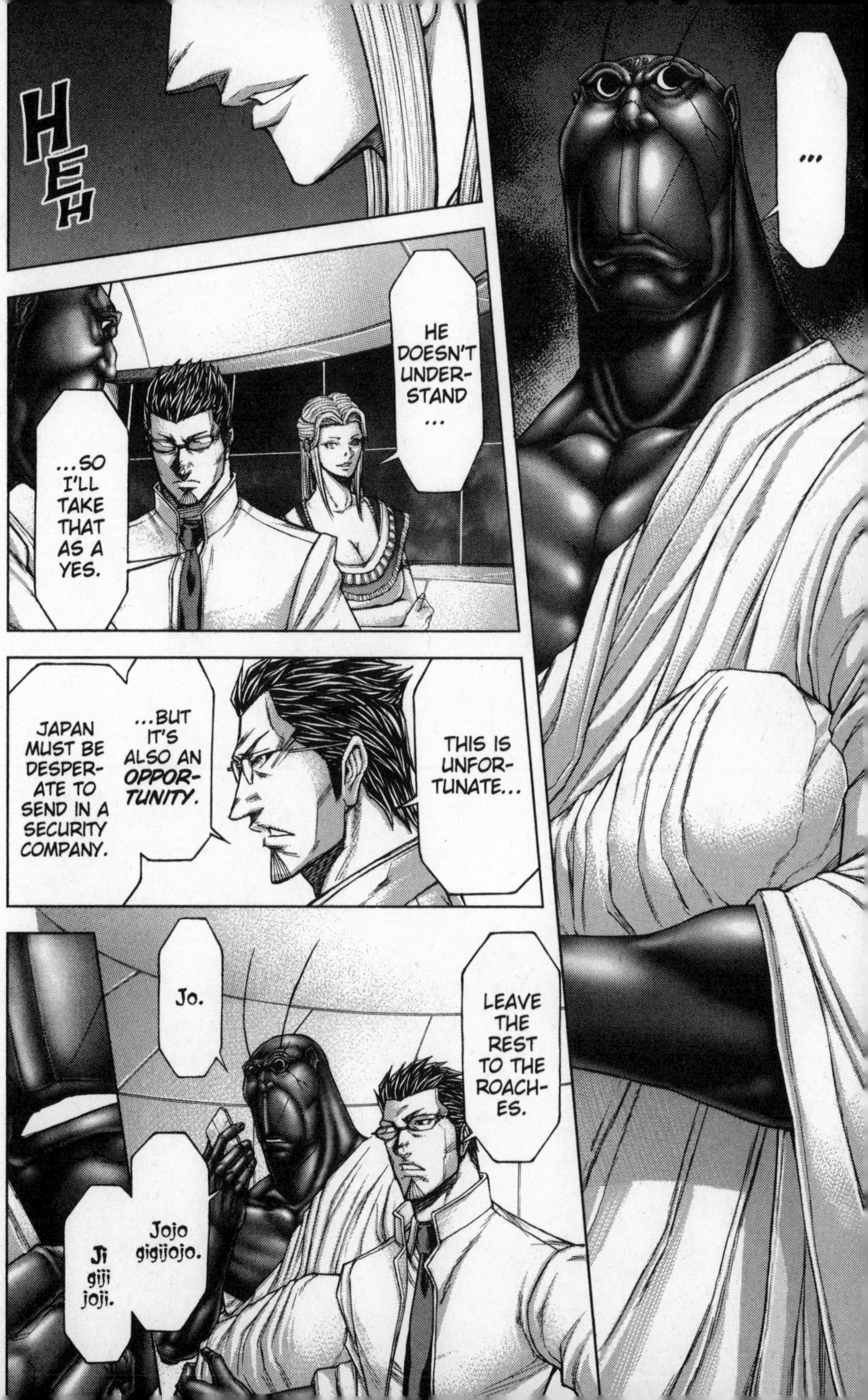
...
HEH
HE DOESN'T UNDER-STAND...
...SO I'LL TAKE THAT AS A YES.
THIS IS UNFORTUNATE...
...BUT IT'S ALSO AN *OPPORTUNITY*.
JAPAN MUST BE DESPERATE TO SEND IN A SECURITY COMPANY.
LEAVE THE REST TO THE ROACHES.
Jo.
Jojo gigijojo.
Ji giji joji.

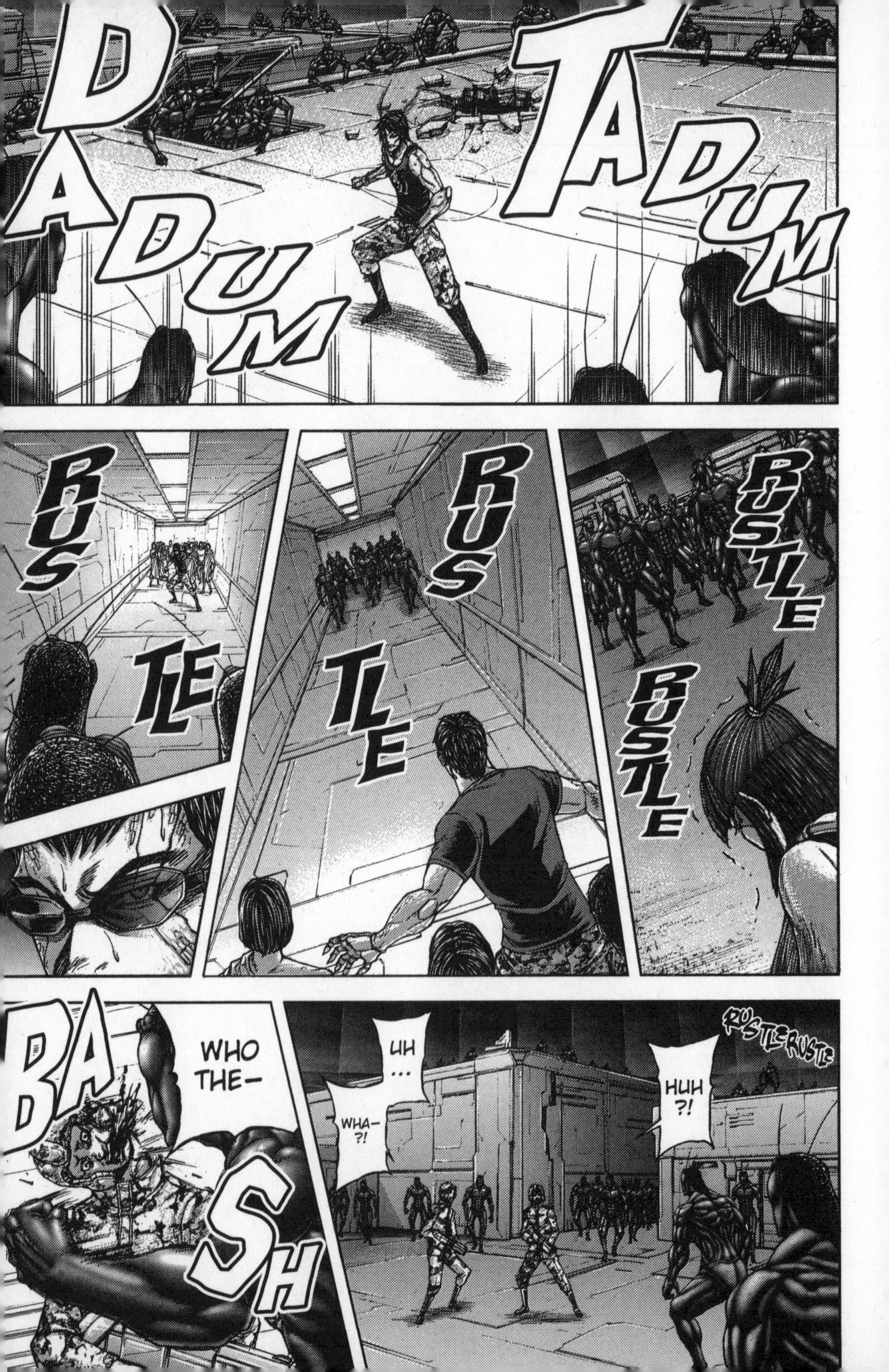
TADUM
DADUM
RUSTLE
RUSTLE
RUSTLE
RUSTLE
RUSTLERUSTLE
HUH ?!
UH …
WHA- ?!
WHO THE-
BASH

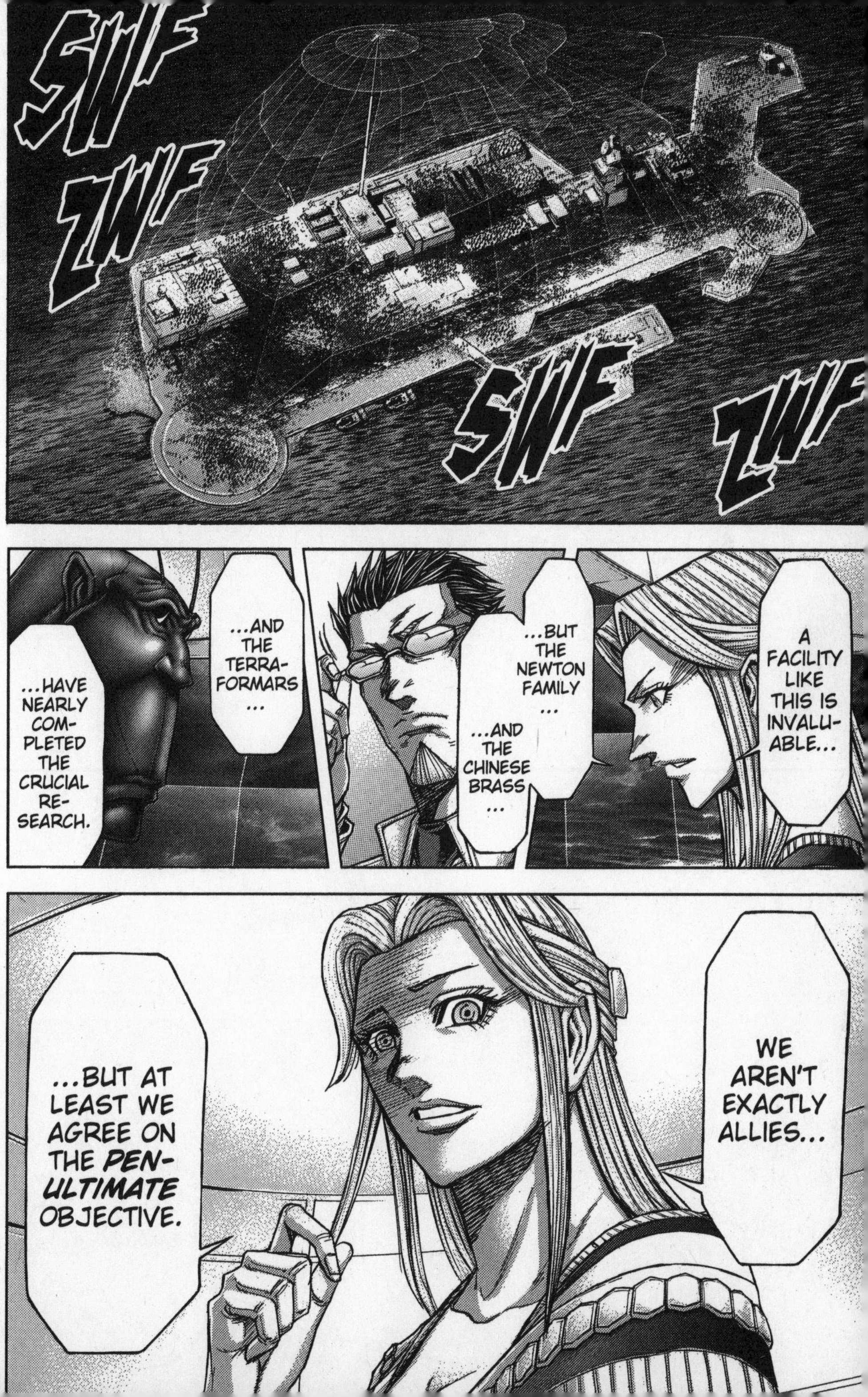
SWF
ZWF
SWF
ZWF
A FACILITY LIKE THIS IS INVALUABLE...
...BUT THE NEWTON FAMILY...
...AND THE CHINESE BRASS...
...AND THE TERRA-FORMARS...
...HAVE NEARLY COM-PLETED THE CRUCIAL RE-SEARCH.
WE AREN'T EXACTLY ALLIES...
...BUT AT LEAST WE AGREE ON THE *PEN-ULTIMATE* OBJECTIVE.

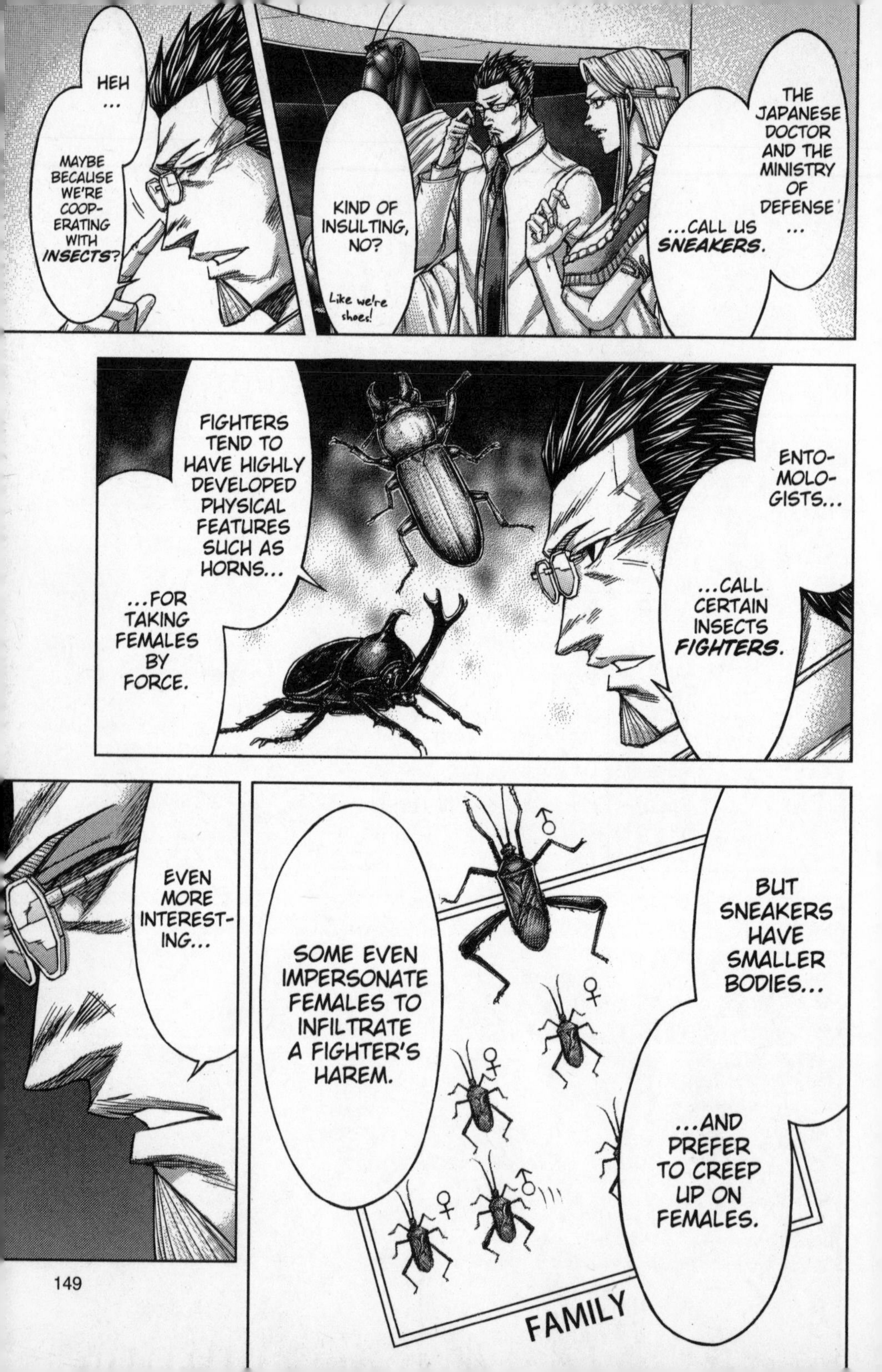
THE JAPANESE DOCTOR AND THE MINISTRY OF DEFENSE ...
...CALL US *SNEAKERS*.
KIND OF INSULTING, NO?
Like we're shoes!
HEH ...
MAYBE BECAUSE WE'RE COOP-ERATING WITH *INSECTS*?
ENTO-MOLO-GISTS...
...CALL CERTAIN INSECTS *FIGHTERS*.
FIGHTERS TEND TO HAVE HIGHLY DEVELOPED PHYSICAL FEATURES SUCH AS HORNS...
...FOR TAKING FEMALES BY FORCE.
BUT SNEAKERS HAVE SMALLER BODIES...
...AND PREFER TO CREEP UP ON FEMALES.
SOME EVEN IMPERSONATE FEMALES TO INFILTRATE A FIGHTER'S HAREM.
FAMILY
EVEN MORE INTEREST-ING...

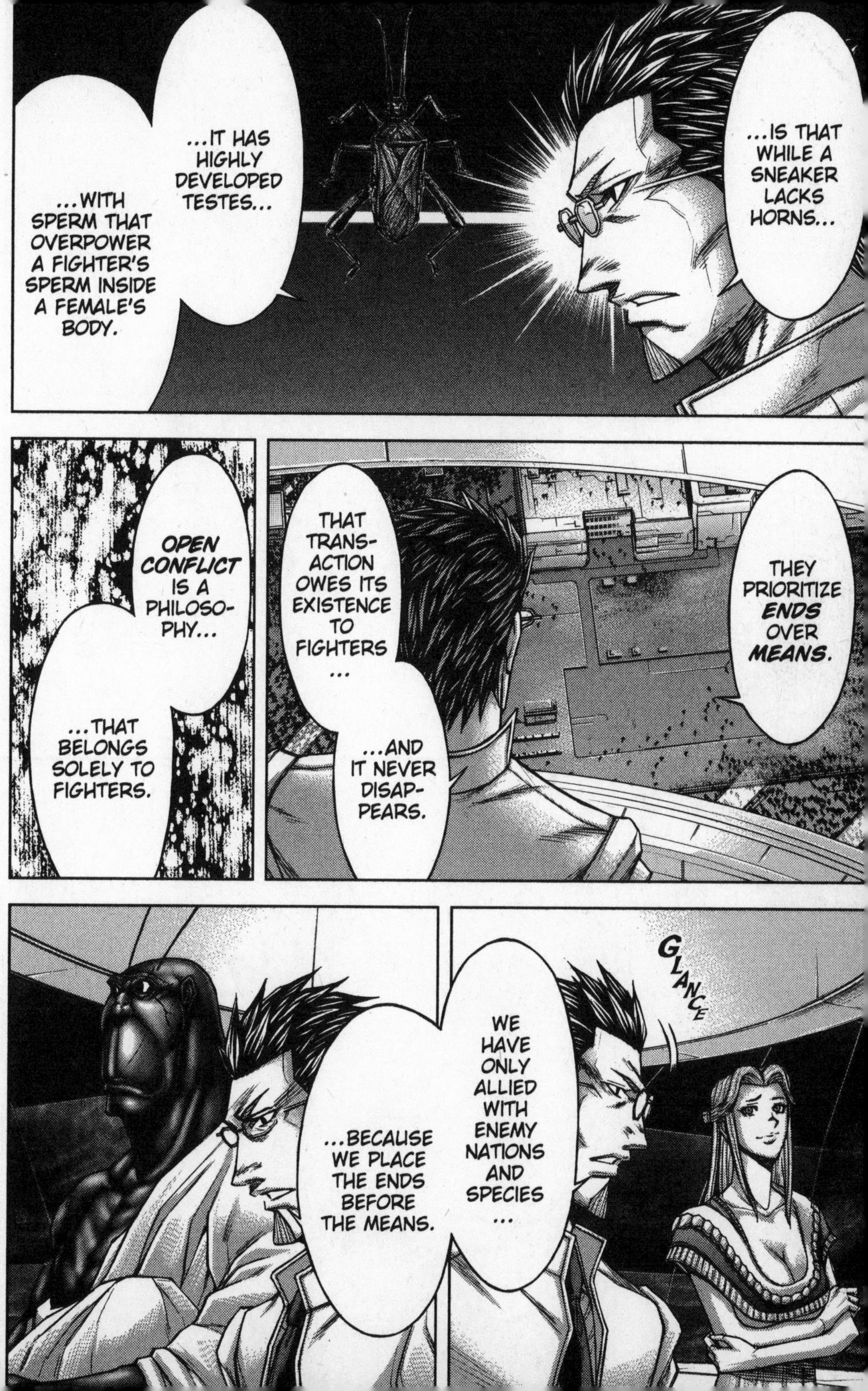
...IS THAT WHILE A SNEAKER LACKS HORNS...
...IT HAS HIGHLY DEVELOPED TESTES...
...WITH SPERM THAT OVERPOWER A FIGHTER'S SPERM INSIDE A FEMALE'S BODY.
THEY PRIORITIZE ***ENDS*** OVER ***MEANS***.
THAT TRANS-ACTION OWES ITS EXISTENCE TO FIGHTERS...
...AND IT NEVER DISAP-PEARS.
OPEN CONFLICT IS A PHILOSO-PHY...
...THAT BELONGS SOLELY TO FIGHTERS.
GLANCE
WE HAVE ONLY ALLIED WITH ENEMY NATIONS AND SPECIES...
...BECAUSE WE PLACE THE ENDS BEFORE THE MEANS.

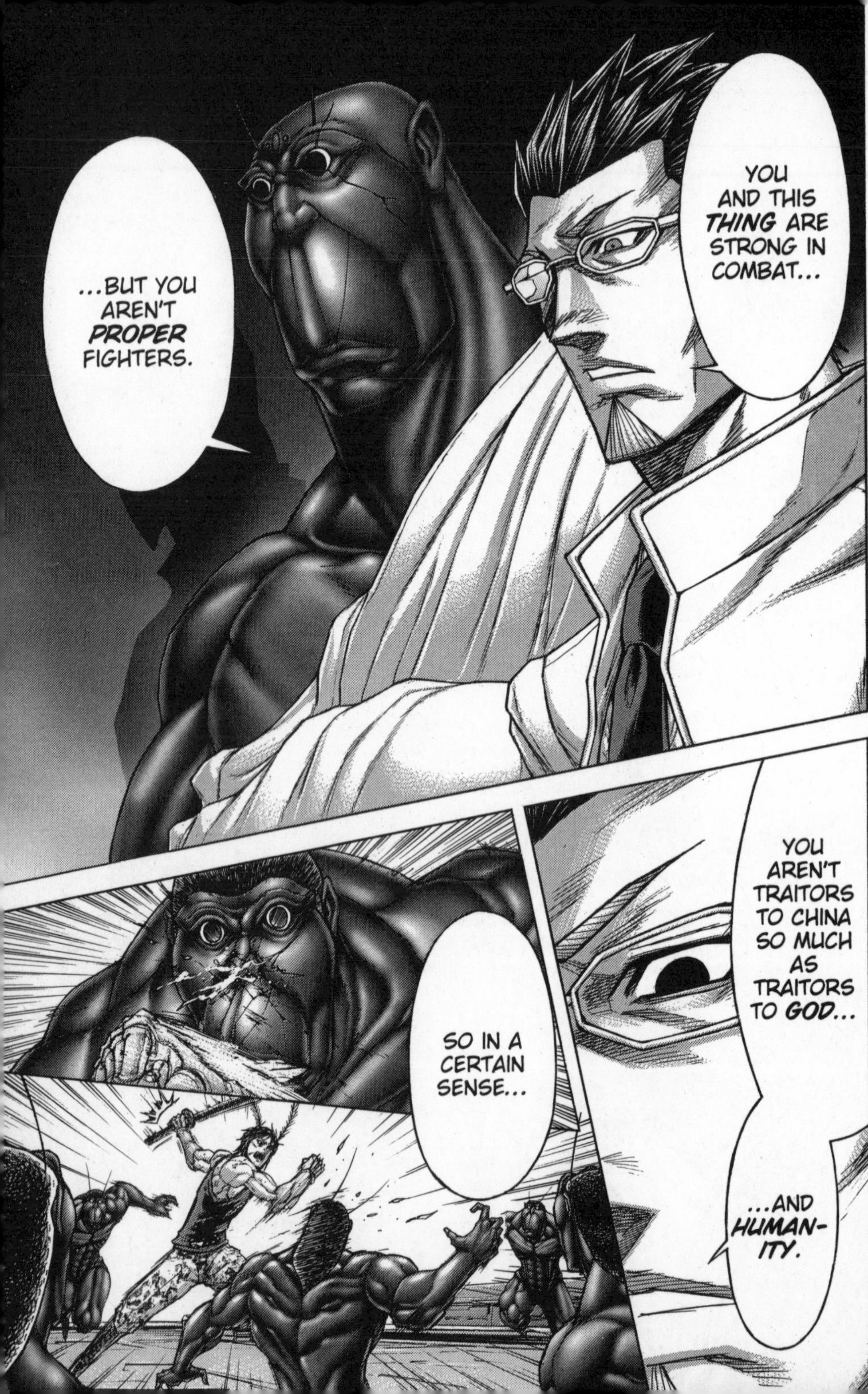
YOU AND THIS *THING* ARE STRONG IN COMBAT...
...BUT YOU AREN'T ***PROPER*** FIGHTERS.
SO IN A CERTAIN SENSE...
YOU AREN'T TRAITORS TO CHINA SO MUCH AS TRAITORS TO ***GOD***...
...AND ***HUMANITY***.

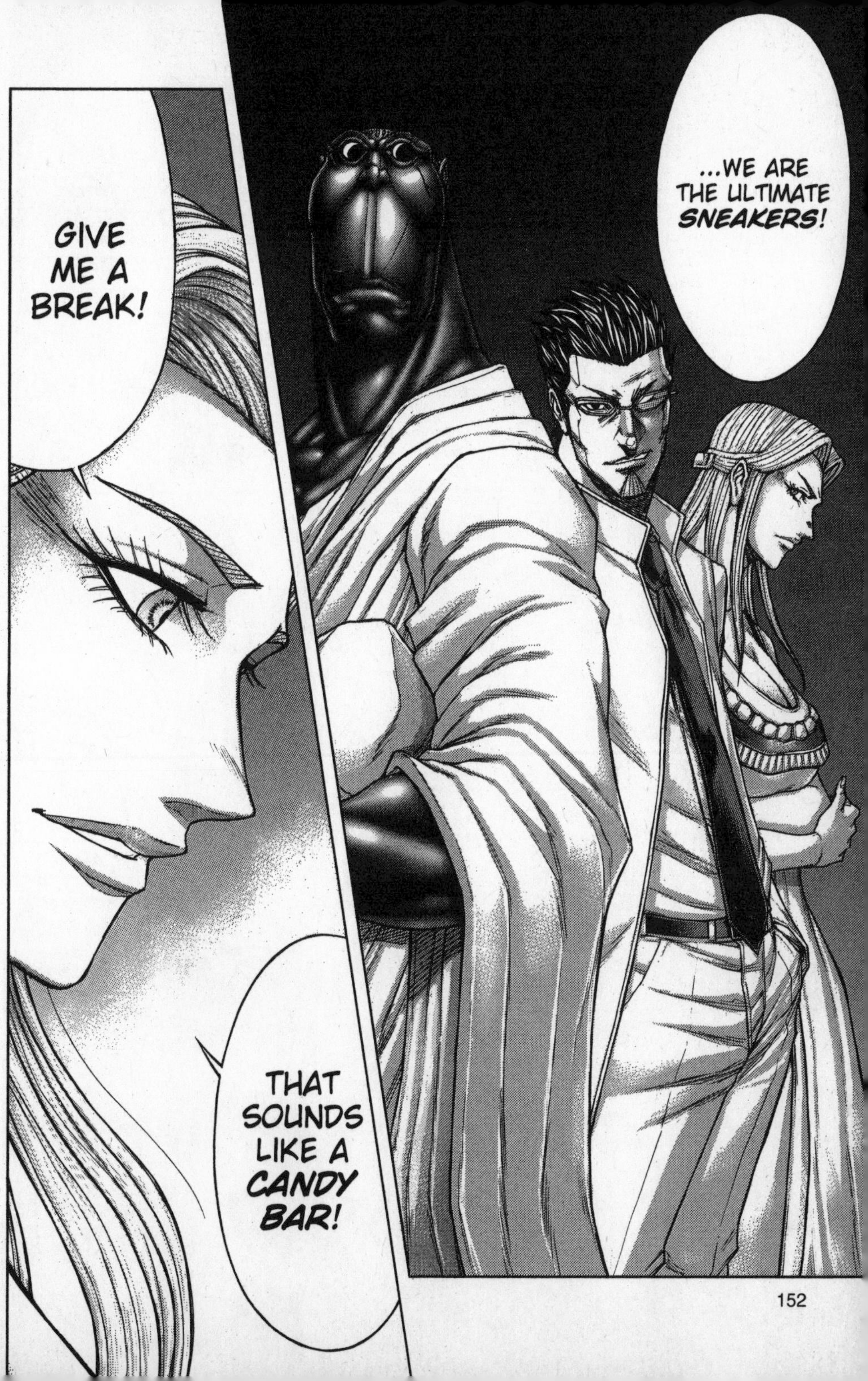
...WE ARE THE ULTIMATE SNEAKERS!
GIVE ME A BREAK!
THAT SOUNDS LIKE A CANDY BAR!

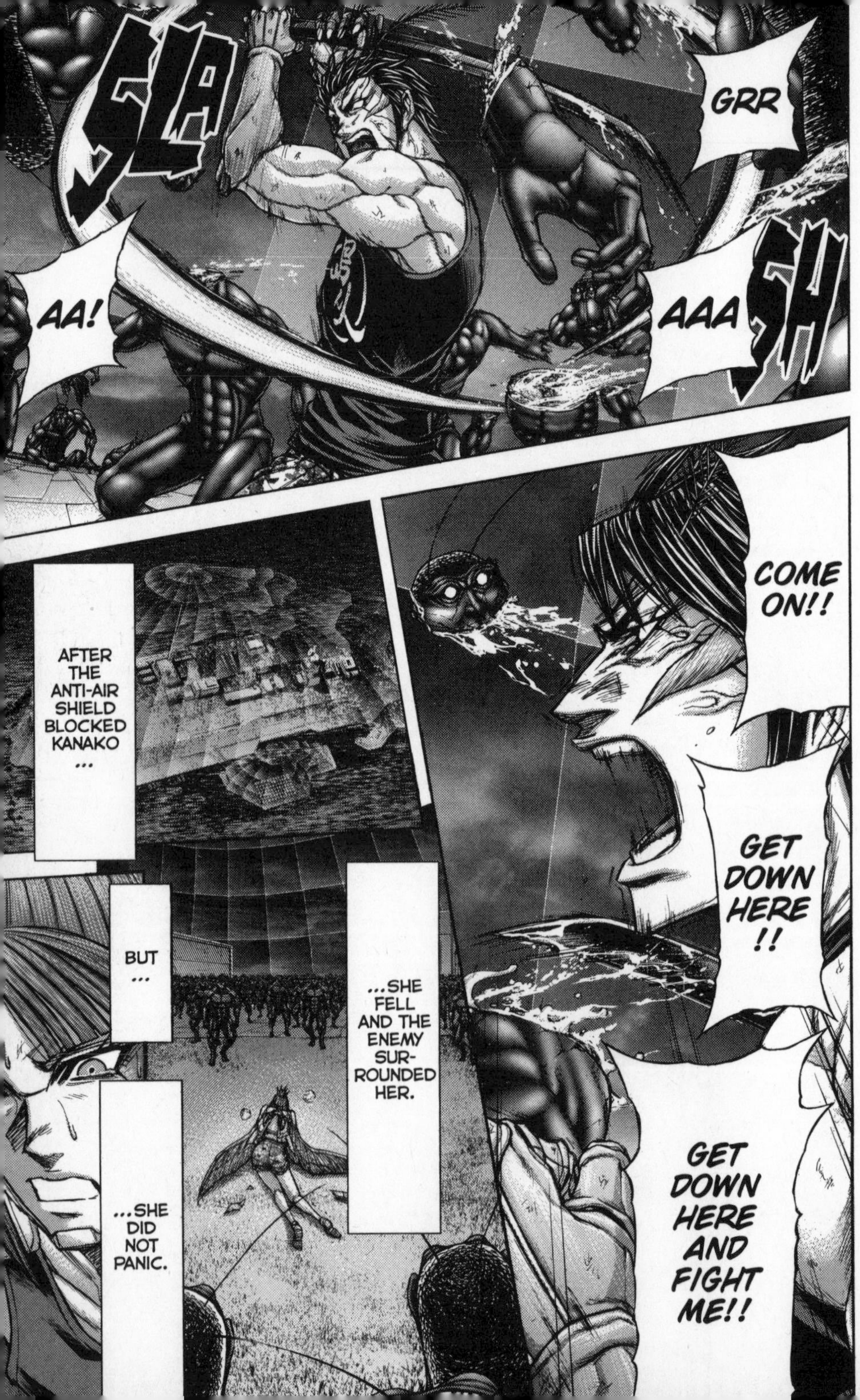
GRR
SH
AAA
SLA
AA!
COME ON!!
GET DOWN HERE!!
GET DOWN HERE AND FIGHT ME!!
AFTER THE ANTI-AIR SHIELD BLOCKED KANAKO...
...SHE FELL AND THE ENEMY SUR-ROUNDED HER.
BUT...
...SHE DID NOT PANIC.

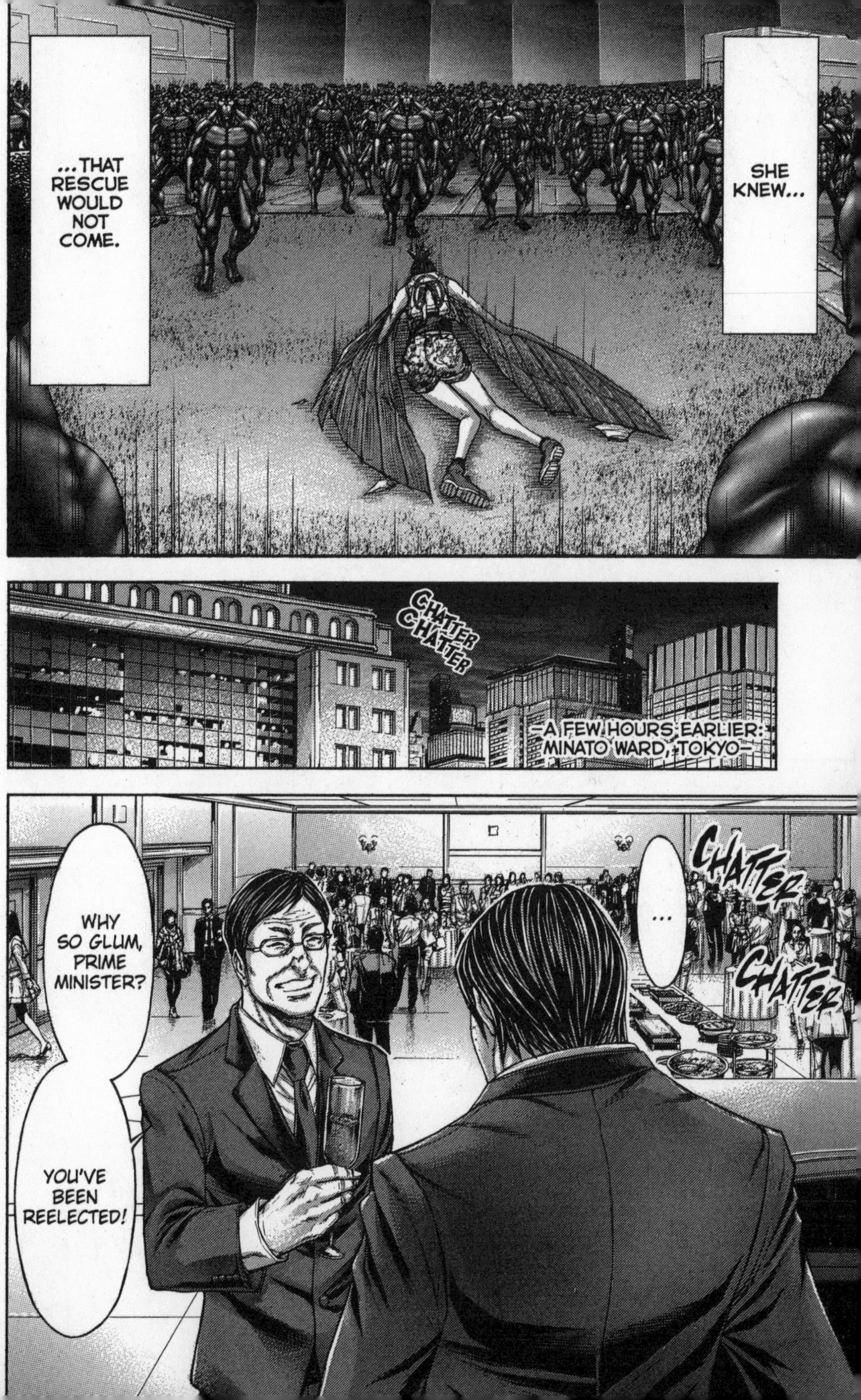
SHE KNEW...
...THAT RESCUE WOULD NOT COME.
CHATTER CHATTER
—A FEW HOURS EARLIER: MINATO WARD, TOKYO—
CHATTER CHATTER
...
WHY SO GLUM, PRIME MINISTER?
YOU'VE BEEN REELECTED!

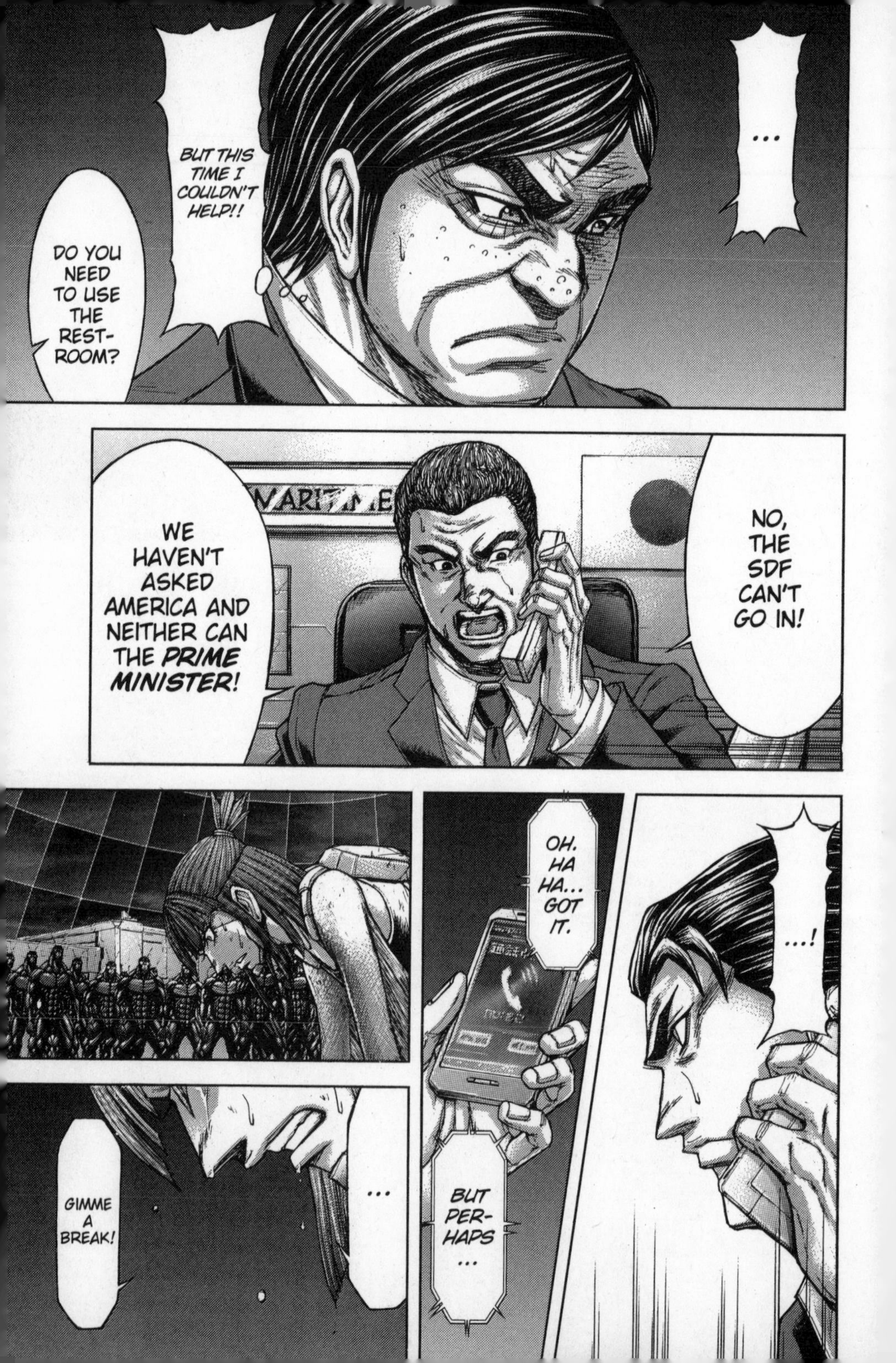
...
BUT THIS TIME I COULDN'T HELP!!
DO YOU NEED TO USE THE REST-ROOM?
NO, THE SDF CAN'T GO IN!
WE HAVEN'T ASKED AMERICA AND NEITHER CAN THE *PRIME MINISTER*!
...!
OH. HA HA... GOT IT.
BUT PER-HAPS ...
...
GIMME A BREAK!

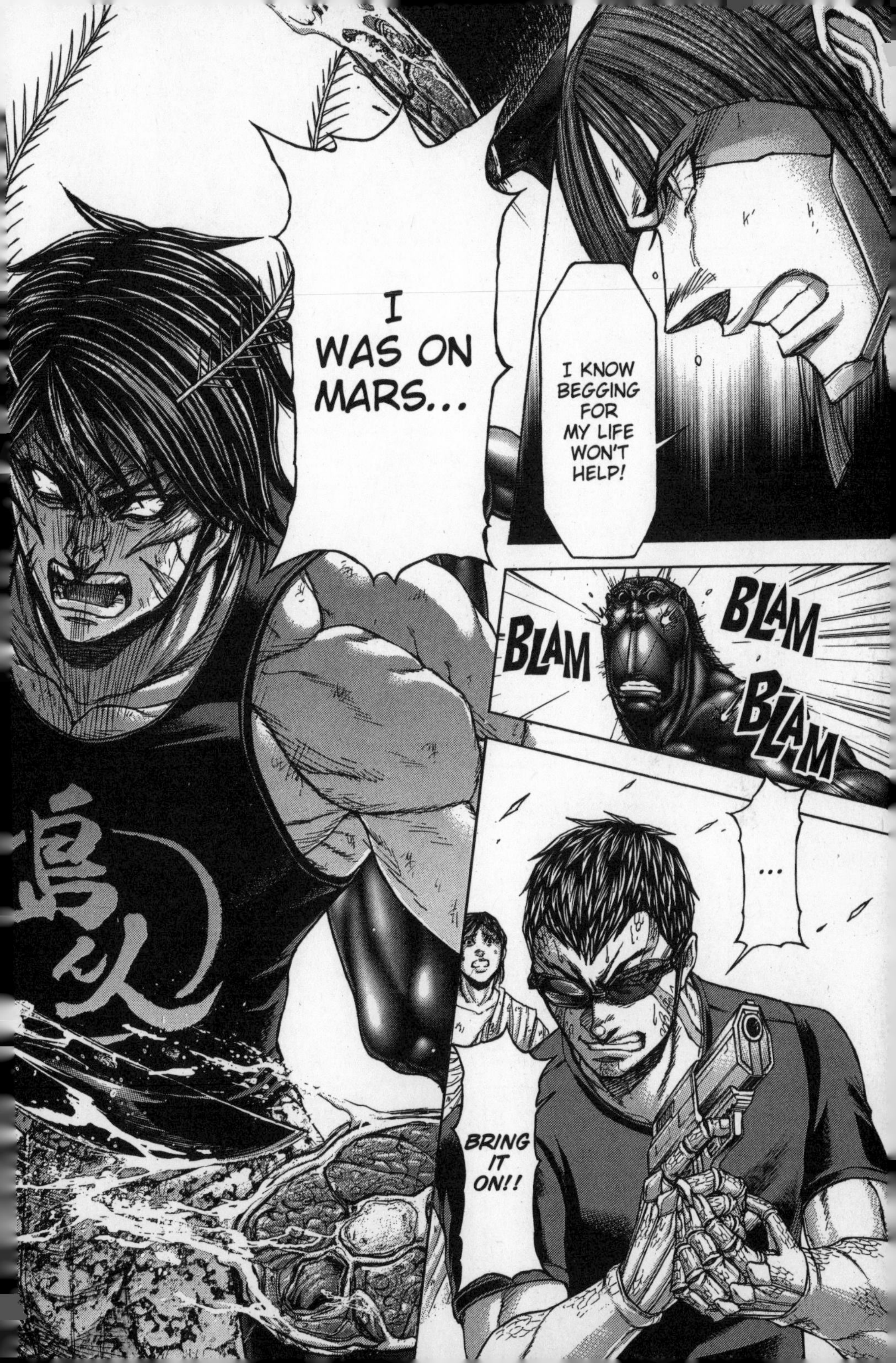
I KNOW BEGGING FOR MY LIFE WON'T HELP!
BLAM
BLAM
BLAM
BLAM
...
BRING IT ON!!
I WAS ON MARS...

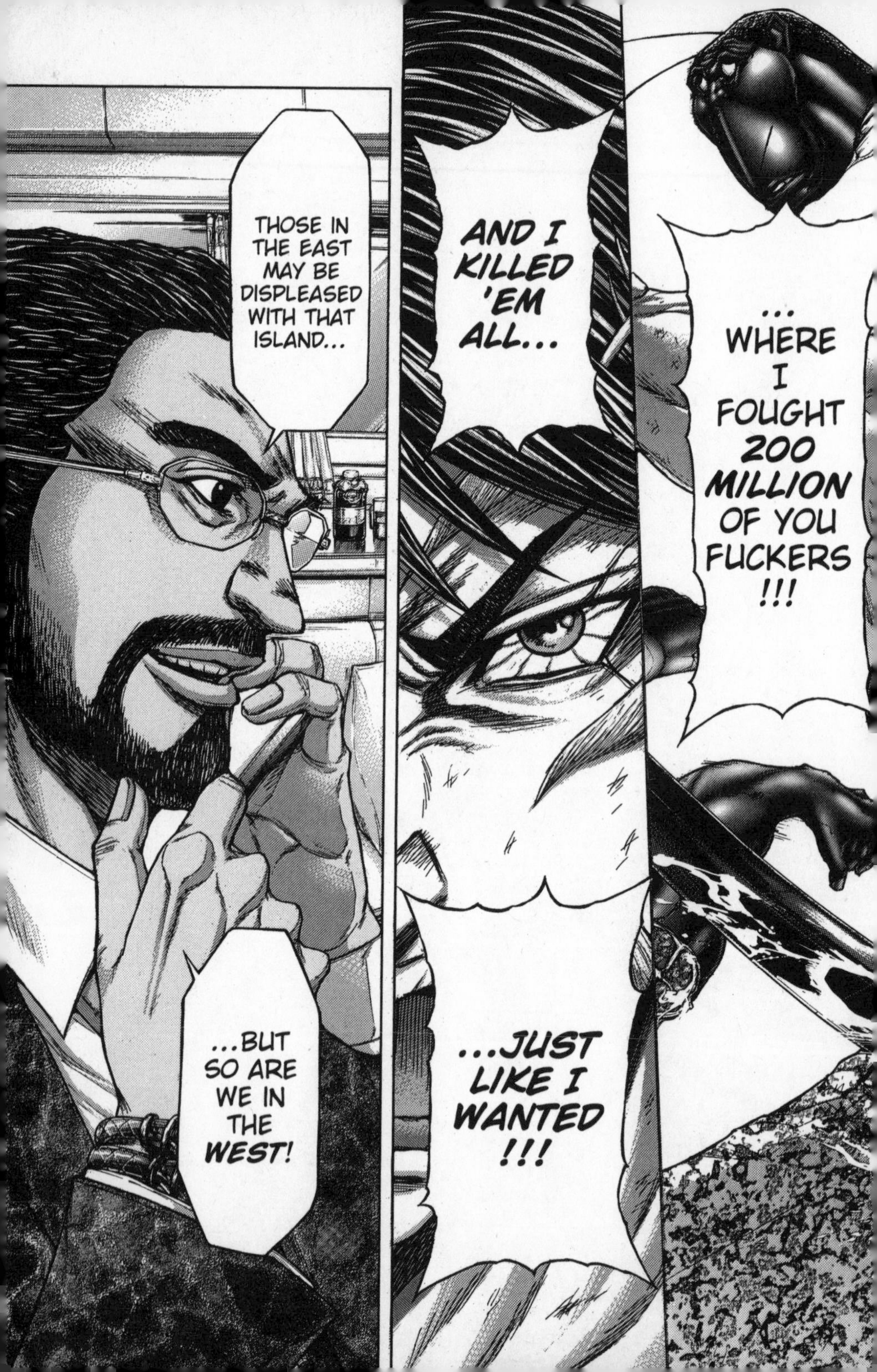
... WHERE I FOUGHT 200 MILLION OF YOU FUCKERS!!!
AND I KILLED 'EM ALL...
...JUST LIKE I WANTED!!!
THOSE IN THE EAST MAY BE DISPLEASED WITH THAT ISLAND...
...BUT SO ARE WE IN THE WEST!

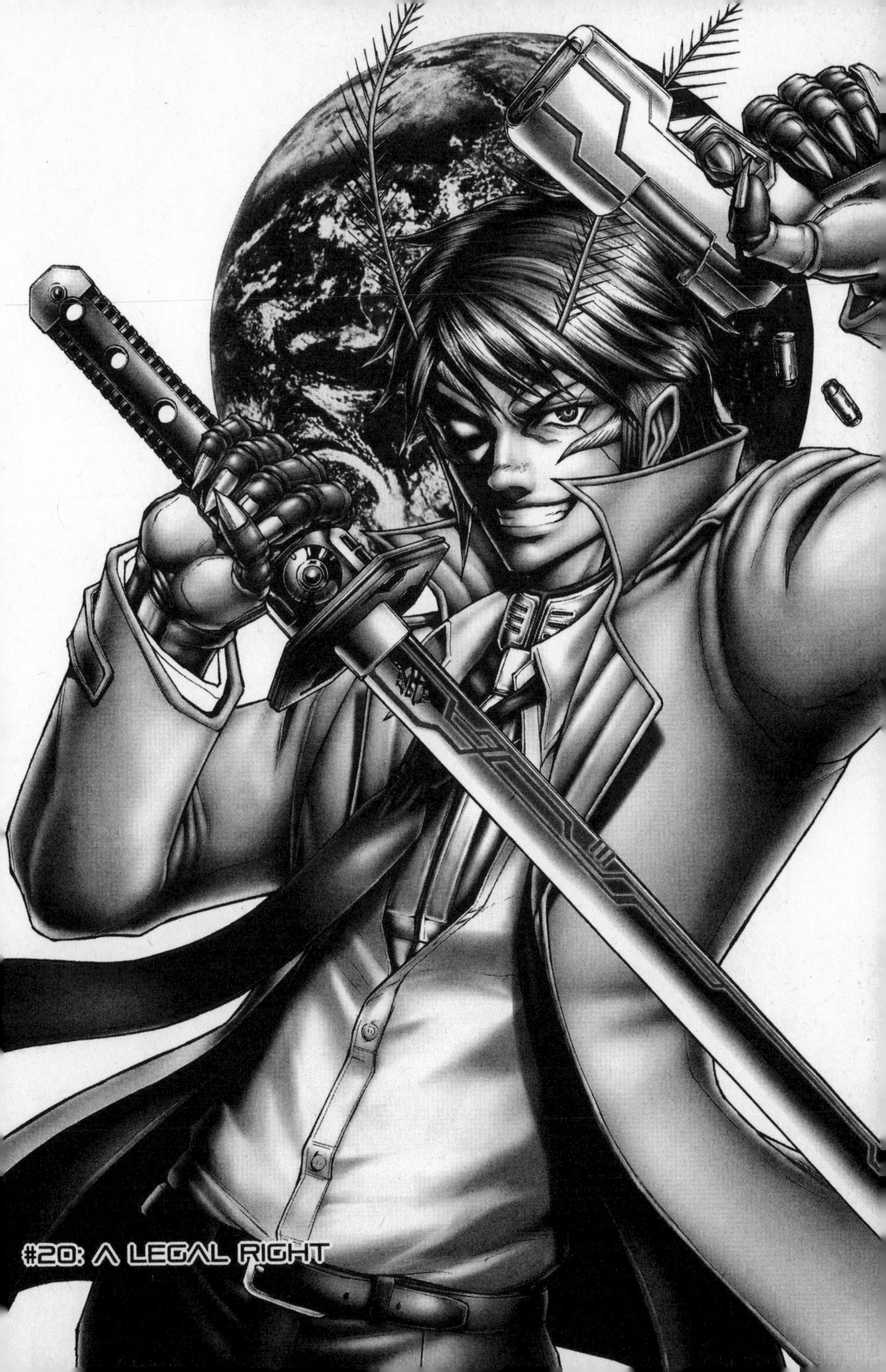
#20: A LEGAL RIGHT

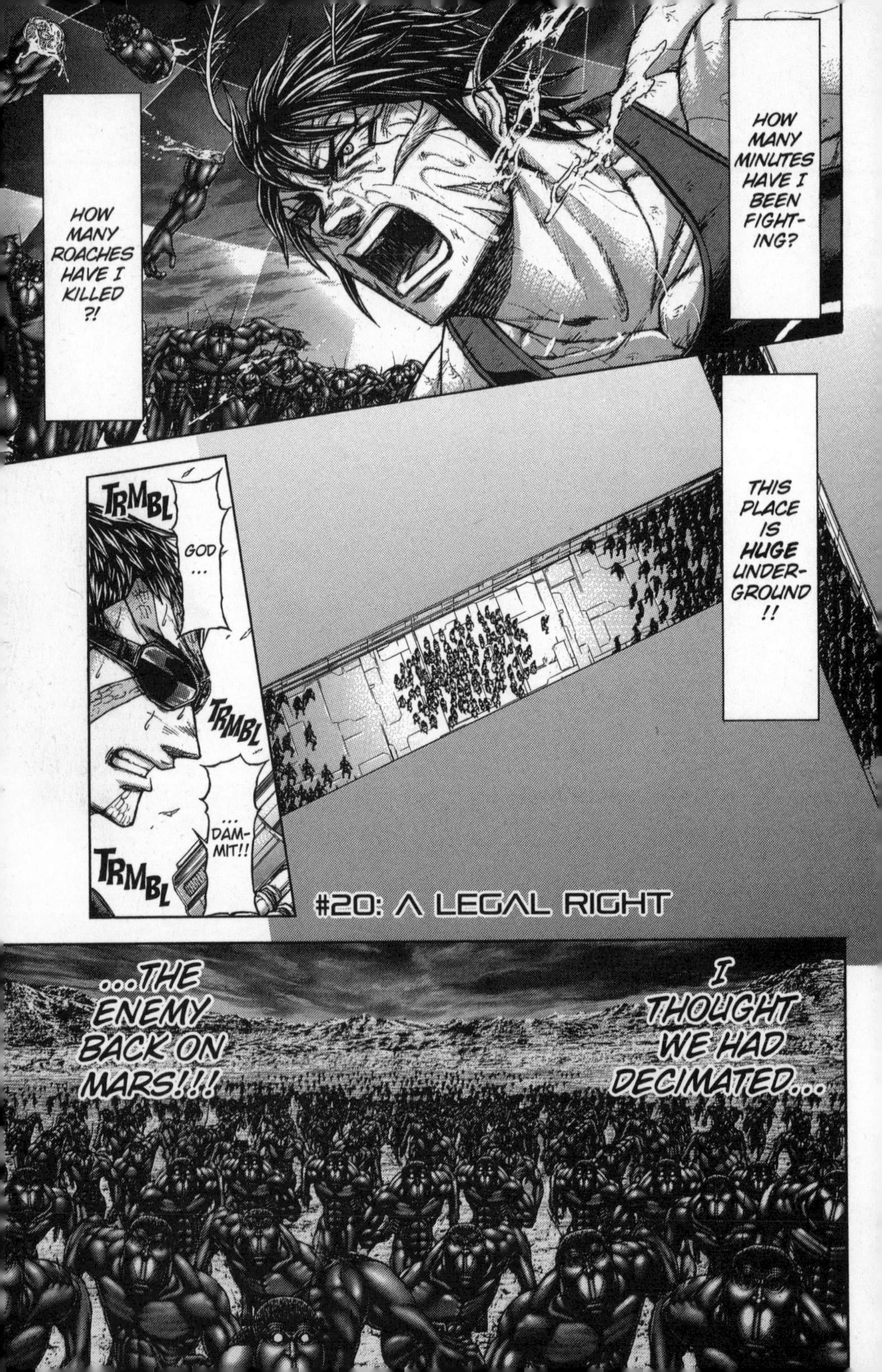
HOW MANY MINUTES HAVE I BEEN FIGHT-ING?
HOW MANY ROACHES HAVE I KILLED ?!
THIS PLACE IS HUGE UNDER-GROUND !!
TRMBL
GOD ...
TRMBL
... DAM-MIT!!
TRMBL
#20: A LEGAL RIGHT
I THOUGHT WE HAD DECIMATED...
...THE ENEMY BACK ON MARS!!!

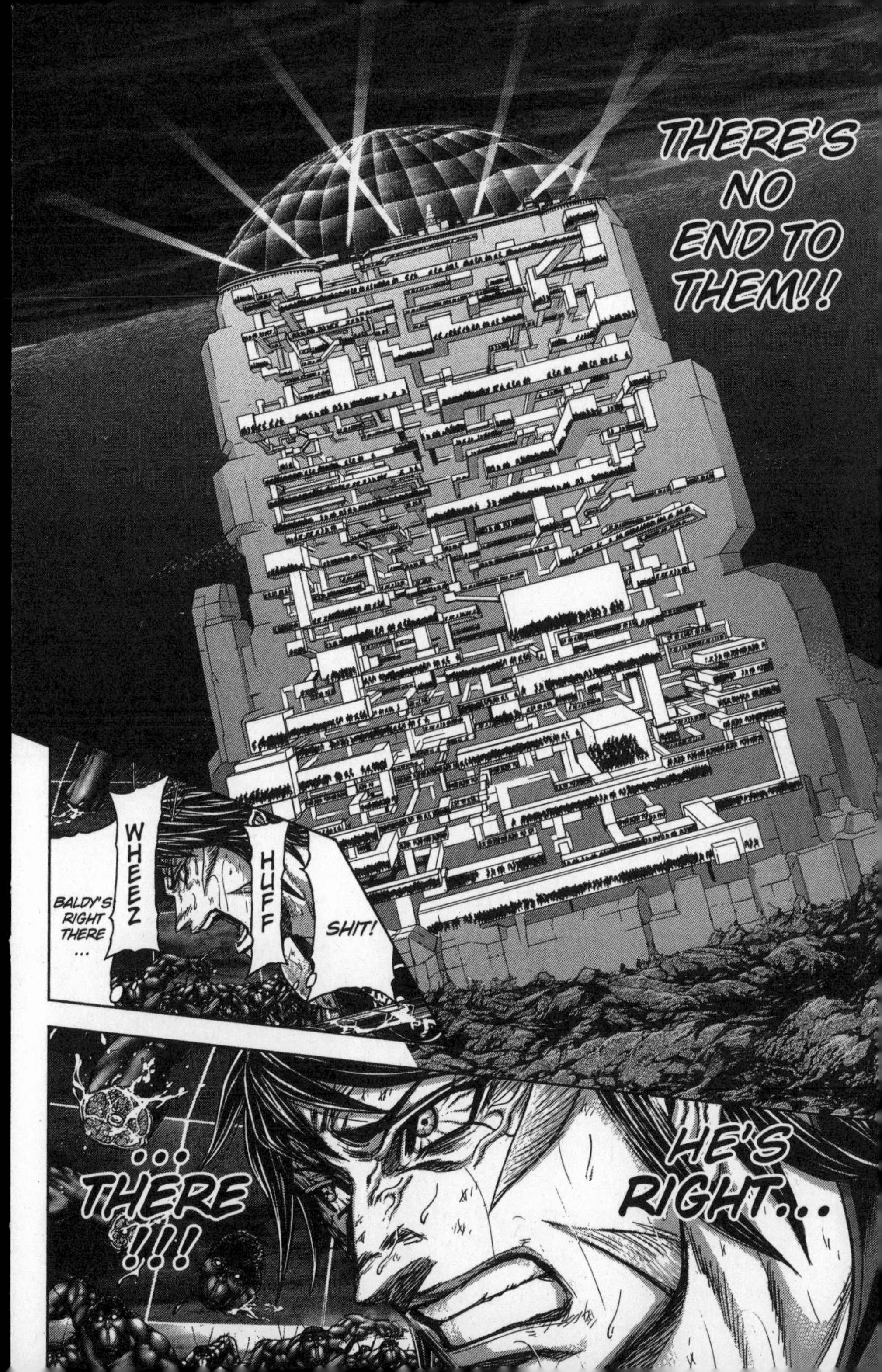
THERE'S NO END TO THEM!!
HUFF
SHIT!
WHEEZ
BALDY'S RIGHT THERE ...
HE'S RIGHT...
...THERE!!!

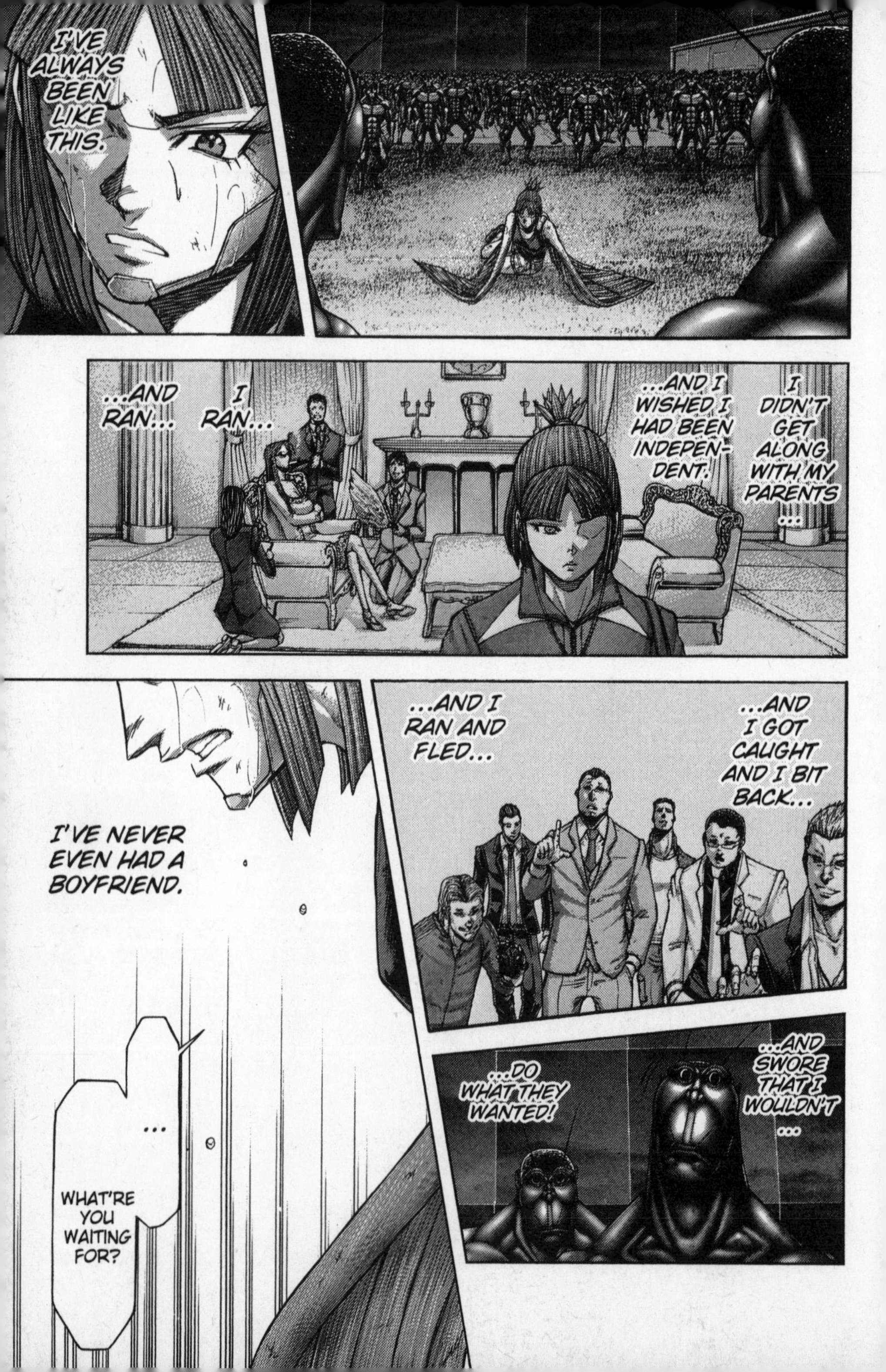
I'VE ALWAYS BEEN LIKE THIS.
I DIDN'T GET ALONG WITH MY PARENTS...
...AND I WISHED I HAD BEEN INDEPEN-DENT.
I RAN...
...AND RAN...
...AND I GOT CAUGHT AND I BIT BACK...
...AND I RAN AND FLED...
...AND SWORE THAT I WOULDN'T...
...DO WHAT THEY WANTED!
I'VE NEVER EVEN HAD A BOYFRIEND.
...
WHAT'RE YOU WAITING FOR?

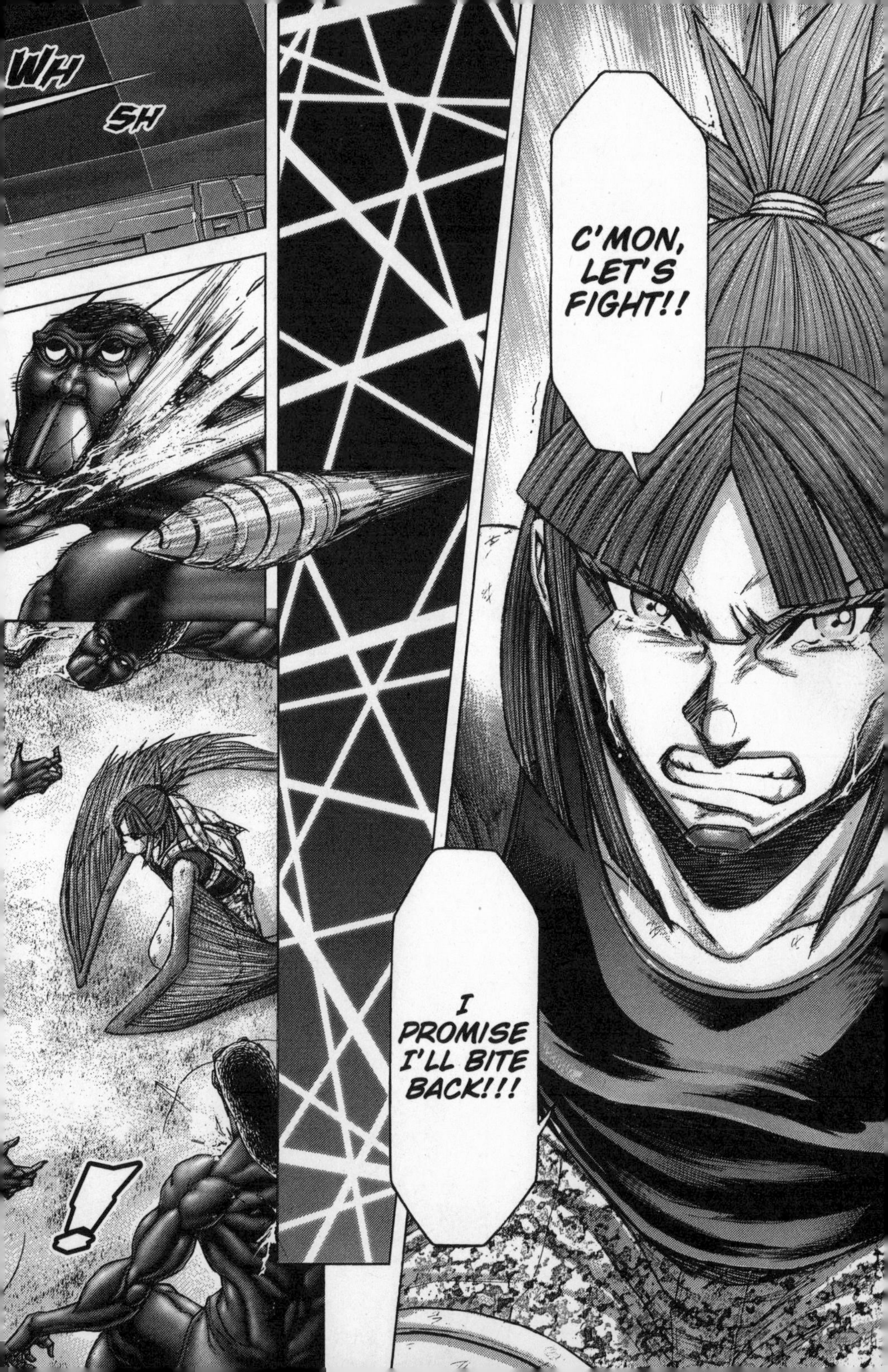
C'MON, LET'S FIGHT!!
I PROMISE I'LL BITE BACK!!!
WH
SH
!

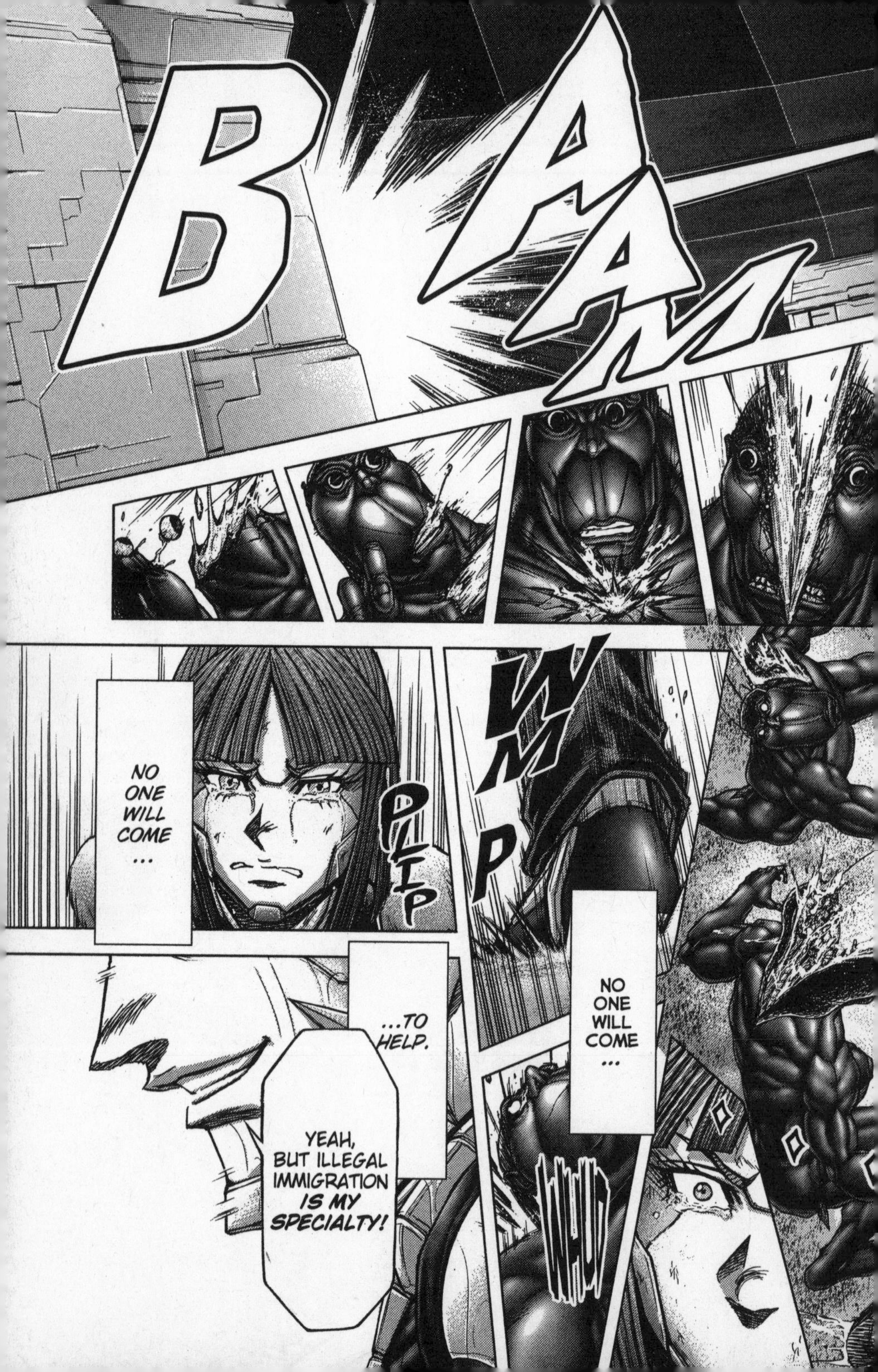
BAM
NO ONE WILL COME...
PLIP
NO ONE WILL COME...
WHUD
...TO HELP.
YEAH, BUT ILLEGAL IMMIGRATION IS MY SPECIALTY!

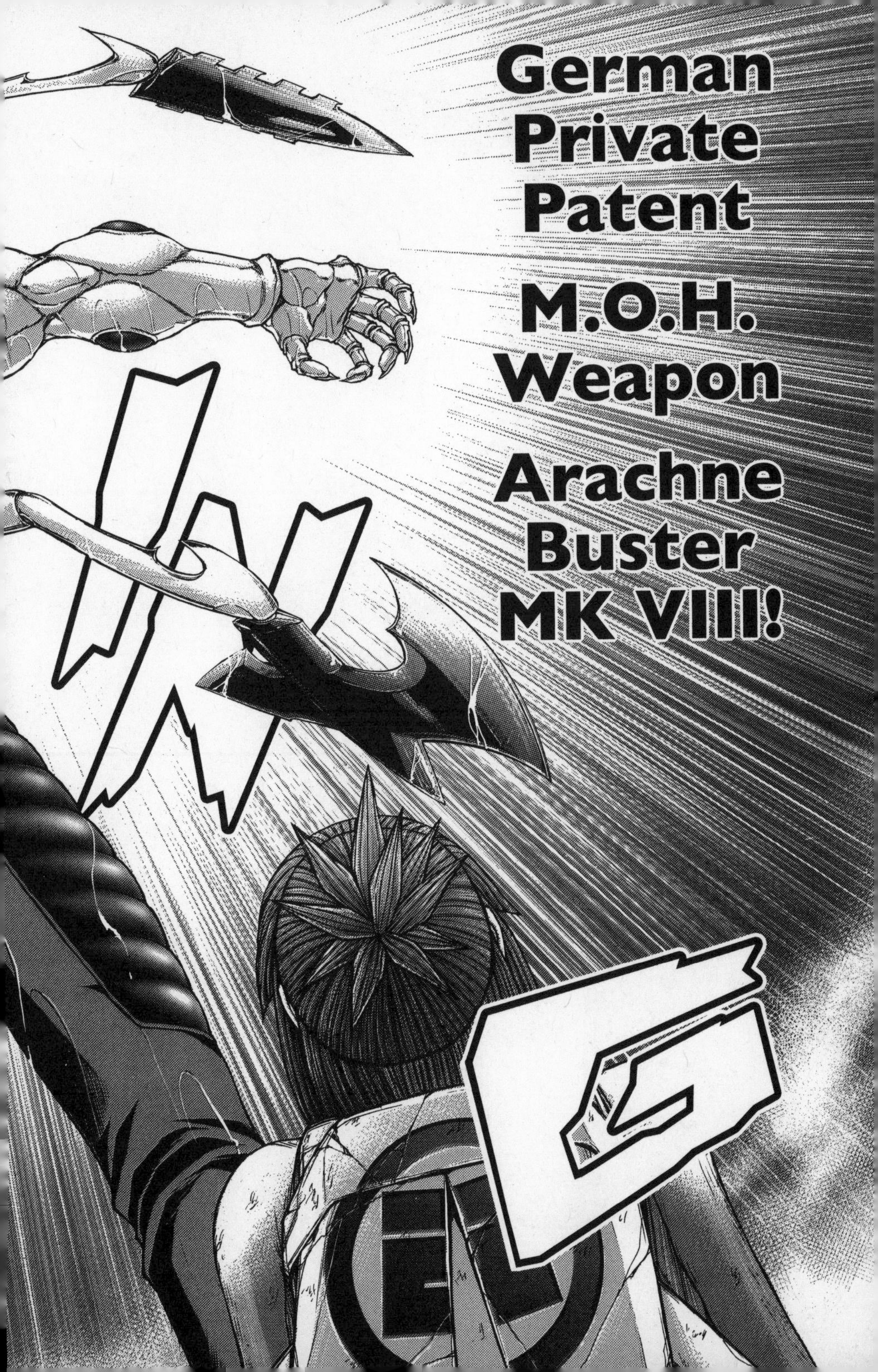
German Private Patent
M.O.H. Weapon
Arachne Buster MK VIII!

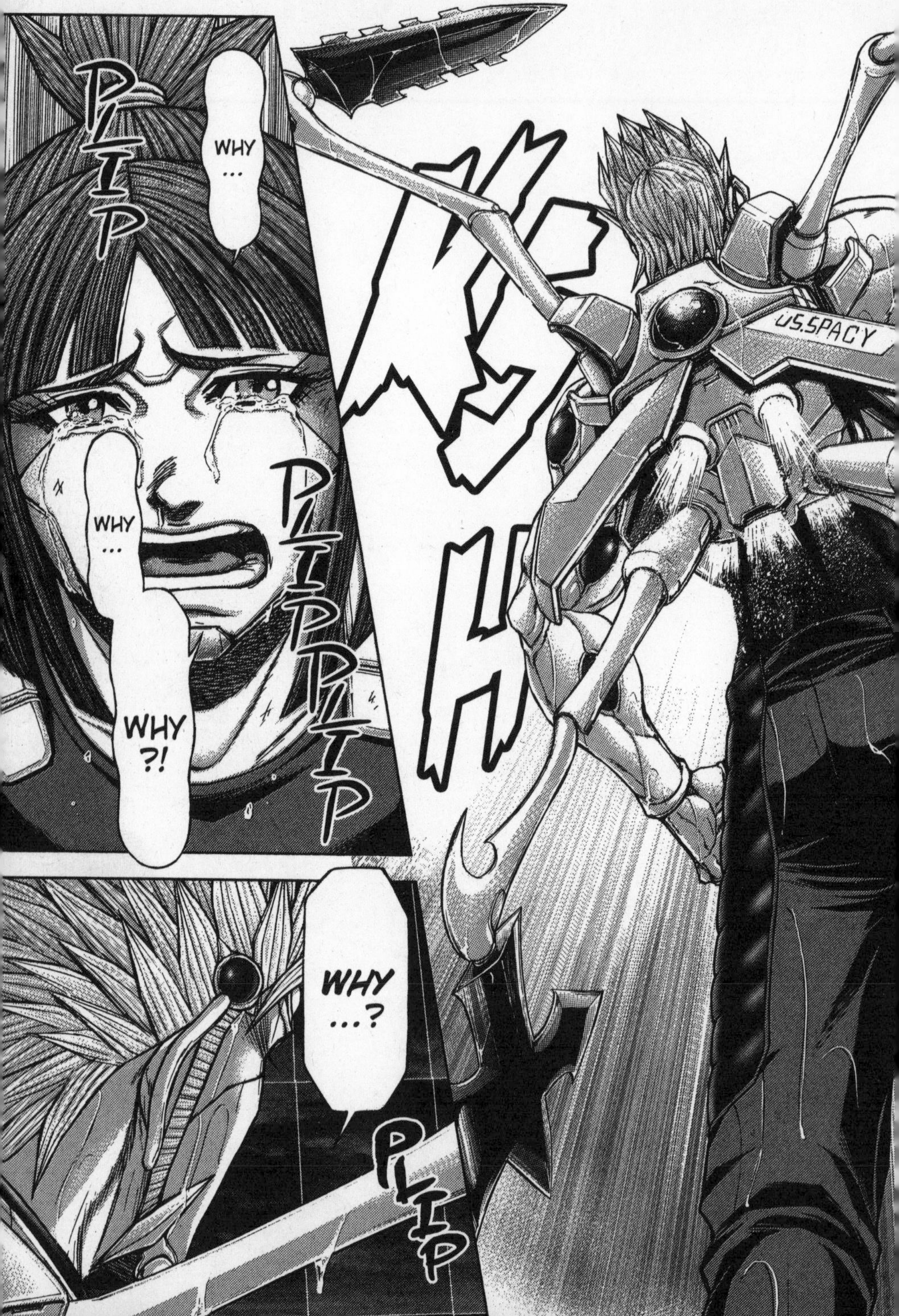
PLIP
WHY ...
WHY ...
WHY ?!
PLIPPLIP
WHY ...?
PLIP

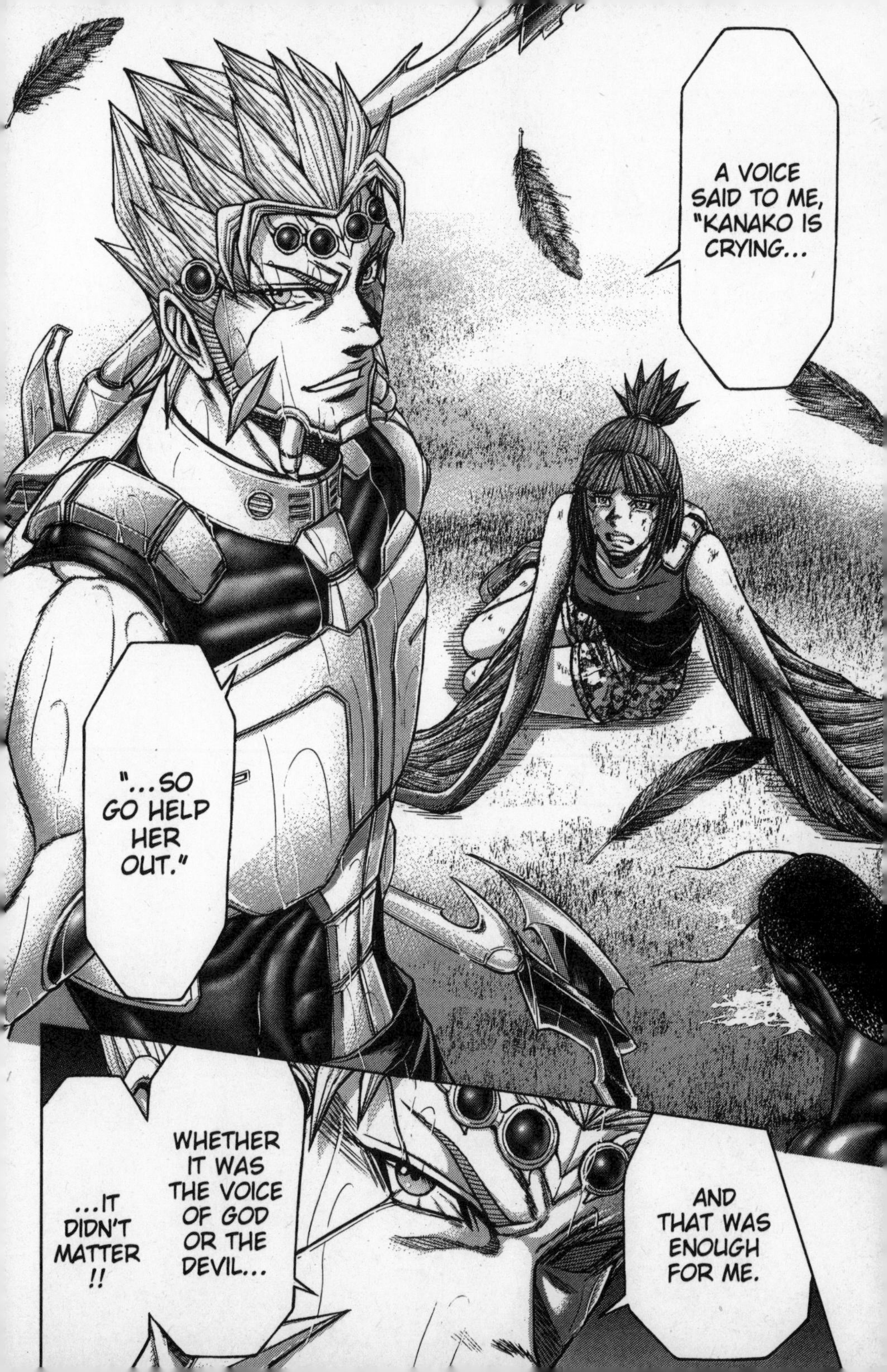
A VOICE SAID TO ME, "KANAKO IS CRYING...
"...SO GO HELP HER OUT."
AND THAT WAS ENOUGH FOR ME.
WHETHER IT WAS THE VOICE OF GOD OR THE DEVIL...
...IT DIDN'T MATTER!!

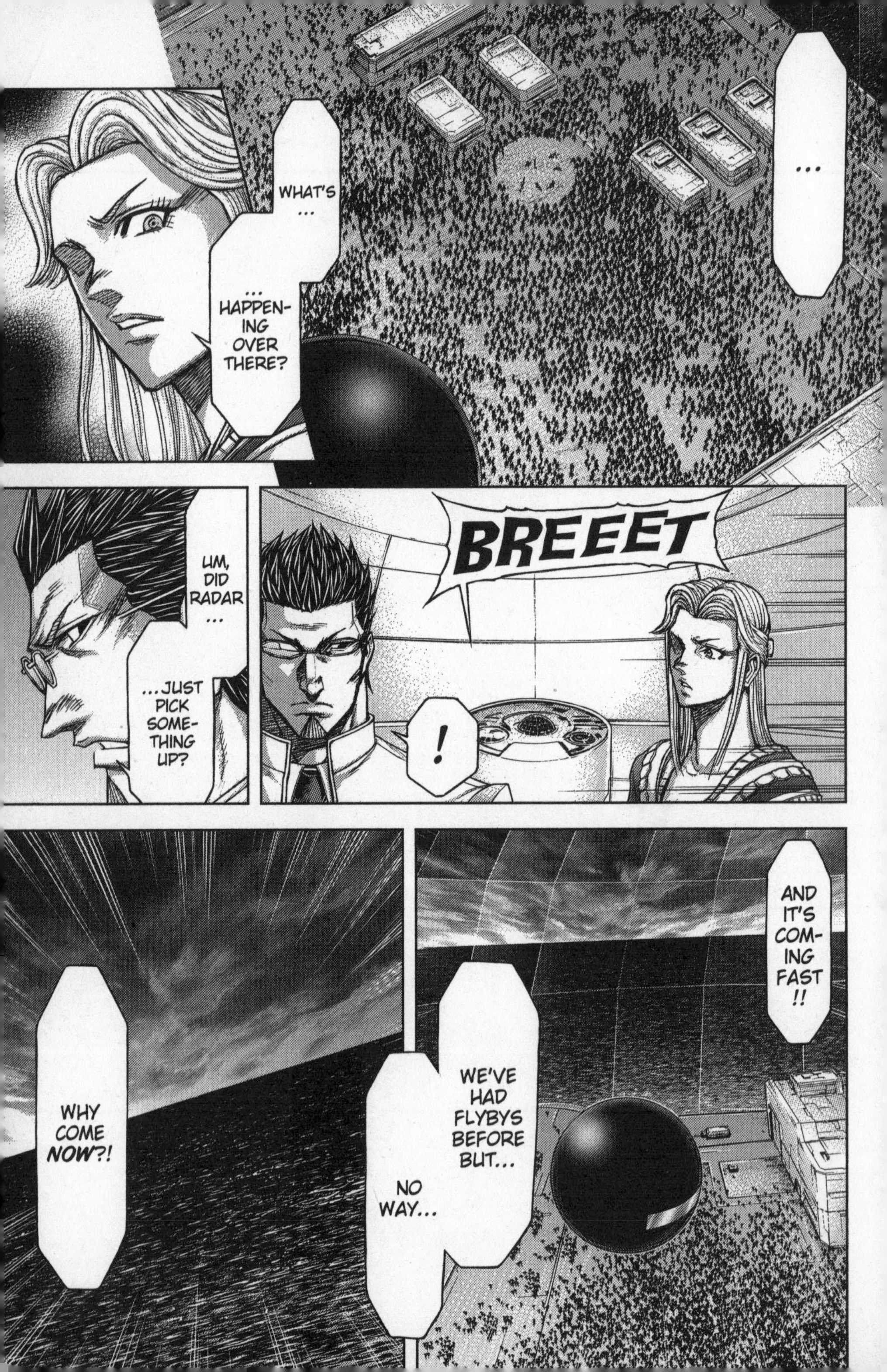
...
WHAT'S ...
... HAPPENING OVER THERE?
BREEET
!
UM, DID RADAR ...
...JUST PICK SOMETHING UP?
AND IT'S COMING FAST!!
WE'VE HAD FLYBYS BEFORE BUT...
NO WAY...
WHY COME *NOW*?!

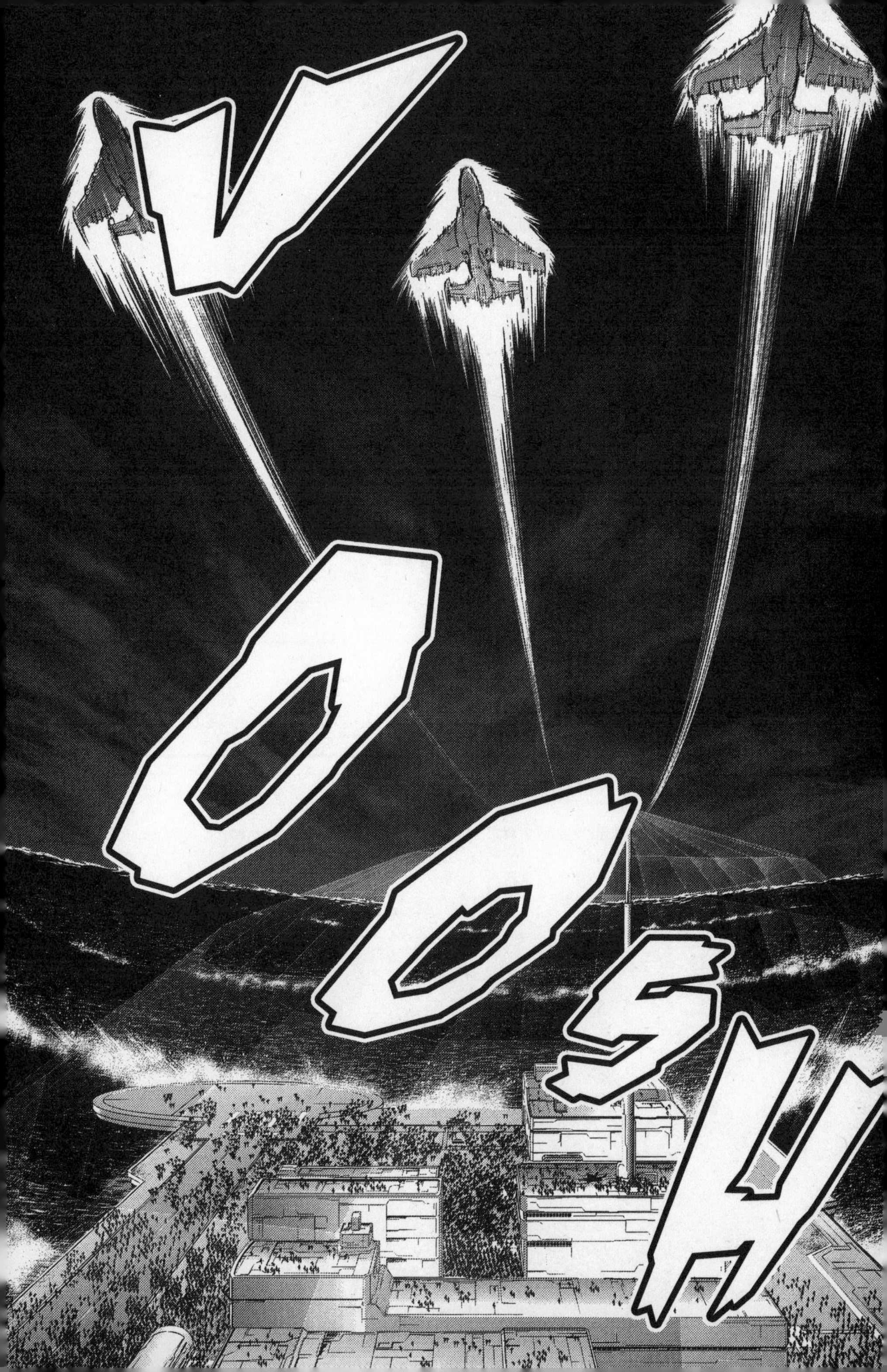
VOOSH

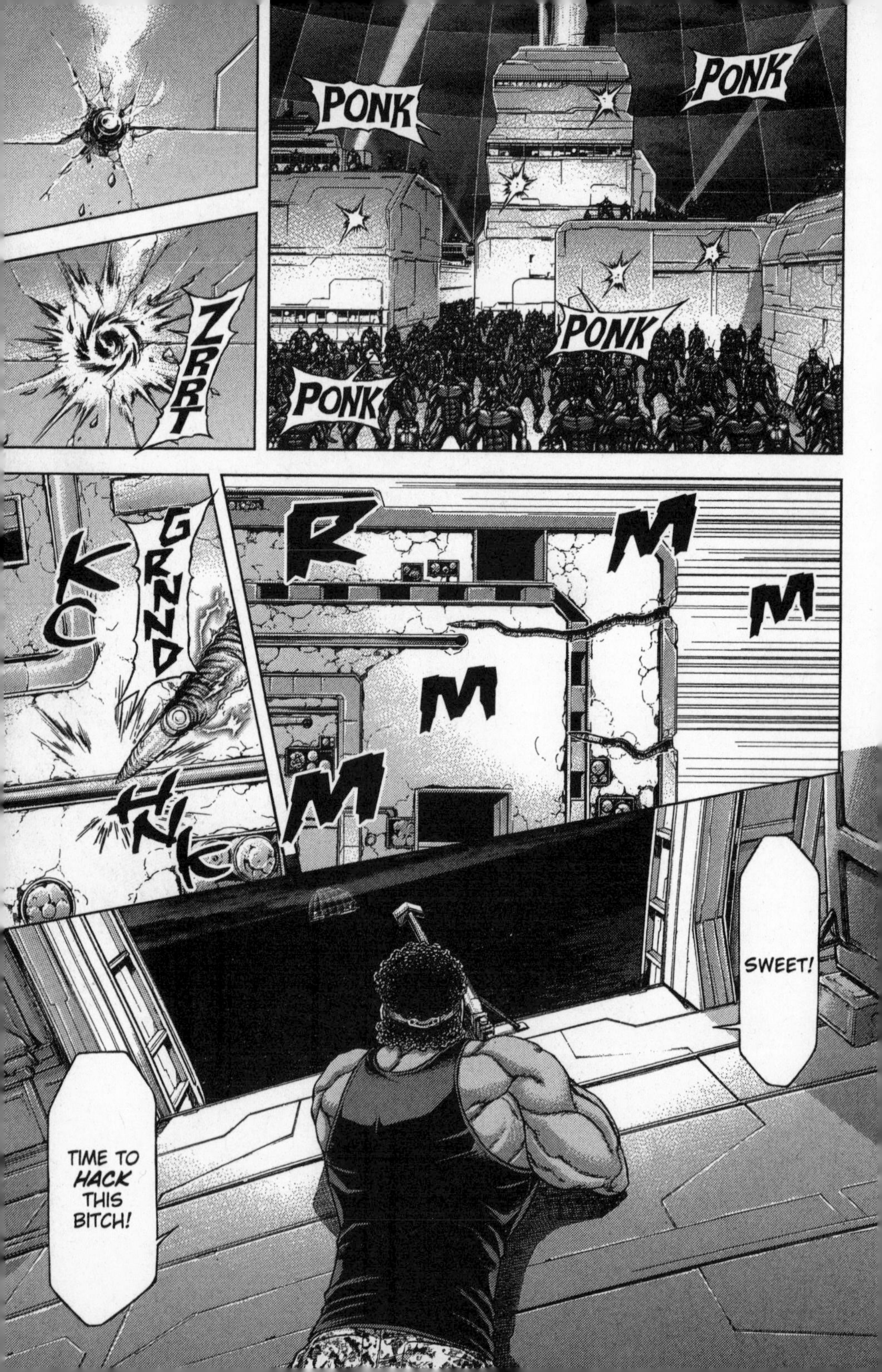
PONK
PONK
PONK
PONK
ZRRRT
RMMMM
GRNND
KC
HNK
SWEET!
TIME TO *HACK* THIS BITCH!

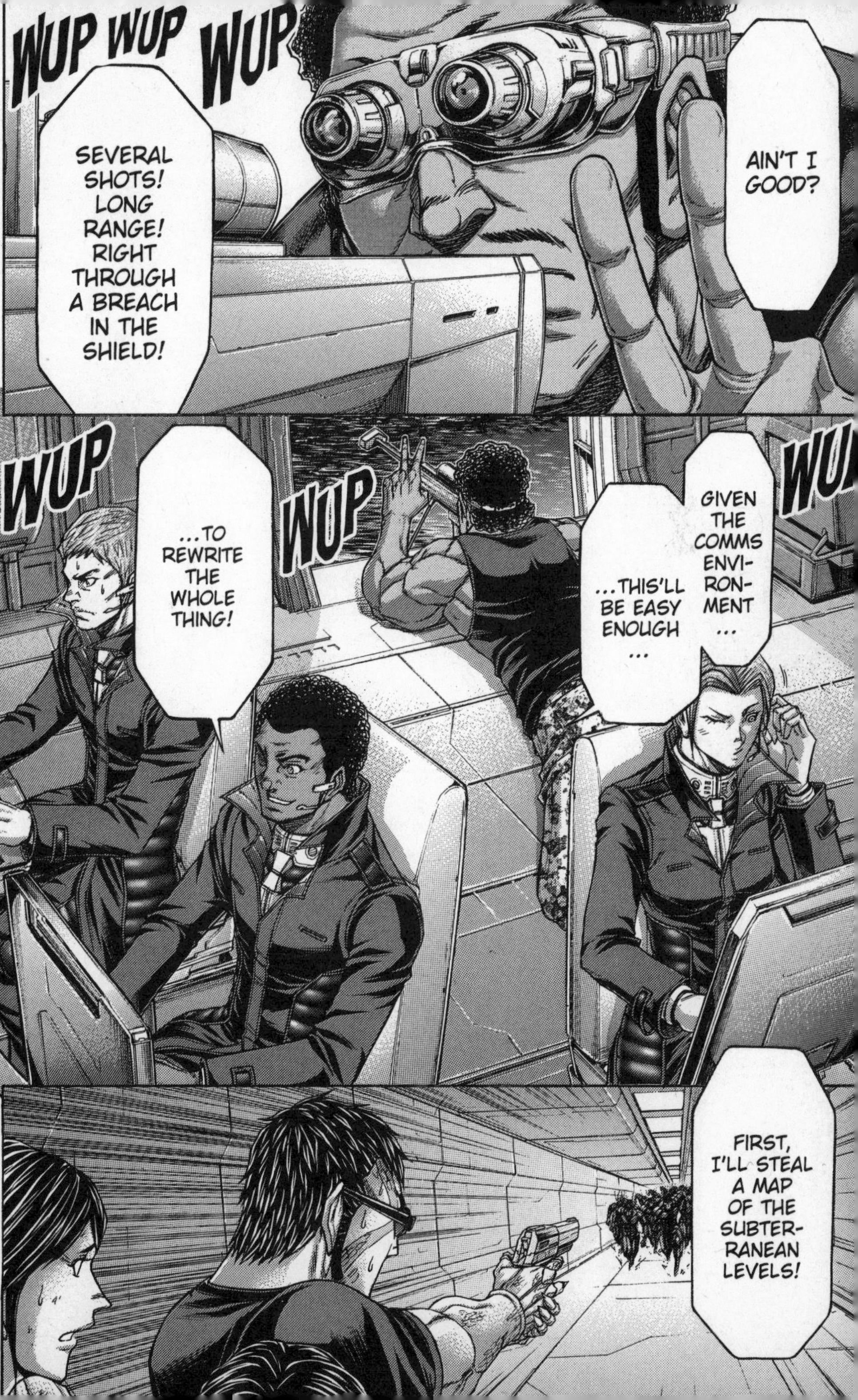
AIN'T I GOOD?
WUP WUP WUP
SEVERAL SHOTS! LONG RANGE! RIGHT THROUGH A BREACH IN THE SHIELD!
GIVEN THE COMMS ENVIRONMENT...
...THIS'LL BE EASY ENOUGH...
WUP
WUP
...TO REWRITE THE WHOLE THING!
FIRST, I'LL STEAL A MAP OF THE SUBTERRANEAN LEVELS!

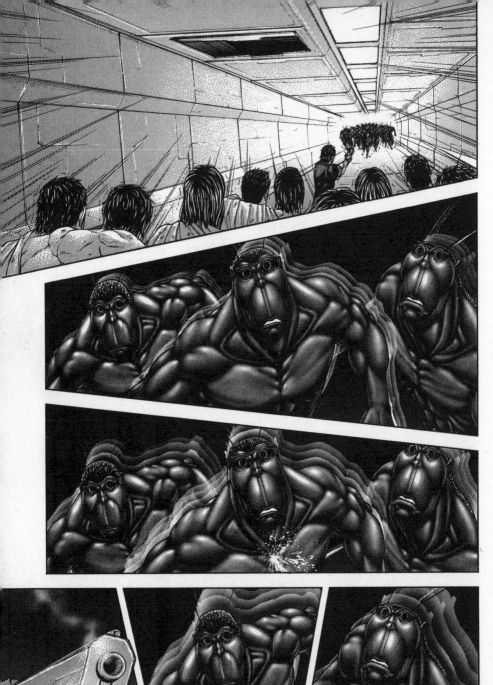

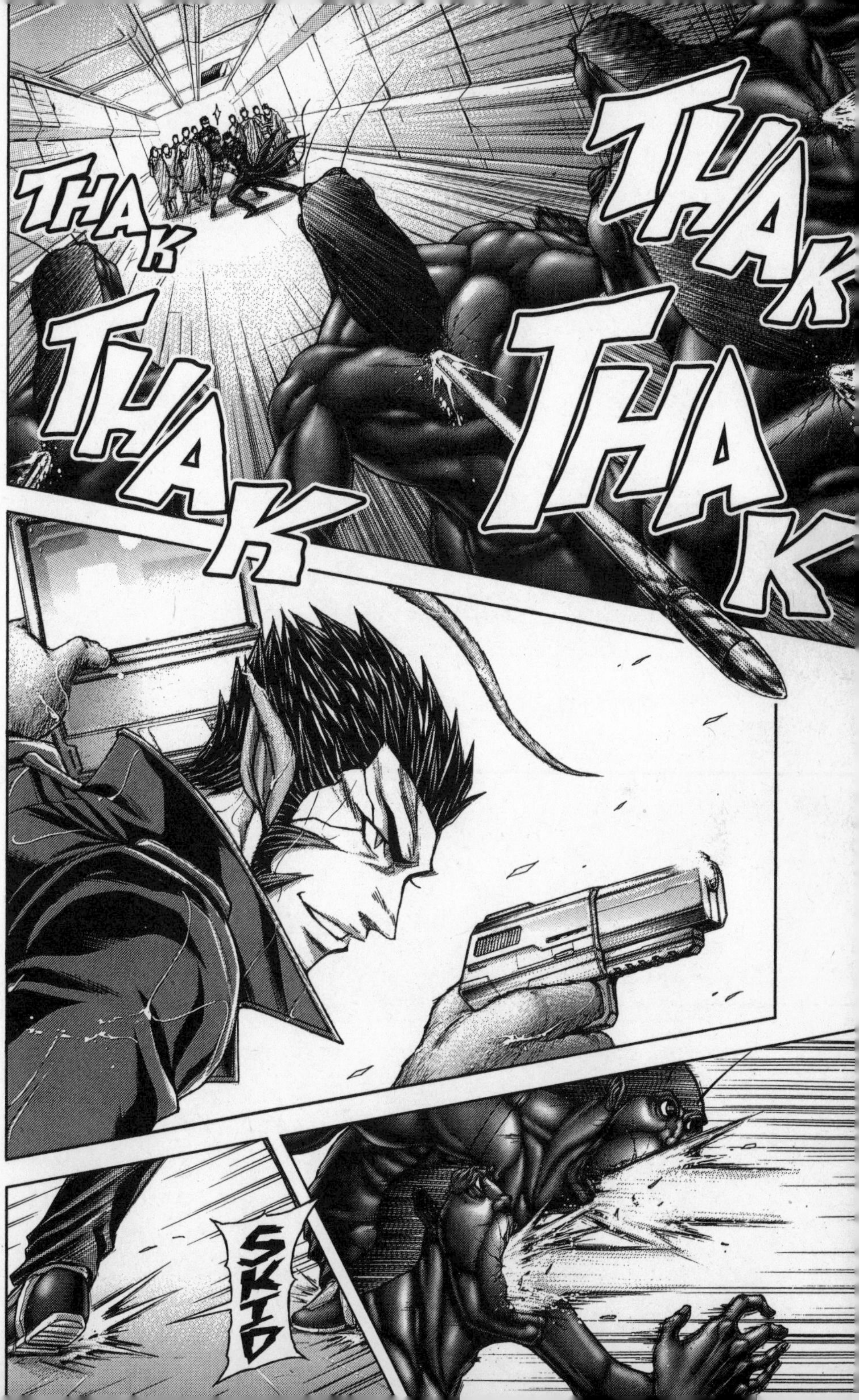
THAK
THAK
THAK
THAK
SKID

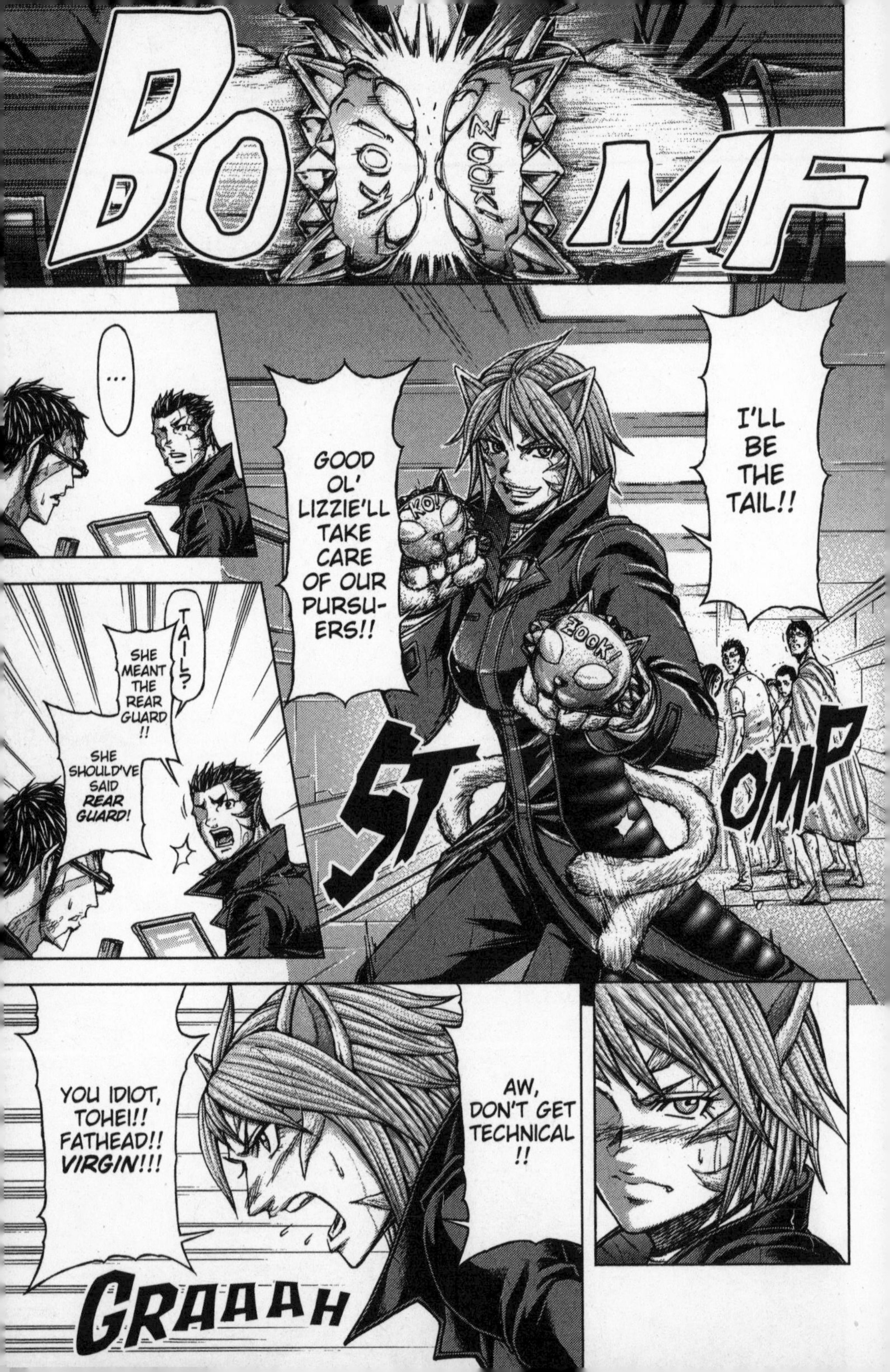
BOOMF
KO!
ZOOK!
I'LL BE THE TAIL!!
GOOD OL' LIZZIE'LL TAKE CARE OF OUR PURSU-ERS!!
STOMP
ZOOK!
KO!
...
TAIL?
SHE MEANT THE REAR GUARD!!
SHE SHOULD'VE SAID *REAR GUARD!*
AW, DON'T GET TECHNICAL!!
YOU IDIOT, TOHEI!! FATHEAD!! *VIRGIN!!!*
GRAAAH

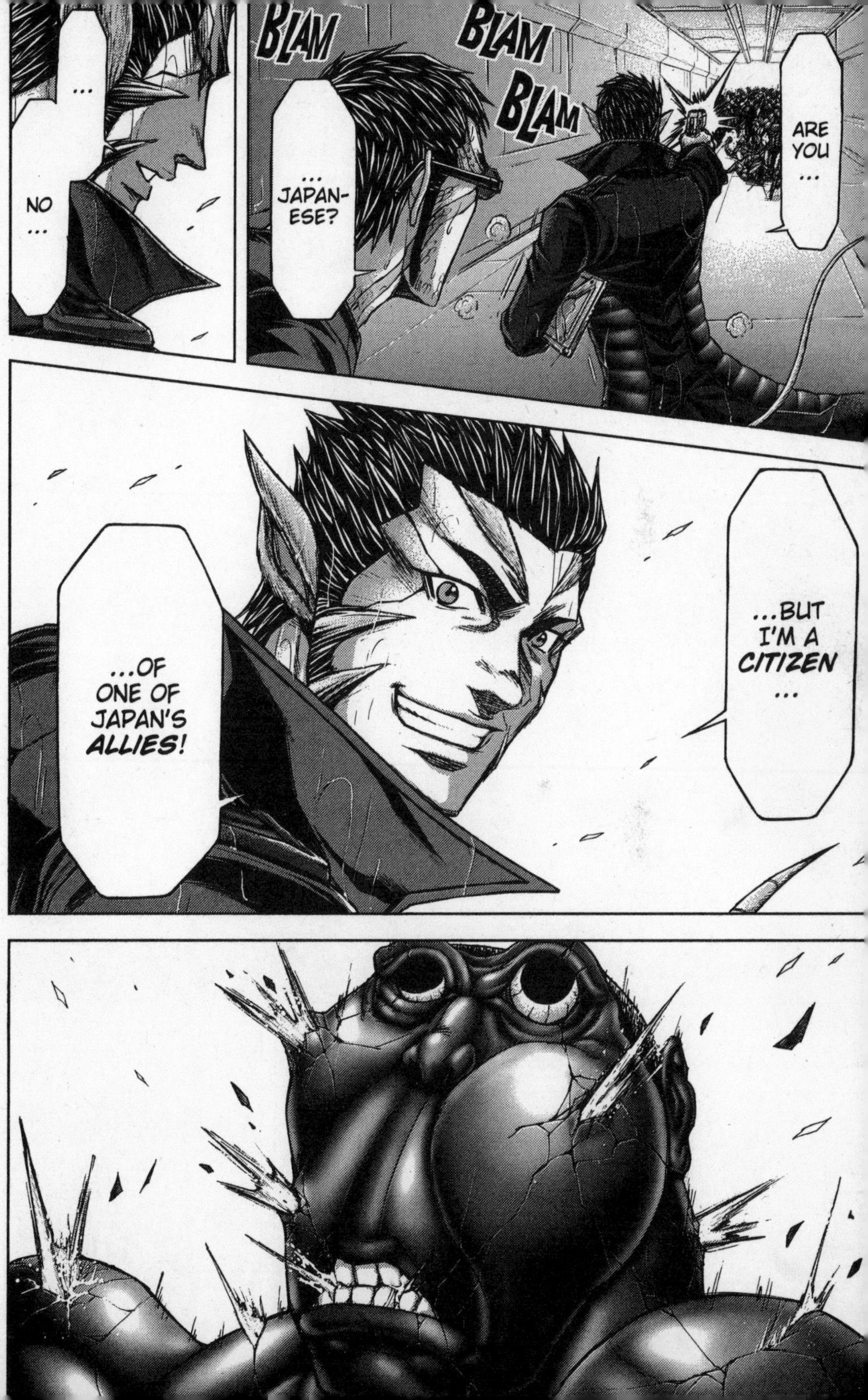
ARE YOU ...
BLAM
BLAM
BLAM
BLAM
... JAPAN-ESE?
...
NO ...
...BUT I'M A *CITIZEN* ...
...OF ONE OF JAPAN'S *ALLIES!*

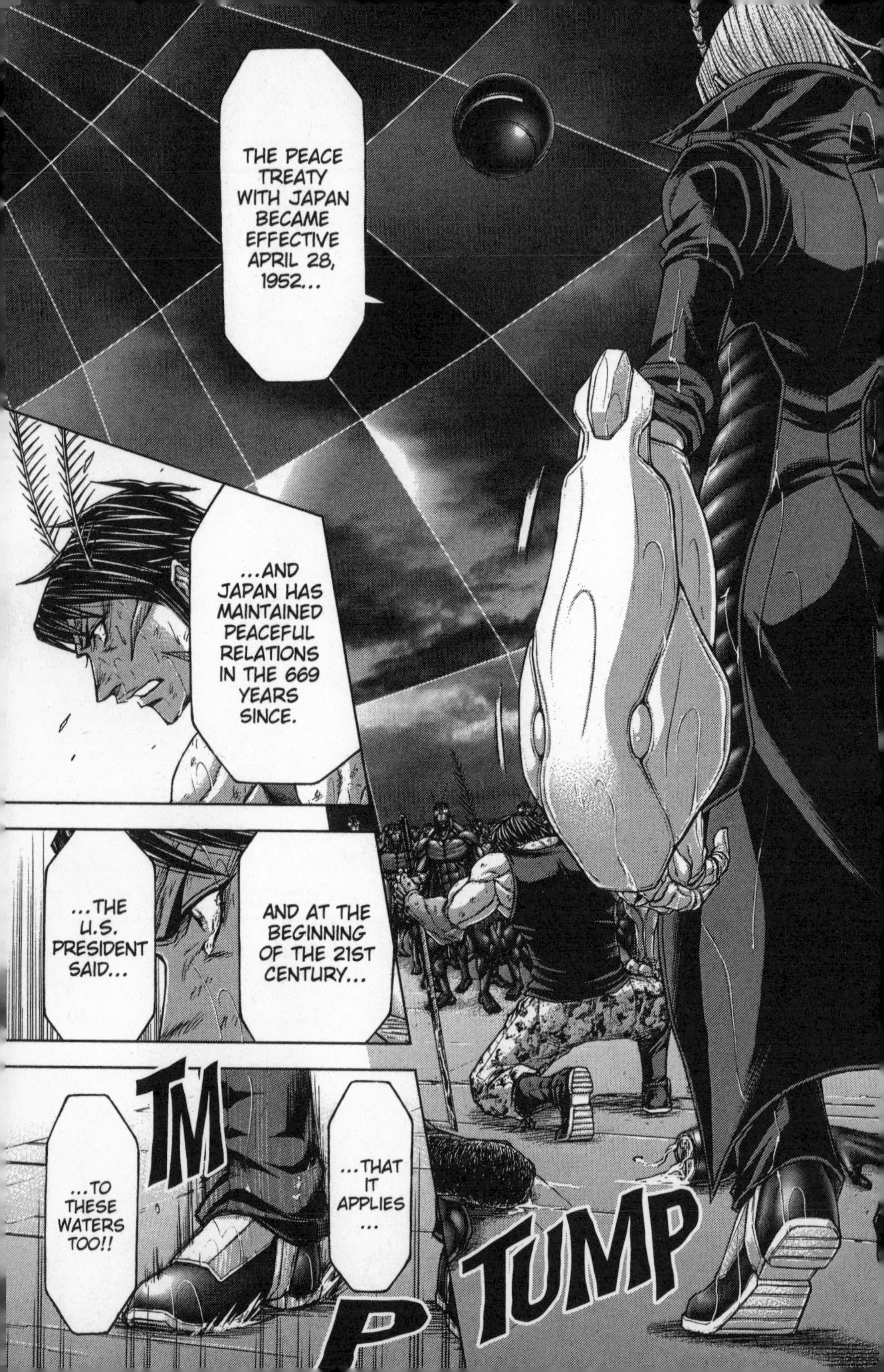
THE PEACE TREATY WITH JAPAN BECAME EFFECTIVE APRIL 28, 1952...
...AND JAPAN HAS MAINTAINED PEACEFUL RELATIONS IN THE 669 YEARS SINCE.
AND AT THE BEGINNING OF THE 21ST CENTURY...
...THE U.S. PRESIDENT SAID...
...THAT IT APPLIES...
...TO THESE WATERS TOO!!
TM
TUMP
P

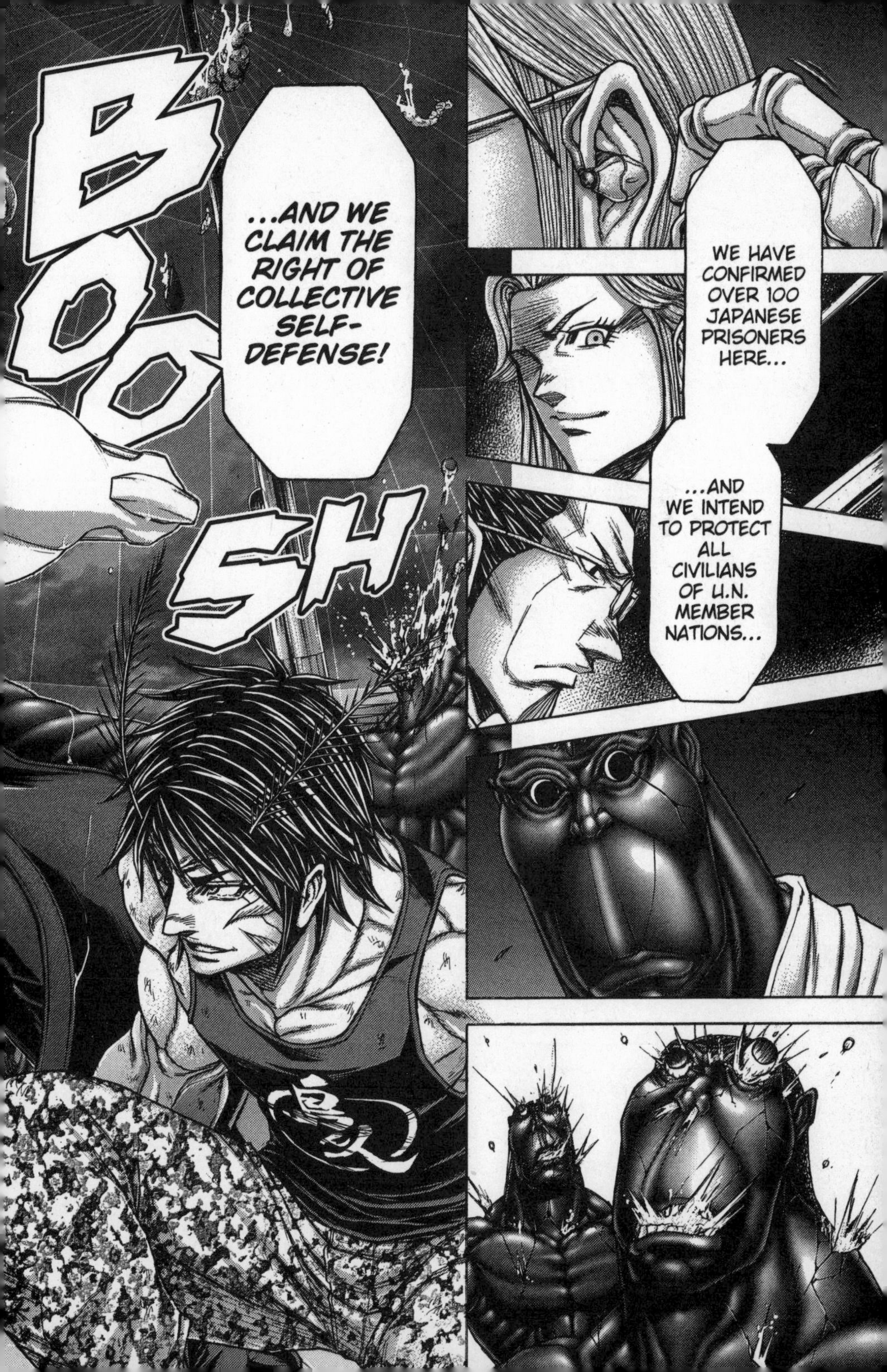
WE HAVE CONFIRMED OVER 100 JAPANESE PRISONERS HERE...
...AND WE INTEND TO PROTECT ALL CIVILIANS OF U.N. MEMBER NATIONS...
...AND WE CLAIM THE RIGHT OF COLLECTIVE SELF-DEFENSE!
BOOSH

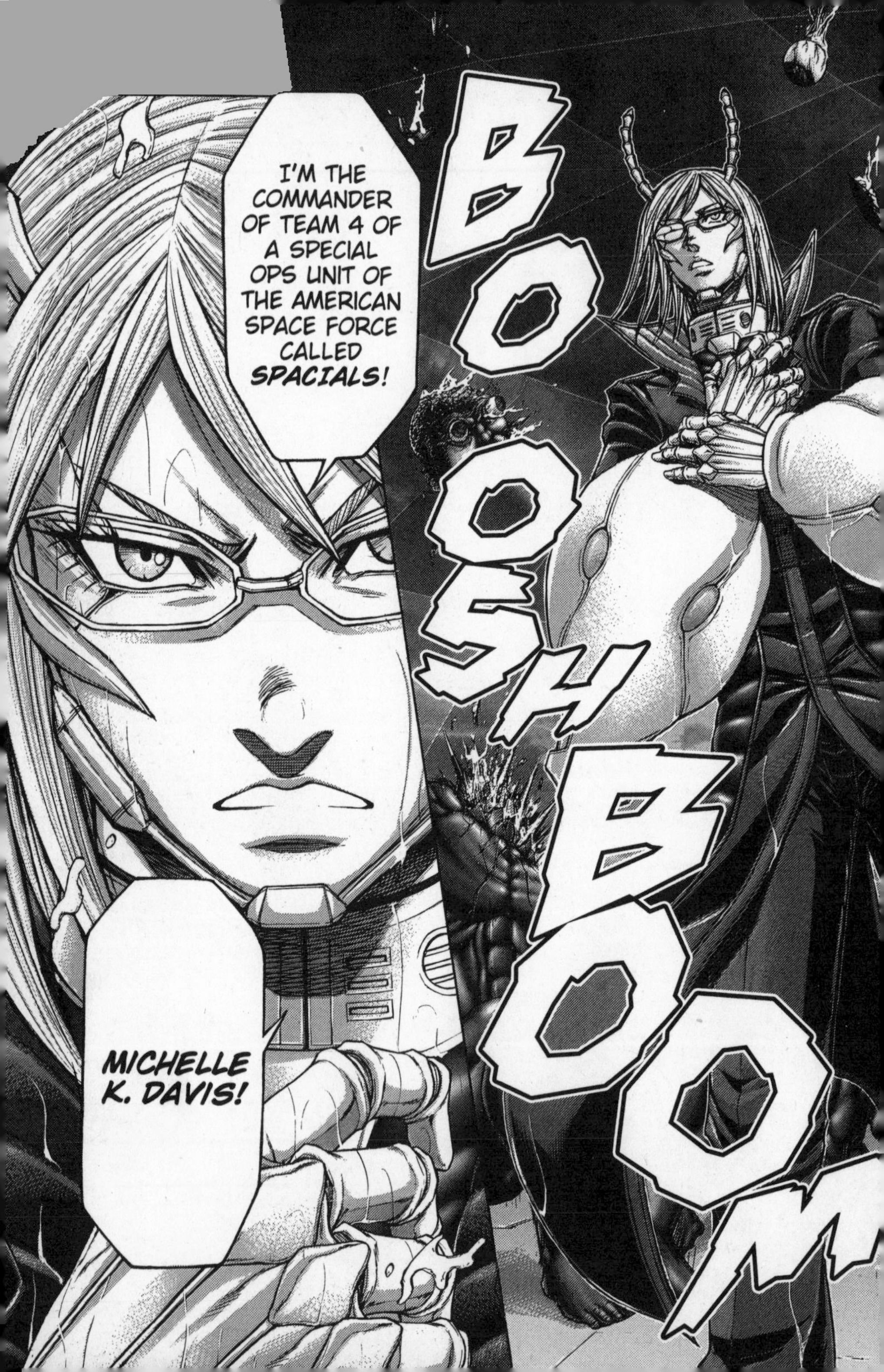
BOOSH
BOOM
I'M THE COMMANDER OF TEAM 4 OF A SPECIAL OPS UNIT OF THE AMERICAN SPACE FORCE CALLED ***SPACIALS!***
MICHELLE K. DAVIS!

TERRA FORMARS

character

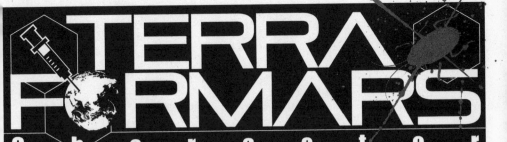

Joichi Hongo ♂

Shizuoka 26 yrs. 180 cm 82 kg

Japan Ranking: 6

Operation Base: Desert Locust

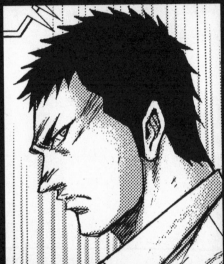

Favorite Foods: Dried fish, miso soup
Dislikes: Rugby teams who don't level the ground after rain.
Eye Color: Black Blood Type: AB
DOB: December 29 (Capricorn)
Favorite thing about aquariums: Touching sea cucumbers

His father was a salaryman and his mother was a housewife. He received good grades and was good at soccer, which made him popular among girls. However, he rarely spoke and was intensely serious, so after about three dates, the girls would lose interest. Another problem is that he tended to consider all girls, including his younger sister, capriciously self-centered, so he kept his distance. Because he grew up in apartments, his dream is to someday have a big house in the country. He can play any position, but he doesn't enjoy commanding others, so he feels more comfortable up front.

Sho Saito ♂

Kanagawa 21 yrs. 168 cm 60 kg

Operation Base: Field Cricket

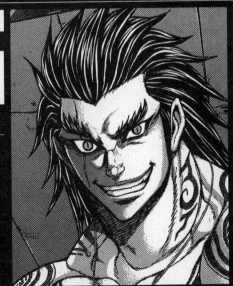

Favorite Foods: Fried chicken
Dislikes: Math
Eye Color: Black Blood Type: O
DOB: November 24 (probably Sagittarius)
Favorite Classics: *The Analects*, elementary school reading

He changed elementary schools a lot and then became classmates with Akari in the fourth grade. He worked for a short time after graduating from junior high, but then he became involved in illegal activities to pay his mother's medical fees and ended up in a gang. Within a few years, he was the boss of multiple gangs in Tokyo. He quickly picked up the English, Chinese and Spanish spoken by his underlings and clients. He's no good at book study, but excels at working with others. He likes women who are up to 20 years older than him.

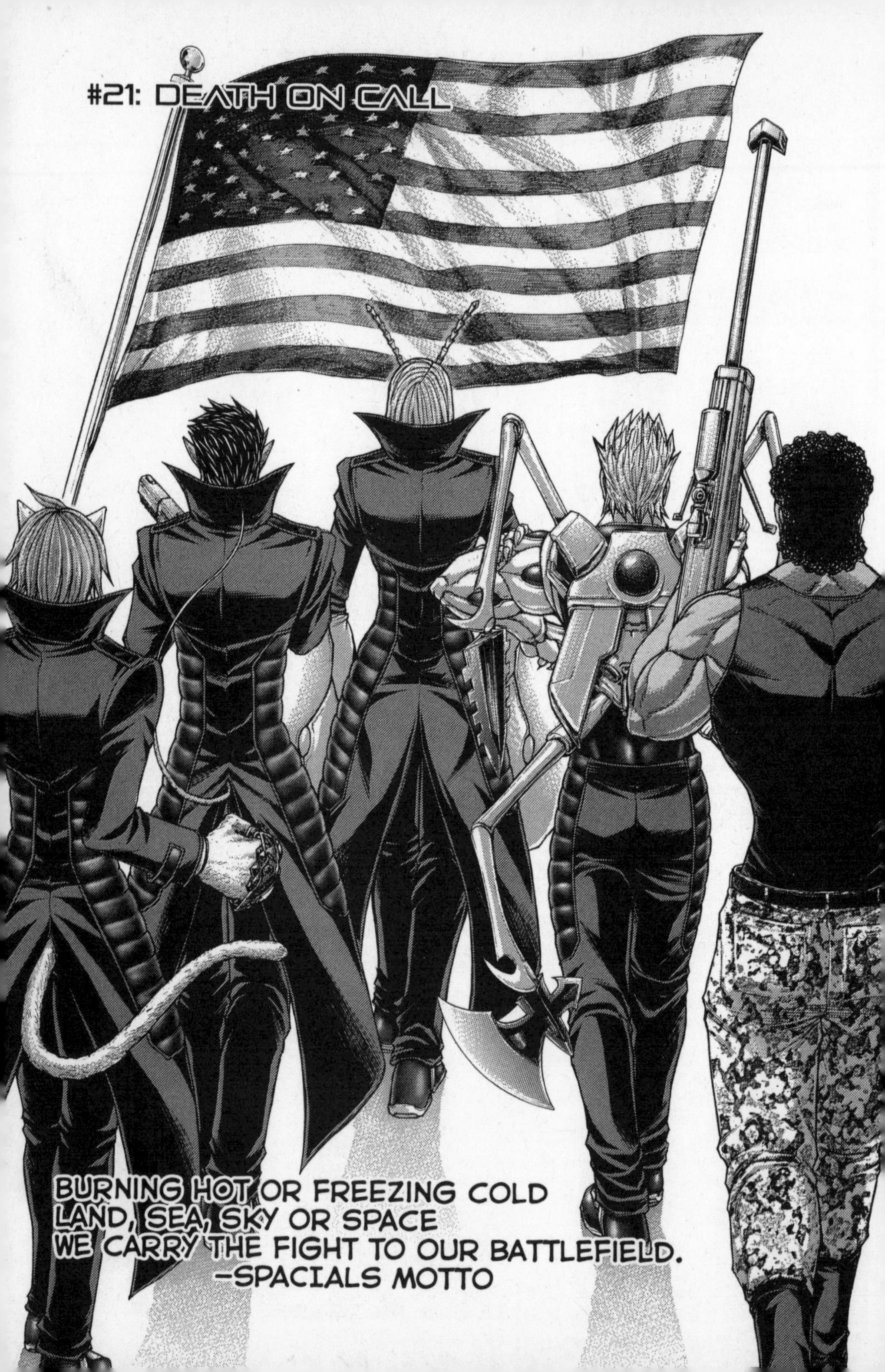
#21: DEATH ON CALL
BURNING HOT OR FREEZING COLD
LAND, SEA, SKY OR SPACE
WE CARRY THE FIGHT TO OUR BATTLEFIELD.
—SPACIALS MOTTO

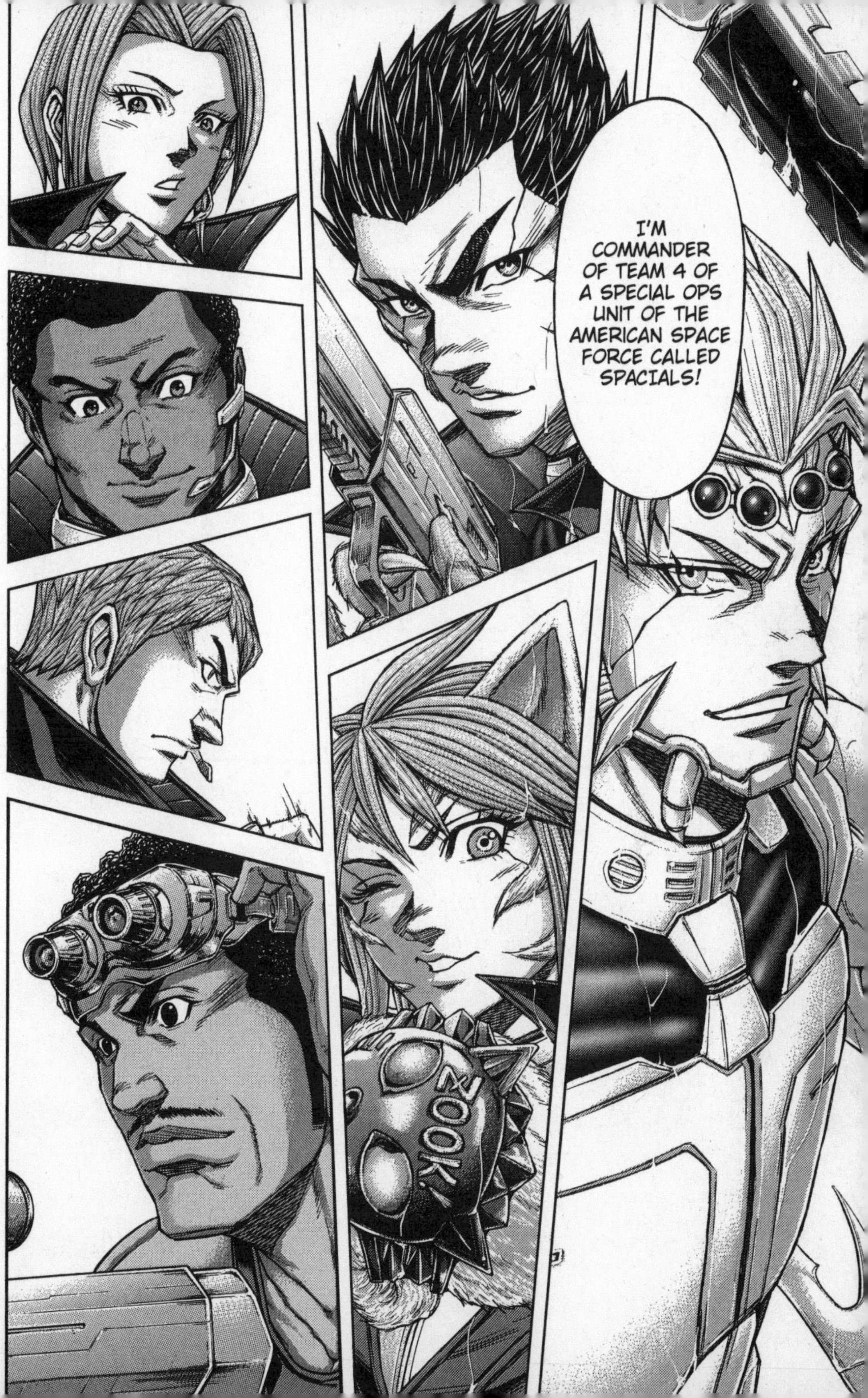
I'M COMMANDER OF TEAM 4 OF A SPECIAL OPS UNIT OF THE AMERICAN SPACE FORCE CALLED SPACIALS!
ZOOK

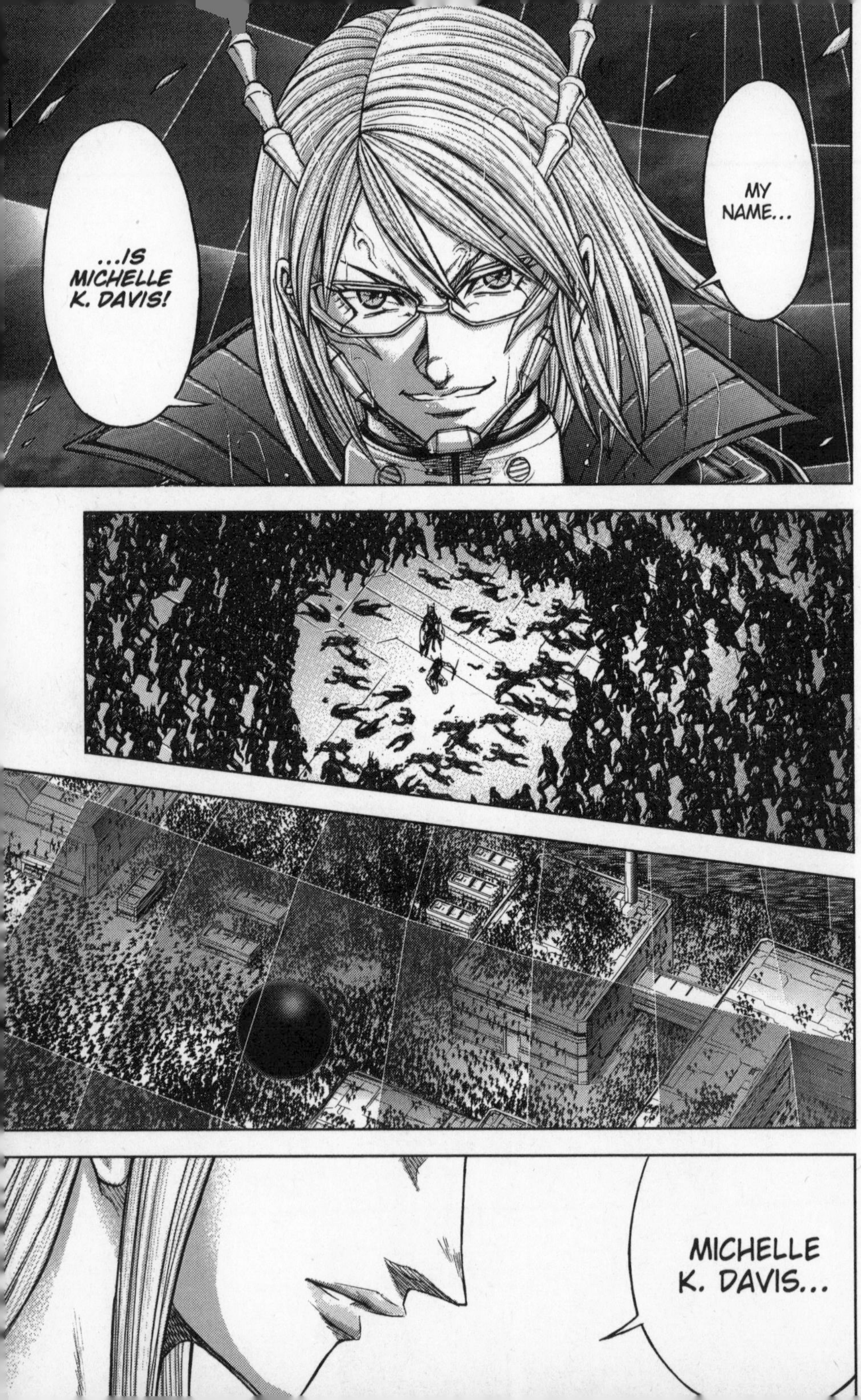
MY NAME...
...IS MICHELLE K. DAVIS!
MICHELLE K. DAVIS...

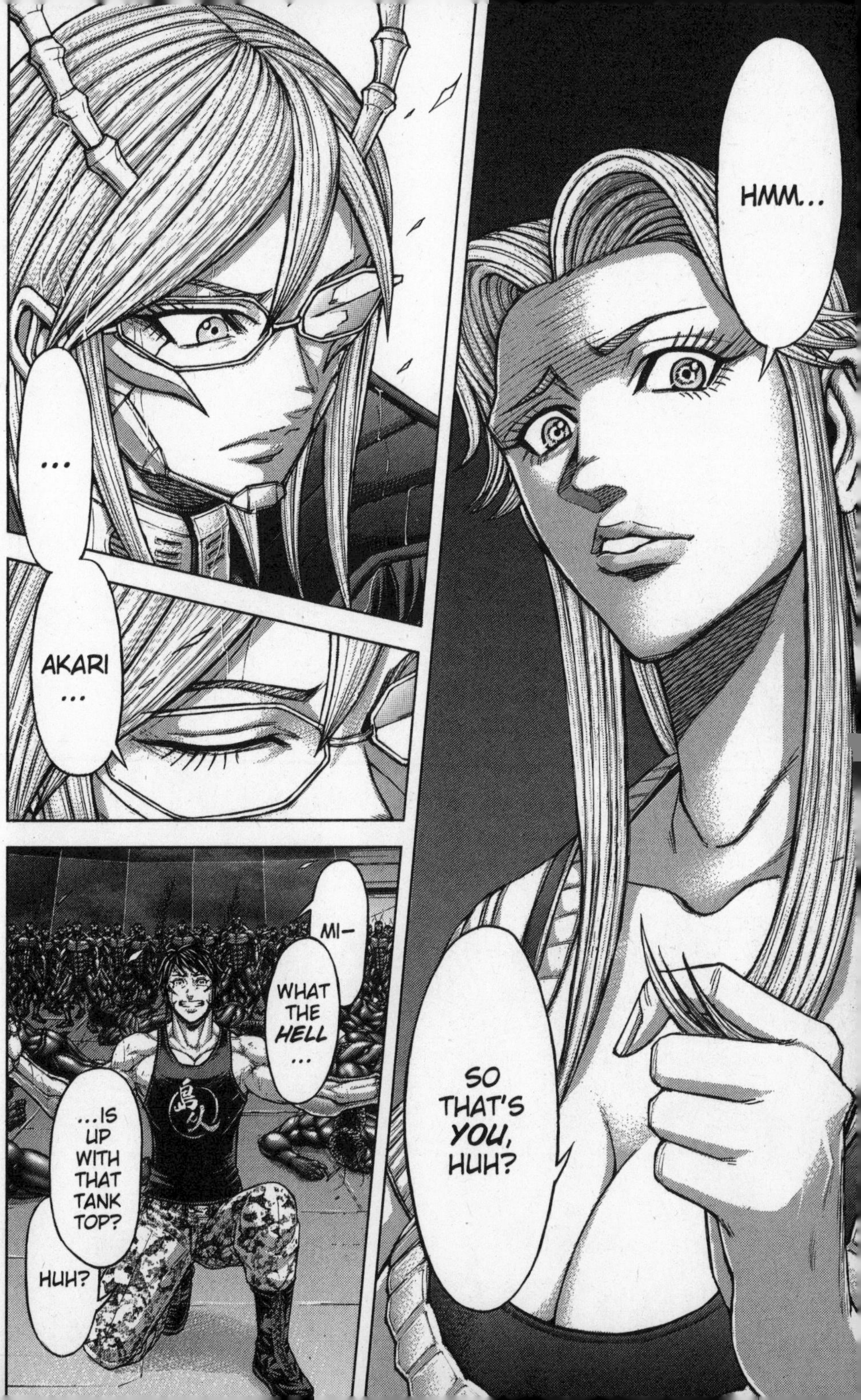
HMM...
SO THAT'S *YOU*, HUH?
...
AKARI ...
MI—
WHAT THE *HELL* ...
...IS UP WITH THAT TANK TOP?
HUH?

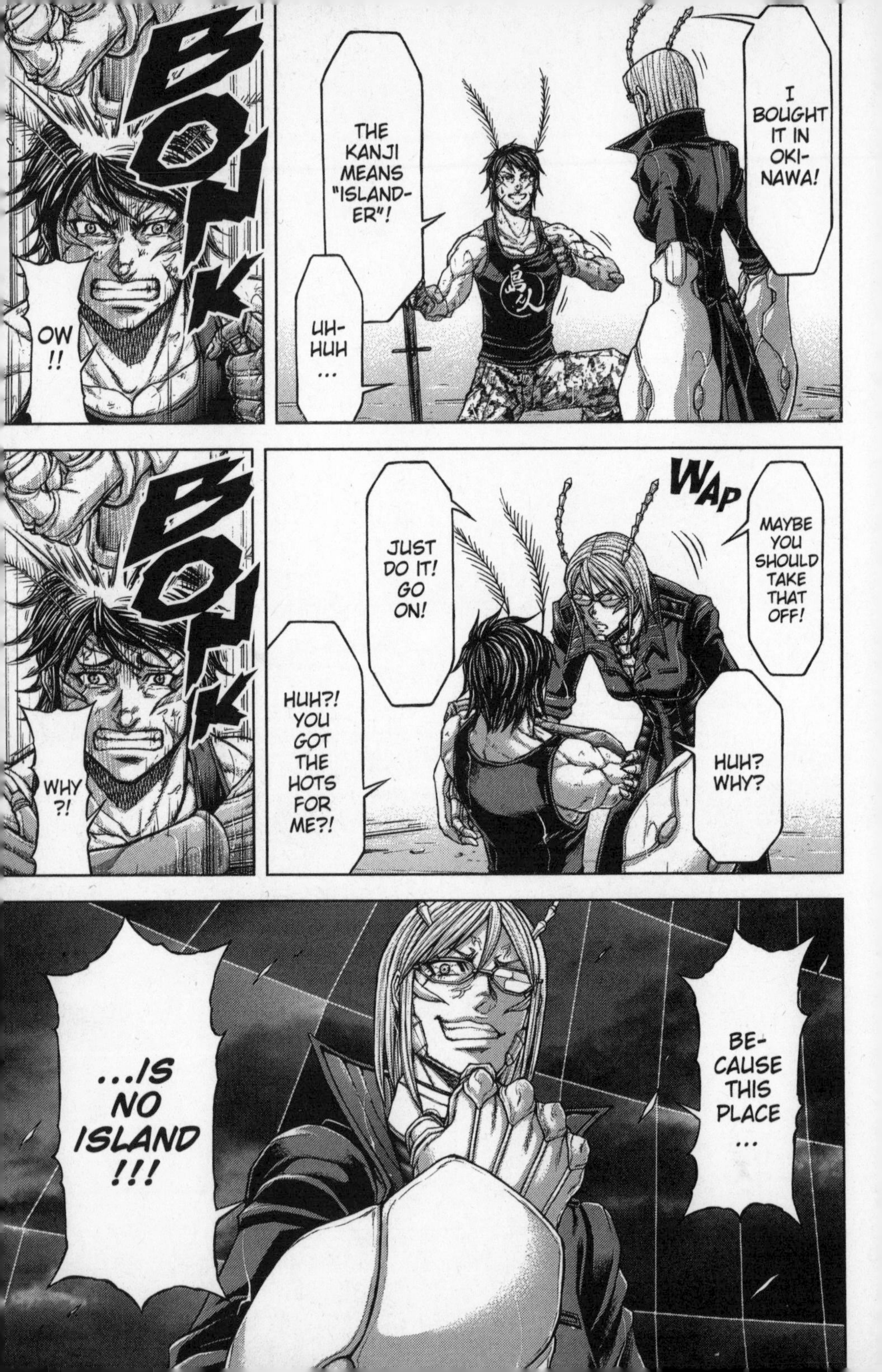
I BOUGHT IT IN OKI-NAWA!
THE KANJI MEANS "ISLAND-ER"!
UH-HUH ...
BONK
OW !!
WAP
MAYBE YOU SHOULD TAKE THAT OFF!
JUST DO IT! GO ON!
HUH? WHY?
HUH?! YOU GOT THE HOTS FOR ME?!
BONK
WHY ?!
BE-CAUSE THIS PLACE ...
...IS NO ISLAND !!!

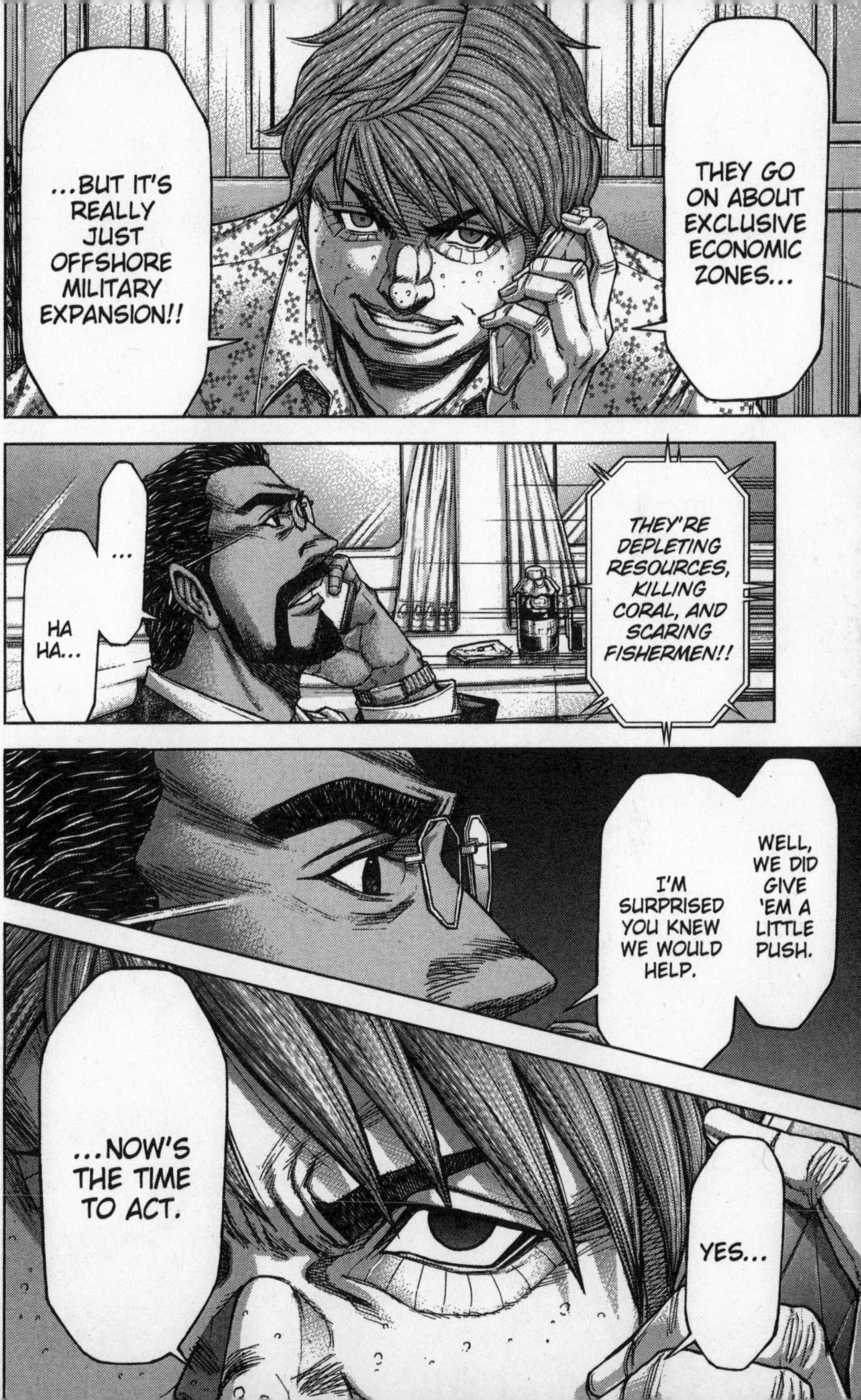
THEY GO ON ABOUT EXCLUSIVE ECONOMIC ZONES...
...BUT IT'S REALLY JUST OFFSHORE MILITARY EXPANSION!!
THEY'RE DEPLETING RESOURCES, KILLING CORAL, AND SCARING FISHERMEN!!
...
HA HA...
WELL, WE DID GIVE 'EM A LITTLE PUSH.
I'M SURPRISED YOU KNEW WE WOULD HELP.
YES...
...NOW'S THE TIME TO ACT.

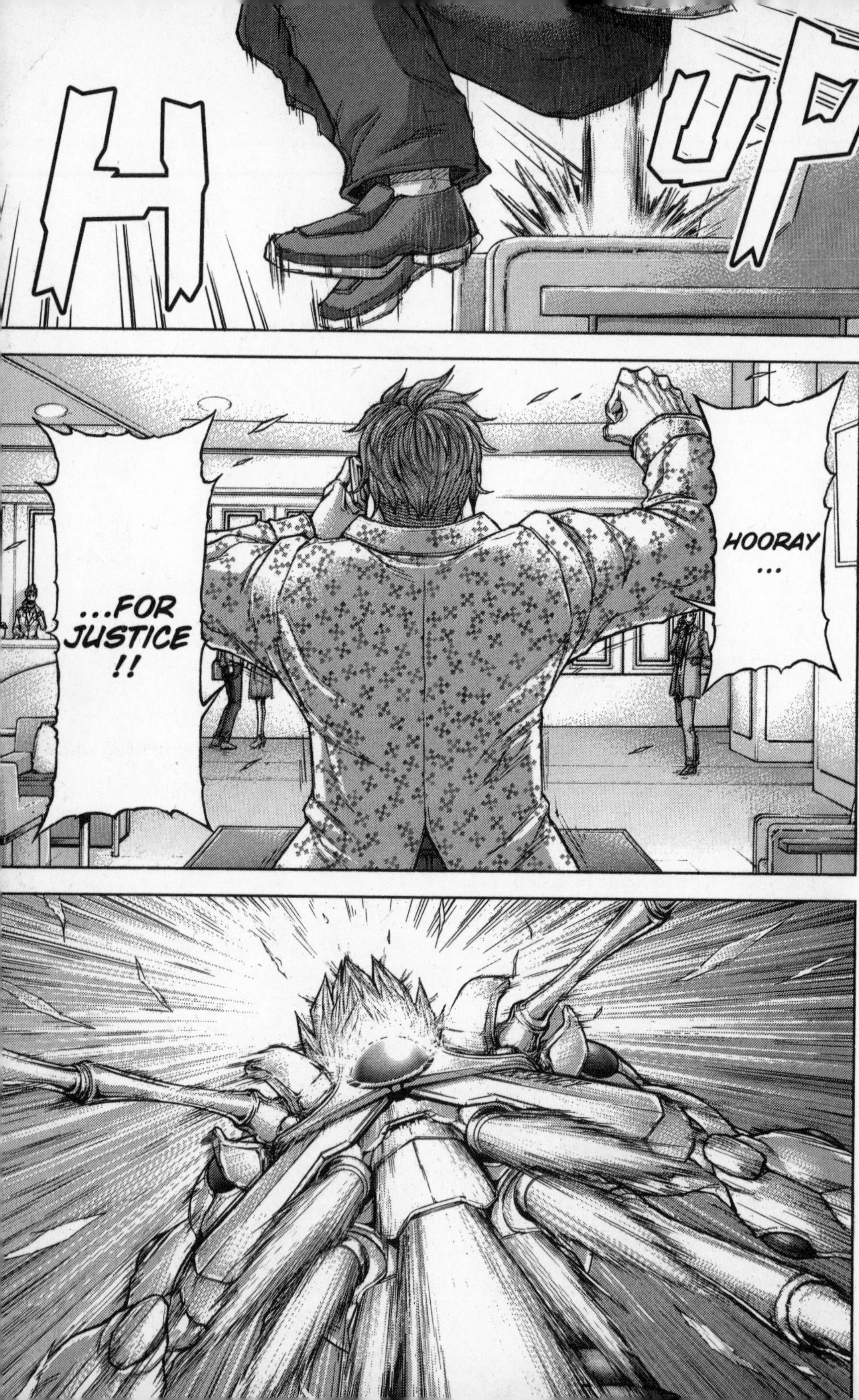
HUP
HOORAY ...
...FOR JUSTICE !!

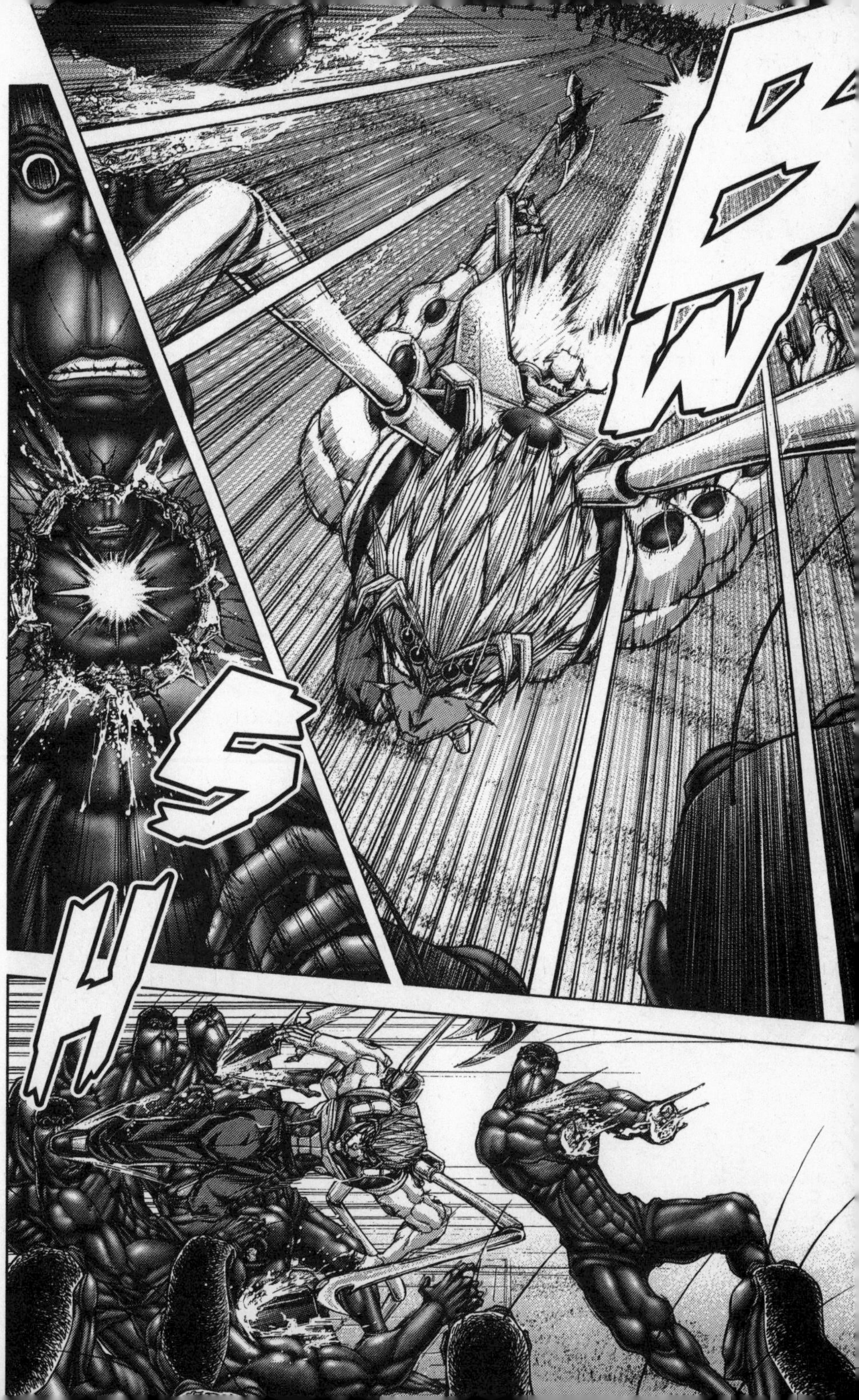

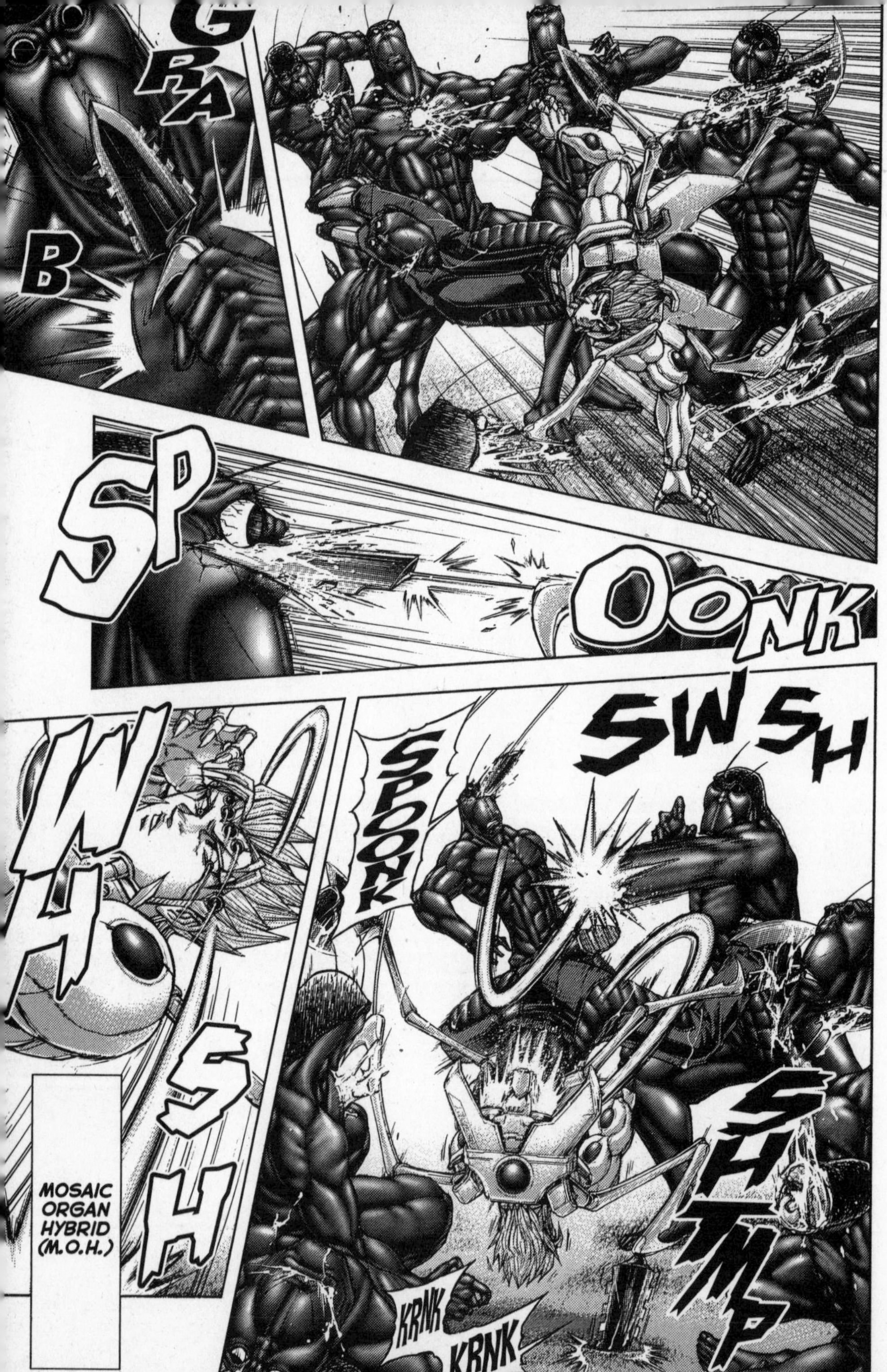
GRAB
SPOONK
SWSH
SPOONK
SHTMP
KRNK
KRNK
WHSH
MOSAIC ORGAN HYBRID (M.O.H.)

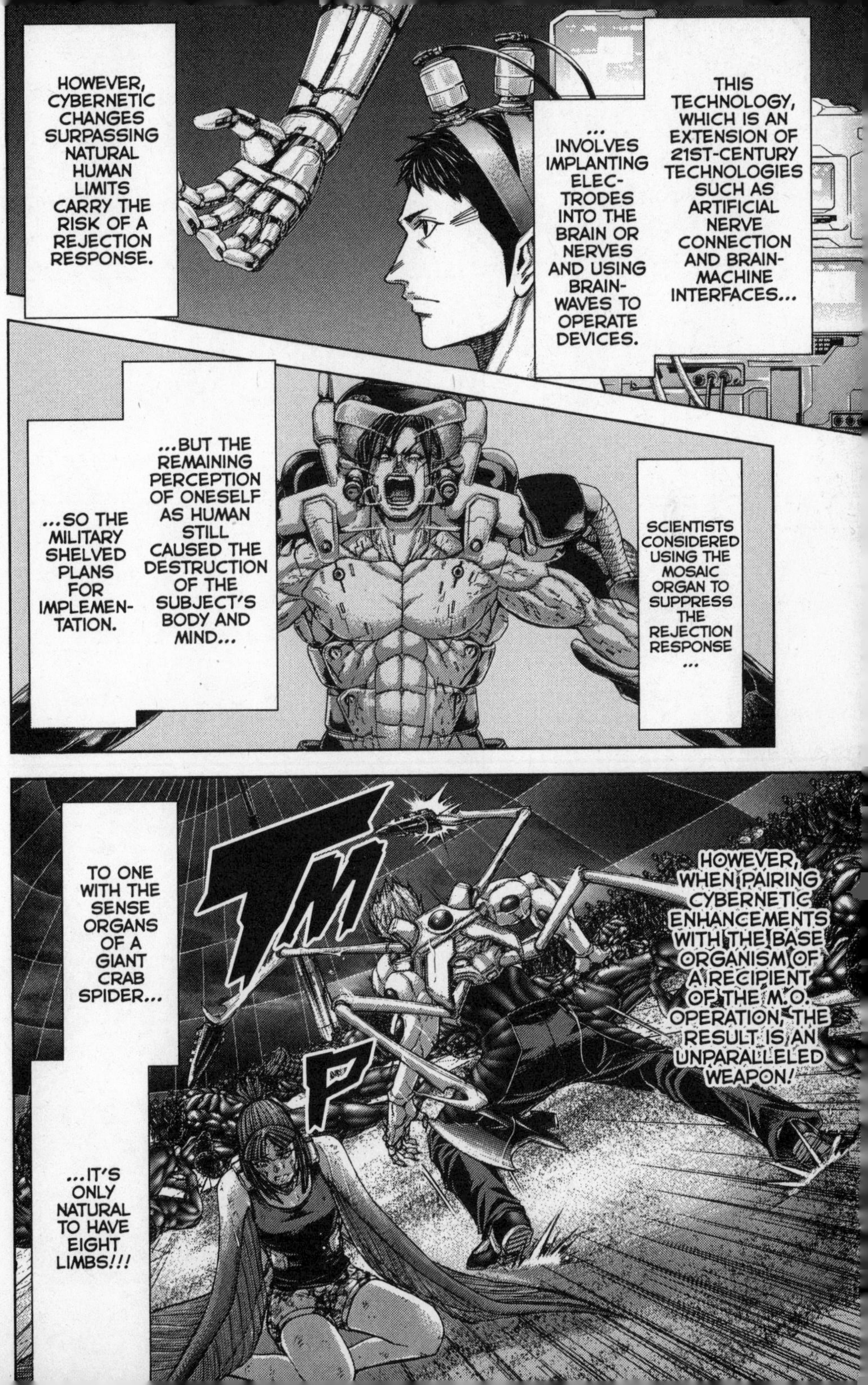
THIS TECHNOLOGY, WHICH IS AN EXTENSION OF 21ST-CENTURY TECHNOLOGIES SUCH AS ARTIFICIAL NERVE CONNECTION AND BRAIN-MACHINE INTERFACES...
...INVOLVES IMPLANTING ELEC-TRODES INTO THE BRAIN OR NERVES AND USING BRAIN-WAVES TO OPERATE DEVICES.
HOWEVER, CYBERNETIC CHANGES SURPASSING NATURAL HUMAN LIMITS CARRY THE RISK OF A REJECTION RESPONSE.
SCIENTISTS CONSIDERED USING THE MOSAIC ORGAN TO SUPPRESS THE REJECTION RESPONSE...
...BUT THE REMAINING PERCEPTION OF ONESELF AS HUMAN STILL CAUSED THE DESTRUCTION OF THE SUBJECT'S BODY AND MIND...
...SO THE MILITARY SHELVED PLANS FOR IMPLEMEN-TATION.
HOWEVER, WHEN PAIRING CYBERNETIC ENHANCEMENTS WITH THE BASE ORGANISM OF A RECIPIENT OF THE M.O. OPERATION, THE RESULT IS AN UNPARALLELED WEAPON!
TM
P
TO ONE WITH THE SENSE ORGANS OF A GIANT CRAB SPIDER...
...IT'S ONLY NATURAL TO HAVE EIGHT LIMBS!!!

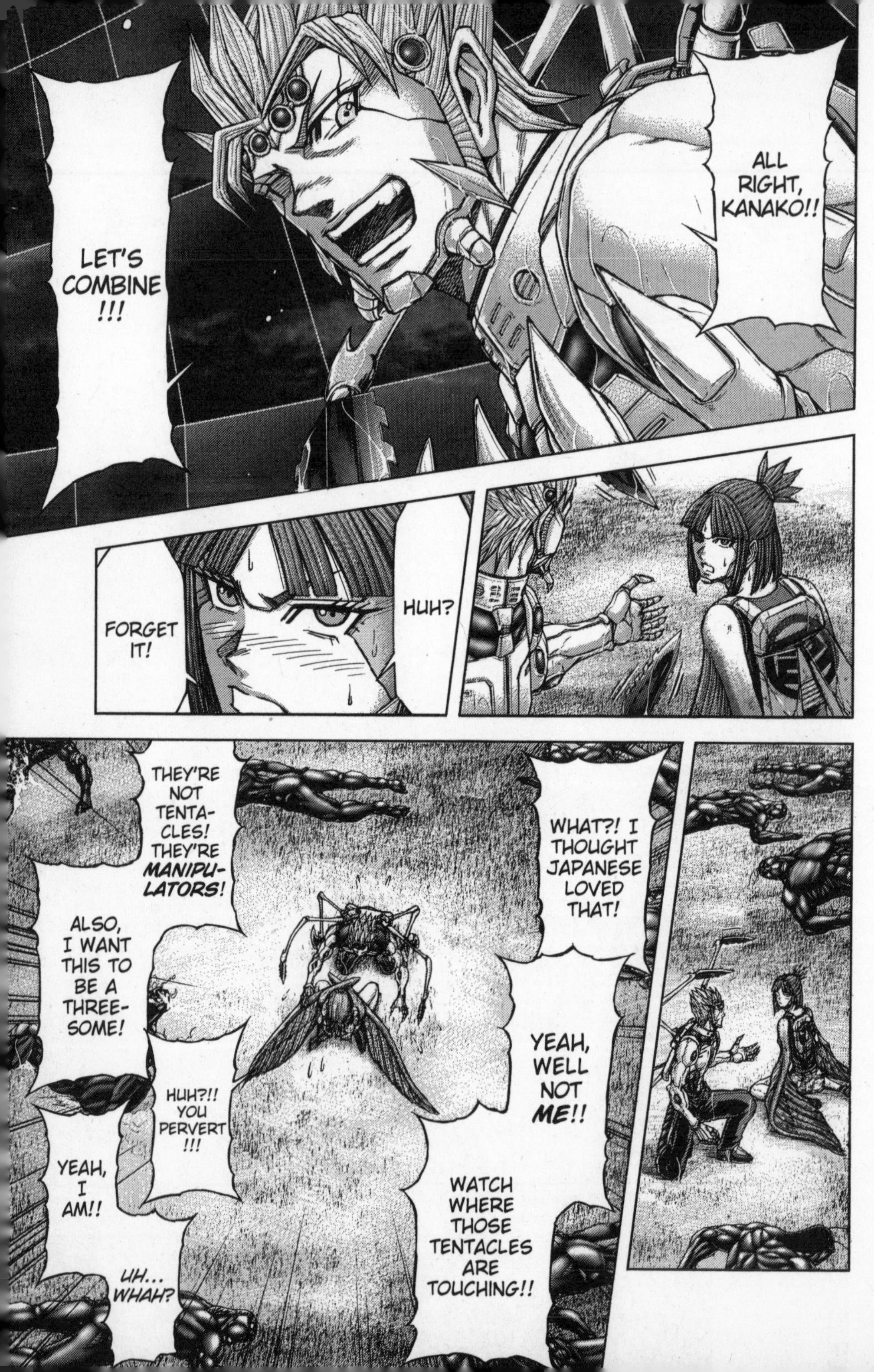
ALL RIGHT, KANAKO!!
LET'S COMBINE!!!
HUH?
FORGET IT!
WHAT?! I THOUGHT JAPANESE LOVED THAT!
YEAH, WELL NOT *ME*!!
WATCH WHERE THOSE TENTACLES ARE TOUCHING!!
THEY'RE NOT TENTACLES! THEY'RE *MANIPULATORS*!
ALSO, I WANT THIS TO BE A THREESOME!
HUH?!! YOU PERVERT!!!
YEAH, I AM!!
UH... WHAH?

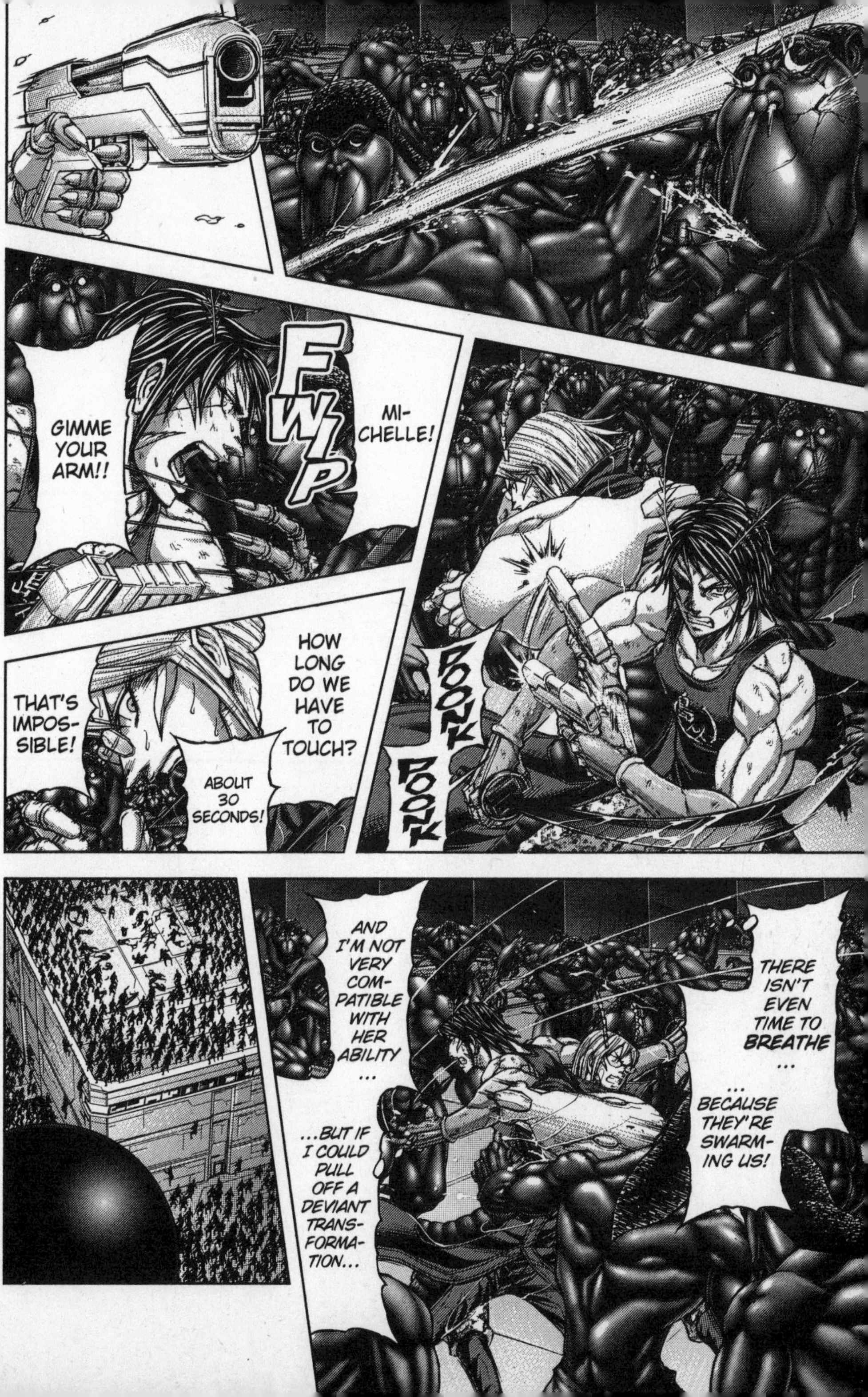
POONK
POONK
MI-CHELLE!
FWIP
GIMME YOUR ARM!!
HOW LONG DO WE HAVE TO TOUCH?
ABOUT 30 SECONDS!
THAT'S IMPOS-SIBLE!
THERE ISN'T EVEN TIME TO BREATHE...
...BECAUSE THEY'RE SWARM-ING US!
AND I'M NOT VERY COM-PATIBLE WITH HER ABILITY...
...BUT IF I COULD PULL OFF A DEVIANT TRANS-FORMA-TION...

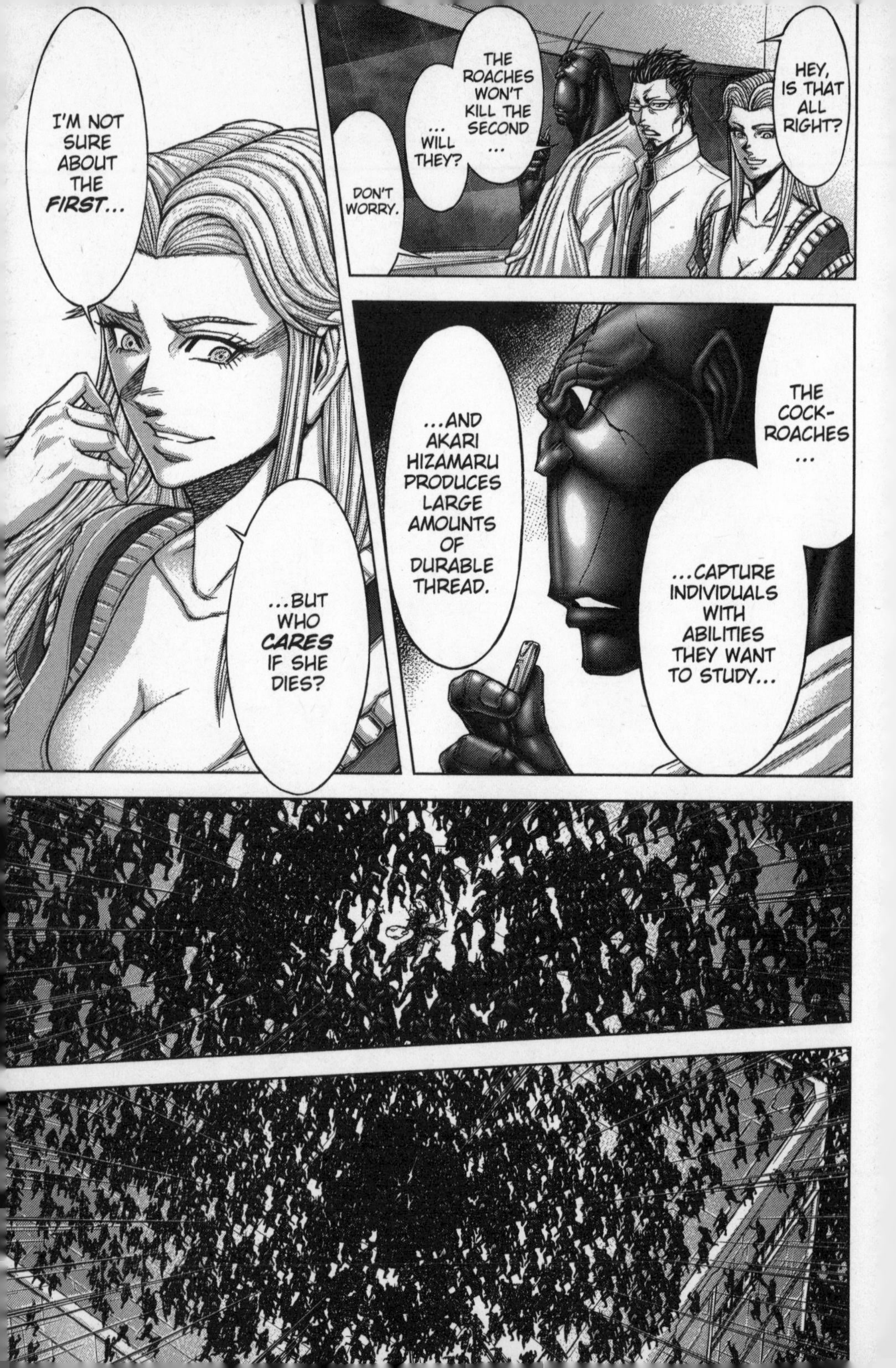
HEY, IS THAT ALL RIGHT?
THE ROACHES WON'T KILL THE SECOND...
...WILL THEY?
DON'T WORRY.
THE COCKROACHES...
...CAPTURE INDIVIDUALS WITH ABILITIES THEY WANT TO STUDY...
...AND AKARI HIZAMARU PRODUCES LARGE AMOUNTS OF DURABLE THREAD.
I'M NOT SURE ABOUT THE *FIRST*...
...BUT WHO *CARES* IF SHE DIES?

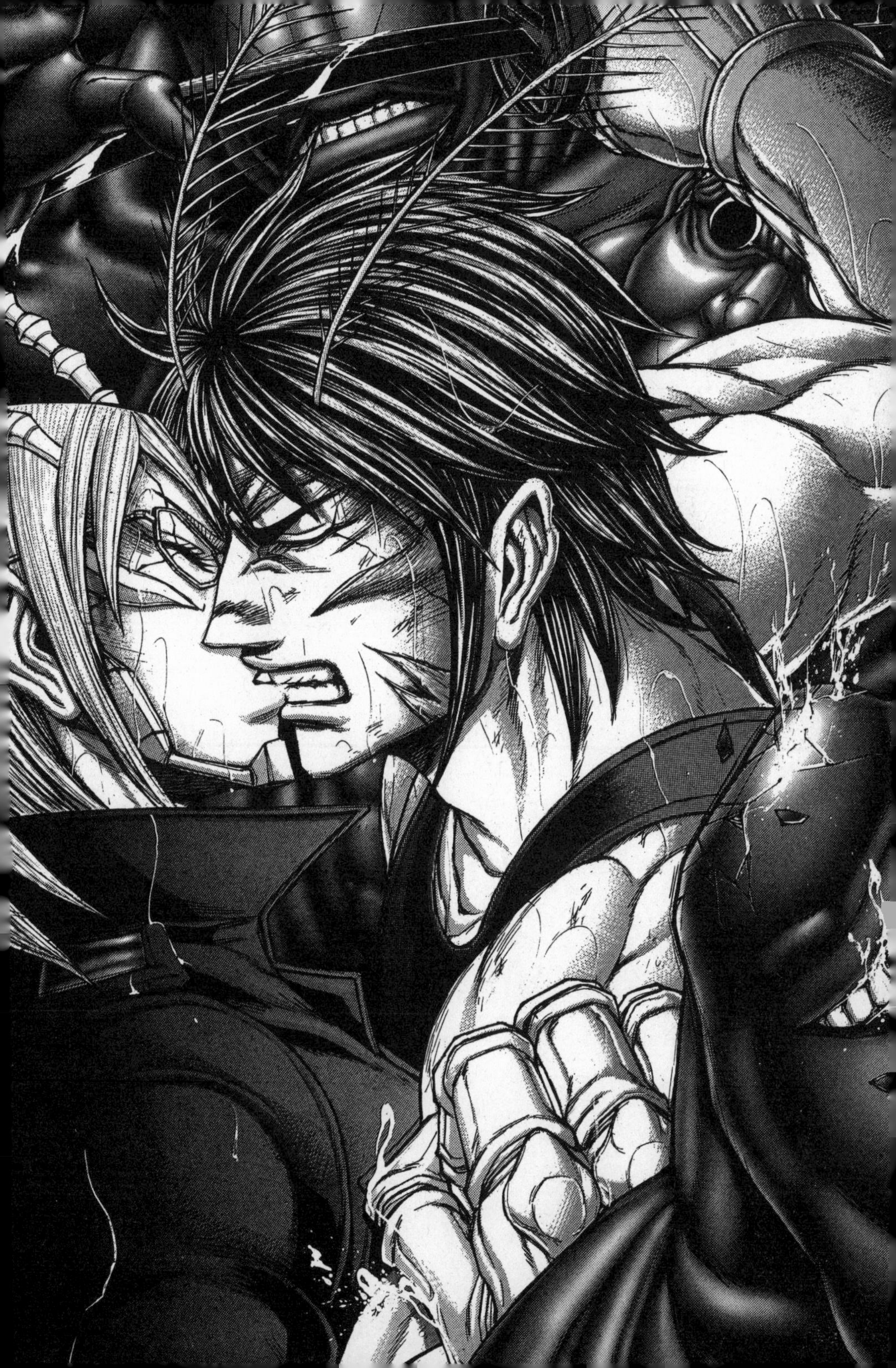

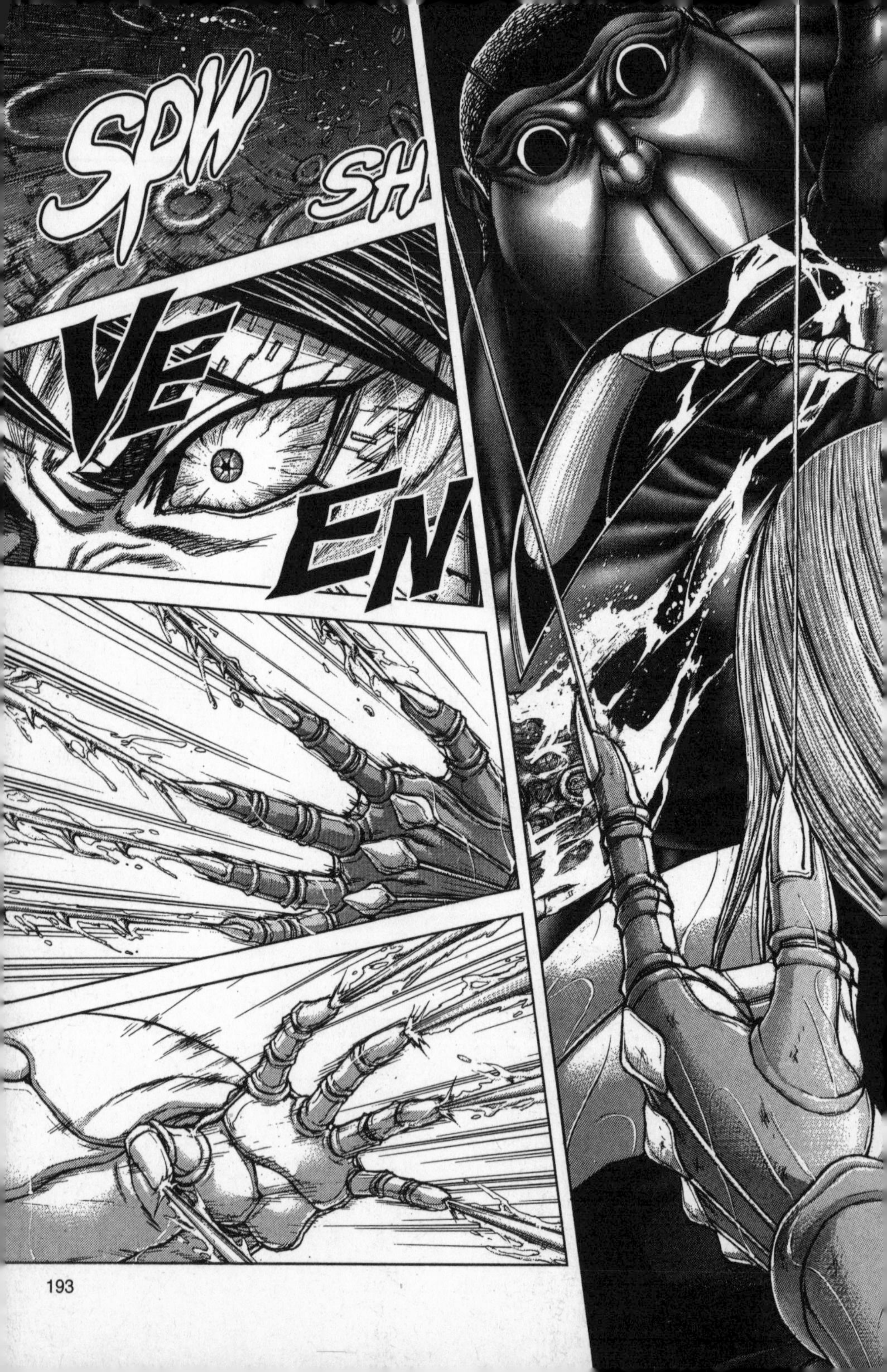
SPW
SH
VE
EM

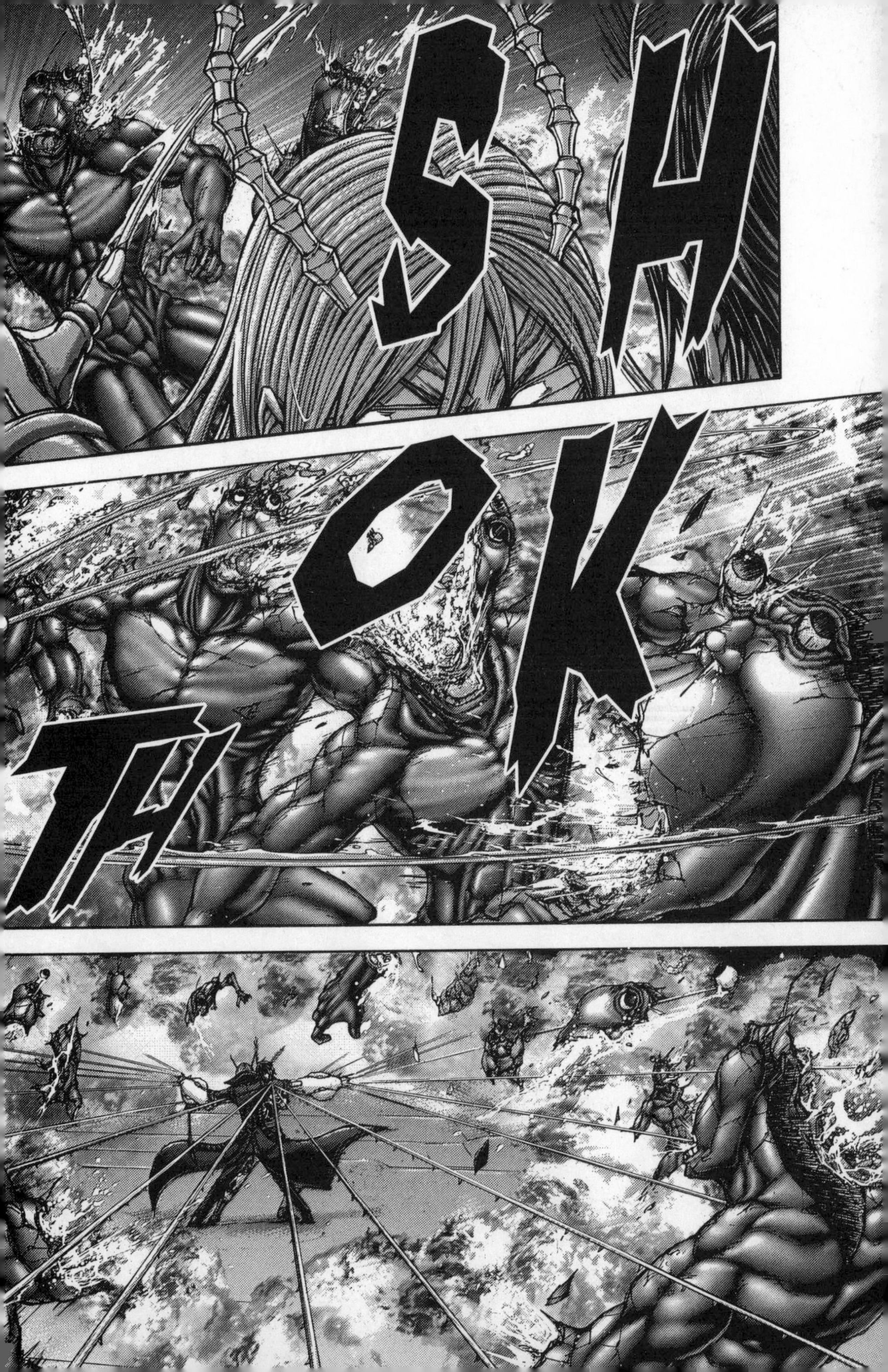
SH
THOK

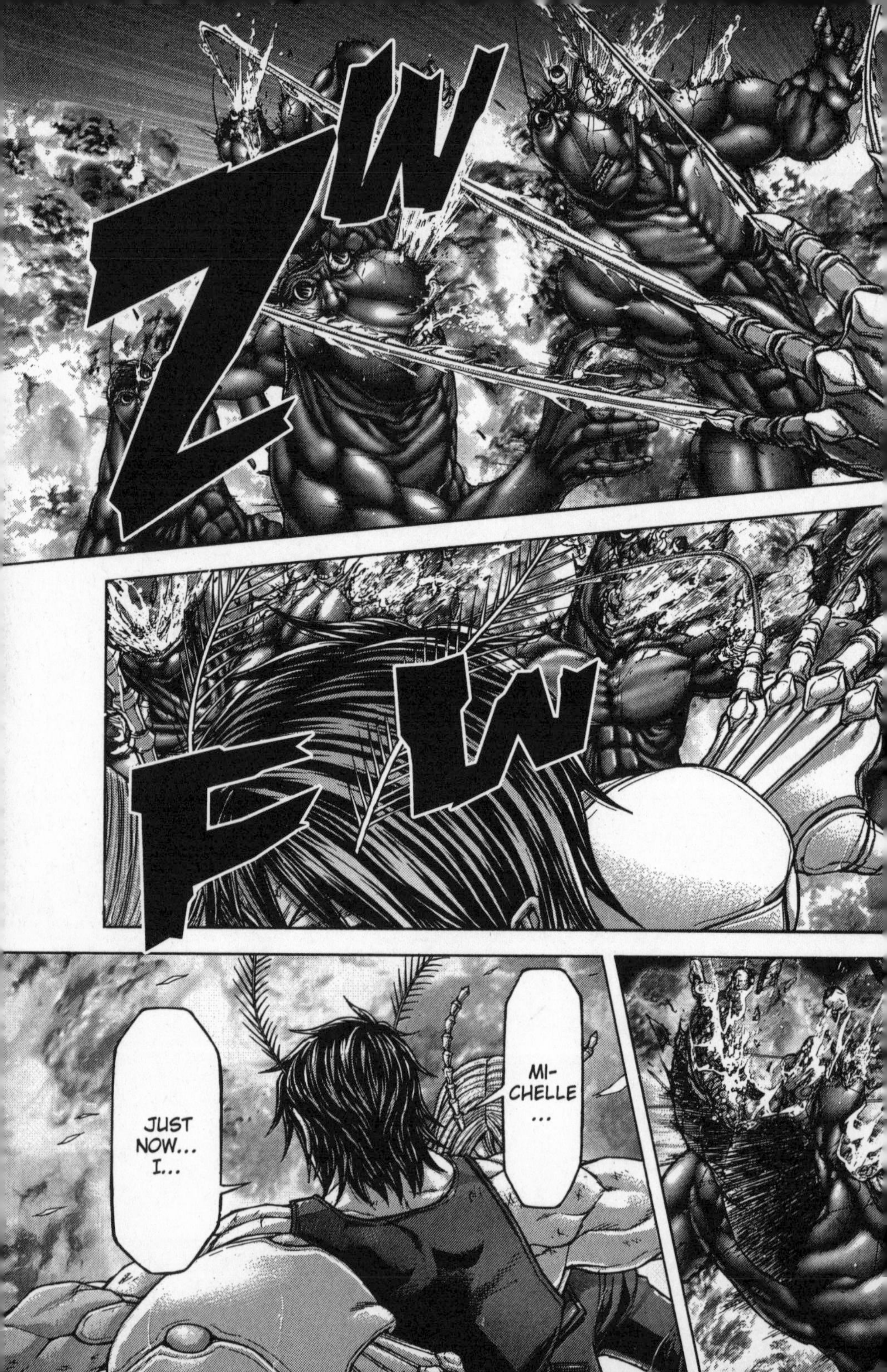
ZW
FW
MI-CHELLE...
JUST NOW... I...

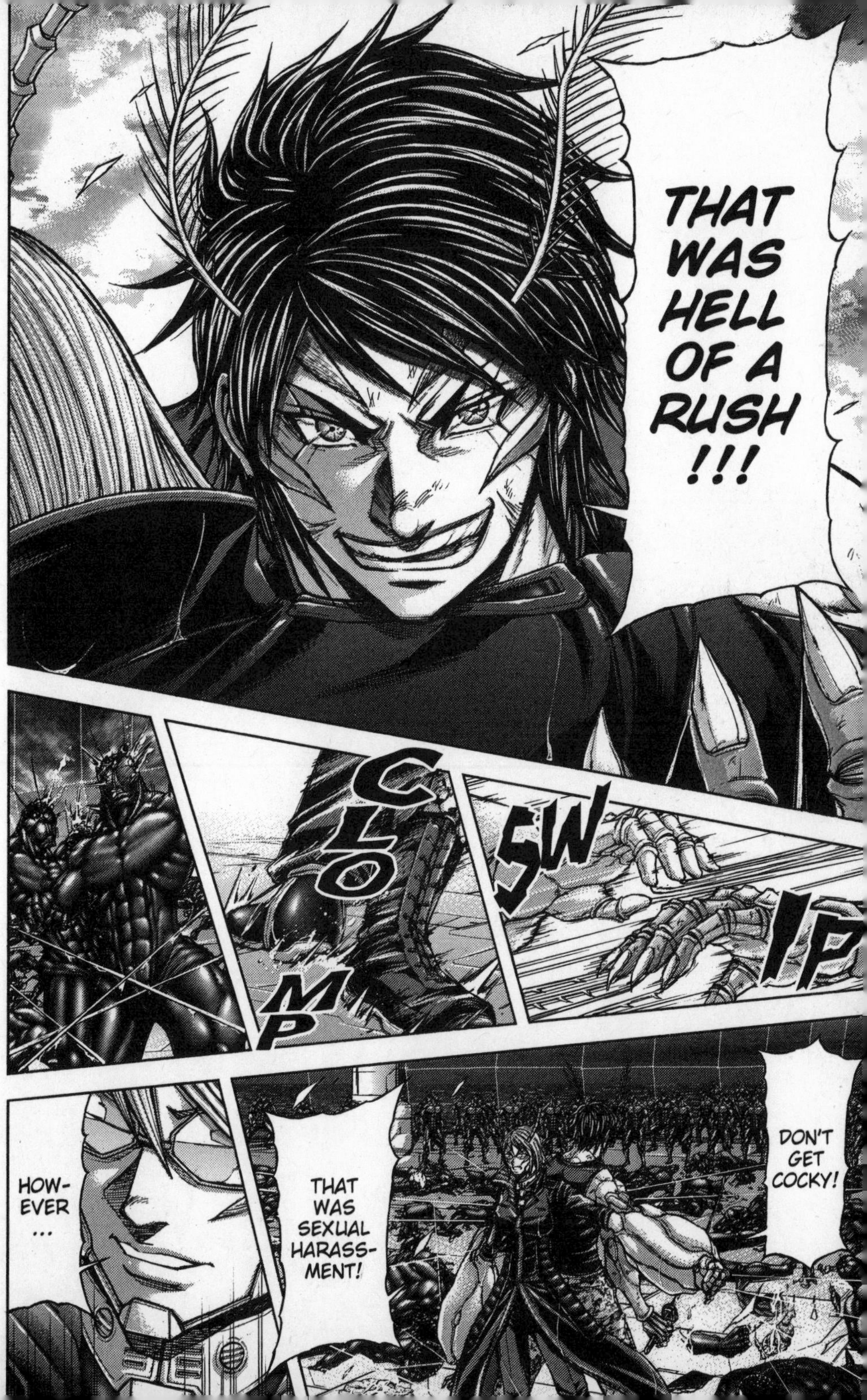
THAT WAS HELL OF A RUSH!!!
SWIP
CLOMP
DON'T GET COCKY!
THAT WAS SEXUAL HARASS-MENT!
HOW-EVER...

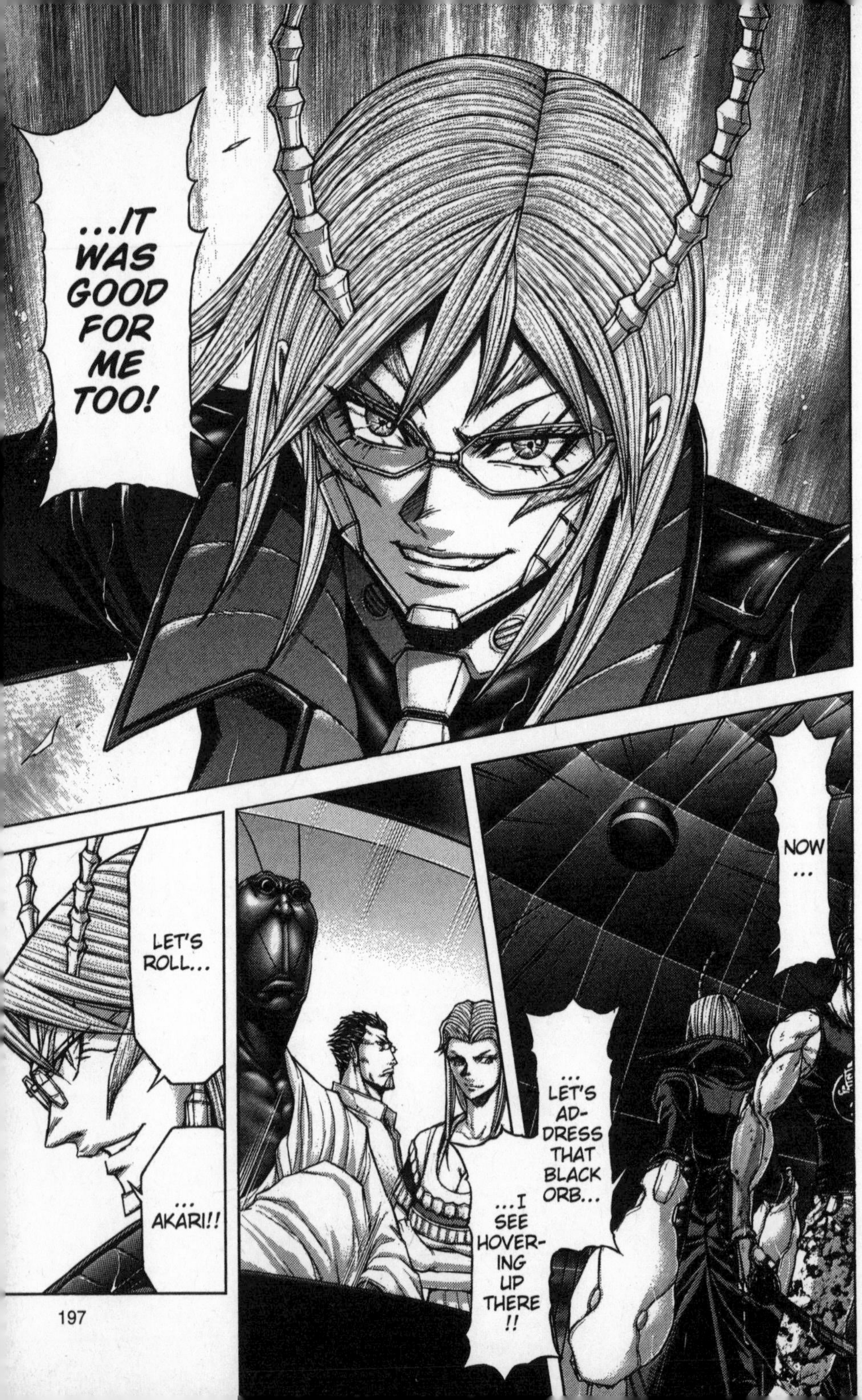
...IT WAS GOOD FOR ME TOO!
NOW ...
... LET'S ADDRESS THAT BLACK ORB...
...I SEE HOVERING UP THERE!!
LET'S ROLL...
... AKARI!!

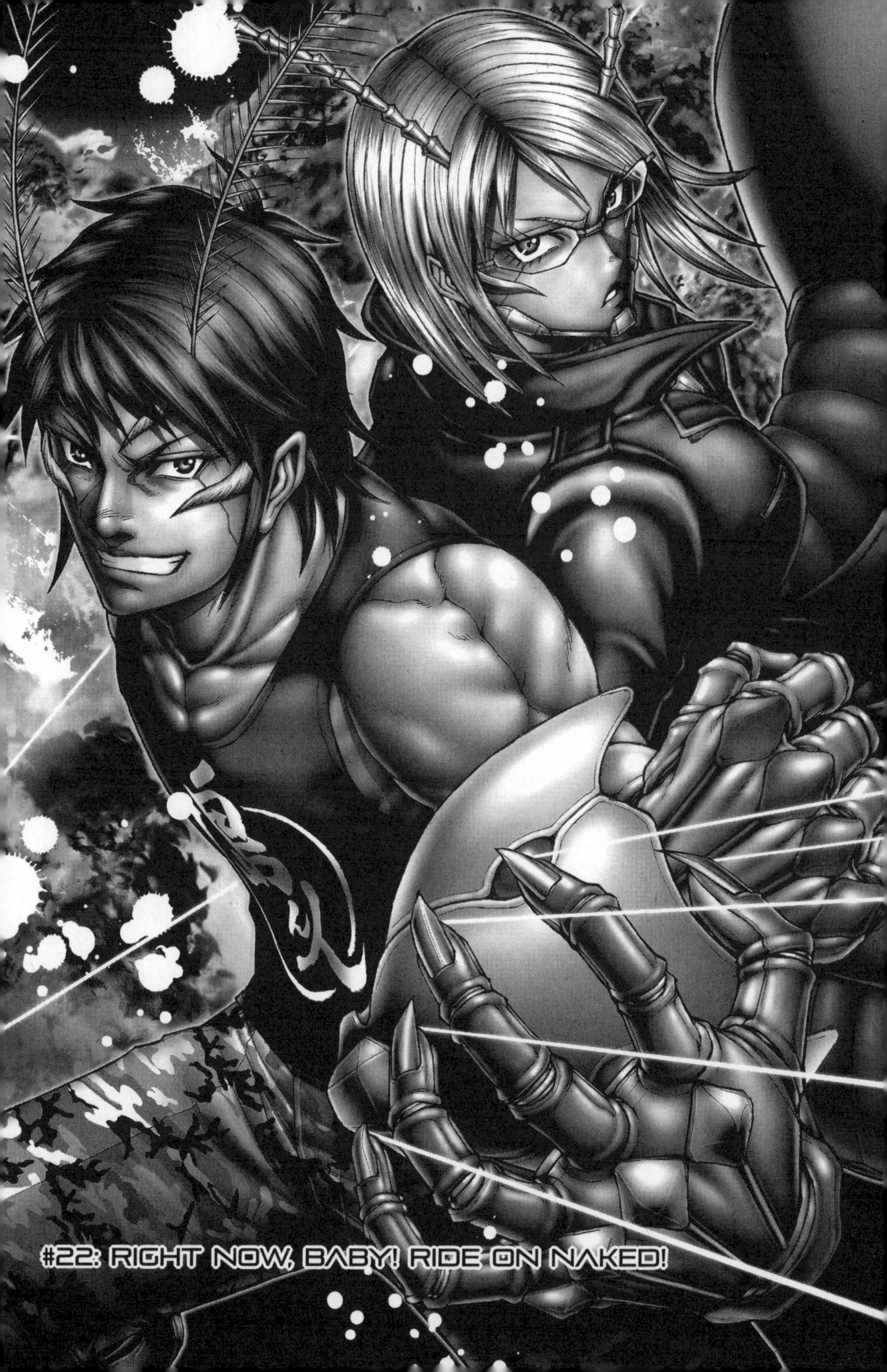
#22: RIGHT NOW, BABY! RIDE ON NAKED!

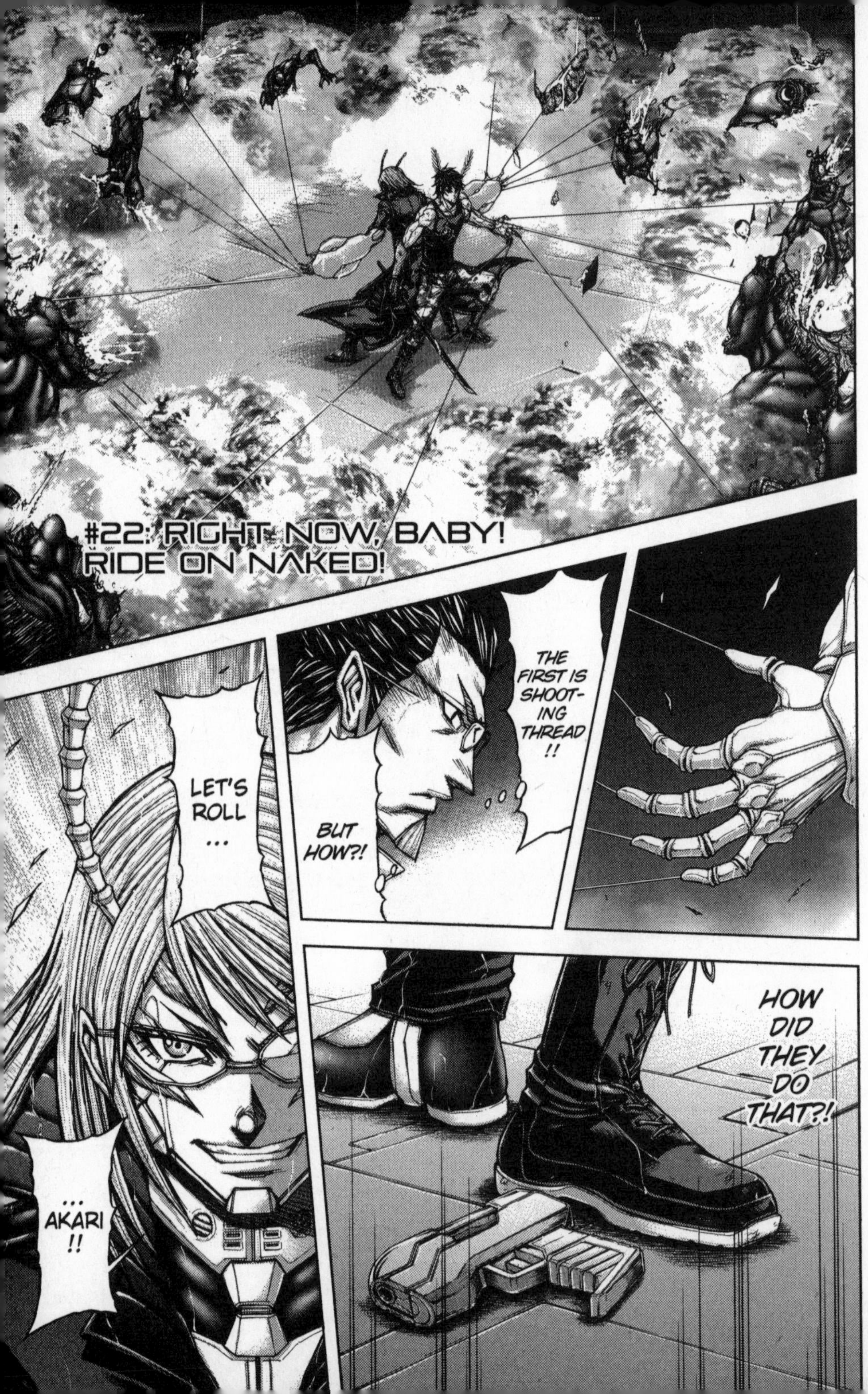
#22: RIGHT NOW, BABY! RIDE ON NAKED!
THE FIRST IS SHOOTING THREAD!!
BUT HOW?!
HOW DID THEY DO THAT?!
LET'S ROLL...
...AKARI!!

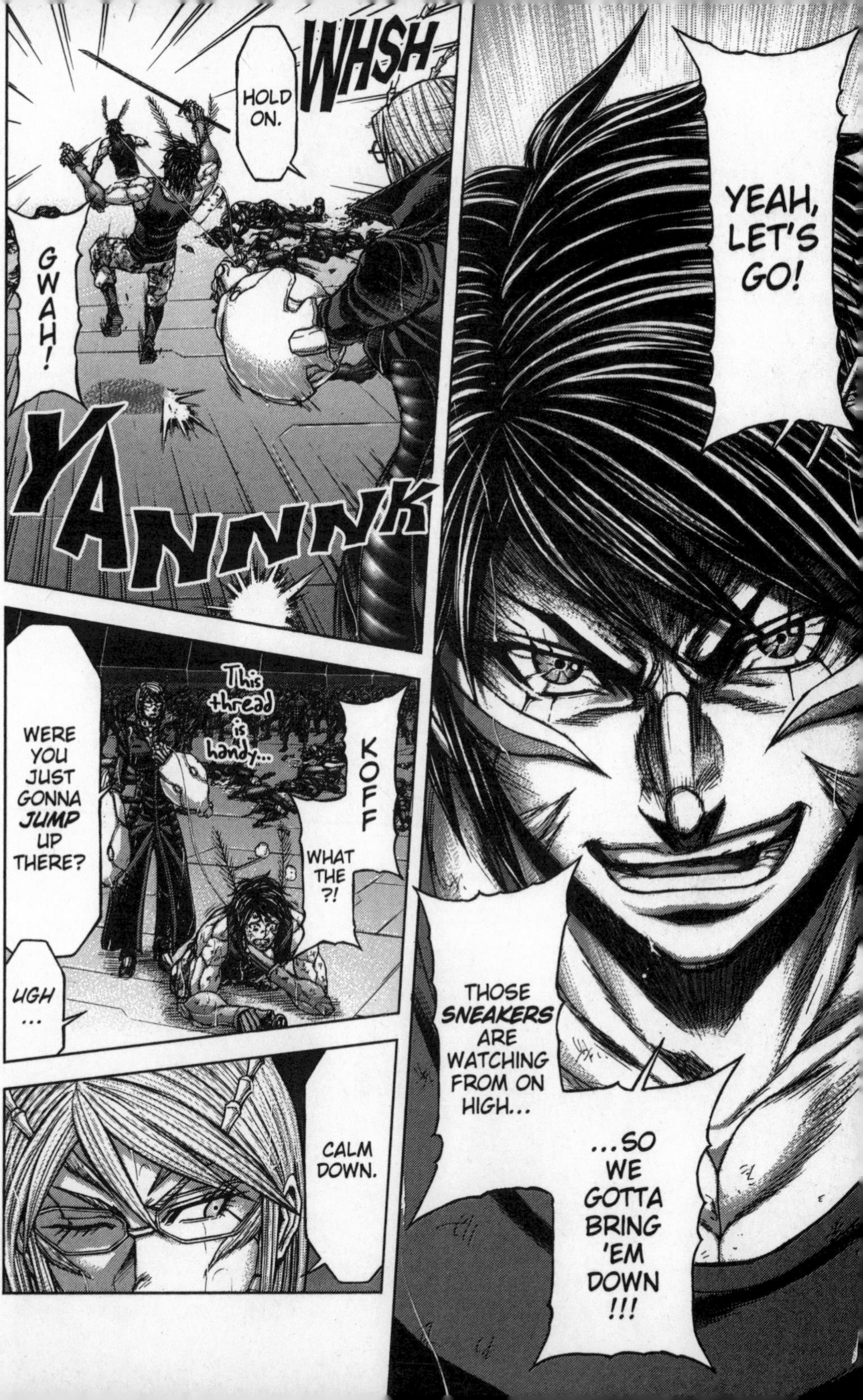
YEAH, LET'S GO!
THOSE SNEAKERS ARE WATCHING FROM ON HIGH...
...SO WE GOTTA BRING 'EM DOWN!!!
WHSH
HOLD ON.
GWAH!
YANNNK
WHAT THE ?!
KOFF
This thread is handy...
WERE YOU JUST GONNA JUMP UP THERE?
UGH ...
CALM DOWN.

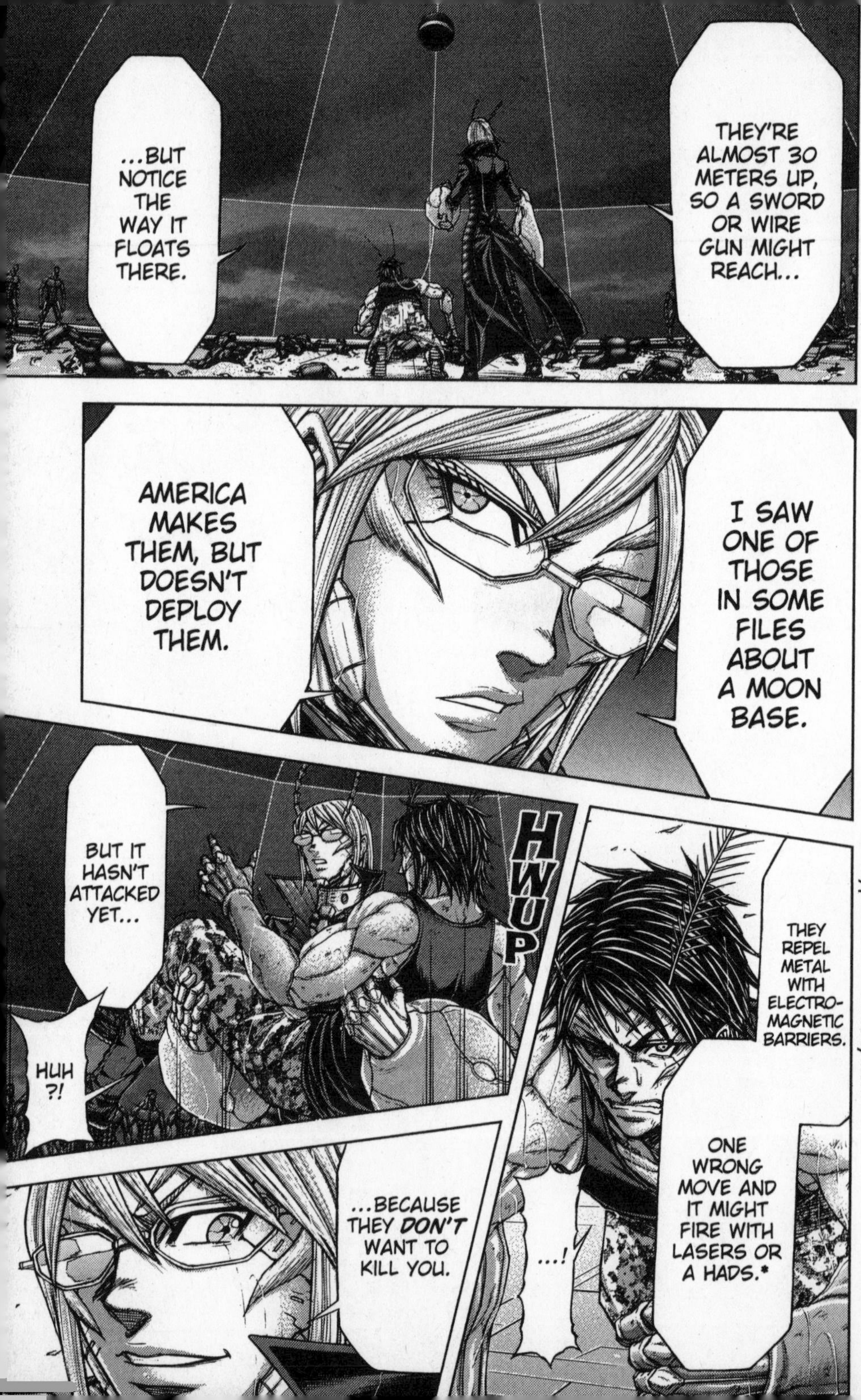

THEY'RE ALMOST 30 METERS UP, SO A SWORD OR WIRE GUN MIGHT REACH...
...BUT NOTICE THE WAY IT FLOATS THERE.
I SAW ONE OF THOSE IN SOME FILES ABOUT A MOON BASE.
AMERICA MAKES THEM, BUT DOESN'T DEPLOY THEM.
THEY REPEL METAL WITH ELECTRO-MAGNETIC BARRIERS.
ONE WRONG MOVE AND IT MIGHT FIRE WITH LASERS OR A HADS.*
...!
BUT IT HASN'T ATTACKED YET...
HWUP
HUH ?!
...BECAUSE THEY DON'T WANT TO KILL YOU.

*Hyperactive Denial System

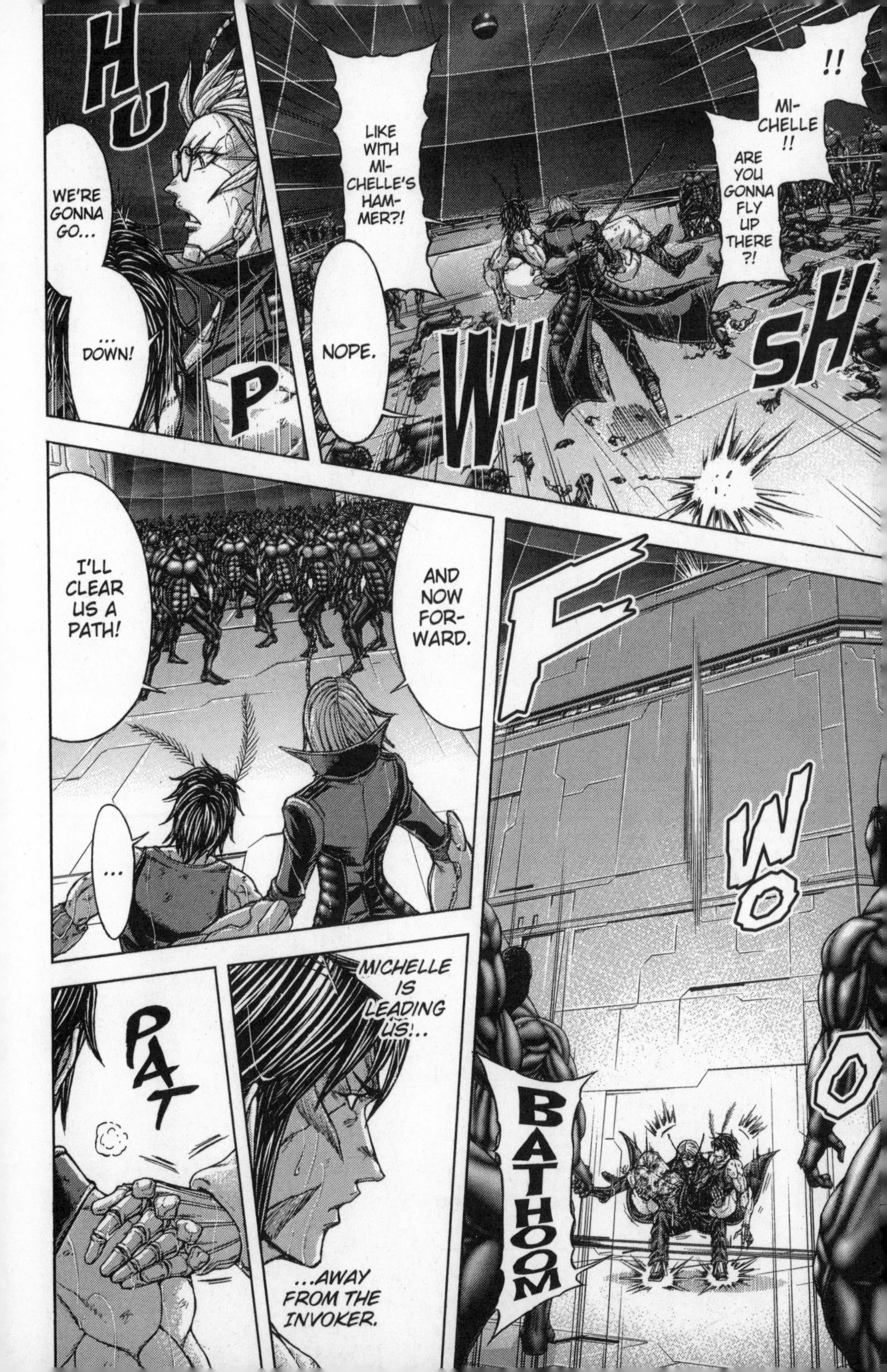
!!
MI-CHELLE!!
ARE YOU GONNA FLY UP THERE?!
LIKE WITH MI-CHELLE'S HAM-MER?!
NOPE.
SH
WH
HU
WE'RE GONNA GO...
...DOWN!
P
F
WO
O
BATHOOM
AND NOW FOR-WARD.
I'LL CLEAR US A PATH!
...
MICHELLE IS LEADING US...
...AWAY FROM THE INVOKER.
PAT

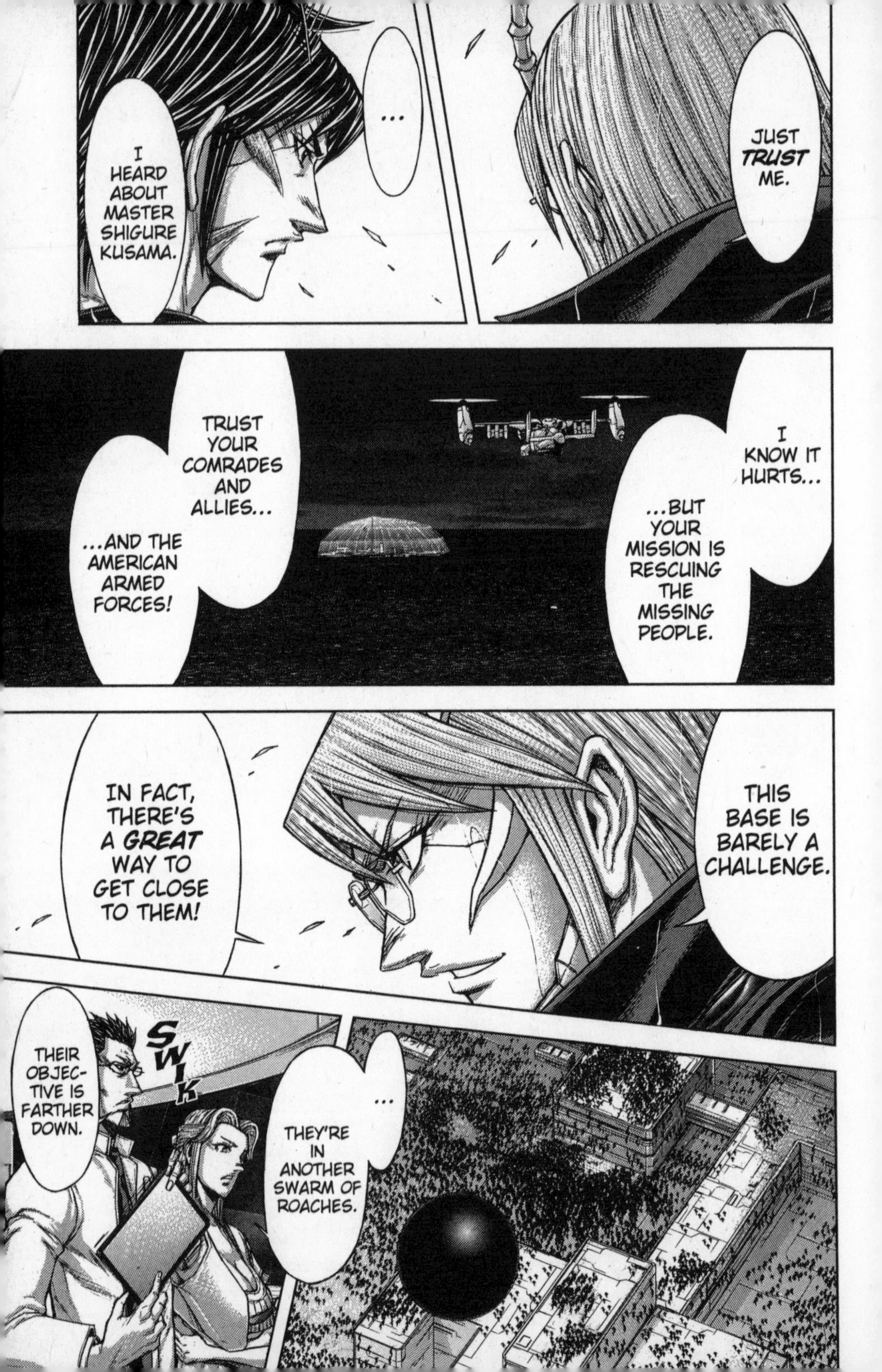
JUST TRUST ME.
...
I HEARD ABOUT MASTER SHIGURE KUSAMA.
I KNOW IT HURTS...
...BUT YOUR MISSION IS RESCUING THE MISSING PEOPLE.
TRUST YOUR COMRADES AND ALLIES...
...AND THE AMERICAN ARMED FORCES!
THIS BASE IS BARELY A CHALLENGE.
IN FACT, THERE'S A GREAT WAY TO GET CLOSE TO THEM!
...
THEY'RE IN ANOTHER SWARM OF ROACHES.
SWIK
THEIR OBJECTIVE IS FARTHER DOWN.

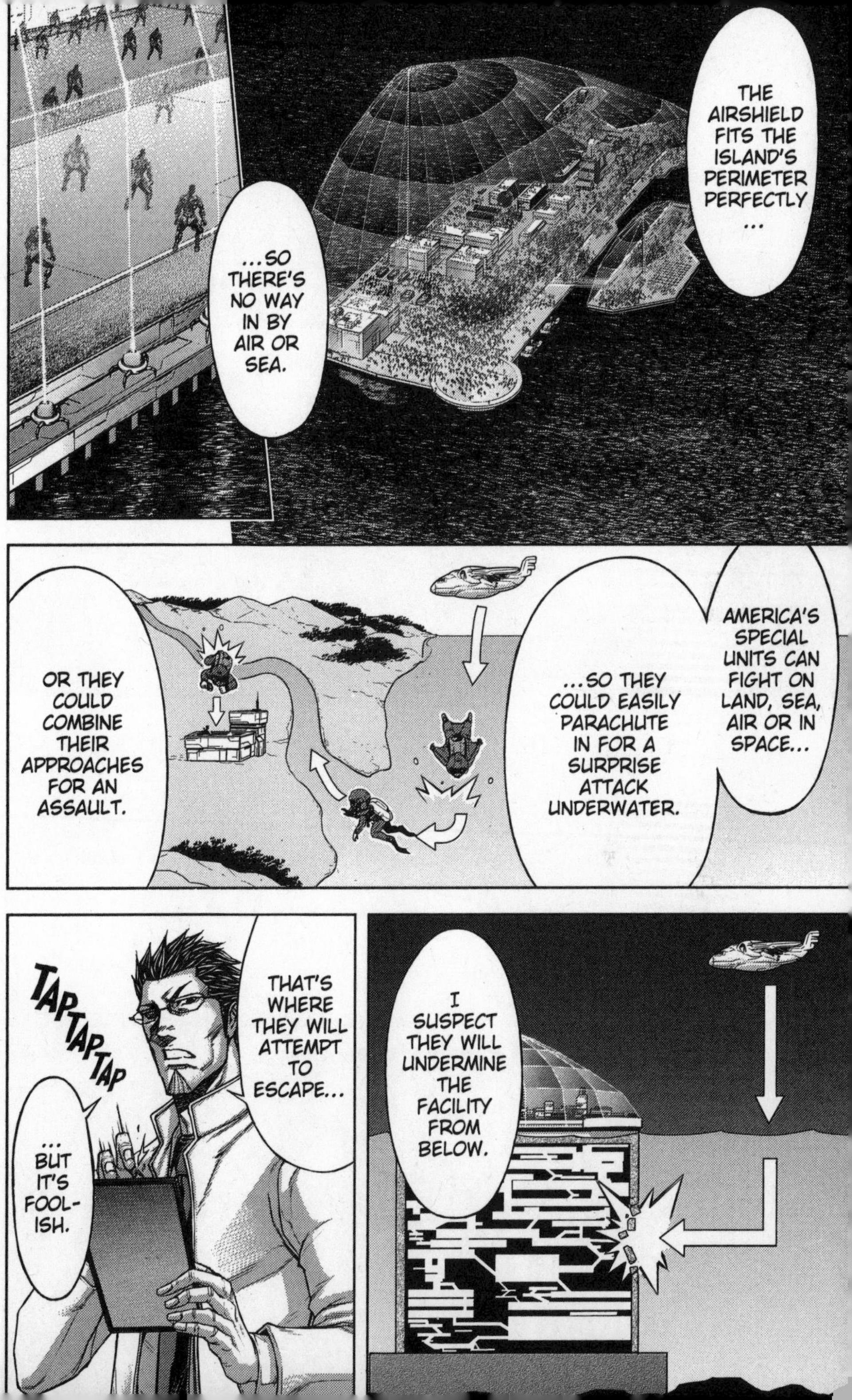
THE AIRSHIELD FITS THE ISLAND'S PERIMETER PERFECTLY ...
...SO THERE'S NO WAY IN BY AIR OR SEA.
AMERICA'S SPECIAL UNITS CAN FIGHT ON LAND, SEA, AIR OR IN SPACE...
...SO THEY COULD EASILY PARACHUTE IN FOR A SURPRISE ATTACK UNDERWATER.
OR THEY COULD COMBINE THEIR APPROACHES FOR AN ASSAULT.
I SUSPECT THEY WILL UNDERMINE THE FACILITY FROM BELOW.
THAT'S WHERE THEY WILL ATTEMPT TO ESCAPE...
TAPTAPTAP
... BUT IT'S FOOL-ISH.

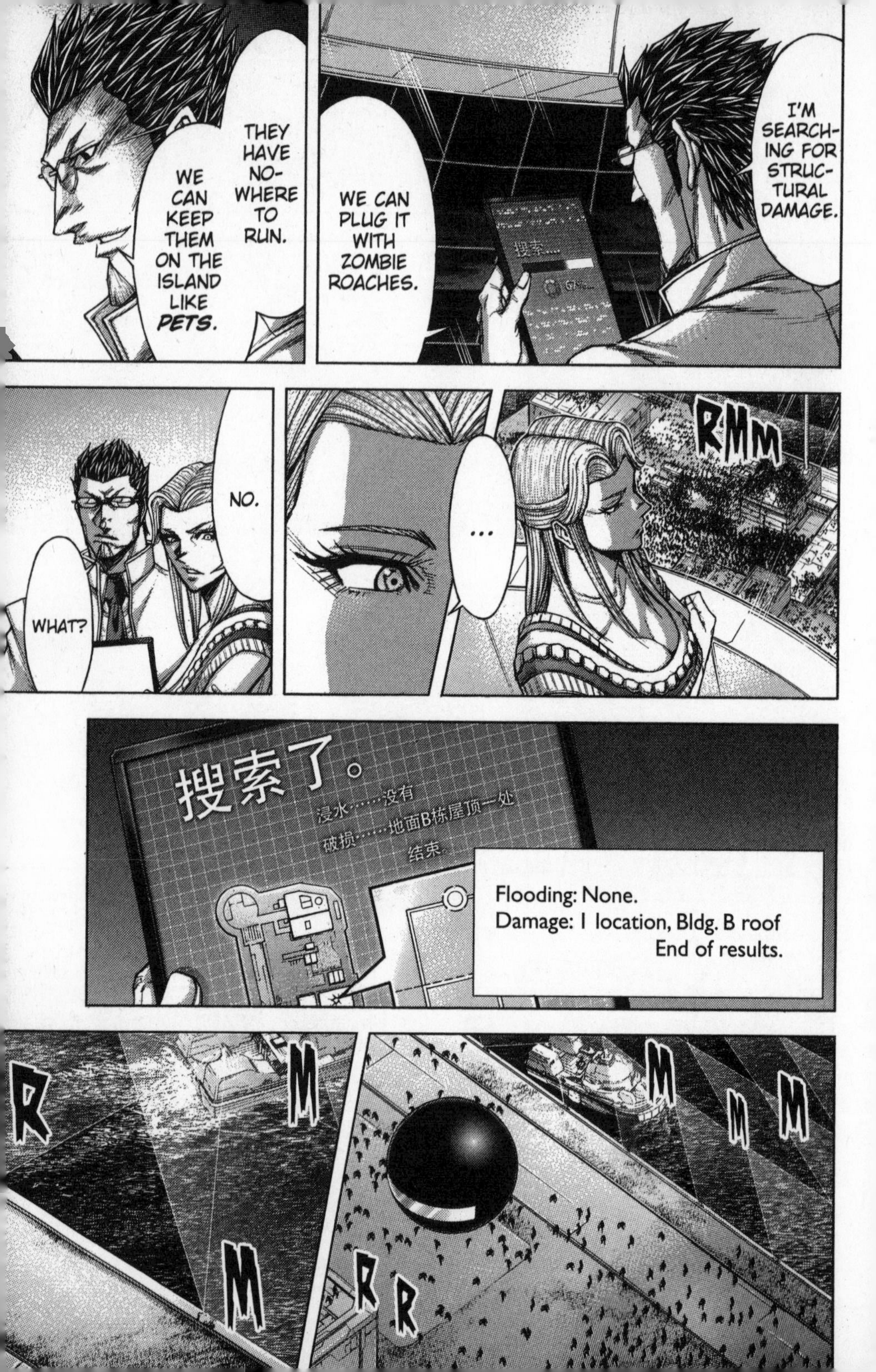
I'M SEARCHING FOR STRUCTURAL DAMAGE.
WE CAN PLUG IT WITH ZOMBIE ROACHES.
THEY HAVE NOWHERE TO RUN.
WE CAN KEEP THEM ON THE ISLAND LIKE *PETS*.
RMM
...
NO.
WHAT?
搜索了。
浸水……没有
破损……地面B栋屋顶一处
结束。
Flooding: None.
Damage: 1 location, Bldg. B roof
End of results.
MMM
RR
R
MM

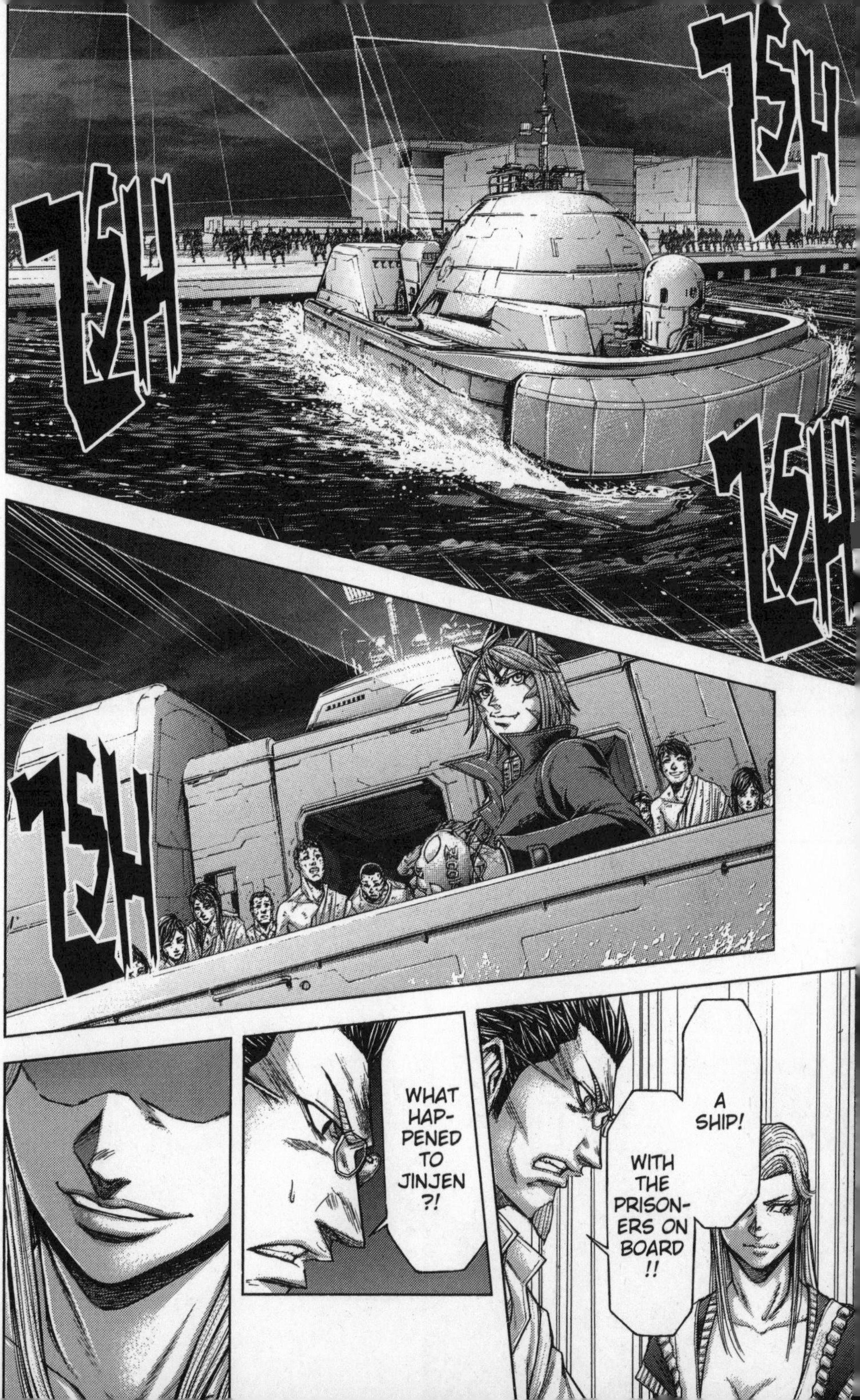
TSH
TSH
TSH
TSH
A SHIP!
WITH THE PRISONERS ON BOARD!!
WHAT HAPPENED TO JINJEN?!

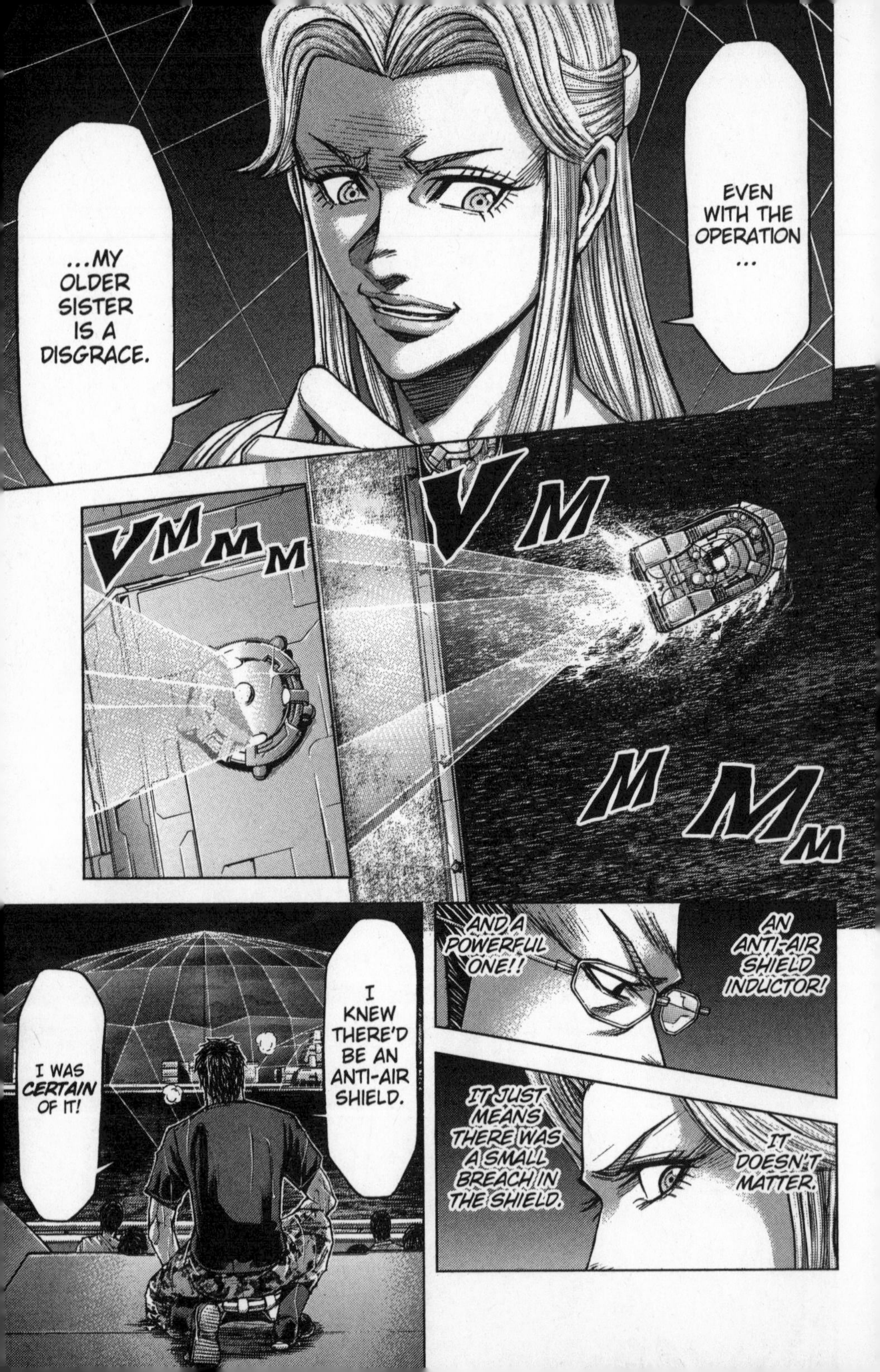
EVEN WITH THE OPERATION ...
...MY OLDER SISTER IS A DISGRACE.
VM
M MM
VMMM
AN ANTI-AIR SHIELD INDUCTOR!
AND A POWERFUL ONE!!
IT DOESN'T MATTER.
IT JUST MEANS THERE WAS A SMALL BREACH IN THE SHIELD.
I KNEW THERE'D BE AN ANTI-AIR SHIELD.
I WAS CERTAIN OF IT!

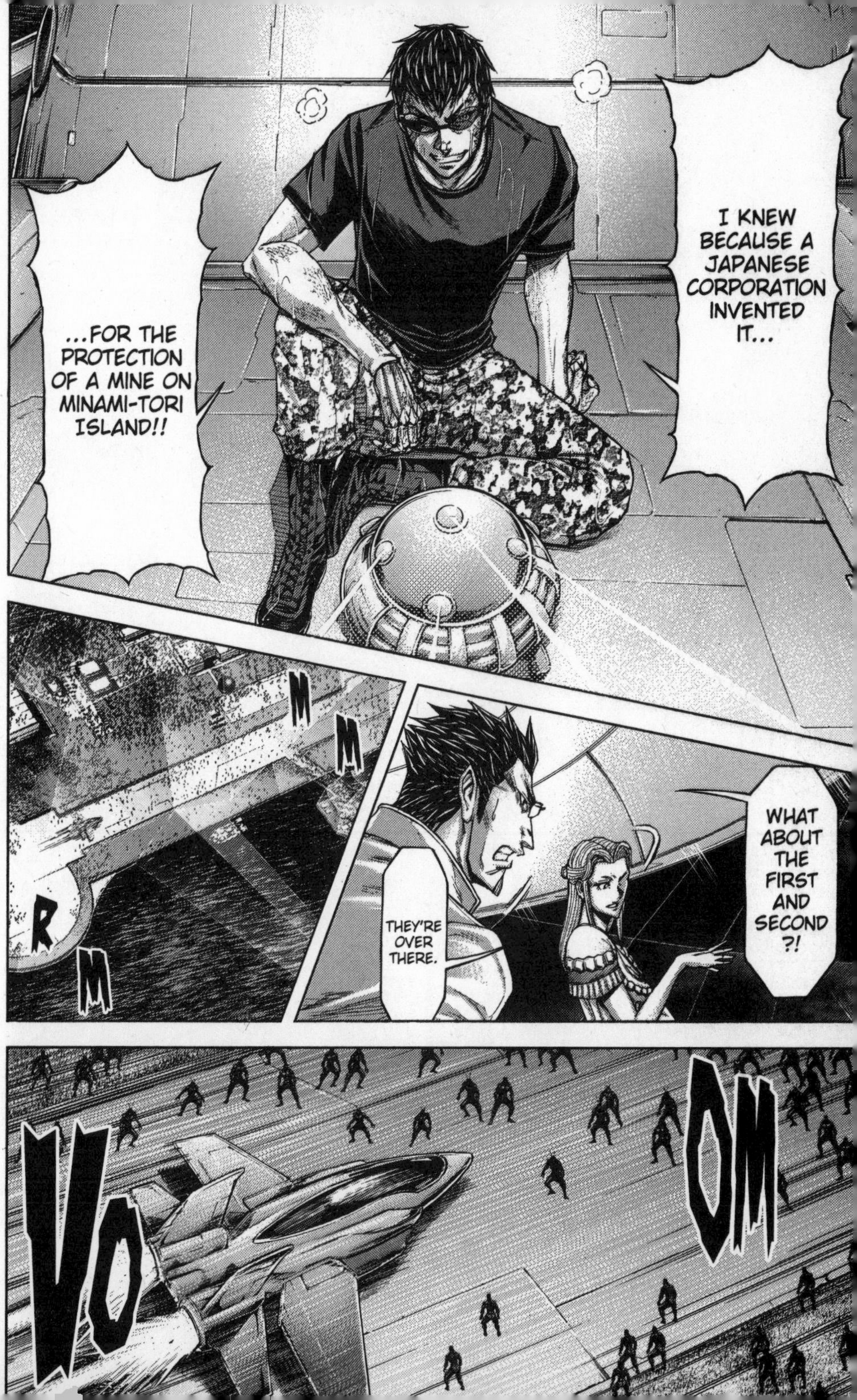
I KNEW BECAUSE A JAPANESE CORPORATION INVENTED IT...
...FOR THE PROTECTION OF A MINE ON MINAMI-TORI ISLAND!!
WHAT ABOUT THE FIRST AND SECOND ?!
THEY'RE OVER THERE.
MMRM
VOOM

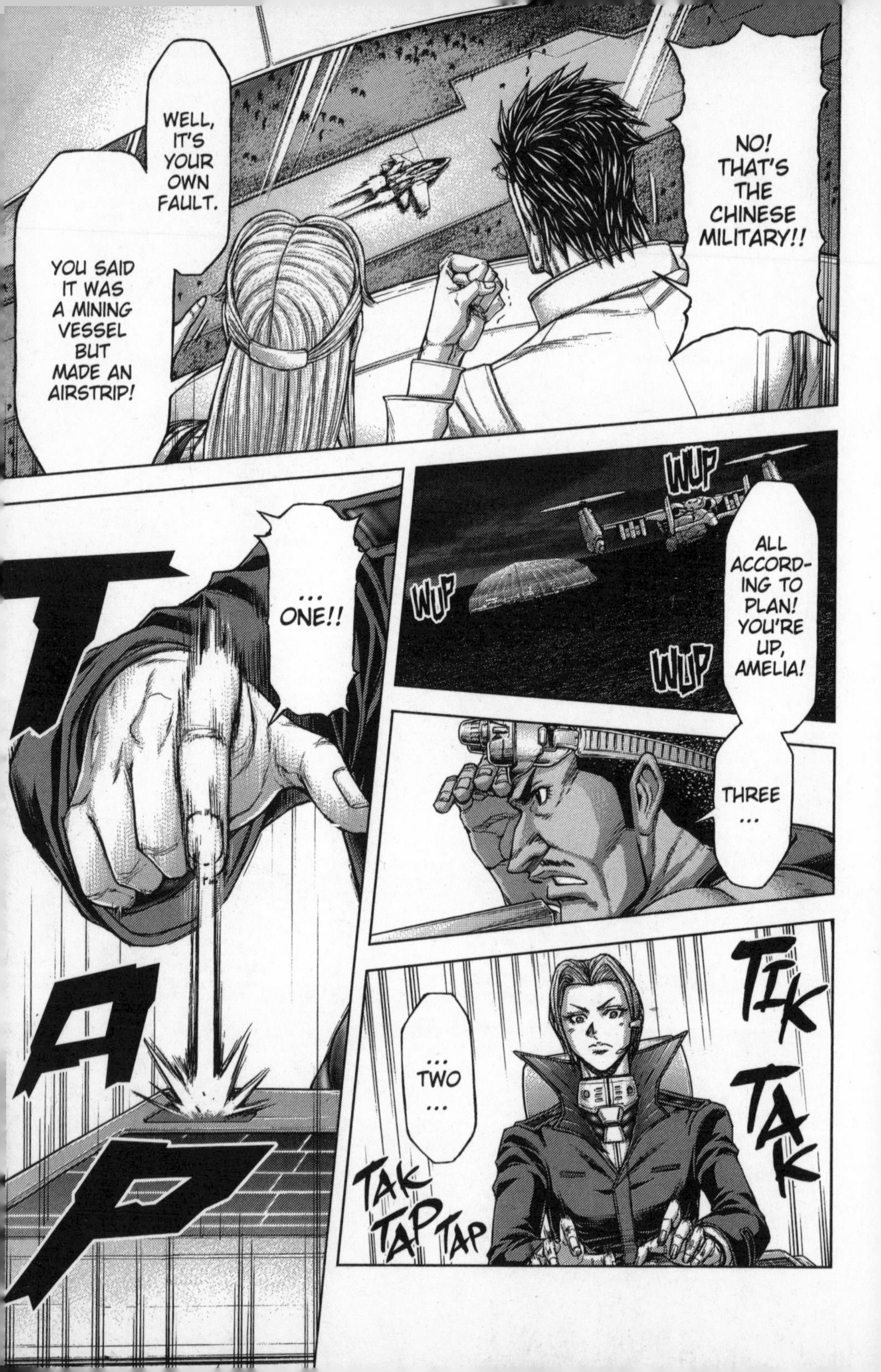
NO! THAT'S THE CHINESE MILITARY!!
WELL, IT'S YOUR OWN FAULT.
YOU SAID IT WAS A MINING VESSEL BUT MADE AN AIRSTRIP!
WUP
ALL ACCORDING TO PLAN! YOU'RE UP, AMELIA!
WUP
WUP
THREE ...
TIK TAK TAK
... TWO ...
TAK TAP TAP
TAP
... ONE!!

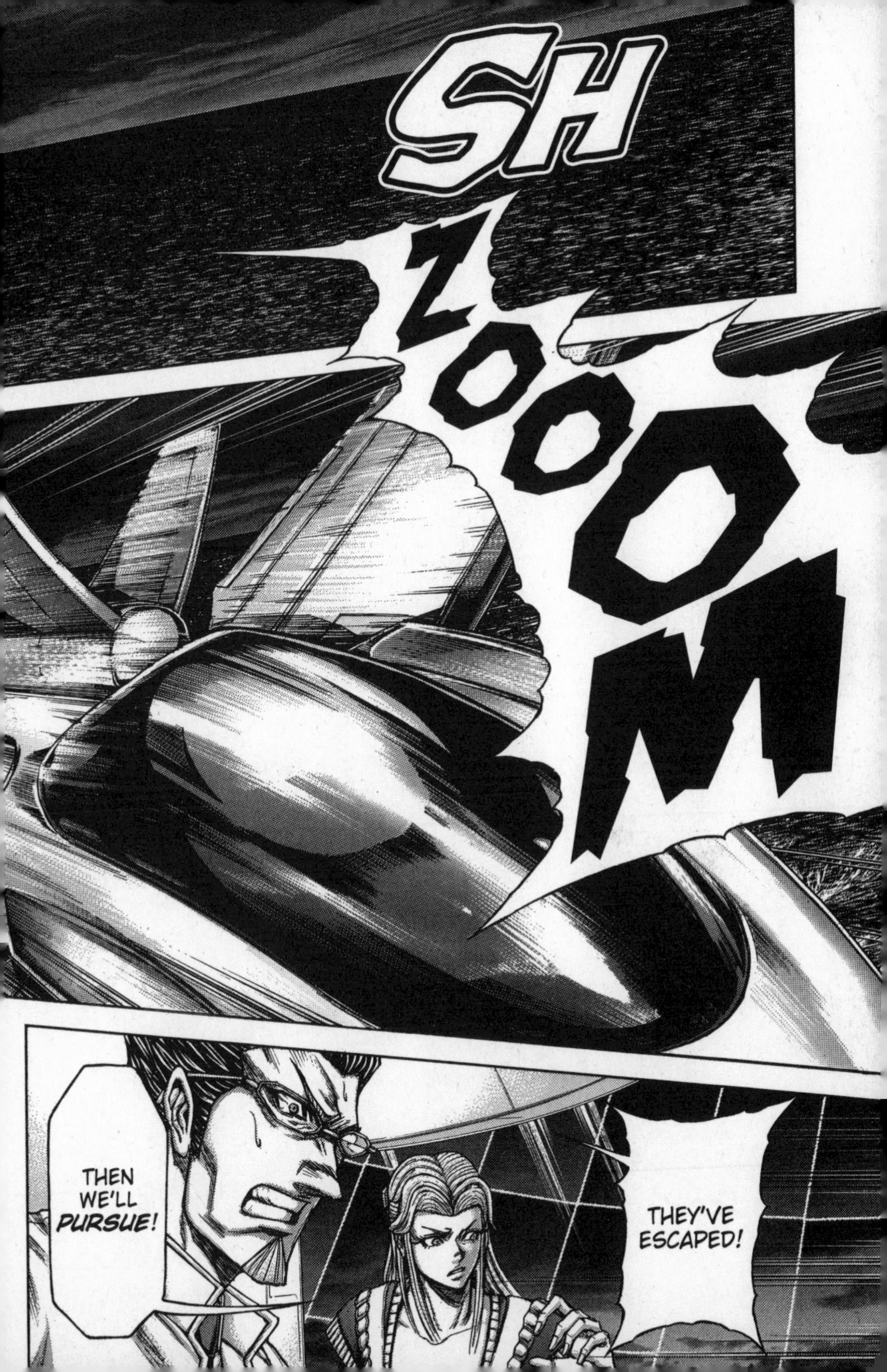
SH
ZOOOM
THEY'VE ESCAPED!
THEN WE'LL *PURSUE*!

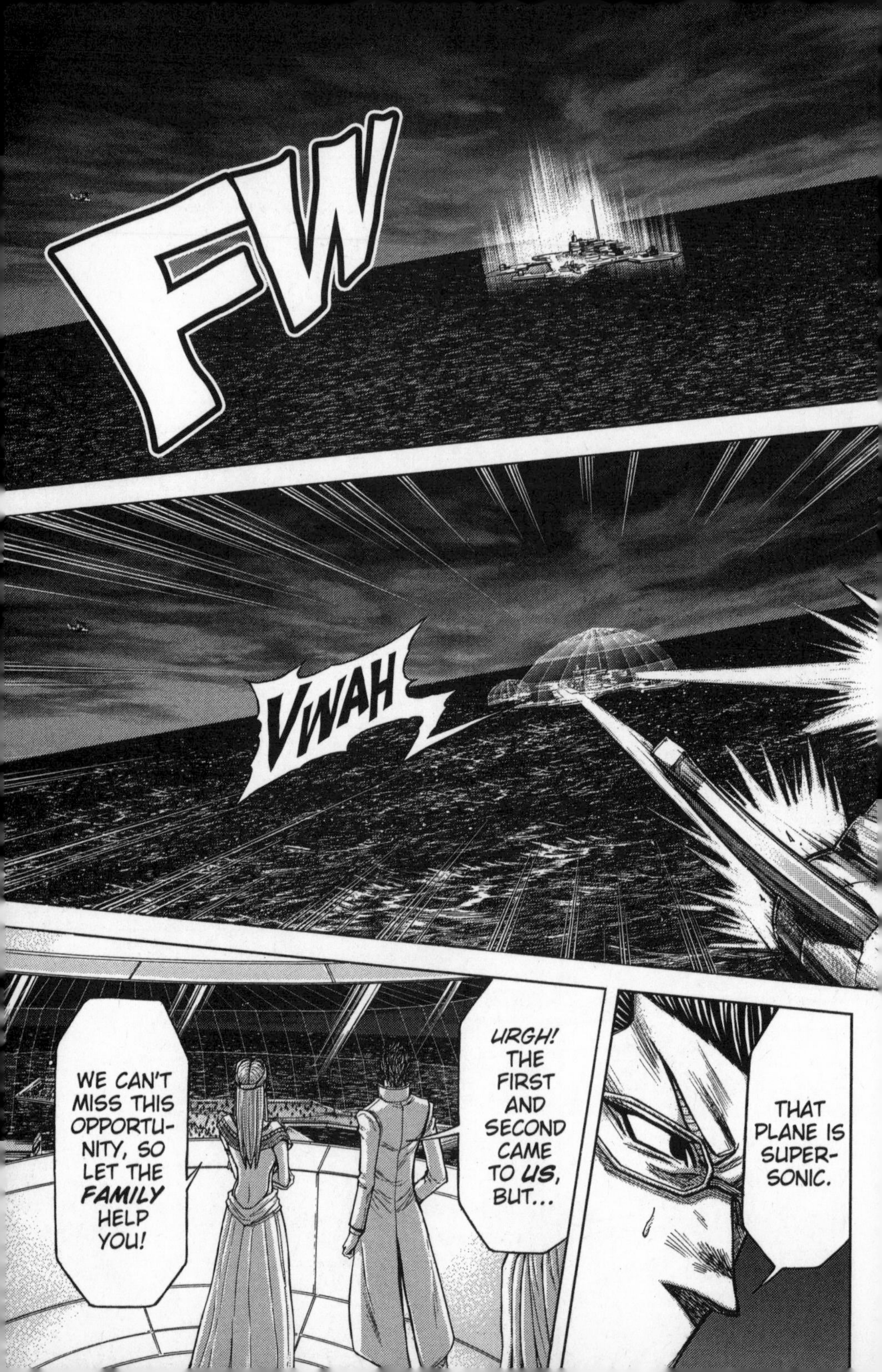
FW
VWAH
THAT PLANE IS SUPER-SONIC.
URGH! THE FIRST AND SECOND CAME TO *US*, BUT...
WE CAN'T MISS THIS OPPORTU-NITY, SO LET THE *FAMILY* HELP YOU!

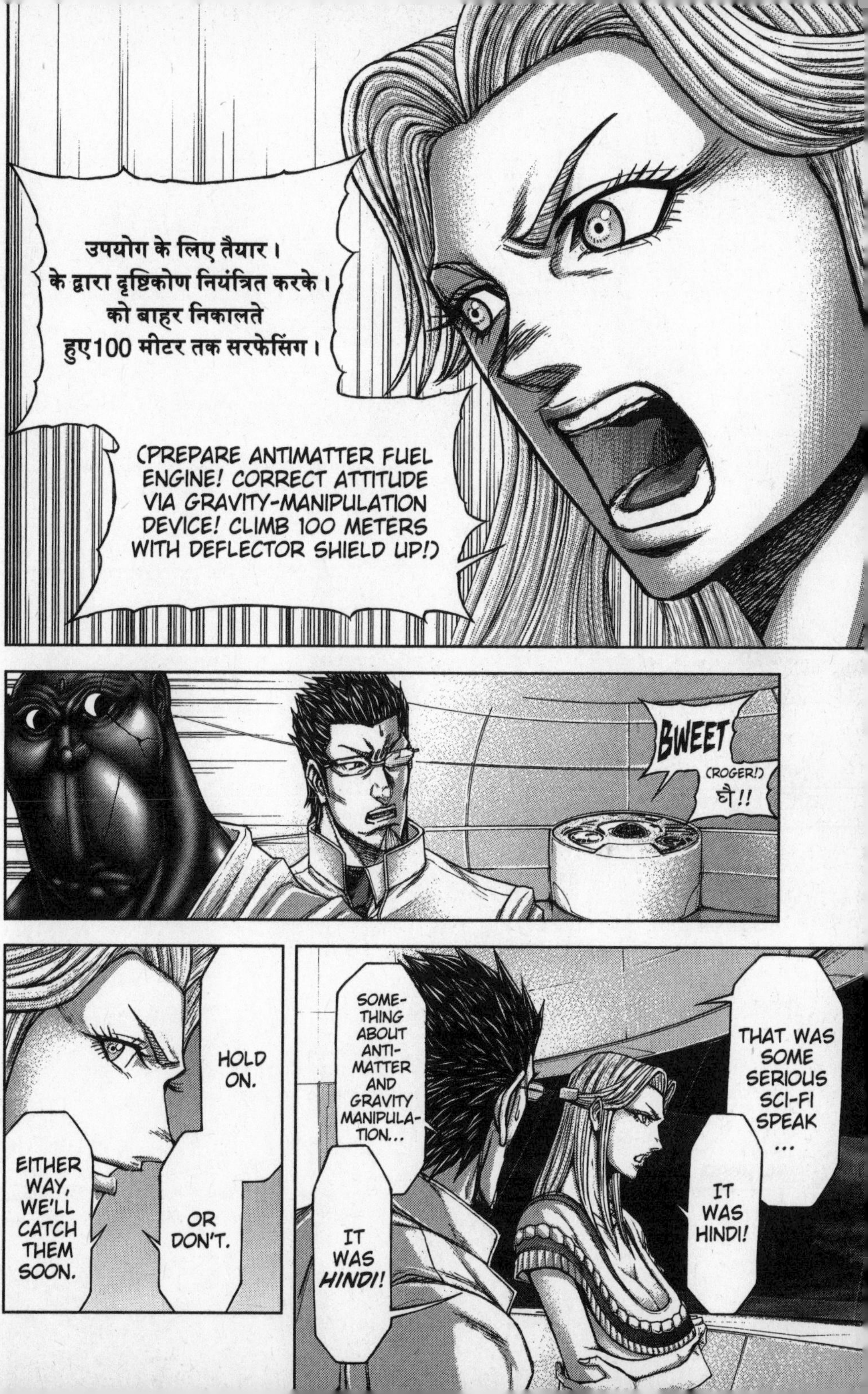

उपयोग के लिए तैयार। के द्वारा दृष्टिकोण नियंत्रित करके। को बाहर निकालते हुए100 मीटर तक सरफेसिंग।
(PREPARE ANTIMATTER FUEL ENGINE! CORRECT ATTITUDE VIA GRAVITY-MANIPULATION DEVICE! CLIMB 100 METERS WITH DEFLECTOR SHIELD UP!)
BWEET
(ROGER!) घौ!!
THAT WAS SOME SERIOUS SCI-FI SPEAK...
SOMETHING ABOUT ANTI-MATTER AND GRAVITY MANIPULATION...
IT WAS HINDI!
IT WAS *HINDI*!
HOLD ON.
OR DON'T.
EITHER WAY, WE'LL CATCH THEM SOON.

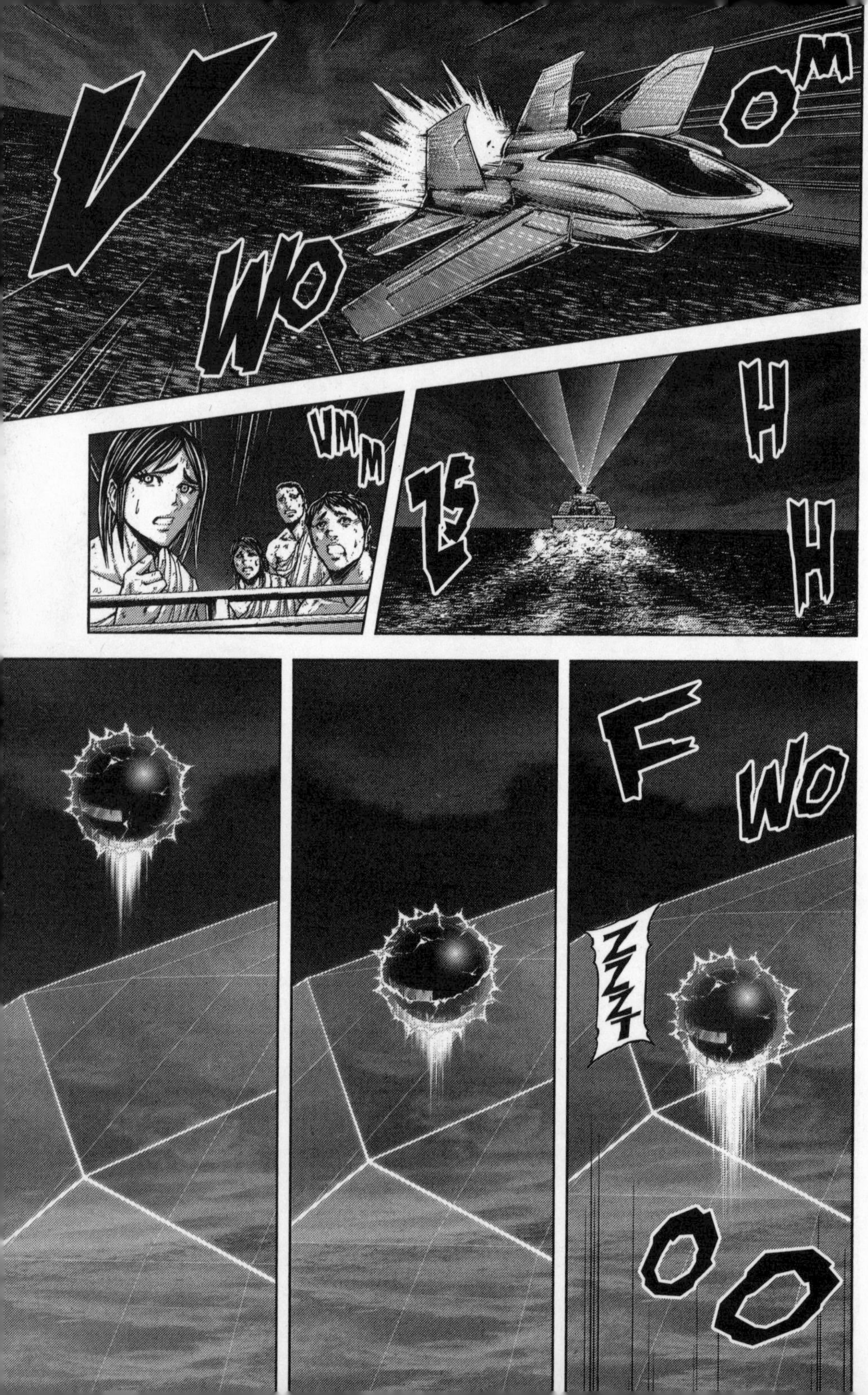
VWOOM
TSHHH
VMMM
FWOOOO
ZZZT

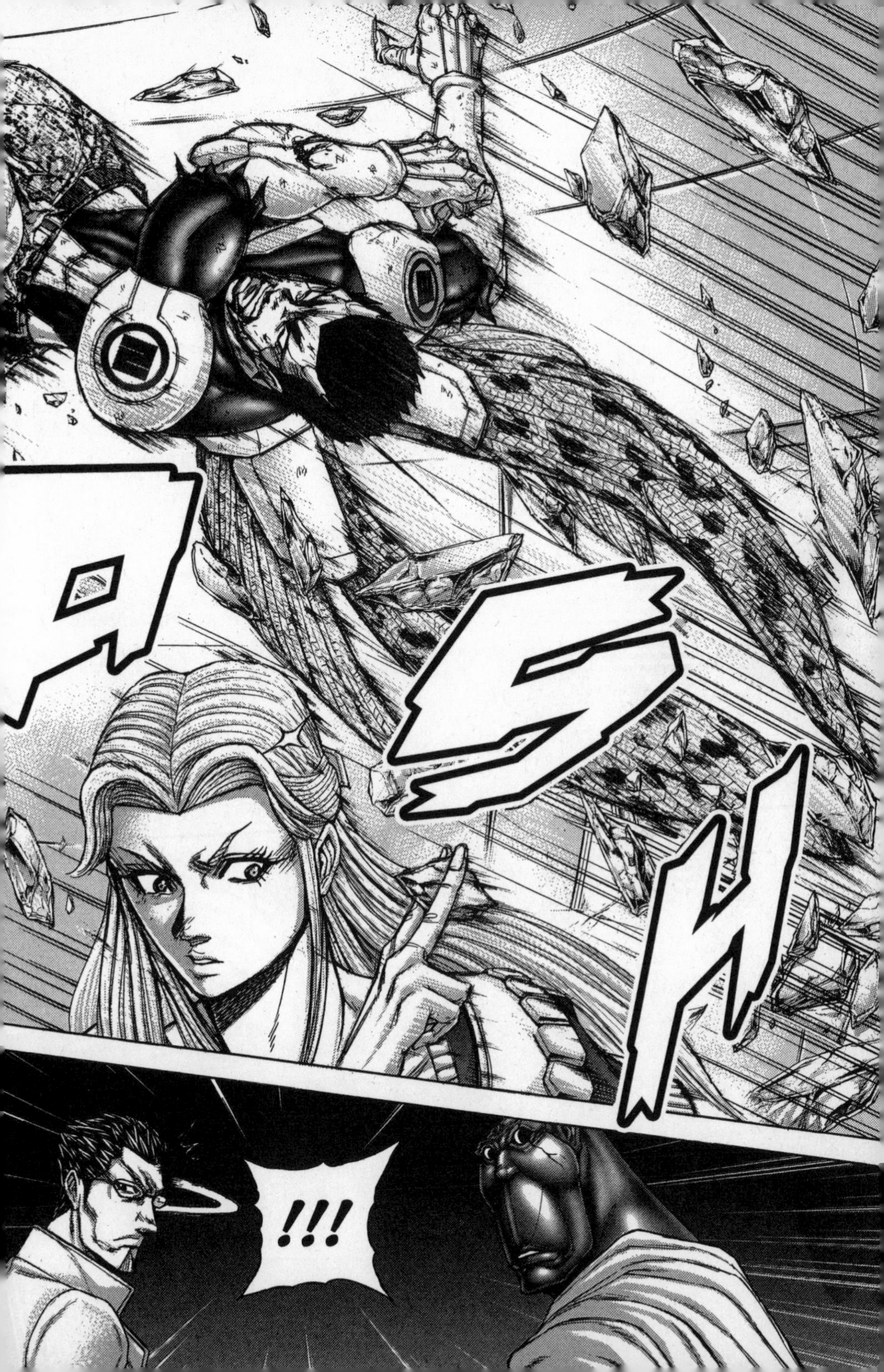
!!!

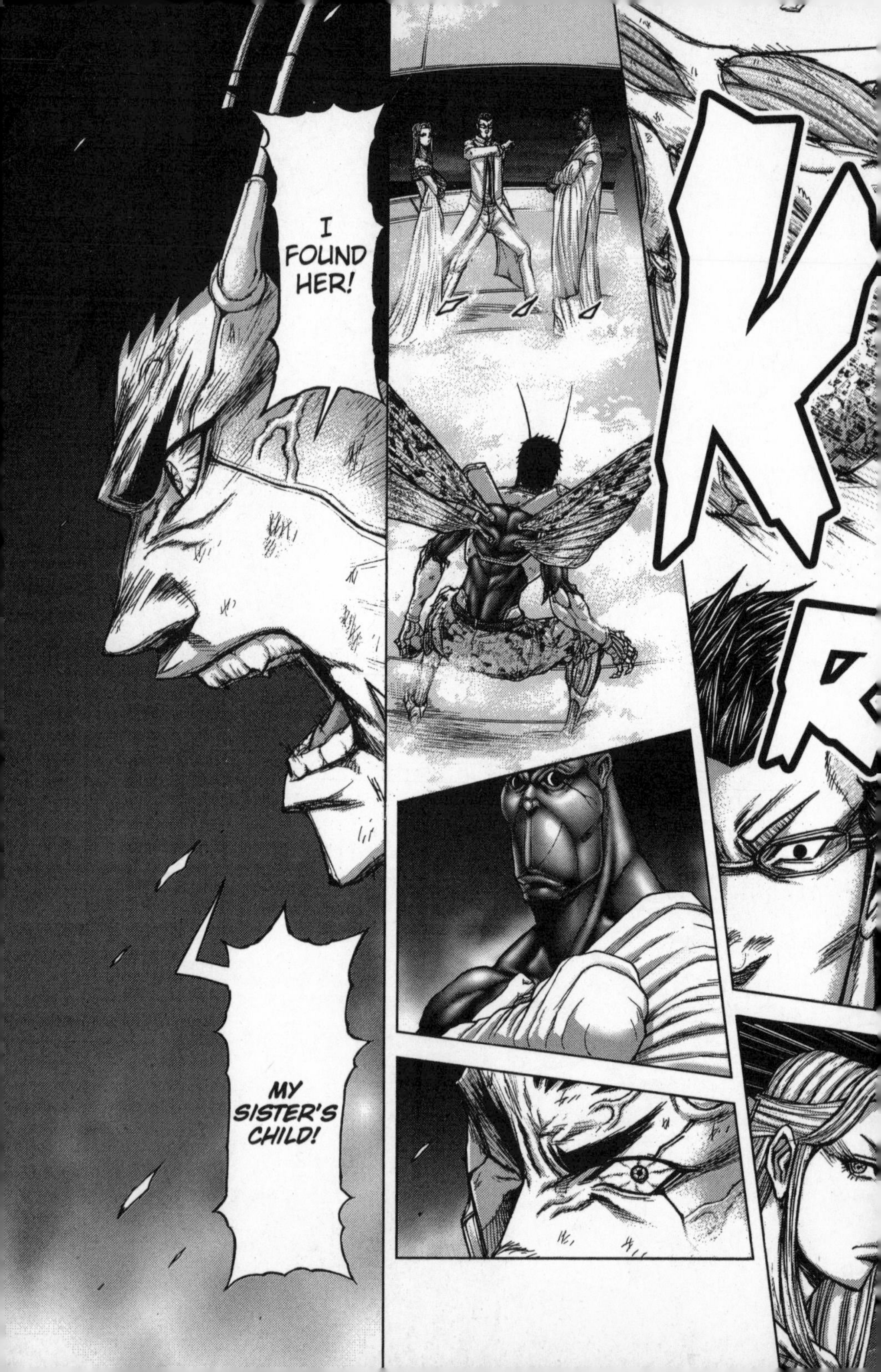
I FOUND HER!
MY SISTER'S CHILD!

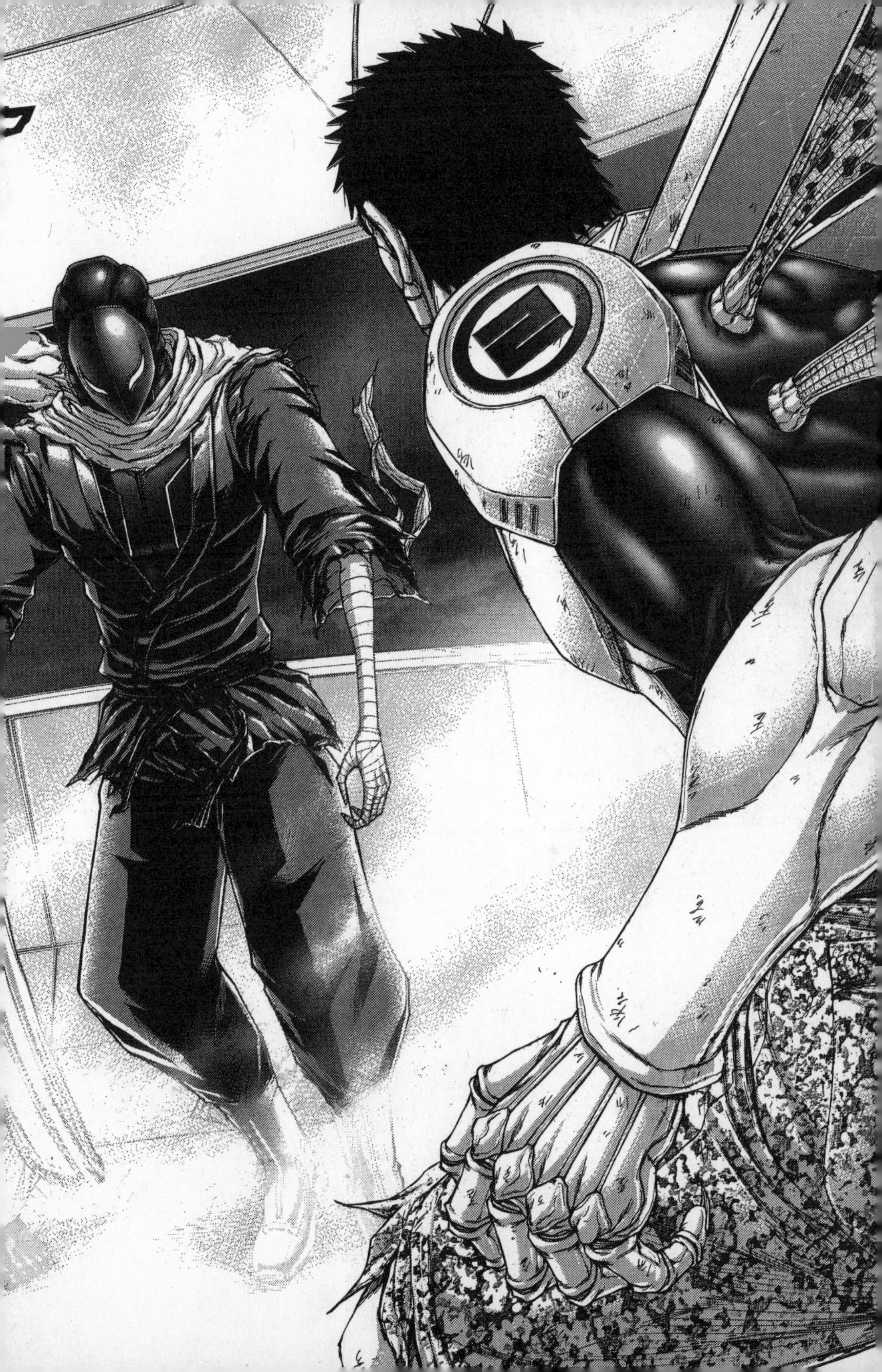

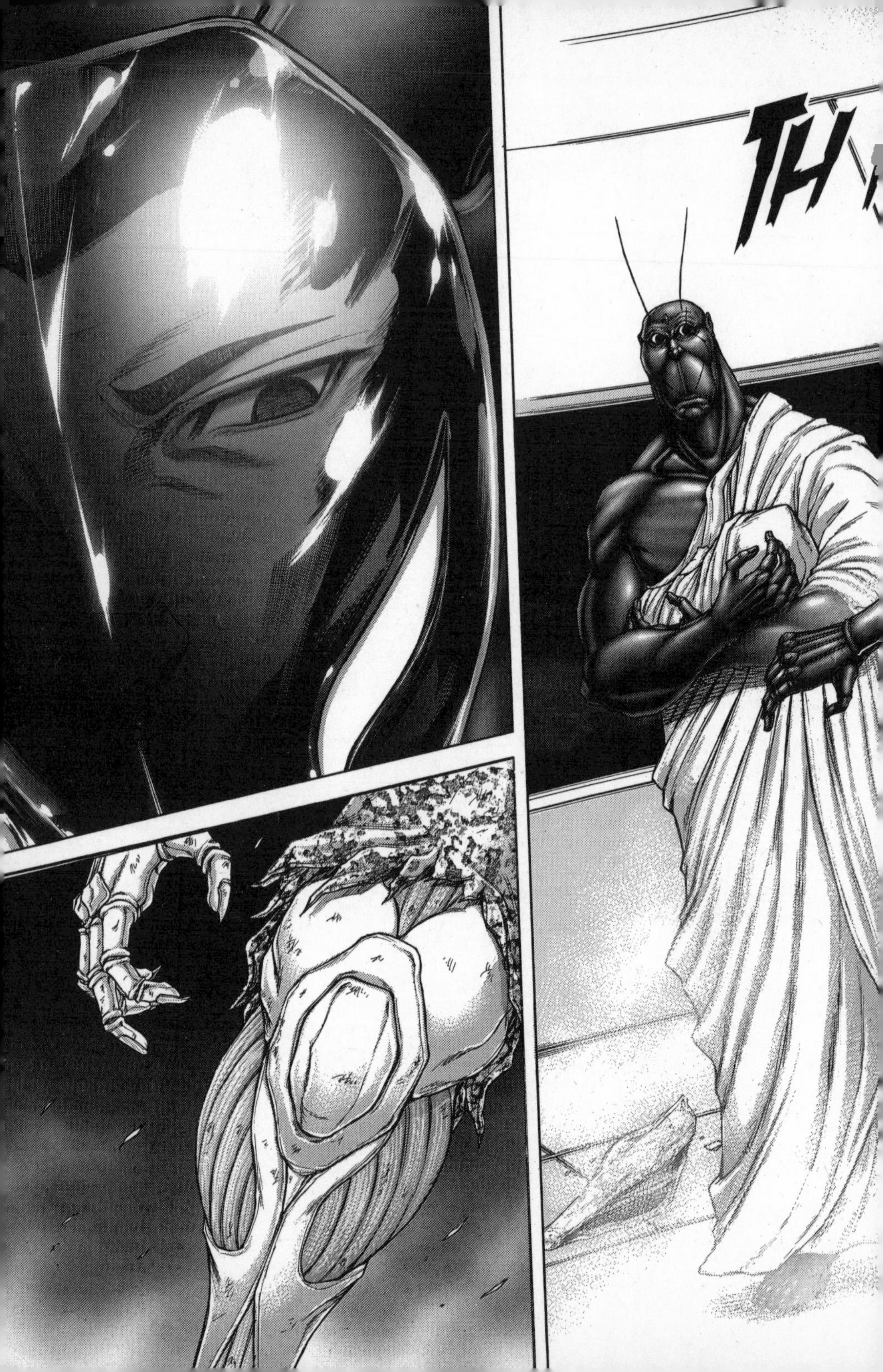
TH

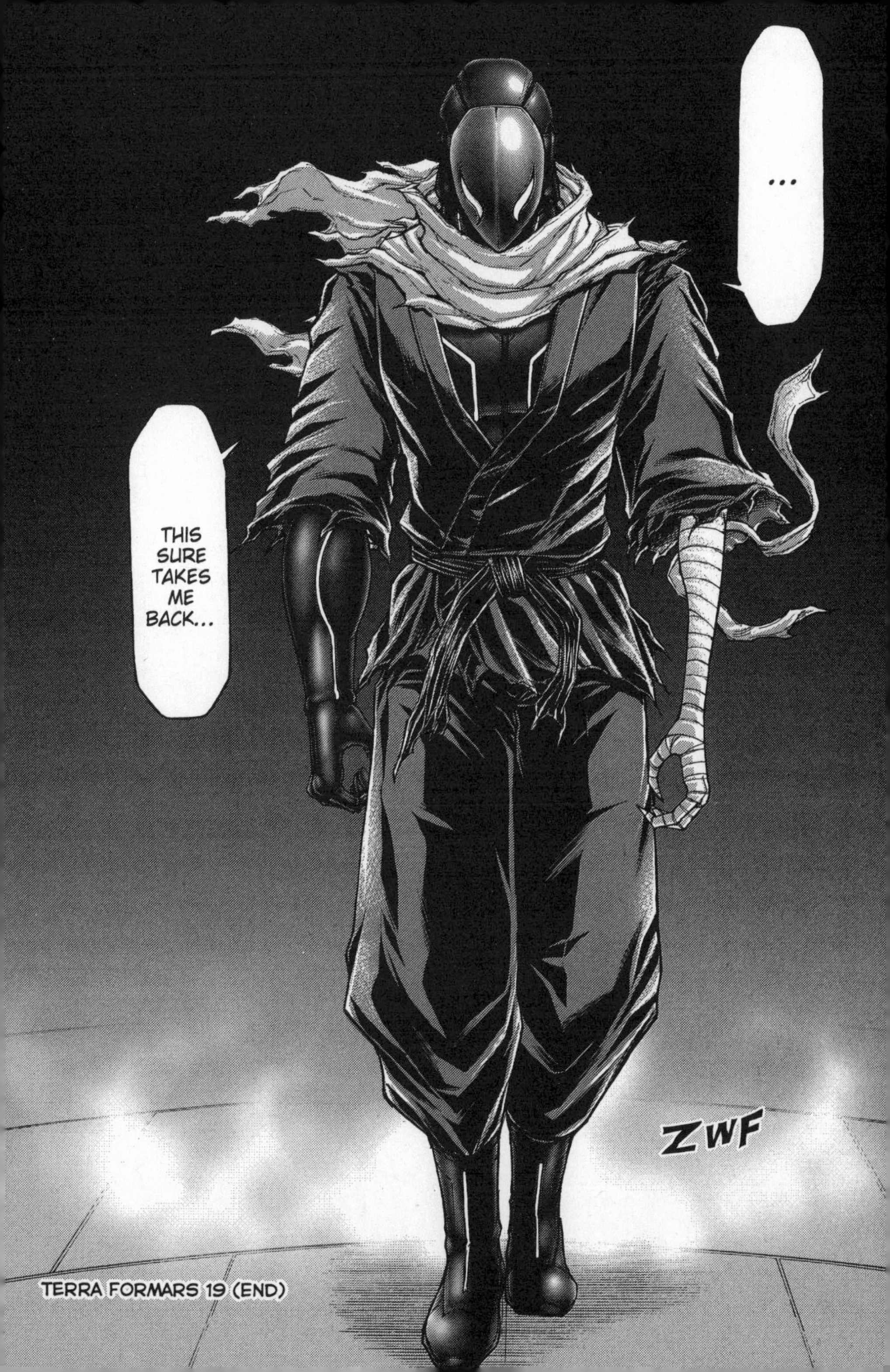
...
THIS SURE TAKES ME BACK...
ZWF

TERRA FORMARS 19 (END)

TERRA FORMARS

Character

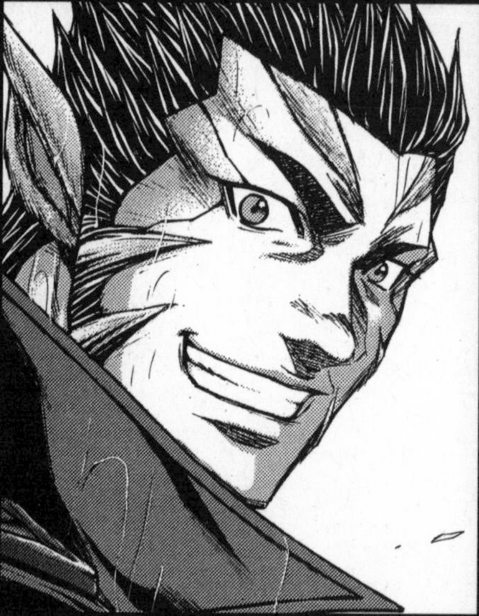

Tohei Tachibana ♂

America (born in Japan) 19 yrs. 176 cm 64 kg

Operation Base: Brown Rat

Favorite Foods: Rice with raw egg
Dislikes: Tough steak
Eye Color: Dark Brown
Blood Type: A
DOB: July 7 (Cancer)

A genius who completed all courses at a four-year university by the time he was 17. His majors were aerospace engineering and information engineering. His computer skills are superb. His dream is to become an astronaut. Karate: 2nd dan.

His parents died when he was a child, so he grew up in an orphanage. When a fire destroyed the place, he sold himself to U-NASA for the funds to rebuild it, and he has never regretted it.

He worries that his partner is the bright and bubbly type.

Elizabeth Rooney ♀

America 19 yrs. 168 cm 52 kg

Operation Base: House Cat

Favorite Foods: Firm steak
Simply Unthinkable: Rice with raw egg
Favorite Boxer: Keiji Onizuka
Eye Color: Blue
Blood Type: B
DOB: May 5 (Taurus)

Former bantamweight high school national boxing champion. Her style is boxer-puncher. When she was 16, she killed an opponent. To compensate and punish herself, she offered herself to U-NASA, and she has never regretted it.

She worries about how her partner never responds to her overtures no matter how much she makes her intentions clear.

"Tohei's a fuckin' chicken-shit virgin bastard! Huh? My bra size?! It's E! What about it?!"

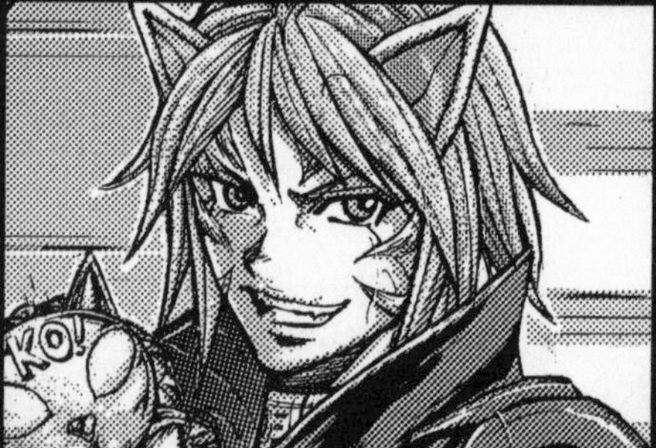
KO!
ZOCK!

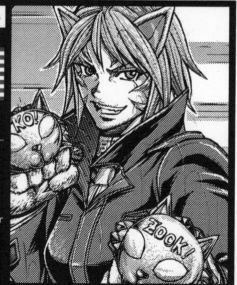

Text: Kenichi Fujihara

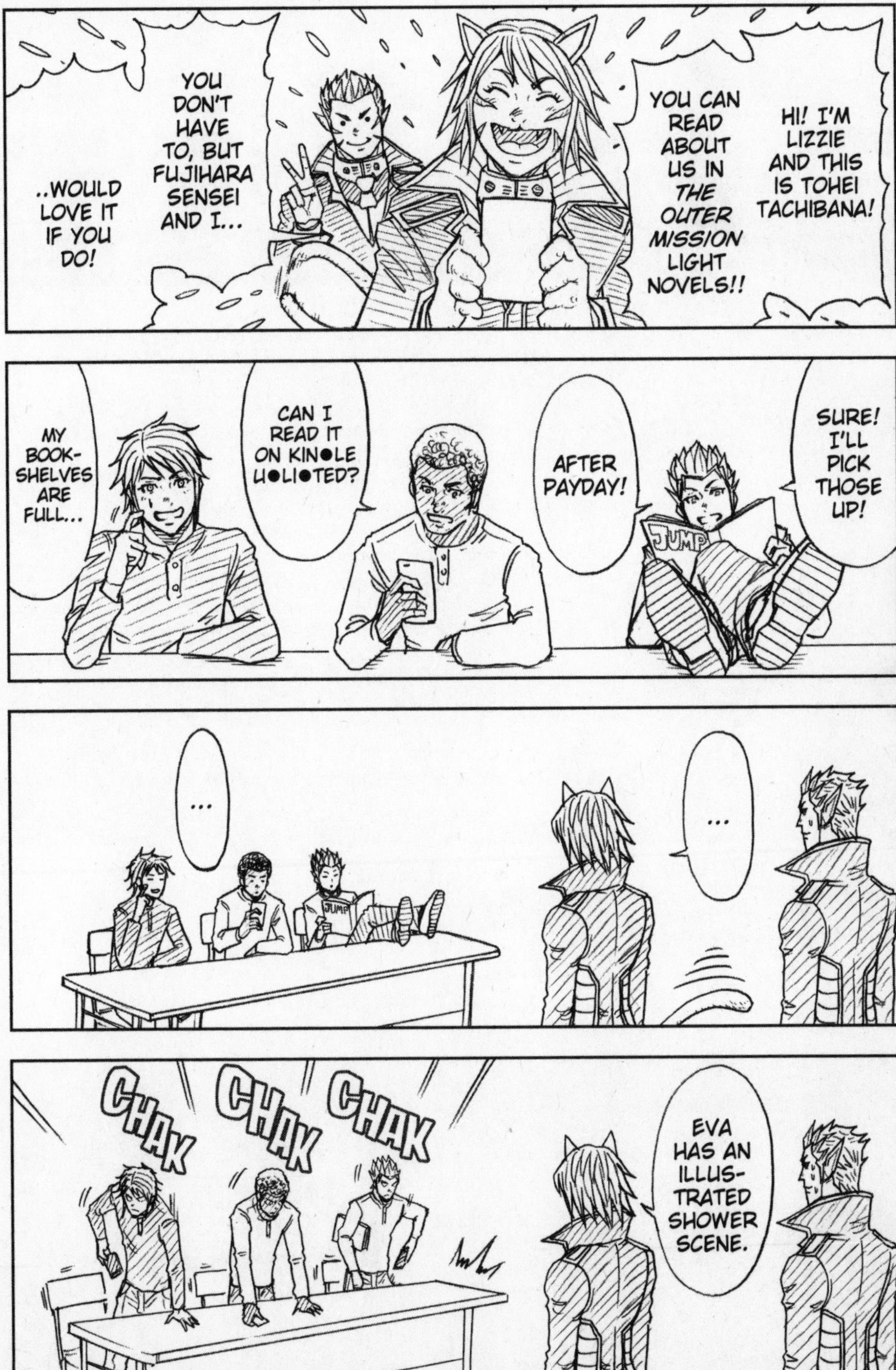
HI! I'M LIZZIE AND THIS IS TOHEI TACHIBANA!
YOU CAN READ ABOUT US IN *THE OUTER MISSION* LIGHT NOVELS!!
YOU DON'T HAVE TO, BUT FUJIHARA SENSEI AND I...
..WOULD LOVE IT IF YOU DO!
SURE! I'LL PICK THOSE UP!
JUMP
AFTER PAYDAY!
CAN I READ IT ON KIN●LE U●LI●TED?
MY BOOK-SHELVES ARE FULL...
...
...
JUMP
EVA HAS AN ILLUS-TRATED SHOWER SCENE.
CHAK
CHAK
CHAK

*I asked author Kenichi Fujihara to write the profiles on the previous page. Sorry for the sudden request! Thanks!!

TERRA FORMARS
Volume 19
VIZ Signature Edition

Story by YU SASUGA
Art by KENICHI TACHIBANA

First published in Japan in 2011 by SHUEISHA Inc., Tokyo.
English translation rights arranged by SHUEISHA Inc.

Translation & English Adaptation/John Werry
Touch-up Art & Lettering/Annaliese Christman
Design/Alice Lewis
Editor/Mike Montesa

Printed in the U.S.A.

Published by VIZ Media, LLC
P.O. Box 77010
San Francisco, CA 94107

10 9 8 7 6 5 4 3 2 1
First printing, October 2017

www.viz.com

VIZ SIGNATURE

RATED M FOR MATURE
PARENTAL ADVISORY
TERRA FORMARS is rated M for Mature and is recommended for mature readers.
ratings.viz.com

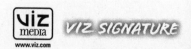

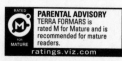

A tale of high
adventure and
survival on the
Japanese frontier!

GOLDEN KAMUY

In the early twentieth century,
Russo-Japanese War veteran Saichi
Sugimoto searches the wilderness of
the Japanese frontier of Hokkaido for
a hoard of hidden gold. With only a
cryptic map and a native Ainu girl to
help him, Saichi must also deal with
every murderous cutthroat, bandit
and rogue who knows about the
treasure!

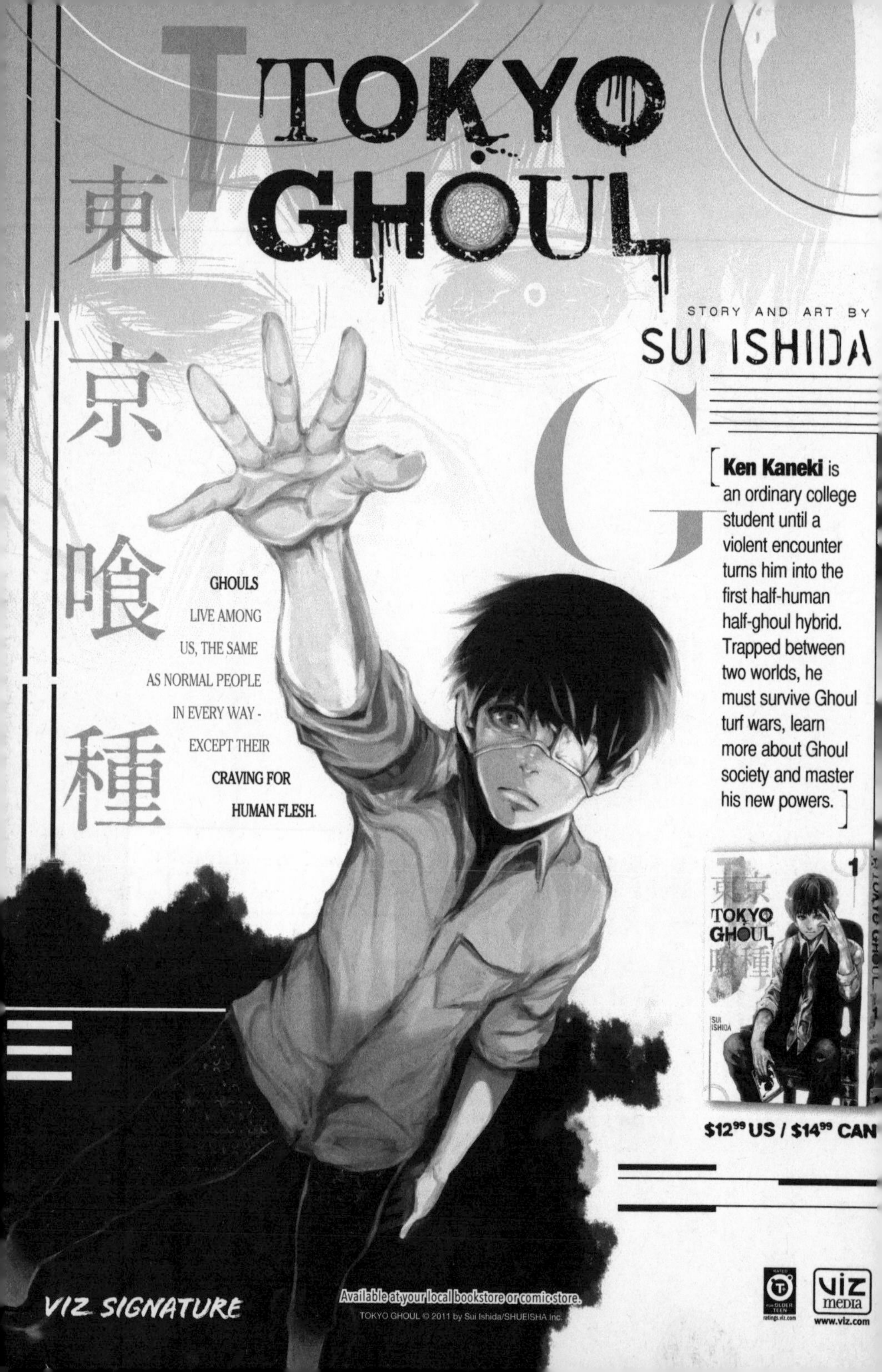
TOKYO GHOUL
東京喰種
STORY AND ART BY
SUI ISHIDA
GHOULS LIVE AMONG US, THE SAME AS NORMAL PEOPLE IN EVERY WAY - EXCEPT THEIR CRAVING FOR HUMAN FLESH.
[Ken Kaneki is an ordinary college student until a violent encounter turns him into the first half-human half-ghoul hybrid. Trapped between two worlds, he must survive Ghoul turf wars, learn more about Ghoul society and master his new powers.]
$12.99 US / $14.99 CAN
VIZ SIGNATURE
Available at your local bookstore or comic store.
TOKYO GHOUL © 2011 by Sui Ishida/SHUEISHA Inc.
RATED T FOR OLDER TEEN
ratings.viz.com
viz media
www.viz.com

Hey! You're Reading in the Wrong Direction!

This is the **end** of this graphic novel!

To properly enjoy this VIZ graphic novel, please turn it around and begin reading from **right to left.** Unlike English, Japanese is read right to left, so Japanese comics are read in reverse order from the way English comics are typically read.

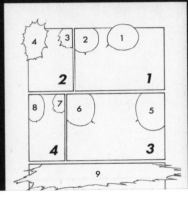

This book has been printed in the original Japanese format in order to preserve the orientation of the original artwork. Have fun with it!